CONCISE ENCYCLOPEDIA OF

ballet

FERDINAND REYNA

Translated by ANDRÉ GÂTEAU

FOLLETT PUBLISHING COMPANY

Chicago

About this book *This edition has been extensively revised and re-edited from the original French edition. Many people helped in this task, and special mention should be made of the following: Arnold Haskell; Marjory Middleton; Peter Williams, Editor Dance and Dancers; The Royal Ballet; London Festival Ballet; Ballet Rambert; Scottish Theatre Ballet.*

© 1967 by Librairie Larousse. English language edition © 1974 by Wm. Collins Sons & Co. Ltd., Glasgow. Published 1974 by Follett Publishing Company. Manufactured in Great Britain.

ISBN: 0-695-80470-7

Library of Congress Catalog Card Number: 73-91737

First Printing

Companion volume to
Concise Encyclopedia of Modern Art

introduction

When I first started to take an interest in ballet over half a century ago the very idea of an encyclopedia of ballet would have been unthinkable. Wisden, of course, Ruff's *Guide to the Turf* and Boxing's *Book of Records* were well established. Ballet lovers stored in their memories all the facts about the dancers they were fortunate enough to see. Very few countries possessed established ballet companies—France, Russia and Denmark—but for most people ballet meant either Pavlova, or Diaghilev's great company.

Today a country without at least one ballet company scarcely exists, and no single volume could contain all the information needed. Every encyclopedia, therefore, is subject to criticism by someone searching for omissions or errors and that is part of the fun, trying to pit one's expertise against that of the compilers who have omitted any mention of one's favourite Fijian ballerina.

The difficulty in compiling such work of reference lies in the rules and exceptions one sets oneself. Exclude the living dancer and it will certainly never date but its value will be greatly diminished, include the living and it will be dated from the moment that it is printed. You can't win!

However, this handy and inexpensive volume seems to me to be well compiled and to contain a number of references not available elsewhere. My memory is not what it used to be and, as I have already written, there is today far too much to remember; the Soviet Union alone has 32 companies and every year sees the emergence of some promising dancer. I am sure that this book will prove of value to me and to all balletomanes.

Arnold Haskell

A

AAKESSON, Birgit (1908–), Swedish dancer and choreographer. She studied with **Mary Wigman** and made her debut in 1934 in Paris. During her early career she toured extensively in Europe and the United States, and in 1957 staged her first productions for the Royal Swedish Ballet. They were *The Minotaur, Rites, Play for Eight* and *Icaros*. In 1963, with **Anthony Tudor** and **Birgit Cullberg**, she assumed responsibility for the artistic policy of the Royal Swedish Ballet.

Abraxas, a ballet in five scenes. Libretto, Heinrich Heine; choreography, Marcel Luipart; music, Werner Egk; decor and costumes, Wolfgang Znamenacek. First performed at the Staatsoper, Munich, 6 June 1948. Principal dancers, Marcel Luipart (Faust), **Solange Schwarz** (Bellastriga), Irina Kladivova (Archiposa). Revived, 8 October 1949, by French choreographer **Janine Charrat** for the Berlin Städtische Oper. Principal dancers, Gabor Orban, Suse Preiser, Janine Charrat. This version had an unprecedented triumph in Germany. Revived at the State Theatre, Hamburg, in 1965. Choreography and production, **Peter van Dijk**; decor and costumes, Eckehard Grübler. Principal dancers, Peter van Dijk, **Marilyn Burr, Nina Vyroubova,** Christa Kempf (Marguerita). The ballet is based on the Faust legend, but departs from tradition by making the devil a woman, Bellastriga, who enlists the aid of Satan's paramour, Archiposa.

abstract ballet or **absolute ballet,** dance in which the movements are expressed for their own sake and are not confined by plot or libretto.

Académie Royale de Danse, L', the first dance academy, established by Louis XIV in Paris, 1661. Louis XIV combined this Académie with l'**Académie Royale de Musique** in 1672, naming **Jean Baptiste Lully** as director. *See* **Ballet, history of.**

Académie Royale de Musique, L', an academy founded in Paris in 1671, with **Jean Baptiste Lully** as director after 1672. The Académie was renamed Théâtre National de l'Opéra in 1871. *See* **Paris Opéra Ballet,** and **Ballet, history of.**

adagio or **adage,** literally at ease, slowly. 1) Sequence of exercises performed slowly with deliberation and designed to develop grace and balance. 2) Portion of a **pas de deux** in classical ballets. It usually depicts a love episode and displays the skill and virtuosity of the ballerina and her partner dancing together.

ADAMA, Richard (Richard Adams, 1928–), American dancer. He studied with **Bronislava Nijinska,** and danced with the Original Ballet Russe (1948), **Grand Ballet du Marquis de Cuevas** (1949–54), and **Maurice Béjart**'s company. From 1955–61 he was first soloist with the Vienna State Opera Ballet; his repertoire included *Giselle, Swan Lake, Les Sylphides, Le Spectre de la Rose* and *Hamlet*. For the Hanover Opera Ballet he revised *Giselle* to follow the original score. In 1963 he became the director of the Bremen State Opera Ballet, Germany, for which he re-created **Taglioni**'s *La Sylphide*.

ADAME MIROIR, a psychological ballet in one act. Libretto and choreography, **Janine Charrat**; music, Darius Milhaud; decor, Paul Delvaux; costumes, Jacques Fath. First performed at the Marigny Theatre, 31 May 1948, by **Les Ballets de Paris de Roland Petit.** Solo dancer,

Roland Petit. Dressed as a sailor, the soloist dances in a corridor of mirrors in which reflections of other dancers appear. The theme is his struggle between consciousness and nightmare.

ADAM ZERO, a ballet in one act. Libretto, Michael Benthall; choreography, **Robert Helpmann**; music, Arthur Bliss; decor, Roger Furse. First performed at the Royal Opera House, Covent Garden, London, 10 April 1946, by Sadler's Wells Ballet. Principal dancers, Robert Helpmann (Adam Zero), **June Brae** and David Paltenghi. The ballet symbolises man's life from birth to death with the Fates dictating the duration and events of his life.

ADAMS, David (1928–   ), Canadian dancer and choreographer. He studied at the Winnipeg Ballet School and later in London where he joined Sadler's Wells Theatre Ballet. From 1946–8 he danced with **International Ballet** and **Metropolitan Ballet** for whom he created one of the male roles in *Designs with Strings*. In 1951 he returned to Canada to join the newly formed National Ballet of Canada. He danced the major roles in *Swan Lake*, *Giselle, Coppélia* and many others. His first choreographic work was *Suite No. 3* for London's **Festival Ballet**, where he was principal dancer. His best known choreographic work is *Barbara Allen* (1960). He joined **The Royal Ballet** (1964) and in 1966 appeared with Margot Fonteyn in a Gala Performance at Lisbon.

ADAMS, Diana (1926–   ), American ballerina and teacher. She studied with **Agnes de Mille,** Edward Caton and **Antony Tudor** in New York. In 1944 she joined **Ballet Theatre** for which she danced *Pillar of Fire, Undertow,* Helen in *Helen of Troy,* Queen of the Wilis in *Giselle* and created the role of Mother in *Fall River Legend.* She joined **The New York City Ballet** in 1950 and danced major roles in *Agon* (1957) and *The Prodigal Son.* She taught at the School of American Ballet, New York. Appeared with Danny Kaye in the film *Knock on Wood.*

Age of Anxiety: performed by New York City Ballet. Ph. New York City Ballet.

ADELAIDE or **Le Langage des Fleurs,** a ballet. Choreography, **Ivan Clustine**; scenario and music, Maurice Ravel (*Valses Nobles et Sentimentales*). First performed at the Théâtre du Châtelet, 1912. Principal dancer, Natasha Trouhanova. Revived in 1917; choreography, Ambrosini. Revived, 1938, at the Paris Opéra; choreography, **Serge Lifar**; decor, Brianchon. This version contained a notable pas de deux by Lifar (The Poet) and **Lycette Darsonval** (The Muse).

AFTERNOON OF A FAUN, THE, *see* **Après-midi d'un Faune, L'.**

AGE OF ANXIETY, a psychological ballet in one act, based on Auden's poem of the same name. Choreography, **Jerome Robbins**; music, Leonard Bernstein; decor, Oliver Smith; costumes, Irene Sharaff. First performed in New York City Center, 26 February 1950, by **The New York City Ballet.** Principal dancers, **Tanaquil Le-Clercq, Francisco Moncion, Todd Bolender, Jerome Robbins.** Four strangers seek security in companionship, but each is ultimately compelled to accept loneliness.

AGLAË or **L'Élève de l'Amour,** a divertissement in one act. Libretto and choreography, **Filippo Taglioni**; music, Keller. First performed, 22 January 1841, at St. Petersburg. Principal dancer, **Maria Taglioni**. Revived, 8 July 1841, at Her Majesty's Theatre, London. Principal dancer, Maria Taglioni. **Anton Dolin** based his 1942 ballet, *Romantic Age*, on *Aglaë*.

AGON, a ballet in one act. Choreography, **George Balanchine**; music, Stravinsky; decor, Nananne Porcher. First produced in New York City Center, 27 November 1957, by **The New York City Ballet.** Principal dancers, **Arthur Mitchell, Edward Villella, Allegra Kent, Violette Verdy.** The same music was used by **The Royal Ballet** for their 1958 production. Choreography, **Kenneth MacMillan**; decor, Nicholas Georgiadis. Principal dancers, **Anya Linden** and **David Blair.** The music

Agon, by Stravinsky: performed by New York City Ballet, with choreography by George Balanchine. Ph. Lipnitzki.

and the original choreography are intricate and interdependent. Balanchine used sarabandes, galliards and branles doubles from the province of Poitou. This succession of rhythms was called 'combat' (*agon*) in the 17th century. The ballet depicts a contest between a boy and a girl dancer.

ALDOUS, Lucette (1939–   ), British ballerina, born in New Zealand. Small but dynamic, she studied in Australia, and in 1955 joined the Royal Ballet School, London. From 1957–63 she danced with Ballet Rambert, moving from soloist to ballerina. She danced principal roles in *Giselle, Coppélia, La Sylphide* and *Don Quixote*. She joined London's **Festival Ballet** in 1963, and **The Royal Ballet** in 1966. She left the Royal Ballet, and joined Australian Ballet.

ALEKO, a ballet in one act, based on Pushkin's poem, *The Gypsies*. Libretto and choreography, **Léonide Massine**; music, Tchaikovsky; decor and costumes, Marc Chagall. First performed in Mexico City, 8 September 1942, by **Ballet Theatre.** The following month it was performed at the Metropolitan Opera House, New York. Principal dancers were **George Skibine** (Aleko), **Alicia Markova** (Zemphira), **Hugh Laing** (Gypsy), **Antony Tudor** (Zemphira's Father). Memorable performances have also been given by **Nora Kaye,** Léonide Massine, **Anton Dolin** and **André Eglevsky.** The ballet depicts the flirtation of Zemphira, a gypsy chief's daughter with two men, and the consequences.

ALEXANDRE LE GRAND, a heroic ballet in prologue, three scenes and epilogue. Libretto and choreography, **Serge Lifar**; music, Philippe Gaubert (*Inscriptions pour les Portes de la Ville*); decor and costumes, P. R. Larthe. First performed at the Paris Opéra, 21 June 1937, by the **Paris Opéra Ballet.** Principal dancers, Serge Lifar (Alexandre), **Yvette Chauviré** (Young Girl from Judea), **Solange Schwarz** (Egyptian Girl), Suzanne Lorcia (Queen of Babylon).

The work shows Alexander the Great setting out to conquer the world, but he is finally poisoned by the Queen of Babylon.

ALGAROV, Youly (1918–), French dancer, born in Russia. He studied under **Eugenia Eduardova, Lubov Egorova** and **Boris Kniasev,** making his debut in Paris in 1937. He was a leading dancer with **Les Ballets des Champs-Elysées** (1945) and **Nouveau Ballet de Monte Carlo,** and created the role of Tariel in *Chota Roustaveli.* In 1952 he became premier danseur étoile of the **Paris Opéra Ballet,** where his repertoire included *Giselle, Jeu de Cartes* and *Suite en Blanc.* Algarov appeared with European companies and gained international fame. In 1965 he became an impresario in Paris.

ALGERANOVA, Claudie (Claudie Leonard, 1924–), British dancer, born in Paris. After studying at the Cone-Ripman School, she joined **International Ballet** (1941), dancing major roles in the classic repertoire. In 1954 she joined **Boro-vansky's** Australian Ballet. She became ballerina at the Lucerne Opera, Switzerland, in 1959, and later joined the Munich State Opera Ballet.

ALGUES, LES, a ballet in four scenes. Libretto, L. B. Castelli; choreography, **Janine Charrat;** music, Guy Bernard; decor, Castelli. First performed at the Théâtre des Champs-Elysées, 20 April 1953, by Ballets de Janine Charrat. Principal dancers, Janine Charrat, **Maria Fris, Peter van Dijk.** A young man feigns madness in order to join his sweetheart, who is a patient in a mental hospital. In this work, the music creates an atmosphere oppressive, dreamlike. It is one of Janine Charrat's major works.

Alhambra Ballets, a term used to denote a series of ballets performed at the Alhambra Theatre, London, between 1871 and 1914. They included *Beauty and the Beast* (1898), *Soldiers of the Queen* (1900) and *Dance Dream* (1911). The dancers included **Pierina Legnani,** Car-

Marie Allard. Ph. Pic.

lotta Mossetti, **Catherine Geltzer** and **Vassily Tikhomirov.** With the **Empire Ballets,** these were the only ballets performed in England at the time. The Danish ballerina, **Adeline Genée,** achieved great success there.

ALLAN, Maude (1883–1956), Canadian dancer, actress, pianist and painter. She studied in San Francisco, Vienna and Berlin. Wishing to recapture Greek plastic art, she danced barefoot in a loose tunic. An innovator of modern dance, she was noted for her appearance in *The Vision of Salome* (1903) in Vienna, to the music of Richard Strauss. She toured extensively, and when her dancing career ended, she taught. Wrote *My Life and Dancing* (1908).

ALLARD, Marie (1742–1802), French ballerina. She studied with **Gaetan Vestris,** making her debut at the Paris

Opéra in 1760. She danced the principal roles in the repertoire of her era, including the title roles in *Sylvia* and *Medea*. Although stout, she was very agile. She was Vestris' mistress and the mother of **Auguste Vestris**. She retired in 1782.

allegro, literally lively, quickly. 1) Any dance or exercise sequence comprising quick, brisk steps. 2) The specific group of brisk exercises which follows the **adagio** exercises in a lesson.

allongé, a position showing the body in an elongated horizontal line; usually an **arabesque.**

ALMA or **La Fille de Feu,** a romantic ballet in four acts. Libretto, Deshayes; choreography, **Fanny Cerito**; music, G. Costa; decor and costumes, W. Grieve. First performed, 23 June 1842, at Her Majesty's Theatre, London. Principal dancers, Fanny Cerito and **Jules Perrot.** An evil spirit, Belfégor, animates the statue of the beautiful Alma, but warns that if she falls in love she will revert to a statue. The ballet is famous for a pas de fascination set by Perrot and danced by him partnered by Cerito.

ALMA MATER, a humorous ballet in one act. Libretto, Edward Warburg; choreography, **George Balanchine**; music, Kay Swift (arranged by Morton Gould); decor, Eugene Dunkel; costumes, John Held, Jr. First produced at the Adelphi Theatre, New York, 1 March 1935, by **The American Ballet.** Principal dancers, Gisella Caccialanza, Heidi Vosseler, **William Dollar,** Charles Laskey. In line with **Lincoln Kirstein**'s view (shared by Warburg) that the company's productions should typify the American way of life, this ballet depicts American college girls and boys at a football match. Characters emerge in the cheer leaders and the students.

ALONSO, Alberto (1917–), Cuban dancer, choreographer and teacher. He was a soloist with the **Ballet Russe de Monte Carlo** (1935–40) and American Ballet Theatre (1940–3; 1945–8). He worked as a choreographer and teacher in Havana at the Sociedad Pro Arte Musicale. In 1948 he collaborated with his sister **Alicia Alonso** in the founding of her company Ballet Alicia Alonso. He was a soloist with the **National Ballet of Cuba** (1959–61). His repertoire includes the title role in *The Prodigal Son*, Gossip in *Paganini* and the title role in *Petrouchka*. As a choreographer, he staged *Carmen* for the Bolshoi Ballet (1968) and *El Guije*, in which he combined classicism and Cuban folklore dances.

ALONSO, Alicia (Alicia Martinez, 1909–), Cuban ballerina, wife of **Fernando Alonso**. Initially a student at Sociedad Pro Arte Musicale, Havana, she later studied with **Alexandra Fedorova, Anatole Vilzak** and Léon Fokine. From 1939–60 she danced with Ballet Caravan, **Ballet Theatre,** Pro Arte (Havana) and **Ballet Russe de Monte Carlo,** moving from soloist to ballerina. In 1948 she formed her own company, Ballet Alicia Alonso, which, in 1955, became the **National Ballet of Cuba.** Her extensive repertoire includes *Les Sylphides*, *Giselle*, *Fall River Legend*, her outstanding Odile in *Swan Lake*, *Romeo and Juliet*, *Aleko* and *Gala Performance*. She has made numerous guest and concert appearances, and has headed her company on tour in the Soviet Union, Manchuria, Mexico, Canada and Paris.

ALONSO, Fernando (1914–), Cuban dancer and teacher. He studied in Cuba and, with **Mordkin, Fedorova** and **Vilzak,** in New York, making his debut with the Mordkin Ballet. He danced with **Ballet Theatre** (1941), Pro-Arte Musicale, Cuba (1941–8), and American Ballet Theatre (1943–8). Among his roles were Peter in *Peter and the Wolf*, and Faun and Ajax in *Helen of Troy*. He became director of Ballet Alicia Alonso (later **National Ballet of Cuba**) in 1948 and, as director and teacher, formed a generation of outstanding dancers. He is married to **Alicia Alonso.**

Josette Amiel: with Peter van Dijk. Ph. Lipnitzki.

AMBOISE, Jacques d' (1934–), American dancer. A pupil of the School of American Ballet, he joined **The New York City Ballet** in 1950, assuming leading roles in 1953. He created roles in *Episodes* and *Movements*, and has danced in *The Nutcracker* and *A Midsummer Night's Dream*. He has choreographed *The Chase* (1963) and *Irish Fantasy* (1964).

American Ballet, The, a company founded by **Lincoln Kirstein** and Edward M. M. Warburg in collaboration with **Balanchine** in 1934. It first appeared in Hartford, Connecticut in December, 1934, and appeared a few months later in New York, presenting seven ballets by Balanchine, including *Songes*, *L'Errante* and *Serenade*. The company became the opera ballet at the Metropolitan Opera in New York in 1935. When attached to the Opera (1935–8) the company staged many modern works, including *Orfeo ed Euridice* (Gluck's opera as a ballet), *Apollon Musagète*, *The Card Party*, and *Le Baiser de la Fée* to music by Stravinsky. The Metropolitan Opera and the American Ballet separated in 1938, and the company was inactive until 1941 when, under Kirstein, it toured South America with members of the Ballet Caravan, becoming The American Ballet Caravan. Balanchine was artistic director, and the repertoire included a number of new works including **Concerto Barocco**. The company disbanded after the tour, but left its mark by preparing the way for **The New York City Ballet**, and by firmly establishing ballet in the United States. Choreographers and dancers include **William Dollar, Todd Bolender, John Taras** and **Lew Christensen**.

American Ballet Caravan *see* **American Ballet, The.**

American Ballet Theatre *see* **Ballet Theatre.**

AMIEL, Josette, French ballerina. She studied at the Conservatoire Français, and made her debut at the Opéra Comique. In 1952 she joined the corps de ballet at the **Paris Opéra Ballet,** becoming première danseuse (1955), and étoile (1958). Her repertoire includes *La Belle Hélène,* **Bourmeister's** *Swan Lake* and **Balanchine's** *Gounod Symphony.* As guest artist she has appeared with Rome Opera Ballet, the Royal Danish Ballet and **Ruth Page's** Chicago Opera Ballet.

AMOR BRUJO, EL, a ballet in one act. Libretto, G. Martinez Sierra; choreography, Pastora Imperio; music, Manuel de Falla. First performed, 15 April 1915, at Teatre Lara, Madrid. Principal dancer, Pastora Imperio (Candelas). Versions have been choreographed by **La Argentinita,** La Méri, **Boris Romanov, Léon Woizikowsky, Serge Lifar** and **Antonio.** There was a revival in 1963 for Jacob's Pillow Dance Festival. Principal dancer, Maria Alba. This is a story of gypsy love inspired by Spanish folklore. The Ritual Fire Dance is a popular solo Spanish dance.

AMOUR ET SON AMOUR, L', a ballet in one act. Choreography, **Jean Babilée;** music, César Franck (*Psyche*); decor, Jean Cocteau. First performed at the Théâtre des Champs-Elysées, 14 December 1948, by **Les Ballets des Champs-Elysées.** Principal dancers, Jean Babilée and **Nathalie Philippart.** The work retells the legend of Cupid and Psyche, and was Babilée's first ballet.

AMOURS DE JUPITER, LES, a ballet in five scenes. Libretto, **Boris Kochno;** choreography, **Roland Petit;** music, Jacques Ibert; decor, Jean Hugo. First performed at the Théâtre des Champs-Elysées, 5 March 1946, by **Les Ballets des Champs-Elysées.** Principal dancers, Roland Petit (Jupiter), Ana Nevada (Juno), **Nathalie Philippart** (Danaë), **Irène Skorik** (Leda), **Ethéry Pagava** (Ganymede), **Jean Babilée** (Mercury). The ballet is based on Ovid's *Metamorphoses.*

AMOURS DES DIEUX, LES, a ballet by Louis Fuzelier and Mouret, in which **Marie Sallé** made her Paris Opéra debut in 1727.

Amsterdams Ballet *see* **Holland, history of ballet in.**

ANDERSSON, Gerd (1932–), Swedish ballerina. A pupil and dancer of the Royal Swedish Ballet, she made her debut in *Abraxas* (1951), and became ballerina in 1958. Her roles included Glove Seller in *Gaieté Parisienne,* Swanilda in *Coppélia* and Princess of the Copper Mountain in *The Stone Flower.* She created the leading female role in *Echoes of Trumpets* (1963).

ANDREANI, Jean-Paul (1929–), French dancer. He studied at the Paris Opéra school with **Serge Peretti,** becoming premier danseur with the company (1948), and étoile in 1953. He created principal roles in **Lifar's** *Blanche Neige* (1951), *Grand Pas* (1953), *Romeo and Juliet* (1955) and *Gounod Symphony* (1959). His repertoire also includes *Swan Lake* and *Pastorale.*

ANDREYANOVA, Elena Ivanovna (1819–57), Russian ballerina. She studied at the Imperial School of Ballet in St. Petersburg and made her debut in 1837, but her performance was eclipsed by the presence of **Marie Taglioni.** In 1842 she danced the title role in the first performance in Russia of *Giselle.*

ANGE GRIS, L', a ballet in one scene. Libretto, the **Marquis de Cuevas;** choreography, **George Skibine;** music, Debussy (*Suite Bergomasque*); decor and costumes, Sebire. First performed at the Casino de Deauville, 20 October 1953, by **Grand Ballet du Marquis de Cuevas.** Principal dancers, **Marjorie Tallchief, Kathleen Gorham,** George Skibine, **Serge Golovine.** At the betrothal of her daughter, a beautiful woman dreams of the man she loved long ago. He returns to her as the angel of death.

ANGIOLINI, Gasparo (1731–1803), Italian dancer, composer and choreographer. He was ballet master of the Vienna Hofoper when Gluck was opera master at the Court Theatre; he choreographed *Don Juan* (1761) and *Semiramis* (1765), to Gluck's music. He succeeded **Hilferding** as ballet master at St. Petersburg in 1766. He argued with **Jean-Georges Noverre** on whether ballet stories should be in the theatre programme.

ANIMAUX MODÈLES, LES, a ballet in prologue, one act and epilogue, based on the fables of La Fontaine. Choreography, **Serge Lifar**; music, Francis Poulenc; decor and costumes, Brianchon. First performed, 8 August 1942, at the Paris Opéra. Principal dancers, Serge Lifar; **Solange Schwarz**, Susanne Lorcia, **Serge Perreti, Yvette Chauviré.** After a rural prologue, the ballet retells six fables of La Fontaine.

ANISIMOVA, Nina (1909–   ), Russian dancer and choreographer. She trained at the Leningrad Ballet School under **Agrippina Vaganova**, and was leading character dancer at the Kirov Theatre, where she won fame for her interpretation of the role of Térèse in *The Flames of Paris*. She was among the first female choreographers in the Soviet Union, and rechoreographed *Coppélia* (1949) and *Schéhérazade* (1950), as well as creating *Gayané* (1945), *Willow Tree* (1957), and other roles. She retired from dancing in 1957.

ANNABEL LEE, a ballet in one act, based on the poem by Edgar Allan Poe. Choreography, **George Skibine**; music, Byron Schiffman; decor and costumes, André Delfau. First performed at the Casino de Deauville, 26 August 1951, by the **Grand Ballet du Marquis de Cuevas.** Principal dancers, **Marjorie Tallchief** (Annabel Lee), George Skibine (Her Lover). Revived, 1957, at the Opéra Comique, Paris, with the same principal dancers. The ballet has been widely performed. Poe's poem is sung during the performance.

ANTIGONE, a ballet in one act, based on the play by Sophocles. Choreography, **John Cranko**; music, Mikis Theodorakis; decor, Rufino Tamayo. First performed at the Royal Opera House, Covent Garden, London, 19 October 1959, by **The Royal Ballet.** Principal dancers, **Svetlana Beriosova** (Antigone), **Donald Macleary** (Haemon), **David Blair** (Polynices), **Michael Somes** (Creon), Gary Burne (Etiocles), **Julia Farron** (Jocasta), **Leslie Edwards** (Oedipus). The ballet shows Creon forbidding burial to the sons of Oedipus. Antigone defies him and buries her brother Polynices by night.

ANTONIA, a ballet in one act. Libretto and choreography, **Walter Gore**; music, Sibelius (*The Bard*, incidental music from *The Tempest*, and 'Festive' from *Scènes Historiques*); decor, Harry Cordwell. First performed at the King's Theatre, Hammersmith, London, 17 October 1949, by Ballet Rambert. Principal dancers, Paula Hinton (Antonia), David Peltenghi (Sebastian), Walter Gore (Rafael). The work depicts a man's grief and desire for revenge when he finds that his loved one has been unfaithful.

ANTONIO (Antonio Ruiz Soler, 1922–   ), Spanish dancer. He studied with Realito, making his debut in 1928 with his cousin Rosario. They toured all over the world until 1953 when Antonio formed his own company. He attempted to unite classic ballet with Spanish dance. His version of *El Amor Brujo* is an example of this.

aplomb, the equilibrium necessary for stability and balance in executing a pose or movement.

APOLLO or **Apollon Musagète,** a ballet in two scenes. Choreography, **George Balanchine**; music, Stravinsky; decor, André Bauchant. First performed at the Théâtre Sarah Bernhardt, Paris, 12 June 1928, by **Diaghilev**'s Ballets Russes. Principal dancers, **Serge Lifar** (Apollo), **Alice Nikitina** and **Alexandra Danilova** (Terpsichore), **Lubov Tchernicheva**

(Polyhymnia), Felia Doubrovska (Calliope). Revived as *Apollon Musagète* with decor by Stewart Chaney at the Metropolitan Opera House, New York, April 1937, for **The American Ballet**. Principal dancers, Lew Christensen, (Apollo), Elise Reiman, Holly Howard, Daphne Vane (The Muses). Revived at the Metropolitan Opera House, New York, 25 April 1943, by **Ballet Theatre**; decor, Pavel Tchelitchev. Principal dancers, **André Eglevsky** (Apollo), Vera Zorina, **Nora Kaye, Rosella Hightower** (The Muses). Revived at New York City Center, 15 November 1951, by **The New York City Ballet**. Principal dancers, André Eglevsky (Apollo), **Maria Tallchief, Tanaquil**

LeClercq, Diana Adams (The Muses). Danced at Copenhagen, 7 January 1957, by the Royal Danish Ballet. Principal dancers, Henning Kronstam, **Kirsten Simone,** Kirsten Petersen. Staged by George Balanchine under the title *Apollon Musagète*, at the Royal Opera House, Covent Garden, London, 15 November 1966, for **The Royal Ballet**. Principal dancers, **Donald Macleary, Svetlana Beriosova,** Georgina Parkinson. Apollo dances with all the Muses in turn, before ascending Olympus to drive his sun chariot across the heavens, the scene which provides the apotheosis.

APPARITIONS, a ballet in prologue,

Apollo: Henning Kronstam, Kirsten Simone and members of the Royal Danish Balle. Ph. Mogens von Havens.

three scenes and epilogue. Libretto, Constant Lambert (after the theme of Berlioz' *Symphonie Fantastique*) ; choreography, **Frederick Ashton**; music, Franz Liszt (orchestrated by Gordon Jacob); decor, Cecil Beaton. First performed at Sadler's Wells Theatre, London, 11 February 1936, by Vic-Wells Ballet. Principal dancers, **Margot Fonteyn** (Woman in Ball Dress), **Robert Helpmann** (Poet), **Harold Turner** (Hussar), Maurice Brooke (Monk). Revived by Sadler's Wells Theatre Ballet in 1947. Principal dancers, Anne Heaton, **John Field**. Seeking inspiration, the poet turns to opium. His subsequent visions are, he realizes, symbols of his own life; disillusioned, he stabs himself. Margot Fonteyn's dancing greatly contributed to the success of this work.

APPLEYARD, Beatrice (1918–), British ballerina and choreographer. She studied with **Ninette de Valois, Karsavina** and **Nijinska**. One of the first members of the Vic-Wells Ballet, she became soloist with the Markova-Dolin Ballet in 1935. In 1951 she took a teaching post in Turkey.

APRÈS-MIDI D'UN FAUNE, L' or **Afternoon of a Faun**, a ballet in one act, based on a poem by Mallarmé. Choreography, **Vaslav Nijinsky**; music, Debussy; decor and costumes, **Léon Bakst**. First performed at the Théâtre du Chatelet, 29 May 1912, by **Diaghilev**'s Ballets Russes. Principal dancer, Vaslav Nijinsky (The Faun). The choreography caused a major scandal, but the ballet has had many revivals throughout the world, with **Serge Lifar, David Lichine** and **Jean Babilée** notable in the role of the Faun. In his version, Lifar omitted the nymphs and danced alone. The original version was revived in 1967 by **Marie Rambert** for Ballet Rambert. Principal dancers, Christopher Bruce, Marilyn Williams. The American choreographer **Jerome Robbins** produced a new version, 14 May 1953, for **The New York City Ballet**. Decor, Jean Rosenthal; costumes, Irene Sharaff. This version was revived at the

Royal Opera House, Covent Garden. 14 December 1971, by **The Royal Ballet**. Principal dancers, **Antoinette Sibley, Anthony Dowell**. Robbins exchanged the original setting for an empty dance studio on a hot afternoon.

arabesque, position in which one leg supports the body and the other is extended to the back. The body stretches forward and one or both arms extend the line of the raised leg. The weight may be carried **pointe** (on the toe), demi-pointe (on the ball of the foot) or on the whole foot.

ARAUJO, Loipa, Cuban dancer. She was a Gold Medal winner at Varna in 1965, and a Silver Medallist and Laureat at the First Moscow International Dance Competition in 1969. She has danced in London, Paris, New York and Moscow.

ARBEAU, Thoinot (Jehan Tabouret, 1519–95), French priest, Canon of Langres. His *Orchésographie*, published in 1588, records, in detail, 16th century society dances, including the musical notation which is now used in **Ashton**'s *Capriol Suite*. The principles of the turned-out legs and feet, later formulated by **Pierre Beauchamp**, are defined through a system of dance notation. A modern translation has been published by **Cyril Beaumont** (London: 1925), and Kamin Dance Publications (New York: 1948).

ARGENTINA, La (Antonia Mercé y Luque, 1888–1936), Argentinian dancer. Her parents were professional dancers, and she started her ballet and Spanish dance training with them when only four, making her debut in 1899 at the Royal Theatre, Madrid. Her first appearances in America (1916 and 1919) were unsuccessful. However, in 1928 she returned, and from then until 1936 made several tours of North America. She also danced at the **Paris Opéra Ballet**, appearing as Candelas in *L'Amour Sorcier*. She was responsible for the revival of Spanish dancing.

La Argentina. Ph. d'Ora.

ARGENTINITA, La (Encarnación López Julves, 1898–1945), Spanish dancer, born in Argentina. She started her training in the Spanish classic dance at the age of four, in Spain, giving her first recitals in 1924. She danced in many countries of Europe. With Federico García Lorca she organized the Madrid Ballet (1932). **Solomon Hurok**, her manager, presented La Argentinita and her group all over the United States and Central and South America (1938). She appeared with **Ballet Theatre** for whom she choreographed *Bolero* and *Goyescas*.

ARGYLE, Pearl (Pearl Wellman, 1910–1947), British ballerina and actress. A **Rambert** pupil, she created several roles in Ballet Club productions, including *The Mermaid* and *Cinderella*. She also danced for Les Ballets 1933 and **The Camargo Society**. She joined Sadler's Wells Ballet in 1935, creating the roles of the Fairy in *Le Baiser de la Fée*, the Serving Maid in

The Gods Go a'Begging and the Queen in *Le Roi Nu*; her finest role was in *Swan Lake*. In 1938 she married and moved to the United States, where she danced in a number of musicals.

ARI, Carina (Carina Janssen, 1897–), Swedish ballerina and choreographer. She studied at the Royal Swedish Ballet School and with **Fokine** when he was in Denmark. She was ballerina of Les Ballets Suédois from 1920–6, when she moved to Paris to become ballet mistress of the Opéra Comique. There she choreographed a number of works, including *Valses de Brahms* and *Jeux de Couleurs*.

AROVA, Sonia (Sonia Errio, 1927–), British ballerina, born in Bulgaria. Her early training was with the Opera Ballet in Sofia, and under **Preobrajenska** and

Sonia Arova. Ph. Iris.

Lifar in Paris. She made her debut with **International Ballet** in 1942, joining Ballet Rambert four years later. For the Metropolitan Ballet, where she went in 1947, she created one of the female leads in *Design with Strings*, and a leading role in *Lovers' Gallery*. She has been guest artist with **Les Ballets des Champs-Elysées**, creating Azucena in *Revenge* (1951); with London's **Festival Ballet**, creating the title role in *The Merry Widow* (1953) and with **Ruth Page**'s Chicago Opera Ballet. She was the first western ballerina to appear with the Komaki Ballet, Japan (1951). In 1962 she partnered **Nureyev** in Paris, in America for his debut (*Don Quixote*), and with **The Royal Ballet**, London (*Swan Lake*). She was guest ballerina at Jacob's Pillow Dance Festival (1962); with the Australian Ballet (1962–3); American Ballet Theatre (1965) and National Ballet, Washington (1963–5). In 1966 she became ballerina and ballet mistress of the Norwegian State Opera Ballet, Oslo. She was appointed director of the Hamburg State Opera Ballet in 1970.

ASHBRIDGE, Bryan (1927–   ), New Zealand dancer. After studying under Kirsova and **Borovansky**, he entered Sadler's Wells School, joining the Sadler's Wells Ballet (now **The Royal Ballet**) in 1948, and becoming soloist in 1954 and principal dancer in 1958. His roles have included Siegfried in *Swan Lake*, Albrecht in *Giselle*, Orion in *Sylvia* and the Prince in *Cinderella*. He has toured widely as guest artist with the Margot Fonteyn Concert Ballet. In 1963 he left The Royal Ballet and returned to New Zealand.

ASHTON, Frederick (1906–   ), British dancer, choreographer and director, born in Ecuador. He studied with **Léonide Massine** and **Marie Rambert**, dancing with Ballet Rambert in 1926. In 1927, with the **Ida Rubinstein** company, he studied choreography under **Nijinska** and Massine. He returned to Ballet Rambert in 1928 and remained until 1935, choreographing not only for the Rambert company but also for **The Camargo Society** and the Vic-

Sir Frederick Ashton. Ph. Dominic.

Wells Ballet. From this prolific period dates his first work, *A Tragedy of Fashion* (1926), and also *La Péri* and *Façade* (both 1931). As chief choreographer of Vic-Wells Ballet (1935–9), he created *Le Baiser de la Fée, Nocturne, Apparitions, Les Patineurs, A Wedding Bouquet* and *Horoscope*. These ballets were wider in range than his previous works, and usually featured **Margot Fonteyn** as principal dancer. His ballets from the years of World War II include *Dante Sonata. The Wise Virgins* and *The Quest*. In 1946 Sadler's Wells Ballet moved to Covent Garden, and here Ashton's works can be categorized into three groups: the abstract ballets, e.g. *Symphonic Variations* and *Homage to the Queen* (celebrating the coronation of Queen Elizabeth II); the one-act dramatic ballets, e.g. *Daphnis and Chloë, Tiresias, Madame Chrysanthème* and *Don Juan*; the spectacular three-act ballets, e.g. *Cinderella, Sylvia* (the first full-length ballet by a British choreographer), *Ondine* and *La Fille Mal Gardée*. Ashton also created works for the **Ballet Russe de Monte Carlo,** Sadler's Wells Theatre Ballet, **The New York City Ballet,** the Royal Danish Ballet, **Teatro alla Scala,** Milan and the Old Vic. In 1952 he became associate director of Sadler's Wells, and on the retirement of **Ninette de Valois** in 1963, was appointed director of what had become **The Royal Ballet.** In this capacity, he re-choreographed *Swan Lake* with **Robert Helpmann.** He created the first work for **Rudolph Nureyev** and Margot Fonteyn, *Marguerite and Armand*, in 1963. Other works for The Royal Ballet include *The Dream* (1964), *Monotones* (1966) and *Enigma Variations* (1968). In 1968 he staged a new version of *Les Noces*. *The Creatures of Prometheus* (1970) marked his retirement from The Royal Ballet. Since 1970 he has choreographed *The Two Pigeons* (1971) and the film ballet *The Tales of Beatrix Potter*.

Ashton's dancing has always taken second place to his work as a choreographer. Among his roles were the Dago in *Façade*, Spectator in *Nocturne* and Carabosse in *The Sleeping Beauty*. He was knighted in 1962, and was made a Companion of Honour (1970).

assemblé, literally an assembling. A jump in which the dancer lands with the feet together (usually in fifth position), having brought them together in the air.

ASSEMBLY BALL, a ballet in one act. Choreography, **Andrée Howard**; music, Bizet (*Symphony in C*); decor Andrée Howard. First performed at Sadler's Wells Theatre, London, 8 April 1946, by Sadler's Wells Theatre Ballet. Principal dancers, **June Brae,** Leo Kersley, Claude Newman. In later productions, **Svetlana Beriosova** and **David Blair** danced the principal roles. The ballet has no real theme, except for romance. There are some Scottish rhythms in the third movement.

ASTAFIEVA, Serafima (1876–1934), Russian dancer and teacher. She studied at the Imperial School of Ballet, St. Peters-burg, and danced at the Maryinsky Theatre. She was a member of **Diaghilev's** Ballets Russes from 1909–11, and later opened a ballet school in London. Among her pupils were **Markova, Dolin, Fonteyn** and **Haskell.**

attitude, position in which the body is supported on one leg, either bent or straight. The other leg is bent backwards, well bent at the knee. The arm on the side of the raised leg is raised above the head, or both arms are raised. In the French and Italian style, the knee is higher than the foot. In the Russian style, the foot is higher than the knee and resembles a slightly bent **arabesque.** The position was inspired by Giovanni Bologna's statue of Mercury.

AUMER, Jean-Pierre (1774–1833), French dancer and choreographer. A pupil of **Jean Dauberval,** he created ballets for the theatres of Porte-Saint-Martin, Lyon, Cassel, Vienna and the Paris Opéra. Among his ballets are *Deux Créoles* (1806), *Les Amours d'Antoine et Cléopâtre* (1808), *Aline* (1818), *La Sonnambula* (1827), *Manon Lescaut* (1830); his was probably the first *La Belle au Bois Dormant* (1829).

Jean-Pierre Aumer. Ph. Reyna.

AURORA'S WEDDING, a divertissement from the last act of *The Sleeping Beauty*. Choreography, **Marius Petipa**; music, Tchaikovsky; decor, **Léon Bakst**; costumes, Nathalie Gontcharova. First performed, 18 May 1922, at the Paris Opéra. Principal dancers, **Vera Trefilova** (Aurora), Pierre Vladimirov (The Prince). The work was taken into the repertoire of **Colonel de Basil's** Ballets Russes de Monte Carlo. Notable performances of Aurora have been given by **Alexandra Danilova, Irina Baronova** and **Tamara Toumanova**. A version by **Anton Dolin**, called *Princess Aurora*, was presented in New York, 26 November 1941, by **Ballet Theatre**. Principal dancers, Irina Baronova, **Alicia Markova, Alicia Alonso, Nora Kaye, Nana Gollner** (Aurora) and Anton Dolin (The Prince).

AUSTRALIA, history of ballet in,
1936–7 Ballet Russe de Monte Carlo visits Australia. Soloists Hélène Kirsova and **Edouard Borovansky** decide to stay.
1939 Borovansky and his wife open a ballet school in Melbourne.
1940 Borovansky presents his first ballets at the Princess Theatre, Melbourne. Kirsova opens a school and forms a company in Sydney.
1941 With Kirsova herself as ballerina, Kirsova Ballet gives its first season, with great success. Tours follow.
1944 Borovansky's company becomes professional with Tamara Tchinarova as ballerina. Tours with *Giselle, Coppélia, Swan Lake, etc* in the repertoire.
1946 Kirsova Ballet is disbanded. Kirsova returns to Europe. Laurel Martyn forms a small company in Melbourne to perform new works and establish a school.
1959 Death, in December, of Edouard Borovansky. **Peggy van Praagh** becomes artistic director of Borovansky Ballet.
1960 Borovansky Ballet is disbanded owing to lack of funds.
1962 Peggy van Praagh becomes artistic director of Australian Ballet, set up under the auspices of the Australian Ballet Foundation. Company is based on Borovansky Ballet with new young Australian dancers and guest artists from major European and American companies.
1962–3 First season of Australian Ballet. Ray Powell is ballet master. **Sonia Arova** and **Erik Bruhn** are guest artists. Harcourt Algeranov, **Kathleen Gorham** and Marilyn Jones are principal regular dancers. The repertoire includes *Swan Lake, Coppélia, Les Sylphides, The Lady and the Fool*. Rex Reed choreographs *The Night is a Sorceress* and *Melbourne Cup*.
1965 Australian Ballet tours Europe, visiting Lebanon, France, England, Scotland and Wales. **Rudolph Nureyev** stages *Raymonda*, **Robert Helpmann** choreographs *The Display* and *Yugen*. Helpmann becomes co-artistic director with Peggy van Praagh. The company subsequently tours the United States.
1970 Nureyev stages and dances in *Don Quixote* for the Adelaide festival.

Australian Ballet *see* **Australia, history of ballet in.**

AUTUMN LEAVES, a ballet in one act. Libretto and choreography, **Anna Pavlova**; music, Chopin (*Nocturne in D flat major* and *Fantaisie Impromptu*); decor, Konstantin Korovine. First performed, 1918, in Rio de Janeiro. Principal dancers, Anna Pávlova (Chrysanthemum), **Alexander Volinine** and Hubert Stowitts. An autumn wind breaks the chrysanthemum from its stalk and whirls it among the fallen leaves. It dies as the sun sets, despite the poet's attempt to revive it. This work was Anna Pavlova's only major essay in choreography.

AVELINE, Albert (1883–   ), French dancer, ballet master and teacher. His entire career has been with the **Paris Opéra Ballet,** where in 1917 he became danseur étoile and ballet master. He danced most of the principal roles in the repertoire of his period, and choreographed *La Grisi* (1935), *Elvire* (1937), *Les Santons* (1938), *Le Festin de l'Araignée* (1939), *Jeux d'Enfants* (1941), *La Grande Jatte* (1950) and *Les Indes Galantes* (1952). He was director of the Opéra ballet school.

B

BABILÉE, Jean (Jean Gutmann, 1923–), French dancer and choreographer. He trained at the Paris Opéra, and danced with local companies in Monte Carlo and Cannes. From 1945 until the company disbanded, he was with **Roland Petit's Les Ballets des Champs-Elysées**, creating the role of the Joker in *Jeu de Cartes*, and dancing in *Le Spectre de la Rose*, the Blue Bird pas de deux, and in *Le Jeune Homme et la Mort*. With the same company he made his debut as a choreographer with *L'Amour et son Amour* (1948), in which his wife, **Nathalie Philippart**, danced Psyche, and *Til Eulenspiegel* (1949). He later joined the **Grand Ballet du Marquis de Cuevas** as guest star (1950); appeared briefly with the **Paris Opéra Ballet** where he created *Hop Frog* (1953); was guest artist at **Teatro alla Scala**, Milan; and, as guest artist with American Ballet Theatre, staged *Til Eulenspiegel*. In 1956 he formed Les Ballets Babilée, choreographing *Balance à Trois*, *Le Boucle* and *Divertimento*.

Baby Ballerinas, the name, originally conceived for publicity purposes, given to **Irina Baronova**, **Tatiana Riabouchinska** and **Tamara Toumanova**, when they headed the Ballets Russes de Monte Carlo in 1932. Their ages then were thirteen, fifteen and fourteen, respectively.

BACCHANALE, a ballet in one act. Libretto, Salvador Dali; choreography, **Léonide Massine**; music, Richard Wagner (from *Tannhäuser*); decor, Dali. First performed at the Metropolitan Opera House, New York, 9 November 1939, by the **Ballet Russe de Monte Carlo**. Principal dancers, **Nathalie Krassovska**, Jeanette Lauret, Milada Mladova, **Nini Theilade**, **André Eglevsky**, Casimir Kokitch, Marc Platov, Christ Volkov.

Surrealist ballet, dealing with the insane dreams of King Ludwig II of Bavaria.

BAISER DE LA FÉE, LE, a ballet in four scenes, based on Hans Andersen's *The Ice Maiden*. Libretto, Stravinsky; choreography, **Bronislava Nijinska**; music (from themes by Tchaikovsky) Stravinsky; decor, **Alexandre Benois**. First performed at the Paris Opéra, 27 November 1928, by the **Ida Rubinstein** company. Revived at the Metropolitan Opera House, New York, 27 April 1937, by **The American Ballet**. Choreography, **George Balanchine**; decor, Alice Halika. Principal dancers, Gisella Caccialanza (Girl), **William Dollar** (Bridegroom), Kathryn Mullony (Fairy), Leda Anchutina (Friend), Annabelle Lyon (Mother). Revived at the Metropolitan Opera House, New York, 10 April 1940, by the **Ballet Russe de Monte Carlo**. Principal dancers, **Alexandra Danilova**, **André Eglevsky**, **Nini Theilade**; again revived at New York City Center, 17 February 1946, by the same company. Principal dancers, Alexandra Danilova, **Frederic Franklin**, Marie Jeanne and **Maria Tallchief**. Revived by Balanchine, 1948, for the Paris Opéra. A new version was produced at the New York City Center, 28 November 1950, by **The New York City Ballet**. Principal dancers, **Tanaquil LeClercq** (Bride), Maria Tallchief (Fairy), **Nicholas Magallanes** (Bridegroom), **Patricia Wilde** (Friend), Beatrice Tompkins (Mother). A version by **Frederick Ashton** was produced at Sadler's Wells Theatre, London, 26 November 1935, by the Sadler's Wells Ballet. Decor, Sophie Fedorovitch. Principal dancers, **Margot Fonteyn** (Bride), **Pearl Argyle** (Fairy), **Harold Turner** (Bridegroom). A version by **Kenneth MacMillan** was staged at the Royal Opera House, Covent Garden, London,

12 April 1960, by **The Royal Ballet.** Decor, Kenneth Rowell. Principal dancers, **Svetlana Beriosova** (Fairy), **Lynn Seymour** (Bride), **Donald MacLeary** (Bridegroom). The ballet depicts a mother and baby boy lost in a snowstorm. The baby is saved by a fairy's kiss, but a spell is cast over him that enables the fairy to reclaim him at the time of his greatest happiness, in order that his life might remain unspoilt. At his wedding the fairy takes him away to live among the immortals.

BAKST, Léon (1866–1924), Russian painter and designer. With **Diaghilev** and **Benois** he founded the *Mir Iskusstva* (World of Art) group of artists and art patrons. He developed a personal style employing bold simplifications and motifs from Russian folk art and created a series of influential designs for Diaghilev's Ballets Russes. These included *Carnaval*, *Schéhérazade*, *L'Après-midi d'un Faune*, *The Sleeping Beauty*.

BAL, LE, a ballet in two scenes. Libretto, **Boris Kochno**; choreography, **George Balanchine**; music, Rieti; decor, Giorgio de Chirico. First performed at the Théâtre de Monte Carlo, 5 July 1929, by **Diaghilev's** Ballets Russes. Principal dancers, **Alexandra Danilova**, **Alice Nikitina, Lydia Sokolova, Anton Dolin, Serge Lifar.** Revived at Essen, 1930, by Ballets Jooss. Choreography, **Kurt Jooss**; decor, Hein Hechroth. Revived, 1935, by Colonel de Basil's **Ballet Russe de Monte Carlo.** Choreography, **Léonide Massine.** In this ballet the decor assumes a greater than usual importance. There are entries from different countries, and a lovers' pas de deux, etc. A young man, in love with a beautiful woman at the ball, persuades her to remove her mask. Unmasked, she is revealed as an old woman, but ultimately this too is a mask hiding the face of a beautiful woman.

BALABINA, Feya Ivanovna (1910–   ), Russian dancer and teacher, Honoured Art Worker of the RSFSR. She studied in Leningrad, and was a soloist (1931–56) with the Kirov Ballet. Her roles include Tao-Hoa in *The Red Poppy*, Kitri in *Don Quixote*, and the title roles in *Esmeralda* and *Cinderella*. From 1947 she taught in Leningrad, becoming coach to the Kirov company in 1953 and artistic director in 1963.

balancé, step, usually in 3/4 time, in which the dancer rocks from foot to foot.

BALANCHINE, George (Georgy Melitonovitch Balanchivadze, 1904–   ), American dancer and choreographer, born in Russia. He studied at the Imperial School of Ballet, St. Petersburg (1914–21), and later joined **Diaghilev's** company in Paris (1924), creating *Apollo, The Prodigal Son, Barabau, The Triumph of Neptune, The Gods Go a'Begging* and *Le Bal.* For **Ballet Russe de Monte Carlo,** he choreographed *Cotillon* and *Le Bourgeois Gentilhomme.* He then founded Les Ballets 1933 at the Théâtre des Champs-Elysées aiming to present new ideas of music, dance and design in the tradition of Diaghilev. Among the ballets he created were *Mozartiana, Songes, Errante,* and *Les Sept Péchés Capitaux.* Principal dancers included **Tamara Toumanova, Nathalie Krassovska** and **Pearl Argyle.** That same year he was invited to organize the School of American Ballet and the American Ballet Company. Here he created *Alma Mater, Le Baiser de la Fée,* and *Card Party.* In 1946, with **Lincoln Kirstein,** he founded the Ballet Society which in 1948 became **The New York City Ballet** with Balanchine as artistic director. His many and notable revivals and new creations for this company included *Orpheus, The Four Temperaments, Bourée Fantasque, Agon, Ballet Impérial, Bugaku* and *Harlequinade;* and, in 1965, his highly successful full-length ballet, *Don Quixote.* On the opening night Balanchine danced the title role. In April 1964 the New York State Theater was opened. At this theatre Balanchine staged *Jewels* (1967), *Who Cares* and *Tchaikovsky Suite No 3* (1970). Balanchine's ballets are in the repertoires of **The Royal**

George Balanchine: with Jean Cocteau. P. Lipnitzki.

Ballet, London, The Royal Danish Ballet, the **Paris Opéra Ballet, Teatro alla Scala,** Milan, the Royal Swedish Ballet, and many others. Balanchine has continued and extended the classical technique of **Marius Petipa.** An advocate of 'pure dance', he believes that nothing in ballet (e.g. decor, costumes, plot) should distract attention from the dancing. He is the author of *Complete Stories of the Great Ballets* (1954). See *Balanchine* (1962) by Bernard Tapei.

BAL DES BLANCHISSEUSES, LE, a ballet in one act. Libretto, **Boris Kochno;** choreography, **Roland Petit;** music, Vernon Duke; decor and costumes, Stanislas Lepri. First performed in Paris, 19 December 1946, by **Les Ballets des Champs-Elysées.** Principal dancers, Roland Petit and Danielle Darmance. The choreography is largely acrobatic, and the ballet has characteristics of musical comedy. Enthralled by street music, an apprentice is surrounded by laundresses, one of whom he loves. He is loved by them all.

BALLABILE, a ballet in one act and six scenes. Choreography, **Roland Petit;** music, Emanuel Chabrier (arranged by Constant Lambert); decor, Antoni Clavé. First performed at the Royal Opera House, Covent Garden, London, 5 May 1950, by Sadler's Wells Ballet. Principal dancers, **Violetta Elvin,** Philip Chatfield, Alexander Grant, Anne Negus, Kenneth Melville. The work is a sequence of impressionistic scenes without a story line. It was Roland Petit's first work for Sadler's Wells Ballet.

ballerina, name derived from an Italian word meaning a female dancer and given to the female soloists in a ballet company once they have reached a specific rank. The term prima ballerina is given to the principal soloist, usually a dancer whose dancing and interpretation of roles has been acknowledged outside of the company of which she is a member. This status corresponds to the étoile star of the Paris Opéra where the name originally meant merely a senior member of the corps de ballet. A still higher rank is that of prima ballerina assoluta, a title accorded to only a selected few in the history of ballet: Legnani and Kchessinska and, in recent years, to Margot Fonteyn and Maya Plisetskaya.

ballet, history of, ballet is a theatrical performance which uses the concerted effects of dance and mime, music and decor, in a highly specialized form. The action may consist of a plot or merely of a situation. Dance was the original element, and, indeed, the word 'ballet' is derived from the Italian 'balletto' or 'ballo', meaning dance.

Ballet first emerged in a recognizable form in Italy during the Renaissance. The ancestors of Italian ballet were the mime-danced actions interpolated in medieval and Renaissance plays, and in traditional folk spectacles. Towards the second half of the 15th century the folk tradition was absorbed by the upper strata of Italian society; courtly masques and entertainments, with mythological themes, became popular. The dance was not choreographed as we know it today, but music was often added later.

A school of dancers and choreographers now flourished at court; early treatises on the dance were published by such masters as Dominic de Piacenza and **Antonio Cornazzano,** who determined the basic principles of choreographic composition and named the steps, of which there were nine. These ideas and the new form of dance had their greatest influence in France, which already had a tradition of courtly *mascarades.* Italian dancing masters, trained at **Cesare Negri'**s school in Milan, appeared at the European courts. The first notable result of this influx was the **Le Ballet Comique de la Reine,** devised in 1581 by Catherine de Medici's Master of Ceremonies, **Beaujoyeux,** to celebrate a betrothal. This was the first important court ballet, which co-ordinated singing, acting and dancing and had choreography based on geometric figures. At this stage, the performers were solely people of the court.

This court ballet, a **ballet de cour,** flourished in France under Henry IV in a form which spread throughout Europe, as far as Denmark and Sweden, in the late 16th and 17th centuries. Ballet-comique gave way to ballet-mascarade, a series of burlesque scenes or entrées in which music and song became more important. Paris and Versailles provided inspiration, while Italy still remained the technical innovator. The golden age of ballet de cour began during the reign of Louis XIV, himself a keen dancer, with the ballet à entrée, as it was now called. Professional dancers had by now taken their place among the courtiers. Sung recitative had replaced declamation, but words had not yet been dispensed with. The dancers' movement was greatly encumbered by heavy costumes, wigs and masks.

This was the era of **Jean Baptiste Lully,** the musician, and **Pierre Beauchamp,** the choreographer. Until now, male dancers had taken the female parts, but Lully was the first to abandon this practice and use women dancers. The foundation of the **L'Académie Royale de Danse** (1661) and L'École de Danse de L'Opera gave an added impetus; the rules of **en dehors** and **en dedans,** and the five positions of the feet were fixed.

Ballet was becoming professional. **L'Académie Royale de Musique** (now the **Paris Opéra Ballet**) opened by Louis XIV with Lully as director, took on the training of dancers. Among the great male dancers of the era were **Jean Balon** and **Louis Dupré,** regarded as the model for the danseur noble; **Marie Camargo** and **Marie Sallé** established the supremacy of the ballerina. These two were responsible for reform of ballet costume, by adopting shorter and lighter dresses, and soft slippers instead of heeled shoes. At the same time in Italy, the virtuoso dancing of **La Barberina** was the culmination of ballet technique. In England, **John Weaver'**s *Loves of Mars and Venus* (1717) was the first ballet to exclude song and speech once and for all.

It was in the 18th century that the form called **ballet d'action** liberated ballet from opera and gave it an independent existence as an art form. **Jean-Georges Noverre** was the originator of this new type of ballet, and his *Lettres sur la Danse et les Ballets* (1760) laid down the basic principles of ballet as we know it today; all elements are subordinated to the theme to create a unified design; the action is expressed entirely in mime. Superfluous gesture and costume are discarded and the dancer completely liberated. Noverre was ballet master at Stuttgart and finally at the Paris Opéra; none of his work has survived, but his most significant works were *La Toilette de Venus*, *Medée et Jason* and *Iphigenie en Tauris*, which he produced with Gluck.

The Austrian, **Hilferding,** the Italian, **Angiolini** and the Frenchmen **Antoine Bournonville** and **Didelot** introduced the ballet d'action to Italy, Russia and Denmark. Dramatic ballet was produced at La Scala, Milan, by **Salvatore Vigano.** Famous choreographers were **Gardel,** who first discarded his mask, and **Dauberval,** with his *La Fille Mal Gardée*, though his choreography has not survived. The greatest dancers were still men, however, such as **Gaetan Vestris** and his son, **Auguste Vestris.** The emergence of romantic ballet in the 19th century is linked with the Romantic movement, which rejected the emphasis on classical form. The new spirit found its expression in more poetic ballet, appealing directly to the emotions of the audience. Supernatural or rustic themes replaced mythology as subject-matter. White became the dominant colour, skin-coloured tights having been introduced and the **tu-tu** appeared at this time. The development of **pointe** work followed the adoption of light heelless shoes, giving the impression that the dancer was airborne. New teaching methods and ballet techniques were codified in **Carlo Blasis's** *Elementary Treatise* (1820).

Romantic ballet is epitomized by the rare spiritual quality of the ballerina **Marie Taglioni** in *La Sylphide*, staged for her by her father **Filippo Taglioni** in 1832. Another version of *La Sylphide*, choreographed by **August Bournonville** in 1836, helped to establish the Royal Danish Ballet as an outstanding ballet company.

Fanny Elssler, a less ethereal, more passionate dancer, brought the character dance into the repertoire. The Italian **Carlotta Grisi** is remembered as the star of *Giselle* (1841), perhaps the greatest of romantic ballets, which alone remains in the repertoire. One of the creators of *Giselle* was Théophile Gautier, a leader of the Romantic movement who did much to inspire and influence ballet. The great dancer and choreographer, **Jules Perrot,** had a success with *La Esmeralda* (1844), in London. Later Paris saw the creation of **Saint-Léon**'s *Coppélia* (1870), but by this time romantic ballet had passed its height; expression and grace had been largely sacrificed to technique. In London, this decline was partly due to a renewed interest in opera.

The centre of interest now shifts to St. Petersburg, where Perrot, Saint-Léon and **Petipa** successively built up a tradition of Russian ballet in the second half of the 17th century. This culminated in *The Sleeping Beauty* with music by Tchaikovsky, staged by Petipa in 1890 at the Maryinsky Theatre (home of the Imperial Ballet from 1889). *The Nutcracker* followed in 1892, and a brilliant revival of *Swan Lake* (1895), which had failed miserably in its first production. Foremost of the Italian dancers engaged at the Maryinsky was **Enrico Cecchetti,** whose **Cecchetti Method** revised ballet teaching, devised a new, logical set of exercises, and co-ordinated disparate elements of the dance. Under the great teacher **Christian Johansson** emerged a new generation of Russian dancers—**Kchessinska, Preobrajenska, Pavlova** and, of the men, **Nicholas Legat** and **Michel Fokine.** The ground was now prepared for the appearance of **Serge Diaghilev,** leader of a progressive group of artists in St. Petersburg, whose arrival at the Théâtre de Châtelet in Paris, in 1909, upset all preconceived ideas and standards. Paris audiences were astounded at the originality and high standard of Diaghilev's productions. He was not content to aim for the best ballet talent in his dancers alone, but also in those who contributed to the ballet. Thus besides the names of **Nijinsky, Karsavina,** Fokine and **Massine,** and all the other famous dancers and choreographers, are those of Stravinsky, Ravel, Poulenc, Picasso, Braque, **Benois** and **Bakst.** Fokine created for Diaghilev the ballets *Polovetsian Dances from Prince Igor, Les Sylphides* and *Petrouchka* ; Nijinsky produced *L'Après-midi d'un Faune* and *Le Sacre du Printemps.* From all these emerges the modern concept of ballet as made up of three composite elements, choreography, music and decor, as laid down by Fokine in **The Five Principles** (1914).

From 1909–20 the Diaghilev company toured all over Europe and America, often in places which had never seen ballet ; these twenty years gave ballet a new impetus. Diaghilev's last ballet was *The Prodigal Son* (1929) ; his later years are remembered for individual dancers such as the English **Lydia Sokolova, Alicia Markova, Ninette de Valois** and **Anton Dolin,** who were to be so important in establishing British ballet.

The great impact on dancing at this time was made by Pavlova, who did not subscribe to Diaghilev's ideas, but to whom the dance was unquestionably supreme. With enormous vitality and dedication, she formed her own company, chiefly of English dancers, and toured extensively. Her best known ballets are *Le Cygne* (1905) and *Autumn Leaves* (1918).

After the deaths of Diaghilev and Pavlova, attention was drawn to Monte Carlo where in 1932 **Colonel de Basil** and **René Blum** formed their Ballet Russe de Monte Carlo, which included as choreographers Massine and **Balanchine.** Many of Diaghilev's former dancers were engaged and his standards adhered to ; soon the company produced its own stars including the famous **Baby Ballerinas.** Of the new ballets the most important were those of Massine, in particular *Les Présages* (1933), performed to Tchaikovsky's Fifth Symphony. It was not long before the company split into two rival companies under de Basil and Blum,

subject to constant intrigues and quarrels ; they continued to tour and had considerable influence. The last important creation (of de Basil's company) was *Graduation Ball* (1940).

It was not until the 1920s that British ballet began to revive, with the foundation of the Royal Academy of Dancing and the Cecchetti Society. In 1930 **Marie Rambert** formed the Ballet Club (to become the Ballet Rambert), encouraging the young choreographers **Frederick Ashton** and **Antony Tudor** ; among the dancers to emerge were **Pearl Argyle, Harold Turner** and **Walter Gore. The Camargo Society,** founded in 1930 to maintain Diaghilev's ideals, produced the new ballets *Job* and *Façade.* In 1931 Ninette de Valois, with the aid of Lillian Baylis, established the Vic-Wells Ballet, headed by Markova and Dolin. The company has since produced dancers such as **Margot Fonteyn, Robert Helpmann, Svetlana Beriosova, Beryl Grey, David Blair** and **Michael Somes.** Its most important new ballet was *The Rake's Progress* (1935), a recreation of Hogarth's London ; de Valois' *Checkmate,* Ashton's *Apparitions* and Helpmann's *Hamlet* were introduced into the repertoire, as well as numerous classical revivals. As the Sadler's Wells Ballet the company toured the provinces and in 1956 received its charter as **The Royal Ballet.** After 1962, the brilliant partnership of **Nureyev** and Fonteyn amazed audiences.

The main centres of ballet today, apart from London and Copenhagen (where the Royal Danish Ballet follows in the steps of Bournonville), are France, Russia and the United States. **Serge Lifar,** one of Diaghilev's discoveries, entered the Paris Opéra in 1929 as choreographer and premier danseur. Over twenty-five years he revitalized the company, creating many new ballets. As a dancer he was often partnered by **Yvette Chauviré,** as leading French ballerina. Other major French companies have been **Les Ballets des Champs-Elysées,** which briefly raised French ballet to great heights in **Petit's** notable *Les Forains* (1945), and the

Grand Ballet du Marquis de Cuevas, a private company started in 1944. Many famous choreographers, including Massine and **Cranko,** have worked for this company. Among its outstanding productions were **Taras**'s *Piège de Lumière* and **Skibine**'s *Idylle* and *Prisoner of the Caucasus.*

In Soviet Russia, Moscow with its Bolshoi Ballet has become the centre of ballet; Leningrad retains the Kirov Ballet (formerly the Maryinsky), the oldest ballet school in Russia. An unbroken tradition has been maintained under such outstanding teachers as **Agrippina Vaganova** and **Vassily Tikhomirov.** From this school have emerged the international ballerinas **Galina Ulanova** and **Marina Semyonova.** Among Vaganova's first roles were *Giselle* and Juliet in *Romeo and Juliet* (1940). Outstanding ballerinas at the Bolshoi since her retirement included **Maximova, Plisetskaya** and **Struchkova**; among male dancers are **Nicolai Fadeyechev** and **Vladimir Vassiliev.** The Kirov has also produced its own stars. Another prominent Moscow company is the Stanislavsky Theatre Ballet, which produced an outstanding full version of *Swan Lake* (1960).

Until recently, the full-length ballet has remained the standard form, with a strong story line realistically presented, following the example of **Alexander Gorsky.** More recently, a series of new ballets have reflected Soviet ideals, among them *The Flames of Paris, The Golden Age* and *The Red Poppy.* A much greater use of folk dance in choreography is designed to appeal to mass audiences. The academies of Moscow and Leningrad are still supreme in producing splendid artists and corps de ballet; extensive research is made into choreography and teaching, and ballet companies now flourish throughout the Soviet Union.

The American contribution to modern ballet has been considerable. After a belated start, the appearance of the de Basil **Ballet Russe de Monte Carlo** in 1933 awakened an interest in ballet. **The American Ballet,** founded by the choreographer Balanchine, presented ballets on American themes, the most successful of which was *Billy the Kid* (1938). Its successor, Ballet Society, was in 1948 transformed into **The New York City Ballet,** the leading company today. Under Balanchine an American style of dancing has developed, rooted in formal classicism and relying on discipline and purity. The school has produced the ballerina **Maria Tallchief,** sister of **Marjorie Tallchief,** and **Jermone Robbins** was artistic director until 1963. The other important American company is **Ballet Theatre,** formed by **Mikhail Mordkin** in 1939. Among its choreographers have been Antony Tudor, Massine and **Agnes de Mille** with *Fall River Legend* (1948); a major success was *Fancy Free* (1944) by Jerome Robbins, who forms an important link with the development of dance choreography in the musical. The American Ballet Russe de Monte Carlo produced the notable *Rodeo* (1942), with music by Copland, which is inspired by the Western. America's latest ballet companies are Ballets: USA (1958), and **Harkness Ballet** (1960).

America has been the motivating force behind the modern dance, which departs from classical ballet by freeing the whole body from technical conventions. **Isadora Duncan** was the originator of free style dancing. Modern dance has been influenced by the Central European schools of **Rudolf von Laban, Mary Wigman** and **Kurt Jooss,** but has also evolved independently. The greatest figure is undoubtedly .**Martha Graham,** whose technique is a highly developed form of modern dance.

The tradition of ballet which began in Renaissance Italy has extended to other countries throughout the world; the history of ballet in these countries will be found under country entries.

BALLET AUX AMBASSADEURS POLONAIS, a divertissement commissioned in 1573 by Catherine de' Medici for the entertainment of Polish envoys. Choreography, **Balthazar de Beau-**

joyeux; music, Roland de Lassus. As in *Ballet Comique de la Reine*, to which it was a pointer, the choreography was arranged on geometric figures. *See* **Ballet Comique de la Reine, Le.**

ballet blanc, classical ballet in which the female dancers wear long white dresses. Examples include *Swan Lake*, *La Sylphide* and *Giselle*. This long dress is also used in **Fokine**'s neo-romantic *Les Sylphides*.

Ballet Caravan *see* **American Ballet, The.**

Ballet Club *see* **Rambert, Marie.**

BALLET COMIQUE DE LA REINE, LE, a ballet commissioned by Queen Catherine de Medici to celebrate her sister Marguerite's marriage. First performed in Paris, 15 October 1581, by dancers from

Le Ballet Comique de la Reine. Ph. Larousse.

the Court. Choreography, **Beaujoyeux**; music, Sieur de Beaulieu; decor and costumes, Jacques Patin. The performance lasted $5\frac{1}{2}$ hours and the choreography was arranged on geometric figures. Based on the legend of Circe, it is regarded as the first important court ballet, and the libretto became an early standard work. Its importance lay in the way the whole work was co-ordinated, as this was the first time anyone had combined music, acting and dancing in one production. It was widely imitated in Italy and France, and greatly influenced the masque in England.

ballet d'action, a form of ballet, developed by **Jean-Georges Noverre,** in which all the main dances and characters were definitely linked to the theme. For the first time, the dance steps, mime, music, costumes, *etc*, were intended to portray the details of the plot.

ballet de cour, a form of entertainment which flourished in European royal courts (except the Russian) in the 16th and 17th centuries. Highly dramatic and theatrical, it was danced by the gentlemen of the court only. The themes were generally mythological or political, or they exalted royalty. Ballet de cour reached its zenith at the French Court, especially with *Le Ballet Comique de la Reine*. In a later development, the ballet-mascarade, the theatrical features were dropped and music, including songs, was given greater prominence. This gave rise to the ballet à entrées, which had a theatrical standard. Still later, women were accepted into the ballet which, abandoned by the courtiers, became professional and more artistic. *See* **Ballet Comique de la Reine, Le.**

BALLET DE LA DÉLIVRANCE DE RENAUD, LE, a **ballet de cour,** including melodrama, dialogue and song. Libretto, Durand; music, de Guedron, G. Bataille, Boesset, Mauduit; mechanical effects and costumes, T. Francini. First performed, 29 January 1617, in the Louvre, Paris. The spectacle had magic, grotesque monsters, fountains and sumptuous costumes. Its

Ballet de la Délivrance de Renaud. Ph. B.N.

significance in the history of French ballet lay in the ingenious use of machinery to achieve scenic effects, and in the singing parts. Louis XIII danced several entrées.

BALLET DE LA DOUAIRIÈRE DE BILLEBAHOUT, a ballet à entrée, danced and sung by Louis XIII of France. Book, Sorel; music, A. Boesset and P. Auger. First danced at the Louvre and then at the Hôtel de Ville de Paris in 1626. Professional dancers, including Marais, only danced some specially choreographed entrées, and never with the gentlemen of the Court. No professional women dancers appeared, but the grand finale was danced by the ladies and gentlemen of the Court.

BALLET DE LA NUIT, a ballet de cour. Plot, Benserade; music, Clémant; mechanical effects, Torelli. Danced in Paris, 1653, by Louis XIV with his courtiers and **Jean Baptiste Lully.** The ballet, which lasted 13 hours, told of the story of Selene and Endymion and depicted scenes after sunset.

Ballet du XXième Siècle *see* **Béjart, Maurice.**

BALLET IMPERIAL, a classical ballet in three movements. Choreography, **George Balanchine**; music, **Peter Tchaikovsky** (*Piano Concerto No. 2 in G major*); decor, Doboujinsky. First performed in New York, 29 May 1941, by American Ballet Caravan. Principal dancers, **Marie Jeanne,** Gisella Caccialanza, **William Dollar.** Staged at the Broadway Theatre, New York, November 1942, for the New Opera Company. Principal dancers, Gisella Caccialanza, Mary Ellen Moylan, William Dollar. Revived in New York City Center, 20 February 1945, by the **Ballet Russe de Monte Carlo.** Principal dancers, **Maria Tallchief,** Mary Ellen Moylan, **Nicholas Magallanes.** Staged at the Royal Opera House, Covent Garden, London, 5 April 1950, by Sadler's Wells Ballet. Balanchine revised the second movement for this production. Decor, Eugene Berman. Principal dancers, **Margot Fonteyn, Beryl Grey, Michael Somes.** Revived 18 October 1963, by **The Royal Ballet.** Decor, Carl Toms. Principal dancers, **Nadia Nerina, Anya Linden, David Blair.** Revived by Balanchine, 1964, for the **New York City Ballet.** Decor, Rouben Ter-Arutunian; costumes, Karinska. Principal dancers, **Suzanne Farrell, Patricia Neary** and **Jacques d'Amboise.** This ballet is a pure dance composition, and follows the music so closely that it has been described as mathematical. The work marked an important point in Balanchine's development.

Ballet International, a company founded by the **Marquis George de Cuevas** in New York, 1944. Its choreographers included **Léonide Massine, Bronislava Nijinska, Boris Romanov,** Edward Caton, **William Dollar,** Antonia Cabos, and **Simon Semenov.** In 1950 the company was joined to the Grand Ballet de Monte Carlo (directed by the Marquis de Cuevas), and became the **Grand Ballet du Marquis de Cuevas.**

Ballet International du Marquis de

Ballet Music. Ph. Lazzari.

Cuevas *see* **Grand Ballet du Marquis de Cuevas.**

Ballet Jooss, see **Jooss, Kurt**

ballet music, in the Middle Ages, the accompaniment to dances such as rondes, farandoles and branles was often provided by the dancers themselves singing traditional airs. Indeed, *ballad* and *ballet* are ultimately the same word and both sprang from the dances and songs of peasant Europe. In the princes' courts of 14th century Italy, where choreographed dance became established, choirs of madrigalists frequently provided the music and any instrumental accompaniment imitated the madrigal style. By the beginning of the 16th century, the lute had become the popular instrument and its music, with its interwoven textures and light rhythms, was easily adapted for dance. By this time it was becoming the practice to join two or more dances of contrasting speed and rhythm, such as a basse dance (slow) with a saltarello (fast), into a single choreographic unit. This, of course, was dance to be danced, not watched. During the second half of the 16th century, the music of viols, violins and the harpsichord gradually replaced that of the lute; the new combination allowed longer harmonic structures with greater variety of texture, but the four and eight bar units of rhythm, reflecting the distant common origin of song and dance, remained. Now dance music was influencing other forms : composers wrote suites (partitas) of stylized dance movements (allemande, courante, minuet, sarabande, jig, and so on) for solo keyboard performance. From its earliest days, ballet as a spectacle was associated with opera, but usually as an entr'acte entertainment. Although **Lully** in the 17th century gave ballet a more central part in his operas, it developed into something with little relevance to the plot, merely providing grand stage effects and an opportunity for exhibition dancing (the rise of the ballerina dates from this time). Composers of the day were expected to include in their scores special dances which would best exhibit a star's talent. Gluck, in his reform of opera in general, and **Jean-Georges Noverre**, in his development of the **ballet d'action,** took a stand against this procedure, insisting that all action on stage, whether danced or mimed, should be relevant to the plot. Their reforms restored to ballet music its interpretive function and, although during the 19th century the personality of the dancer was a major force in the world of ballet, the status of the composer was truly established. Opera composers continued to insert ballets in their operas, but ballet and ballet music were now firmly established in their own right.

In the first half of the 19th century, when ballet was separating itself from opera, ballet music lost its appeal for major composers and the bulk was produced by theatrical composers of little consequence outside the theatre. Outstanding among these were Léo Délibes (1836–91) who, as well as operas, wrote *La Source*, *Coppélia* (1870) and *Sylvia*, and Adolphe Adam (1802–56) who composed *Giselle*, *La Fille du Danube* and *Le Corsaire*. In Russia, ballet did not suffer so badly, and the standards set by Gluck and Noverre were maintained, especially during the long reign of **Marius Petipa** who worked with Peter Tchaikovsky (1840–93) in the production of *The Nutcracker*, *The Sleeping Beauty* and *Swan Lake*. Tchaikovsky's brilliant talent for orchestration and dramatic writing was given full rein in these works which still survive today in both the ballet and the concert repertoire.

By the end of the 19th century, ballet had become one of the most conservative of the arts, but within a decade, from 1911, **Diaghilev**'s Ballets Russes changed all this and made ballet a major international art form. Although he respected the best in ballet and music of the past, Diaghilev pursued a policy of commissioning fresh work from the newest and best of contemporary composers and artists. Because of his talent for detecting real genius in others, this policy was so successful that it was to the ballet that the music public looked for the avant-garde in the 1920s and '30s. The furore caused by the first performance of Stravinsky's *The Rite of Spring* extended well beyond the confines of ballet circles. Between 1909 and 1929, the most eminent composers worked for Diaghilev, creating new departures in ballet and music. Some even believe that Stravinsky and Ravel wrote their best music for Diaghilev. A notable feature of Diaghilev's new ballets was that many of them were shorter and employed smaller ensembles in accompaniment than was usual in 19th century productions. Later ballet companies followed Diaghilev's lead in approaching the foremost composers of the day for their scores.

It is perhaps significant of the place held by music in ballet as an art form that only those works whose scores are considerable musical achievements in their own right retain their place in the repertoire, the only apparent exception being perhaps *Giselle*. This may be because, of all the elements of ballet, music seems to have travelled farthest from the rude accompaniment of early dance. Both, however, share one obvious feature—rhythm. The rhythms of the tom-tom and of Tchaikovsky fulfil similar functions and those are not primarily to provide rhythm to dance to, for dance can easily create its own rhythm, but to create a rhythm to which the expression or action unfolds, to lighten and stylize the world of dance, framing it off from the reality which it is transmuting. What the music accompanies is not merely the individual movements of the dance but the actions of the ballet, inner as well as outer. Indeed, obvious, immediate, appreciable rhythm may be absent from ballet music, as in Stravinsky's later works. **Fokine,** at first baffled by the score of *Petrouchka,* was eventually intrigued enough to create new dance forms to translate its movement. Music integrates the elements of ballet; it gives the action relevance, proportion, progression and heightened tension, on a plane removed from and more significant than reality.

Among the notable composers who have written ballet music are the following: Mozart (*Les Petits Riens*), Beethoven (*Die Geschöpfe des Prometheus*), Adam (*Giselle*), Délibes (*Coppélia, Sylvia*), Tchaikovsky (*The Nutcracker, Swan Lake, The Sleeping Beauty*), Richard Strauss (*The Legend of Joseph*), Satie (*Parade*), De Falla (*El Amor Brujo, The Three-Cornered Hat*), Ravel (*Daphnis and Chloë*), Bartók (*The Wooden Prince, The Miraculous Mandarin*), Milhaud (*L'Homme et son Désir, The Creation of the World, Le Train Bleu, The Bells*), Poulenc (*Les Biches, Aubade, Les Animaux Modèles*), Shostakovitch (*The Golden Age*), Honegger (*Amphion*), Vaughan Williams (*Job*), Cohen (*The Green Table*), Auric (*Les Fâcheux, Les Matelots, La Concurrence, La Chambre*), Stravinsky (*The Firebird, Petrouchka, The Rite of Spring, Les Noces, Persephone, Le Baiser de la Fée, Le Renard, Orpheus, Agon, Apollon Musagète, Jeu de Cartes*), Prokofiev (*The Prodigal Son, Romeo and Juliet, Cinderella, The Stone Flower*), Bliss (*Checkmate, Miracle in the Gorbals*), Copland (*Billy the Kid, Appalachian Spring*), Khachaturian (*Gayané*), Ibert (*Les Amours de Jupiter*), Arnold (*Rinaldo and Armida*), Rawsthorne (*Madame Chrysanthème*), Britten (*Prince of the Pagodas*), Henze (*Ondine*).

Ballet Rambert *see* **Rambert, Marie.**

Ballet Russe de Monte Carlo, a ballet company founded by **René Blum** and **Colonel de Basil** in 1931. Blum first formed the company as the Ballets de Théâtre de Monte Carlo, and when de Basil joined him the name was changed to René Blum and Colonel de Basil Ballets Russes de Monte Carlo. After two seasons the name was changed to the singular. Its choreographers included **Balanchine** and **Massine.** Among its dancers were **Alexandra Danilova,** and the **Baby Ballerinas, Irina Baronova, Tamara Toumanova** and **Tatiana Riabouchinska.** The company toured extensively, and in 1935 it was booked into the New York Metropolitan Opera House by the American impresario Hurok. René Blum retired from the management of the company in 1934, and left it completely in 1936. Shortly after, quarrels between de Basil and Massine resulted in Massine's leaving the company (now Colonel de Basil's Ballet Russe de Monte Carlo) in 1938. Massine went to Monte Carlo, where in 1936 Blum had formed a company, the René Blum Ballets Russes de Monte Carlo. Blum then formed another ballet company with Massine as artistic director. The company became the Ballet Russe de Monte Carlo. A number of de

Igor Stravinsky. Ph. Lipnitzki.

Basil's people left to join Massine, including Danilova and Toumanova. Other dancers with the new company included **Alicia Markova** and **Serge Lifar**. After further quarrels, de Basil's company went to London, where its name was changed to the Royal Covent Garden Ballet Russe and later to the Original Ballet Russe. Both companies toured extensively in the 1940s. The Original Ballet Russe was disbanded in 1947, and the Ballet Russe de Monte Carlo became inactive after 1963.

Ballet Society *see* **New York City Ballet, The.**

Ballet Theatre, a ballet company established in New York in 1939. It grew out of the Mordkin Ballet, which was founded by **Mikhail Mordkin** in 1937. It was financed by co-founder Lucia Chase, and directed by Richard Pleasant, and the repertoire included *Les Sylphides* and *Carnaval* (**Fokine**), *The Lilac Garden* (**Antony Tudor**) and *La Fille Mal Gardée* (**Bronislava Nijinska**). The company was re-organized again in 1941 (following the resignation of Pleasant), with **Alicia Markova** and **Irina Baronova** as ballerinas. Between 1941 and 1948 the company danced a number of seasons at the Metropolitan Opera House, New York, and in Mexico City, and in 1946 visited the Royal Opera House, Covent Garden, London. In the 1950s it toured extensively in Europe, the US and South America. In 1957 its name was changed to American Ballet Theatre. In 1960 it became the first American company to tour the Soviet Union. In 1965 American Ballet Theatre celebrated its 25th anniversary with a successful season at the New York State Theater, of which the major achievement was Jerome Robbins' *Les Noces*. It subsequently held seasons at the New York State Theater. In 1966 the company made an extensive tour of the US and Canada, and in 1970 it again visited Covent Garden. Leading dancers of the company have included **Adolph Bolm, Patricia Bowman, Lucia Chase, Karen Conrad, Leon Danielian, Anton Dolin,**

William Dollar, Maria Karnilova, Nora Kaye, Andrée Howard, Eugene Loring, Hugh Laing, Nina Stroganova, Antony Tudor, Alicia Alonso, John Kriza and **Jerome Robbins.**

Ballet Théâtre de Paris *see* **Béjart, Maurice.**

Ballets 1933, Les *see* **Balanchine, George.**

Ballets de Monte Carlo, a ballet company founded by Sergei Denham (formerly the director of the **Ballet Russe de Monte Carlo**) in Monte Carlo in 1966, under the patronage of Prince Rainier III of Monaco. **Léonide Massine** was appointed choreographer.

Ballets de Paris de Roland Petit, Les, a French company founded by **Roland Petit** in Paris, 1948, after he left **Les Ballets des Champs-Elysées**. The first season at the Théâtre Marigny opened with *Les Demoiselles de la Nuit*, in which **Margot Fonteyn** created the leading role. *L'Oeuf à la Coque* and *Carmen* (1949) followed. Among its dancers were **Renée Jeanmaire, Nina Vyroubova, Colette Marchand** and **Gordon Hamilton.** After seasons in Paris and New York, the company finally closed in 1959 with Cyrano de Bergerac.

Ballets de Théâtre de Monte Carlo *see* **Ballet Russe de Monte Carlo.**

Ballets des Champs-Elysées, Les, a French company founded by **Roland Petit, Boris Kochno** and **Irène Lidova** in Paris, 1945. Petit was ballet master, principal male dancer and choreographer until 1947, when he left the company. The company disbanded in 1949, but it is remembered for the high degree of originality of its members. Its dancers included **Jean Babilée, Nina Vyroubova** and **Youly Algarov,** and its repertoire included *La Sylphide*, (revival), the melodramatic *Le Jeune Homme et la Mort* and *Le Bal des Blanchisseuses*.

Ballets Russes *see* **Diaghilev, Serge** and **ballet, history of.**

Ballets Jooss *see* **Jooss, Kurt**

Ballets: USA *see* **Robbins, Jerome.**

ballon, elasticity in jumping and the ability to remain in the air for long enough to execute movements.

ballonné, an upward spring and bouncing step. The working leg is raised knee-high, either front, back or side, and the foot brought sharply to the front of the knee or calf of the supporting leg which lands bent in line with the foot; the accent of this movement is the strike of the foot against the supporting leg.

ballotté (tossed) or **pas ballotté,** a throwing up of the working leg with **développé** movement into an open

Jean Balon. Ph. B.N.

position. Start at fifth position, draw foot up side of leg, **fondu** supporting leg while the working leg developpés, lower to point tendu. This can be done at the barre in adage or sauté. In the sauté movement the dancer starts with the left foot behind the knee of the supporting leg, springs upward, simultaneously crossing one leg in front of the other (**passé**) to the **cou-de-pied.** He alights on the left foot, at the same time turning out the thigh of the working leg until it is at right angles to the body (développé), the toe in line with the knee of the supporting leg. The toe is then fully extended to the side, front and back.

BALON or **BALLON, Jean** (1676–1739), French dancer and choreographer. He made his debut in *L'Oronthée* (1688) and entered the Paris Opéra in 1691. He succeeded **Pierre Beauchamp** as choreographer to Louis XIV in 1687 and, for the court, created *L'Inconnue* and *Les Eléments.* His mimed version of Corneille's *Les Horaces* (1708) foreshadowed **Noverre's** **ballet d'action.** For **Marie Camargo's** debut he revived **Rameau's** *Caractères de la Danse* (1726).

BALUSTRADE, a ballet in four movements. Choreography, **George Balanchine**; music, Stravinsky (*Concerto for Violin and Orchestra*); decor, Pavel Tchelichev. First performed in New York, 22 January 1941, by Original Ballet Russe. Principal dancers, **Tamara Toumanova, Roman Jasinski, Paul Petrov.** Only three performances were given.

BANNERMAN, Kenneth (1936–), British dancer. After studying with Marjory Middleton in Edinburgh, he joined the Ballet Rambert School, and later Ballet Rambert (1956), with which he became a leading dancer, appearing in both classical and modern roles which include James in *La Sylphide* (1960), Elder Son in *Place in the Desert*, Franz in *Coppélia*, and roles in *Night Shadow*. He left the company in 1966.

BARABAÜ, a ballet in one scene,

Libretto, Vittoria Rieti; choreography, **George Balanchine**; music, Vittoria Rieti; decor and costumes, Maurice Utrillo. First performed at the Coliseum Theatre, London, 1925, by **Diaghilev's** Ballets Russes. Principal dancers, **Léon Woizikowsky, Serge Lifar, Alexandra Danilova**. The work depicts the gaiety and exhilaration of life in a sunny Italian village. A new version by **Ninette de Valois** was given by Sadler's Wells Ballet in 1935.

BAR AUX FOLIES-BERGÈRE, a ballet in one act. Libretto (based on Manet's painting and characters from Toulouse-Lautrec) and choreography, **Ninette de Valois**; music, Chabrier (*Dix Pièces Pittoresque*); decor, William Chappell. First performed at the Mercury Theatre, London, 15 May 1934, by Ballet Rambert. Principal dancers, **Alicia Markova** (La Goulue), **Pearl Argyle** (La Fille au Bar), Diana Gould (Grille d'Egout), **Frederick Ashton** (Valentin), Oliver Reynolds (Le Vieux Marcheur). The highlights are the Can-Can and the solo by La Goulue.

BARBERINA, La (Barberina Campanini, 1721–99), Italian ballerina and a pupil of Rinaldi Fossano. She was presented at the Académie Royale, Paris in 1739 and on this occasion **Rameau** composed four dances especially for her. She danced at Versailles, Covent Garden, Dublin and Berlin.

BARI, Tania (1936–), Dutch ballerina. She studied in Rotterdam and Paris, and in 1955 joined **Maurice Béjart**'s Ballet Théâtre de Paris and later his Ballet du XXième Siècle with which she is leading soloist. Her repertoire includes *Le Sacre du Printemps* and *L'Étranger*.

BARISHNIKOV, Mikhail (1948–), Russian dancer. After studying in Riga and Leningrad, he joined the Kirov Ballet. As a principal dancer, his repertoire includes *Coppélia, Giselle* pas de deux, *Flames of Paris* and *Don Quixote*. In 1970 he appeared in the title role in Konstantin

B

Sergeyev's *Hamlet*. He won first prize in the junior section at Varna, Bulgaria (1966), and was Gold Medallist and Laureat at the First Moscow International Dance Competition (1969).

BARN DANCE, a ballet in one act. Libretto and choreography, Catherine Littlefield; music (folk tunes), David Guion, John Powell, Louis Gottschalk; decor, A. Pinto; costumes, S. Pinto. First performed in Philadelphia, 23 April 1937, by the Littlefield Ballet Company. Principal dancers, Dorothie Littlefield, Thomas Cannon. Revived at the Metropolitan Opera House, New York, 9 May 1944, by **Ballet Theatre**. Principal dancers Dorothie Littlefield, Thomas Cannon, later replaced by **Nana Gollner** and **Paul Petrov**. The work depicts the spirited capers of a barn dance in an American village.

BARNES, Clive (1927–), British writer and critic, resident in the United States. In England he wrote for *Dance and Dancers, New Statesman* and *The Times*. He was London correspondent of the New York *Dance Magazine*, ballet critic of the *Daily Express* (1956–65) and *The Spectator* (1959–65). He moved to New York in 1965 as dance critic of the *New York Times*. His published works include *Ballet in Britain Since the War* (1953) and *Ballet Here and Now* (1961).

BARON NAHUM (1906–56), British ballet photographer. Collections of his works were published as *Baron at the Ballet* (1950) and *Baron Encore* (1952).

BARONOVA, Irina (1919–), Russian ballerina. She studied with **Olga Preobrajenska** in Paris, becoming soloist at the **Paris Opéra Ballet** in 1930. Her technical virtuosity and personality impressed **Balanchine**, and she became a **Baby Ballerina** of the original Ballets Russes de Monte Carlo (1932), continuing with the several Ballet Russe de Monte Carlo companies until 1940. She was ballerina of **Ballet Theatre** (1941–2); with **Massine**'s Ballet Russe Highlights

C

(1945); and guest artist with Original Ballet Russe (1946). She created roles in *Helen of Troy, Le Beau Danube,* and danced in *Swan Lake, Les Présages, Coppélia, La Fille Mal Gardée, Petrouchka* and Queen of Shernakhan in *Le Coq d'Or.* She retired from dancing in 1946, and took up the teaching of mime at the Royal Academy of Dancing, London.

barre, in a dance studio, a handrail fixed to the wall, which the dancer uses for support and balance in the execution of exercises. Usually at a height of three feet six inches from the floor.

BARTHOLIN, Birger (1900–), Danish dancer, choreographer and teacher. He studied with **Michel Fokine, Nicholas Legat** and **Alexander Volinine.** Among his productions were Prokofiev's *Classical Symphony* and *Romeo and Juliet* (1937). He was ballet master of the National Opera Ballet, Helsinki and the National Opera Ballet, Oslo, and later took a teaching post in Copenhagen.

battement, any one of a number of leg exercises of a beating nature.

batterie, any movement in which the calves of the legs beat together during a leap. In grande batterie, the elevation is large (the leap is high) and the movement includes the **cabriole, sissonne** battue and **assemblé.** In petite batterie, the elevation is smaller and the movement includes the **entrechat** and **brisé.**

battu, step involving a beating movement of the calves.

BAYADÈRE, LA, a ballet in three acts, based on Indian dramas. Libretto, **Marius Petipa** and Sergei Khudekov; choreography, Marius Petipa; music, Leon Minkus; decor, K. Ivanov, P. Lambin, O. Allegri, A. Kwapp. First performed at the Maryinsky Theatre, St. Petersburg, 23 January 1877, by the theatre company. Principal dancer, Yekaterina Vazem. Revived at the Kirov Theatre, 13 December

1932, by **Agrippina Vaganova** and, 10 February 1941, by Vladimir Ponomaryov (with new dances by **Vakhtang Chabukiany**). Principal dancers, **Natalia Dudinskaya,** Chabukiany. This version was performed in England, Canada and the United States by the Kirov Ballet in 1961. The Kingdom of the Shades scene was restaged, following Petipa's choreography, at the Royal Opera House, Covent Garden, London, 1963, by **Rudolph Nureyev.** Principal dancers, **Margot Fonteyn,** Rudolph Nureyev. The story is of love, intrigue and murder. The original version closed with the collapse of a temple in which the murderess and her lover die, but this scene was omitted from later versions.

BAYOU, a ballet in one scene. Choreography, **George Balanchine**; music, Virgil Thomson (*Arcadian Songs and Dances*); decor and costumes, Dorothea Tanning. First performed in New York, 1952, by **The New York City Ballet.** The choreography evokes the mysteries of a country where life, plants, rivers and seas have a hidden destiny. The inhabitants are called from the depth of the forest by spirit Bayou.

BEACH, a humorous ballet in one scene. Libretto, René Kerdyck; choreography, **Léonide Massine**; music, Jean Françaix; decor and costumes, Raoul Dufy. First performed at the Théâtre de Monte Carlo, 1933, by Ballet Russe de Monte Carlo. Principal dancers, **David Lichine,** Léonide Massine, **Tatiana Riabouchinska, Irina Baronova.** The work depicts the gods of the sea as bathers on a popular beach.

BEAUCHAMP, Pierre (1636–1705), French dancer and teacher. He was ballet master to the court of Louis XIV, and in 1671 became ballet master of **L'Académie Royale de Musique.** At court he choreographed the ballets of **Lully** and Molière, often appearing in them with the king. One of these, *Triomphe de l'Amour,* was the first to include women as dancers. Beauchamp introduced the **turn-out** and, although his system of dance notation was never published, he is generally credited with establishing the **five positions,** the basis of all ballet steps.

BEAU DANUBE, LE, a ballet in one act. Libretto and choreography, **Léonide Massine;** music, Johann Strauss, Josef Lanner; decor, Vladimir and Elizabeth Polunin; costumes, Comte Etienne de Beaumont. First performed at the Théâtre de la Cigale, Paris, 17 May 1924, by Soirées de Paris. Principal dancer, **Lydia Lopokova** (Street Dancer). Revived at the Théâtre de Monte Carlo, 5 April 1933, by **Ballet Russe de Monte Carlo.** Principal dancers, **Alexandra Danilova** (Street Dancer), Léonide Massine (Hussar), **Tatiana Riabouchinska** (Young Girl), **Irina Baronova** (Seamstress), **David Lichine** (Dandy). Performed, June 1938, at the Drury Lane Theatre, London. Massine has staged the ballet for the Royal Danish Ballet and London's **Festival Ballet.** In Vienna, a street dancer meets a former sweetheart, the Hussar, who is strolling with his fiancée. She fails to attract the Hussar, who is reunited with his fiancée. This is one of Massine's most popular ballets.

BEAUGRAND, Léontine (1842–1925), French ballerina. She studied at the Opéra School and made her debut in **Marie Taglioni**'s *Le Papillon* (1860). She danced *Diavolino* in 1864, and succeeded Giuseppina Bozzachi as Swanilda in *Coppélia* (1871), a role originally created for her. Famed for her elevation.

BEAUJOYEUX, Balthasar de (Baldassarino da Belgiojoso, died 1587), Italian violinist and choreographer who became valet de chambre to Catherine de Medici in Paris. He organized royal entertainments for Charles IX, and in 1581 produced *Le Ballet Comique de la Reine* to celebrate the marriage of the Duc de Joyeuse and the sister of the Queen. *See* **Ballet Comique de la Reine, Le.**

BEAUMONT, Cyril William (1891–), British writer and publisher,

Chairman of the Imperial Society of Teachers of Dancing. An authoritative and prolific writer on the dance, his London book-store 'Under the Sign of the Harlequin' was well known to ballet lovers. He was ballet critic of *Dancing World* (1921–4), *The Sunday Times* (1950–9) and editor of *Dance Journal* (1924). He helped to codify Cecchetti's method, and initiated the founding (1922) of the Cecchetti Society. A few of his many published works are *Serge Lifar* (1928), *The Complete Book of Ballets* (1937), *The Sadler's Wells Ballet* (1946), *Ballets Past and Present* (1955). He has translated the *Orchésographie* of **Thoinot Arbeau.** He became a Chevalier of the Légion d'Honneur in 1951, and was awarded the OBE in 1962.

BECK, Hans (1861–1952), Danish dancer, teacher and choreographer. He studied with **August Bournonville** at the Royal Danish Ballet School, making his debut in 1879, and becoming a soloist with the company in 1881. From 1894–1915 he was ballet master at the Royal Danish Ballet, where, due to his care and energy, the Bournonville ballets have been preserved intact. The best known of his productions is *The Little Mermaid.*

BEDELLS, Phyllis (1893–), British ballerina and teacher. She studied with **Genée, Bolm, Cecchetti** and **Anna Pavlova,** making her debut as child solo dancer in *Alice in Wonderland* (1906). From 1907–16 she danced at the Empire Theatre, becoming prima ballerina. She was prima ballerina during the Covent Garden Opera season of 1920, with **Anton Dolin** during the London Coliseum season (1926–7), with her own company (1928); and was an original member of **The Camargo Society** (1930). Her farewell performance was in 1935 at the London Hippodrome. She founded her own school in 1925, and became vice-president of the Royal Academy of Dancing. She is author of *My Dancing Years* (1954).

BÉJART, Maurice (1928–), French

dancer and choreographer. He made his debut in 1945 at the Marseille Opéra Ballet where he had studied, later becoming a pupil of **Léo Staats** in Paris. From 1947–9 he toured Europe with **Les Ballets de Paris de Roland Petit**; was principal dancer with **International Ballet,** London, for the 1949–50 season; and was guest artist with the Royal Swedish Ballet during 1951 and 1952. In 1954, with the writer Jean Laurent, he formed Les Ballets de L'Étoile, for which he choreographed and danced in his major work *Symphonie pour un Homme Seul* (1955), set to *musique concrète* (music mirroring the noise to which the 20th century is subjected). His choreographic style combines the classic with modern, and he uses speech, song, spectacular costumes and has captured a young, enthusiastic audience. Success with Stravinsky's *Le Sacre du Printemps* led to his appointment as ballet director of the Théâtre Royale de la Monnaie, Brussels, now known as Les Ballets du XXième Siècle. His *Romeo and Juliet* was presented at a Gala Performance at the Royal Circus, Brussels in 1966. As choreographer he created Salvador Dali's *Gala* in Venice and the Bacchanale in *Tannhäuser* at Bayreuth (both 1961). In 1967 he staged Flaubert's *The Temptation of St. Anthony,* and in 1971 his company had a season at the London Coliseum, where *Firebird* and *The Rite of Spring* were among the ballets he presented. For Les Ballets du XXième Siècle he has created a number of works including *Nijinsky—Clown of God* (1971), *Les Fleurs du Mal* and *Cocteau and the Dance* (both 1972).

BELLE AU BOIS DORMANT, LA *see* **Sleeping Beauty, The.**

BELLS, THE, a ballet in five parts, based on the poem by Edgar Allan Poe. Libretto and choreography, **Ruth Page**; music, Darius Milhaud; decor, Isamu Noguchi. First performed in Chicago, 26 April 1946, by Chicago University Composers' Series. Principal dancers, Ruth Page, Jerome Andrews. Presented at New York City Center, 16 September 1946, by **Ballet Russe de Monte Carlo.** Principal dancers **Frederic Franklin,** Ruth Page, and later **Ruthanna Boris.** The five parts of the work are Silver Bells (merriment), Golden Bells (wedding), Brazen Bells (terror, despair, anger), Iron Bells (solemnity, groaning) and Dance of the Ghouls.

BELOVED, THE or **La Bien-Aimée,** a ballet in one act. Libretto, **Alexandre Benois**; choreography, **Bronislava Nijinska**; music, Schubert and Liszt (arranged by Milhaud); decor, Benois. First performed at the Théâtre National de l'Opéra, 22 November, 1928, by the Paris Opéra Ballet. Principal dancers, **Ida Rubinstein, Anatole Vilzak.** Revived by Nijinska, 1937, for the Markova-Dolin company. Decor, George Kirsta. Principal dancers, **Alicia Markova, Anton Dolin.** Revived, 1941, for **Ballet Theatre.** Decor and costumes, Nicolas de Molas. Principal dancers, Alicia Markova, Anton Dolin. The ballet shows a poet re-enacting his youth with his Muse.

BELSKY, Igor (1925–   ), Russian dancer and choreographer, Honoured Artist of the RSFSR. He studied in Leningrad, joining the Kirov Ballet in 1942. His roles include Chief Warrior in *Prince Igor*, Tybalt in *Romeo and Juliet*, Nur-Ali in *The Fountain of Bakhchisarai* and Mako in *Path of Thunder*. As a choreographer his works include *Coast of Hope* (1959) and *Swan Lake* for the Dutch National Ballet.

BENESH, Rudolf (1916–   ), British painter. He published a system of **dance notation,** *Introduction to Benesh Dance Notation* (1955). In 1962 he founded the College of Choreology, London.

BENNETT, Alexander (1930–   ), British dancer. He was a pupil of Marjorie Middleton, and first danced with the Edinburgh Ballet Club. He joined Ballet Rambert in 1951, and became principal dancer in 1953. From 1957 he was principal dancer with Sadler's Wells Theatre Ballet and **The Royal Ballet,** returning to

Ballet Rambert in 1963. His roles have included Albrecht in *Giselle*, Florimund in *Sleeping Beauty* and Master of Tregennis in *The Haunted Ballroom*.

BENOIS, Alexandre (1870–1960), Russian painter, art historian and scenic designer. With **Léon Bakst** and **Serge Diaghilev**, he founded the journal *The World of Art*. He collaborated in the founding of Diaghilev's Ballets Russes. He made his debut as scenic designer at the Maryinsky Theatre with the decor for *Sylvia* and *Cupid's Revenge* (both 1901) and *Le Pavillon d'Armide* (1907) for which he also created the libretto and costumes. Benois's association with Diaghilev's company was a major contribution to the greater cohesion and unity between dancer, composer and painter. For Ballets Russes, he designed costumes and decor for *Les Sylphides* (1909), the controversial costume **Nijinsky** wore in *Giselle* (1910) and *Petrouchka* (1911), for which he wrote the libretto with Stravinsky. For the **Ida Rubinstein** company in 1929, he designed costumes and decor for *La Bien Aimée*, *Les Noces de Psyche et L'Amour* and *La Valse*; for Original Ballet Russe *Graduation Ball* (1940); for **Ballet Russe de Monte Carlo** *The Nutcracker* (1940) and *Raymonda* (1946); for the **Grand Ballet du Marquis de Cuevas** *Enchanted Mill* (1948); and for London's **Festival Ballet** *Graduation Ball* and *The Nutcracker* (1957). Among his publications are *Reminiscences of the Ballet Russe* (London: 1941) and *Memoirs* (London: 1960).

BERIOSOV, Nicholas (1906–), Lithuanian dancer and choreographer. He studied ballet in Czechoslovakia, and his ~~early career was with the Prague Opéra~~ Ballet and the Lithuanian National Ballet, Kaunas. In 1935 he joined **René Blum's** company in Monte Carlo, working with **Fokine.** He toured with **Ballet Russe de Monte Carlo** (1938), was ballet master with the **Marquis de Cuevas's Ballet International** (1944, 1956, 1961–2), his own Grand Ballet (1947), **Metropolitan Ballet,** London (1947), **Teatro alla**

Scala, Milan (1950–1) and London's **Festival Ballet** (1951–4), staging *Petrouchka, The Nutcracker, Schéhérazade, Prince Igor* and his own version of *Esmeralda*. He was ballet director with the Stuttgart Ballet and in 1962 became director of the Finnish National Ballet for which he staged a number of major works. Ballerina **Svetlana Beriosova** is his daughter.

BERIOSOVA, Svetlana (1932–), British ballerina, born in Lithuania. Taken to the United States in 1940, she studied with her father **Nicholas Beriosov** and **Anatole Vilzak,** making her debut in 1941 with Original Ballet Russe. In 1947 she appeared as guest artist with the Ottawa Ballet Company in *Les Sylphides* and *The Nutcracker*. She danced with the **Grand Ballet du Marquis de Cuevas** (1947) and Metropolitan Ballet (1948–9) and created a role in **Taras's** *Design with Strings*. In 1950 she joined Sadler's Wells Theatre Ballet as joint ballerina, moving to **The Royal Ballet** as soloist in 1952, and becoming ballerina in 1955. She has been a great inspiration to **Ashton.** Her repertoire includes the leading female roles in *Rinaldo and Armida* (1955), *The Prince of*

Svetlana Beriosova in Giselle. Ph. Dominic.

the Pagodas (1957), *Antigone* (1959), *Le Baiser de la Fée* (1960), *Perséphone* (1961), *Les Noces* (1966), *Enigma Variations* (1968) and *Jazz Calendar*. She has been guest artist in Italy, Germany and Yugoslavia.

BESSMERTNOVA, Natalia Igorevna (1941–), Russian dancer, wife of **Yuri Grigorovich**. She was a Gold Medallist at Varna in 1965. In 1961 she joined the Bolshoi Ballet and became ballerina. Her repertoire includes *Giselle, Pages from Life* and *Chopiniana*.

BESSY, Claude, French ballerina. She studied at the Paris Opéra school, making her debut with the **Paris Opéra Ballet** in 1941, and becoming étoile in 1956. Her technical ability was evident in **Lander's** *Études* (1952), and she has danced the principal roles in the classical repertoire. She created Romantic Love in *The Shadow* (1953), 3rd Movement in *Symphonie Fantastique* (1957), Chloë in *Daphnis and Chloë* (1959) and the ballerina roles in *Pas de Deux* (1960) and *Symphonie Concertante* (1962). She has danced with American **Ballet Theatre** and been guest ballerina with Bolshoi Theatre Ballet. In 1970 she was appointed the first woman dance director of the Paris Opéra Ballet.

BICHES, LES or **The House Party,** a plotless ballet in one act, with singing and speaking parts. Choreography, **Bronislava Nijinska**; music, Francis Poulenc; decor and costumes, Marie Laurencin. First performed at the Théâtre de Monte Carlo, 6 January 1924, by **Diaghilev's** Ballets Russes. Principal dancers, **Vera Nemtchinova,** Bronislava Nijinska, **Lubov Tchernicheva, Alexandra Danilova, Ninette de Valois,** Felia Dubrovska, **Anatole Vilzak, Alice Nikitina, Léon Woizikowsky,** Nicholas Zverev, Natalie Komarova. Revived in England, 1937, for the Markova-Dolin company, under the title *The House Party*. Principal dancers **Alicia Markova, Anton Dolin.** Revived, 1947, for **Grand Ballet du Marquis de Cuevas.** Principal dancers, **Marjorie Tallchief, George Skibine.** Revived by Nijinska, 2 December 1946, for **The Royal**

Claude Bessy. Ph. Lipnitzki.

Ballet, England. Principal dancers, Georgina Parkinson (La Garçonne), **Svetlana Beriosova** (Hostess), **David Blair,** Keith Rosson, Robert Mead (Athletes). The work depicts a sophisticated house party in the 1920s which demonstrates to the jeunesse doré the superficiality of their way of life. This is regarded as one of Nijinska's best works.

BIEN-AIMÉE, LA *see* **Beloved, The.**

BIG CITY, THE, a ballet in three scenes. Libretto and choreography, **Kurt Jooss;** music, Alexander Tansman (*Sonatine Transatlantique*) ; decor, Hein Heckroth. First performed at the Opera House, Cologne, 21 November 1932, by Ballet Jooss. Principal dancers, Mascha Lidoltt Sigurd Leeder, Ernst Uthoff. The ballet depicts the evil aspect of life in big cities and a young girl's disillusionment after she deserts her sweetheart for a libertine.

Les Biches: programme by Marie Laurencin for Diaghilev's Ballets Russes production. Ph. Giraudon.

BILLY THE KID, a contemporary American ballet in one act. Libretto, **Lincoln Kirstein**; choreography, Eugene Loring; music, Aaron Copland; decor and costumes, Jared French. First performed at the Chicago Opera House, 16 October 1938, by Ballet Caravan. Principal dancers, Eugene Loring (The Kid), **Marie-Jeanne** (Mother and Sweetheart), Lew Christensen (Sheriff Garrett), **Todd Bolender** (Alias). Revived at the Majestic Theatre, New York, 13 February 1941, by **Ballet Theatre.** Principal dancers, Eugene Loring, **Alicia Alonso,** Richard Reed, David Nillo. Typifying the American way of life in days gone by, the ballet has a stylized form and atmosphere, and depicts cowboys, Mexican dancers, pioneers and gold diggers.

BIRDS, THE, a comedy ballet in one act. Libretto and choreography, **Robert Helpmann**; music, Ottorino Respighi (*The Birds*) ; decor, Chiang Lee. First performed at the New Theatre, London, 24 November 1942, by Sadler's Wells Ballet. Principal dancers, **Beryl Grey** (Nightingale), **Alexis Rassine** (Dove), Moyra Fraser (Hen). The ballet depicts the loves and jealousies of the birds.

BIRTHDAY OFFERING, a ballet in one act. Choreography, **Frederick Ashton**; music, Alexander Glazounov (arranged by Robert Irving). First performed at the Royal Opera House, Covent Garden, London, 5 May 1956, by Sadler's Wells Ballet. Principal dancers, **Margot Fonteyn, Beryl Grey, Violetta Elvin, Nadia Nerina,** Rowena Jackson, **Svetlana Beriosova, Elaine Fifield, Michael Somes,** Alexander Grant, Brian Shaw, Philip Chatfield, David Blair, Desmond Doyle, **Bryan Ashbridge.** The work was created to celebrate the 25th birthday of Sadler's Wells Ballet, and was taken into the repertoire.

BJØRNSSON, Fredbjørn (1926–), Danish dancer and choreographer. He trained at the Royal Danish Ballet School, graduated into its company, and became soloist in 1949. One of Denmark's greatest stars, his roles include Franz in *Coppélia* and Thief in *Carmen*. It is as a mime and character dancer that he has achieved his greatest success, as in *The Lesson* and *The Miraculous Mandarin*. He worked with **Balanchine, Robbins, Martha Graham** and **Robert Joffrey** in New York (1961), and staged *Napoli* for New Zealand Ballet in 1962. He has choreographed *Bag Taeppet* (1954), *Skaelmeri* (1957) and *Lykke pa Rejsen* (1959).

BLACHE, Jean-Baptiste (1765–1834), French dancer and choreographer. He danced at the Paris Opéra for five years before embarking on a career as ballet master in Montpellier, Lyon, Marseille and Bordeaux. He choreographed *La Noce Villageoise*, *La Fête Indienne*, *The Barber of Seville* and *Mars and Venus*.

BLAIR, David (David Butterfield, 1932–   ), British dancer, Commander of the Order of the British Empire. He studied at Sadler's Wells School and joined Sadler's Wells Theatre Ballet in 1947. In 1953 he became a soloist with **The Royal Ballet,** becoming principal dancer in 1955. In 1961 he succeeded **Michael Somes** as **Margot Fonteyn**'s official partner. He danced **Ashton**'s pas de deux in *Cinderella* and created Captain Belaye in *Pineapple Poll*, Harlequin in *Harlequin in April* and Mercutio in *Romeo and Juliet* (1964). He also dances the classic repertoire and has appeared in *Les Biches, Romeo and Juliet, La Fille Mal Gardée* and *Song of the Earth*. He has been guest artist at **Teatro alla Scala,** Milan, and has toured Australia, Turkey and Spain with Margot Fonteyn's Concert Ballet. In the United States, he staged *Swan Lake* (1965) and *The Sleeping Beauty* (1966) for Municipal Ballet, Atlanta, Georgia.

BLAND, Alexander *see* **Lloyd, Maude.**

BLASIS, Carlo (1795–1878), Italian dancer, choreographer and teacher. He studied with **Jean Dauberval**, and, as premier danseur at **Teatro alla Scala,**

Carlo Blasis. Ph. Lipnitzki.

Milan, worked with **Salvatore Vigano.** From 1826–30 he was soloist and choreographer at the King's Theatre, London, and from 1837–53 was director of the Royal Academy of Dance at **Teatro alla Scala.** He trained many famous dancers of the period, including **Fanny Cerito, Carlotta Grisi, Sofia Fuoco** and **Carolina Rosati.** His *Elementary Treatise* (1820), was republished in 1944 as *An Elementary Treatise Upon the Theory and Practice of the Art of Dancing*; it codified ballet technique and remains today the basis for the classic dance. He also wrote *The Code of Terpsichore* (1828), republished in 1830.

BLISS, Herbert (1923–60), American dancer and teacher. He studied at the Kansas City Conservatory of Music and the School of American Ballet. He joined **Ballet Russe de Monte Carlo** in 1944 and danced Champion Roper in *Rodeo*, Czardas in *Raymonda* and in the pas de trois in *Ballet Imperial*. In 1947 he danced with Ballet Society, and remained with the company as a soloist when it became **The New York City Ballet.** His repertoire included *Serenade* and *La Valse*. His teaching came to a tragic end when he was killed in a car crash.

BLUEBEARD, a ballet in two prologues, four acts and three interludes. Libretto and choreography, **Michel Fokine**; music, Offenbach (from his comic opera *Bluebeard*); decor, Marcel Vertès. First performed in Mexico City, 27 October 1941, by **Ballet Theatre**. Performed in New York, 12 November 1941. Principal dancers, **Anton Dolin** (Bluebeard), **Alicia Markova** (Floretta), **Irina Baronova** (Boulotte), Ian Gibson, **George Skibine** (Prince Sapphire). The work deals light-heartedly with the grim story of Bluebeard and his seven wives.

BLUM, René (1884–1944), French ballet impresario. On the death of **Diaghilev** (1929), Blum became director of the Ballets de L'Opéra de Monte Carlo; in 1932 the company agreed to join with the Paris Russian Opera, under the management of **Colonel de Basil,** to form the René Blum and Colonel de Basil Ballet Russe de Monte Carlo. Blum left this partnership in 1936 and founded the René Blum Ballets Russes de Monte Carlo with **Fokine** as first choreographer and ballet master. In 1938 Blum collaborated with **Léonide Massine** to form a company, **Ballet Russe de Monte Carlo.** He was co-director until 1940, and died in the Auschwitz concentration camp in 1944.

BOGATYRI, a ballet in three scenes, based on Russian folk-lore. Libretto and choreography, **Léonide Massine**; music, Alexander Borodin; decor, Nathalie Gontcharova. First performed at the Metropolitan Opera House, New York, 20 October 1948, by **Ballet Russe de Monte Carlo.** Principal dancers, **Alexandra Danilova, Mia Slavenska, Nathalie Krassovska, Frederic Franklin.** The decor was used by **Bronislava Nijinska** for her ballet, *Ancient Russia*. The Bogatyri were the famous warriors who served the early Russian rulers. The ballet depicts one of their adventures. The choreography used large groups, mass movement and peasant dances.

BOGOMOLOVA, Liudmila (1932–), Russian ballerina, Honoured Artist of the RSFSR. She studied at the Bolshoi school (1945–51), joined the Bolshoi company and took on solo parts after only a few seasons. Her roles have included Proposed Bride in *Swan Lake*, Olia in *Little Stork*, Kitri in *Don Quixote*, Mistress of the Copper Mountain in *The Stone Flower*, Jeanne in *The Flames of Paris*, Madelon in *Fadette* and Suimbike in *Shurale*.

BOLENDER, Todd (1919–), American dancer and choreographer. He entered the School of American Ballet in 1936, studying under **Balanchine** and **Anatole Vilzak.** He was soloist with Ballet Caravan (1937, 1941), and Littlefield Ballet. He founded American Concert Ballet with Mary Jane Shea and **William Dollar,** for which he choreographed *Mother Goose Suite* (1943). During the 1944 season he was a member of **Ballet Theatre,** and in 1945 a guest artist with **Ballet Russe de Monte Carlo,** choreographing *Comedia Balletica*. He became a member of Ballet Society in 1946, and remained as one of the leading male dancers when it became **The New York City Ballet.** He created roles in *The Four Temperaments*, *Symphonie Concertante*, and *The Pied Piper*. He also choreographed *The Miraculous Mandarin* (1951), *Souvenirs* (1955), and *The Creation of the World* (1960). He has been guest choreographer in Turkey, and America. He became director of ballet at the Frankfurt Opera House in 1967.

BOLERO, a plotless ballet in one act. Choreography, **Bronislava Nijinska**; music, Maurice Ravel; decor, **Alexandre Benois.** First performed at the Paris Opéra, 22 November 1928, by the **Ida Rubinstein** Company. Principal dancers, Ida Rubinstein, **Anatole Vilzak.** Nijinska produced a new version, 1934, in Paris. Revived, 30 October 1944, for **Ballet Inter-**

national. Principal dancers, Viola Essen, Alexander Iolas, David Ahdar. Staged, 1934, by **Harald Lander** for Royal Danish Ballet, and by **Serge Lifar,** 1941, for the Paris Opéra. **Anton Dolin** based a solo dance on *Bolero* at Sadler's Wells Theatre in 1932. In this work, Spanish dances are adapted to the ballet.

BOLM, Adolph (1884–1951), Russian dancer and choreographer. He studied at the Russian Imperial Ballet School, becoming soloist at the Maryinsky Theatre in 1910. He organized and danced in the first tours of **Anna Pavlova** (1908, 1909) ; and danced with **Diaghilev**'s Ballets Russes (1909, 1910). His roles were Chief Warrior in *Polovetsian Dances from Prince Igor,* the mime role of Pierrot in *Carnaval,* and Tsarevitch in *The Firebird.* He left the Maryinsky Theatre in 1911, rejoined Diaghilev's company, and toured with them as premier danseur, choreographer and ballet master until 1918. His Ballet Intime toured America for several seasons. After staging *Le Coq d'Or* (1918) and *Petrouchka* (1919) for the Metropolitan Opera, he was engaged by Chicago Grand Opera Ballet where he presented *Birthday of the Infanta* (1919) and *Krazy Kat* (1920). He staged *Apollon Musagète* for Colón Opera, Buenos Aires (1928), and established a ballet school for the San Francisco Opera Company, where he was choreographer and ballet master from 1933–9. He joined **Ballet Theatre** in its initial season (1939), and staged *Peter and the Wolf* in addition to his previous works. He was ballet master and régisseur-general (1942–1943). His last work was *The Firebird,* after which he taught and worked in films in Hollywood.

Bolshoi Ballet *see* **Russia, history of ballet in.**

BONNEFOUS, Jean-Pierre (1945–   ), French dancer. He studied at the Paris Opéra school, becoming premier danseur étoile by 1966. His repertoire includes leading roles in *Daphnis and Chloë, The Four Temperaments* and *The Nutcracker.*

BORCHSENIUS, Valborg (Valberg Jorgensen, 1872–1948), Danish ballerina and ballet mistress. A pupil and dancer at the Royal Theatre School, Copenhagen, she became soloist in 1895, and later ballerina, partnering **Hans Beck.** Although she retired in 1918, she returned to help **Harald Lander** stage the **Bournonville** ballets which she had danced, including *Napoli, La Sylphide, Far From Denmark, La Ventana, Folk Tale* and *Kermesse in Bruges.* She was one of the Royal Theatre School's greatest teachers.

BORIS, Ruthanna (1918–   ), American ballerina and teacher. She studied under Léon Fokine and at the Metropolitan Opera School of Ballet, where she made her debut as soloist in *Carmen* (1935), becoming première danseuse in 1939. She joined **Ballet Russe de Monte Carlo** in 1943 and became ballerina. Her repertoire

Jean Balon. Ph. B.N.

included *Frankie and Johnny*, *Les Sylphides*, *Raymonda*, and *Coppélia*, and she choreographed *Cirque de Deux* (1947), and *Quelques Fleurs* (1948). For **The New York City Ballet** she choreographed *Cakewalk* (1951), *Kaleidoscope* (1953), and *Will o' the Wisp* (1953). Among the ballets she created as director of the Royal Winnipeg Ballet were *The Comedians* and a re-worked version of *Kaleidoscope*. In 1965 she became associate professor of drama and director of dance at the University of Washington, Seattle.

BÖRLIN, Jean (1893–1930), Swedish dancer and choreographer. He studied at the Theatre Royal, Stockholm (1902), and entered the corps de ballet of the opera to become second dancer in 1913. He left the company in 1918 to work with **Fokine**, and was engaged as premier danseur and choreographer by Rolf de Maré when he formed his Ballets Suédois (1920) and produced a number of avant-garde works, including *Les Vierges Folles* (1920), *L'Homme et son Désir* (1921) and *La Création du Monde* (1923).

BOROVANSKY, Edouard (1902–59), Czech dancer, choreographer and teacher who brought ballet to Australia. After studying at the Prague National Theatre School he joined the **Pavlova** company. From 1932–9, he was soloist with Colonel de Basil's **Ballet Russe de Monte Carlo** and danced character parts. In 1939 the company toured Australia where Borovansky opened a school. In 1944 the Borovansky Ballet Company staged its first season. Their productions included *Giselle* and *Coppélia*. The company had many difficulties, was reformed in 1959, and is now the Australian Ballet.

Borovansky Ballet *see* **Australia, history of ballet in.**

BOUBLIKOV, Timofeï Semenovitch (1744–1815), Russian dancer, choreographer, and dancing master. He studied dance at the school for cadets established by the Russian court in 1738. This was the forerunner of the Imperial Ballet School, St. Petersburg. From 1765–7 he danced in Vienna, but returned to Russia where he was largely responsible for introducing folk dancing into the world of theatrical dancing.

BOUCANIERS, LES *see* **Jovita.**

BOURGEOIS GENTILHOMME, LE, a ballet in two scenes, based on Molière's play. Libretto and choreography, **George Balanchine**; music, Richard Strauss; decor, Eugene Berman. First performed at New York City Center, 23 September 1944, by **Ballet Russe de Monte Carlo.** Principal dancers, **Nicholas Magallanes** (Cleonte), Michel Katcharov (Jourdain), **Nathalie Krassovska** (Daughter). A similar ballet was staged at Monte Carlo, 3 May 1932, by René Blum Ballets. A five-act comedy ballet had been produced in Chambord, 14 October 1670, and in Paris, 29 November 1670. Music, **Lully.**

BOURMEISTER, Vladimir Pavlovitch (1904–71), Russian dancer and choreographer, Honoured Art Worker of the RSFSR. He was a pupil at the Lunacharsky Theatre Technicum in Moscow (1925–9), and became leading soloist with the Moscow Art Theatre of Ballet. He choreographed a new version of *Le Corsaire* (1931). In 1941 he was appointed chief choreographer and ballet master of what had become the Stanislavsky and Nemirovich-Danchenko Lyric Theatre Ballet—a notable company with some 36 dancers. His productions for this company included *The Merry Wives of Windsor* (1942), *Swan Lake* (1953), *Schéhérazade* (1944) and *Le Carnaval* (1946). In 1960 his *Swan Lake* was staged at the **Paris Opéra Ballet,** and in 1961 he choreographed *Snow Maiden* for London's **Festival Ballet.**

BOURNONVILLE, Antoine (1760–1843), French dancer and choreographer,

Bournonville: Napoli. Ph. Reyna.

father of **August Bournonville**. He studied with **Jean-Georges Noverre**, and danced in his ballets in Vienna, Paris and London. In 1782 he became danseur at Stockholm where he choreographed his first ballet, *Les Meuniers Provençaux* (1785). He went to Copenhagen in 1792, dancing in many of **Galeotti**'s ballets and succeeding Galeotti as dance director at Copenhagen in 1816. He remained in this post until 1823.

BOURNONVILLE, August (1805–79), Danish choreographer, dancer, ballet master and teacher. At the age of eight he was accepted into the Royal Danish Ballet School, where he studied under **Vincenzo Galeotti,** making his debut in 1813. In 1820 a scholarship enabled him to travel to Paris and study under **Auguste Vestris,** as well as other French teachers. He became soloist at the Paris Opéra in 1823, where he partnered **Marie Taglioni**. His first ballet was *The Soldier and the Peasant* (1829), which was created for the Royal Danish Ballet on his return to Copenhagen where he was soloist and choreographer for 25 years. During this time he created some 50 ballets as well as divertissements for operas and plays. Today about ten of his ballets are still performed. Among his best known are *La Sylphide* (1836), *Toreadoren* (1840),

Konservatoriet eller et Avisfrieri (1849) *Kermessen i Brugge* (1849), *Et Folkesagen* (1854), and *Far From Denmark* (1860). He retired in 1877, and was knighted. Bournonville's influence on the development of the Danish Ballet was immense. At a time when the role of the male dancer was degenerating into that of a *porteur*, Bournonville, a brilliant dancer, created many roles for himself which maintained vigorous male dancing. This continues to give Danish male dancers an outstanding position in the field of ballet. His autobiography is *My Theatre Life*.

bourrée, pas de, a short walking step in which the weight is transferred three times from foot to foot. There are 23 variations.

bourrée couru, pas de, a succession of short, even, running steps akin to the **bourrée,** on demi-pointe or whole foot; a linking step.

BOURRÉE FANTASQUE, a plotless ballet in one scene and three movements. Choreography, **George Balanchine**; music, Emanuel Chabrier; decor and costumes, Barbara Karinska. First performed in New York City Center, 1 December 1949, by **The New York City Ballet**. Principal dancers, **Tanaquil LeClercq, Jerome Robbins, Maria Tallchief,**

Nicholas Magallanes, Janet Reed, Herbert Bliss. Revived at the Festival Hall, London, 18 August 1960, by London's **Festival Ballet**. Principal dancers, **Marilyn Burr, Belinda Wright**, Olga Ferri, **John Gilpin**, Ronald Emblem. Revived, 18 December 1963, by Paris Opéra Ballet. A lively spectacle of three unrelated pieces, satirising the dance.

BOUTIQUE FANTASQUE, LA, a ballet in one act. Choreography, **Léonide Massine**; music, Rossini (arranged and orchestrated by Ottorino Respighi); decor, André Derain. First performed at the Alhambra Theatre, London, 5 June 1919, by **Diaghilev**'s Ballets Russes. Principal dancers, **Enrico Cecchetti** (Shopkeeper), **Lydia Lopokova, Léonide Massine** (Can-Can Dancers), **Lydia Sokolova, Léon Woizikowsky** (Tarantella Dancers), **Stanislas Idzikowsky** (Snob), **Nicholas Zverev** (Cossack Chief). Others to dance the Can-Can with Massine have included **Tamara Karsavina, Vera Nemtchinova, Alexandra Danilova**. Revived, 1933, for **Colonel de Basil**'s Ballets Russes; 1938, for **Ballet Russe de Monte Carlo**; 1943, for **Ballet Theatre**; 1947, for Sadler's Wells Ballet. The work depicts love and revolt in a toyshop when two dolls come to life. It is one of Massine's most successful works.

BOWMAN, Patricia, American ballerina and teacher. She studied with **Fokine, Mordkin, Legat** and **Egerova** in New York, Paris and London. Between 1937 and 1940 she was ballerina at Roxy Theatre, Mordkin Ballet and **Ballet Theatre** dancing classical and vaudeville roles. The repertoire includes *Les Sylphides* and *Carnaval*. She took a teaching post in New York in 1955.

BRABANTS, Jeanne, Belgian dancer and choreographer. She studied in Belgium, England, France, Germany and Denmark. She danced from 1939–58, at the same time staging productions at the Royal Flemish Theatre, Antwerp. Her works have been given in Europe and South America.

Appointed (1951) head of the ballet school at the Royal Flemish Opera, and (1970) director of Ballet van Vlaanderen.

BRAE, June (June Bear, 1917–), English dancer. She studied with Goncharov in China and with **Legat** in London, making her debut with Ballet Club. As principal dancer for Sadler's Wells Ballet (1936–42), she created the role of Black Queen in *Checkmate* with **Helpmann** as Red King. She later created Ballerina in *Adam Zero* and, for Sadler's Wells Theatre Ballet's first season (1946), danced the leading role in *Assembly Ball*, Alice in *The Haunted Ballroom* and Bride in *La Fête Étrange*.

BRAHMS, Caryl, English writer and ballet critic. He edited *Footnotes to the Ballet* (1936). Among his many publications are *Robert Helpmann, Choreographer* (1943) and *A Seat at the Ballet* (1951).

bras, ports de, positions of, or exercises for, the arms. There are five basic positions, the names of which vary according to the system of teaching.

BREGVADZE, Boris (1926–), Russian dancer, Peoples' Artist of the RSFSR. He studied in Leningrad with **Boris Shavrov** (1944–7) and took the role of Andrei in *Tatiana*. He then became a leading dancer with the Kirov Theatre Ballet, where his roles included Solor in *La Bayadère*, Mercurio in *Romeo and Juliet*, the title parts in *Othello* and *Spartacus* and other roles.

BREXNER, Edeltraud (1927–), Austrian ballerina. She studied at the Vienna State Opera Ballet School (1934–44), becoming soloist in 1953 and prima ballerina in 1957. As soloist, her first roles were Salome Pockerl in *Titus Feuerfuchs* (1950) and Bellastriga in *Abraxas* (1953). She has danced principal roles in *The Legend of Joseph, Giselle, Les Sylphides, Swan Lake* and many others. She has toured with the company in Europe and the United States.

BRIANSKY, Oleg (1929–), Belgian dancer. He studied under **Katchourovsky, Gsovsky** and **Volkova,** and became leading dancer with **Les Ballets des Champs-Elysées** in 1947. He joined **Les Ballets de Paris de Roland Petit** in 1949, and London's **Festival Ballet** in 1951. He created Devil in *Vision of Marguerite,* Gennaro in *Napoli* and Phoebus in *Esmeralda,* and took the principal roles in *Swan Lake, Schéhérazade, The Nutcracker* and *Polovetsian Dances from Prince Igor.* He danced with **Ruth Page**'s Chicago Opera Ballet for three seasons (1955–8), and on tour partnered **Tamara Toumanova, Alicia Markova, Nathalie Krassovska** and **Beryl Grey.** In 1960 Briansky became premier danseur with London's Festival Ballet. Among works he has choreographed are *Pièces Brillantes* and a pas 'de deux from *Romeo and Juliet.* He left Festival Ballet to dance in the United States.

BRIANZA, Carlotta (1867–c 1930), Italian ballerina. She studied under **Carlo Blasis,** and made her debut at the Arcadia Theatre, St. Petersburg, in 1887. She went as guest artist to the Maryinsky Theatre, and danced in *Haarlem Tulip* with **Enrico Cecchetti** (1889). She is remembered for her role as Princess Aurora in the Petipa-Tchaikovsky *The Sleeping Beauty* in 1890. In 1891 she returned to Italy to dance and teach; her last appearance was as Carabosse in **Diaghilev**'s elaborate 1921 London production of *The Sleeping Beauty.* She was professor of dance at L'Opéra Comique, Paris.

brisé or **pas de brisé,** a movement in which the dancer leaps upward from one foot, beats the legs together while in the air, then lands on one or both feet.

BRITTON, Donald (1929–), British dancer. He studied at Maddocks School, Bristol, and later at Sadler's Wells School, joining its Theatre Ballet in 1946, and the Sadler's Wells Ballet in 1947. He became a principal dancer with **The Royal Ballet;** his roles have included The Rake in *The Rake's Progress,* Captain Belaye in *Pineapple Poll* and Blue Skater in *Les Patineurs.* He created a memorable role in *The Burrow* (1958).

BRONZE HORSEMAN, THE, a ballet in four acts, based on the poem by Pushkin. Libretto, Pyotre Abolimov; choreography, **Rotislav Zakharov;** music, Reinhold Glière; decor, Mikhail Bobyshov. First performed in Leningrad, 14 March 1949, by Kirov Theatre Ballet. Principal dancers, **Konstantin Sergeyev** (Yevgeny), **Natalia Dudinskaya** (Parasha). Repeated, 27 June 1949, at the Bolshoi Theatre, Moscow. Principal dancers, **Mikhail Gabovich, Galina Ulanova.** Yevgeny loses his sweetheart, Parasha, during a flood, and goes mad. He believes that the Bronze

The Bronze Horseman: Raisa Struchkova and Konstantin Sergeyev. Ph. Photo Off. Cult. Sov.

Horseman (a statue of Peter the Great) is hunting him down.

BRUHN, Erik (1929–   ), Danish dancer and choreographer. He studied at the Royal Danish Ballet School, joined the company in 1947 and became a soloist in 1949. As guest artist, he has danced with American **Ballet Theatre** (1949–51, 1955–8, 1960–1), **The New York City Ballet** (1959–60, 1963–4), **The Royal Ballet** (1962), Australian Ballet (1962–1963), Royal Swedish Ballet (1964) and National Ballet of Canada (1966). His many roles included James in *La Sylphide*, Don José in *Carmen*, Albrecht in *Giselle* and Siegfried in *Swan Lake*. He staged **Bournonville**'s *La Sylphide* for the National Ballet of Canada (1964). He was appointed director of ballet at the Royal Swedish Opera House in 1967. In 1971 he resigned from his post and retired from dancing.

BUCKLE, [**Christopher**] **Richard** [**Sandford**] (1916–   ), British writer and critic. He founded the magazine *Ballet* (1939). He has been ballet critic of *The Observer* (1948–55) and *The Sunday Times* (1959–   ). He wrote *The Adventures of a Ballet Critic* (1953), *In Search of Diaghilev* (1955), *Modern Ballet Design* (1955) and *Nijinsky* (1971).

BURR, Marilyn (1933–   ), Australian ballerina. She studied at the Australian Ballet School, making her debut in 1948 with the National Ballet Company. She joined London's **Festival Ballet** in 1953, and was promoted to ballerina. She has danced Queen of the Wilis and the title role in *Giselle*, Sugar Plum Fairy in *The Nutcracker*, Kupava in *The Snow Maiden*, and Zobeide in *Schéhérazade*. She created Ingrid in *Peer Gynt*. In 1963 she became ballerina with the Hamburg State Opera Ballet.

C

cabriole, a step in which the dancer leaps in the air, one leg extended front, back or side, and beats the other leg upward against it, thus pushing it higher, before he alights. It can be taken to side, in front or behind.

CAGE, THE, a ballet in one act. Libretto and choreography, **Jerome Robbins**; music, Stravinsky (*Concerto in D for Strings*); decor, Jean Rosenthal; costumes, Ruth Sobotka. First performed at New York City Center, 14 June 1951, by **The New York City Ballet.** Principal dancers, **Nora Kaye** (Novice), **Nicholas Magallanes** (Second Intruder), Yvonne Mounsey (Queen), Michael Maule (First Intruder). The ballet depicts the destruction of man by woman, based on the way some female insects kill the male.

CAHUSAC, Louis de (c 1706–59), French ballet master and dance historian. His book *La Danse Ancienne et Moderne* (Paris, 1754) anticipated the reforms of **Jean-George Noverre** and is a complete record of the dance up to that time. Among the ballets he produced for the Académie Royale were *Zaïs* (1747) and *Naïs* (1749). Between 1744 and 1756 he collaborated on *L'Algérien, Les Fêtes de l'Himen et de l'Amour* and *Zoroastre.*

CAMARGO, Marie (Marie Ann de Cupis de Camargo, 1710–70), French ballerina. She studied at the Paris Opéra with **Françoise Prévost** and made her Paris debut in 1726 in *Les Caractères de la Danse.* She is as well remembered for her reforms as for her dance technique. She shortened the length of the skirt, allowing the dancer greater freedom of movement, and removed the heels of the dancing shoes. She developed the **90° turn-out,** the **cabriole** and the entrechat-quatre.

She danced in *Ajax, Le Jugement de Paris* and *Les Fêtes Grecques et Romaines.* **The Camargo Society** was founded in London in 1930 to encourage ballet in England.

Camargo Society, The, a society founded in London in 1930, after the death of **Serge Diaghilev.** The aims of the society were to create a national ballet, maintaining interest in older ballets as well as encouraging young English dancers and choreographers to create new works. Among the works performed for the Camargo Society were *Pomona* and *Façade* by **Frederick Ashton,** *Job* and *La Creation du Monde* by **Ninette de Valois,** and *Adam and Eve* by **Antony Tudor.** During the time of the Camargo Society's existence, the Ballet Rambert and the Sadler's Wells (now Royal) Ballet were being created. The Camargo Society was dissolved in 1933.

CANADA, history of ballet in.

1938 Gweneth Lloyd and Betty Farrally establish a ballet school and small company in Winnipeg, Manitoba.

1939 First public performances by the Winnipeg company.

1948 Winnipeg company sponsors first Canadian Ballet Festival to become an annual (until 1954) convention of non-professional companies.

1949 Winnipeg Ballet becomes a professional company.

1950 National Ballet of Canada is founded in Toronto. **Celia Franca** is appointed artistic director. Choreography by Grant Strate and **David Adams.**

1952 Les Grands Ballets Canadiens is formed in Montreal to give television performances. **Ludmilla Chiriaeff** is director and choreographer. On tour, the company is at first known as Ballets

Chiriaeff. Kay Ambrose is appointed artistic director of National Ballet of Canada.

1953 The Winnipeg company becomes the Royal Winnipeg Ballet. National Ballet of Canada visits the United States and appears at Jacob's Pillow Dance Festival. Eric Hyrst becomes premier danseur and choreographer of Les Grands Ballets Canadiens.

1954 Royal Winnipeg Ballet suffers a disastrous fire.

1956 Ruthanna Boris becomes artistic director and choreographer of Royal Winnipeg Ballet. She injects new life into the company.

1957 Canada Council starts making funds available to the three companies and to the (semi-professional) Classical Ballet Concert Group of Ottawa.

1958 Arnold Spohr becomes director of Royal Winnipeg Ballet.

1959 Les Grands Ballets Canadiens makes its US debut at Jacob's Pillow Dance Festival.

1962 Les Grands Ballets Canadiens become the first Canadian company to stage *La Fille Mal Gardée.*

1964 Anna-Marie and David Holmes join Les Grands Ballets Canadiens as leading dancers. **Brian Macdonald** is appointed choreographer of Royal Winnipeg Ballet which makes its first tour of the United States.

1966 First full-length Canadian ballet, *Rose Latulippe,* staged for Royal Winnipeg Ballet by Brian Macdonald. The company subsequently tours the USSR.

CAPRICCIO ESPAGÑOL, a ballet in one act. Libretto and choreography, **Léonide Massine** and **La Argentinita**; music, Nicholas Rimsky-Korsakov; decor, Mariano Andreù. First performed at the Théâtre de Monte Carlo, 4 May 1939, by **Ballet Russe de Monte Carlo.** Principal dancers, La Argentinita, **Mia Slavenska** and **Nathalie Krassovska** (Gypsy Girl), Léonide Massine and **Frederic Franklin** (Gypsy Youth), **Alexandra Danilova** (Peasant Girl), **Michel Panaiev** (Peasant Youth). The ballet was taken into the

B

repertoire of American Ballet Theatre in 1943, with Massine and **Nora Kaye** in the leading roles. Massine also staged it for **International Ballet** in London in 1951. It comprises five divertissements.

CAPRICES DU CUPIDON ET DU MAÎTRE DE BALLET, LES, a comic **ballet d'action** in one act. Choreography, **Vincenzo Galeotti**; music, Jens Lolle. First performed in the Royal Theatre, Copenhagen, 31 October 1786, by the Royal Danish Opera, and still in the repertoire of the Royal Danish Ballet. Revived by **Harald Lander,** 2 February 1952, for the **Paris Opéra Ballet** with decor by Chapelain-Midy. Cupid pairs off blindfolded couples in national costume with the wrong partners. The choreography is practically unchanged from the original. See illustration p. 46.

CAPRICHOS, a ballet in four episodes and an epilogue, based on four of Goya's etchings. Libretto and choreography, Herbert Ross; music, Béla Bartók (*Contrasts for piano, clarinet and violin*); decor, Helen Pons. First performed in Hunter College Playhouse, New York, 24 January 1950, by Choreographer's Workshop. Taken into the repertoire of **Ballet Theatre** at the New York City Center, on 26 April 1950. Principal dancers, Charlyne Baker, Jenny Workman, **Nana Gollner,** Eric Braun, Peter Gladke, Ruth Ann Koesun, **John Kriza,** Mary Burr, Jack Beaber, Scott Douglas, Jenny Hicks, Vernon Lusby and Ralph McWilliams.

CARACOLE *see* **Divertimento No. 15.**

caractère, danse de (formerly danse comique), non-stylized folk or national dance, or one based on a mode of living, eg trade. It is not strictly part of the classical ballet.

CARD GAME or **Jeu de Cartes,** a ballet in one act. Choreography, **George Balanchine**; music, Igor Stravinsky; decor, Irene Sharaff. First performed in the Metropolitan Opera House, New York,

D

Decor for Les Caprices du Cupidon et du Maître de Ballet: by Chapelain-Midy.
Ph. M. Vaux.

27 April 1937, by **The American Ballet.**
Principal dancer, William Dunbar (Joker).
Revived with the title of *Poker Game* by
Ballet Russe de Monte Carlo in 1940.
Principal dancer, **Frederic Franklin.**
Revised and performed by **The New York
City Ballet** in the New York City Center,
15 February 1951. Principal dancers,
Todd Bolender, Janet Reed (Queen of
Hearts). A new version was performed by
Les Ballets des Champs-Elysées in the
Théâtre des Champs-Elysées, 12 October
1945, with the title, *Jeu de Cartes.*
Choreography, **Janine Charrat;** decor,
Pierre Roy. Principal dancer, **Jean Babilée.**
Yet another version was choreographed by
Ludmilla Chiriaeff for Grands Ballets
Canadiens. The theme of the ballet is the
havoc produced by the Joker in each hand
of cards.

CARMEN, a ballet in one act and five

scenes, based on the opera by Bizet.
Choreography, **Roland Petit;** music,
Georges Bizet; decor, Antoni Clavé. First
performed at the Prince's Theatre, London,
21 February 1949, by **Les Ballets de
Paris de Roland Petit.** Principal dancers,
Roland Petit (José), Serge Perrault
(Escamillo), **Renée Jeanmaire** (Carmen).
Petit also staged the ballet for the Royal
Danish Ballet, January 1960, in Copen-
hagen. Principal dancers, **Kirsten Simone**
(Carmen), **Flemming Flindt** (José),
Henning Kronstam (Escamillo). **Ruth
Page** presented a revised version, 1959
for Chicago Opera Ballet. One of Petit's
outstanding works, *Carmen* was criticized
by musicians but was a success in Paris,
London, and the USA. The pas de deux in
Carmen's room and the fight between
Carmen and José before the stabbing were
highlights of Petit's production. In 1967 a
version was created for the Bolshoi Ballet

by **Alberto Alonso**, with **Maya Pliset-skaya** as Carmen. The following year this version was produced in Cuba, with **Alicia Alonso** in the title role. The music was arranged and orchestrated by Schedrin. The ballet deals in symbols, and life and death are played out in the arena. A new version was created by **John Cranko** with music by Wolfgang Fortner (*Bizet Collage*). First performed 28 February 1971, by the Stuttgart Opera Ballet. Principal dancers, **Marcia Haydée**, Egon Madsen, Richard Cragun.

CARNAVAL, LE, a ballet in one act. Libretto and choreography, **Michel Fokine**; music, Robert Schumann; decor, **Léon Bakst**. First performed for charity in the Pavlova Hall, St. Petersburg, 1910. Principal dancers, **Tamara Karsavina,** Leon Leontiev, Vera Fokina, Ludmila Scholler, **Bronislava Nijinska,** Alfred Bekefy, Vasily Kiselev, Alexander Shiriaiev, Vsevolod Meyerhold. First stage performance in the Teater des Westens, Berlin, 20 May 1910, by **Diaghilev**'s Ballets Russes. Principal dancers, Tamara Karsavina, **Vaslav Nijinsky, Adolph Bolm. Stanislas Idzikowsky** later took over Nijinsky's role of Harlequin in the Diaghilev company and danced it for Sadler's Wells Ballet. The ballet was revived by Michel Fokine in 1940 for American Ballet Theatre with Adolph Bolm as Pierrot. The theme is

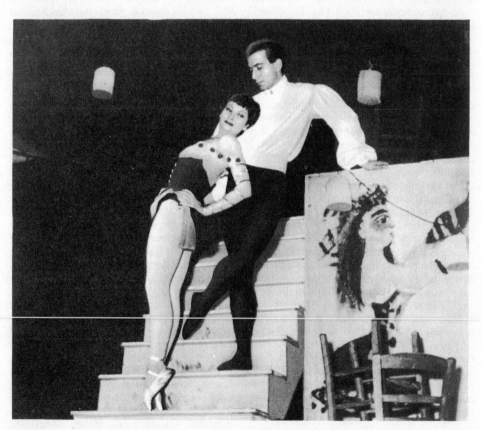

Carmen: Renée Jeanmaire and Roland Petit. Ph. Lipnitzki.

a ball at which dancers and guests enjoy a masquerade dressed as characters from commedia dell'arte.

Carnival of the Animals, orchestral suite by Saint-Saëns from which the cello solo provided music for the solo *The Dying Swan* and for a ballet. Choreography and decor, **Andrée Howard.** First performed in the Mercury Theatre, London, 26 March 1943, by Ballet Rambert. *See* **The Dying Swan.**

CARROLL, Elisabeth (Elisabeth Pfister, 1937–), American dancer, born in Paris. She became soloist with Monte Carlo Opera Ballet in 1951. Two years later she joined **Ballet Theatre,** and was promoted to first soloist in 1961. Her repertoire included *Graduation Ball, Les Sylphides, Les Patineurs, Peter and the Wolf, Bluebeard* and *Gala Performance.* She created the leading female role in *Points on Jazz* (1961). She joined Robert Joffrey Ballet in 1962 and **Harkness Ballet** in 1964.

CARTER, Alan (1920–), British dancer, choreographer and teacher. After studying with **Astafieva** and **Nicholas Legat,** he was soloist with Sadler's Wells Ballet (1938–40), dancing a large repertoire and creating the title role in *Harlequin in the Street* and one of the Gemini in *Horoscope.* He joined the newly-formed Sadler's Wells Theatre Ballet (1946), where he choreographed *The Catch* to Bartók, *House of Shadows* and *Vier Mal Vier.* In 1948 he became director and choreographer of St. James Ballet (the touring company of The Arts Council of Great Britain). He was ballet master and choreographer at the Empire Theatre, London (1951–3). As ballet director and choreographer at Bayerische Staatsoper, Munich (1954–9), he staged versions of *The Miraculous Mandarin, Prince of the Pagodas* and *Ondine.* While guest teacher at **The Royal Ballet** in 1962, he choreographed *Toccata.* In 1964 he became ballet director at Wuppertal Opera Germany.

CARTER, Jack (1923–), British dancer and choreographer. He studied at the Sadler's Wells School and later danced with the Sadler's Wells Opera Ballet, and the Original Ballet Russe. With Ballet Rambert he staged a number of works for Ballet Workshop. From 1954–7 he choreographed in Amsterdam, where he created his dramatic ballet *Witch Boy* (1956) based on *The Dark Side of the Moon.* From 1957 he became associated with London's **Festival Ballet,** and was appointed resident choreographer (1965). For this company he has staged his own versions of *Swan Lake* (1966) and *Coppélia* (1968); his own ballets include *Beatrix* (1966) and *Cage of God*, which he produced for Western Theatre Ballet. In 1970 he created *The Unknown Island* to celebrate the Berlioz centenary year. He has also danced and choreographed throughout Europe and South America.

CASSE-NOISETTE *see* **Nutcracker, The.**

CASTOR ET POLLUX, a ballet based on the mythological opera by **Jean Philippe Rameau.** Performed at l'Académie Royale, Paris, in 1772. Principal dancers, **Gaetan Vestris** and **Maximilien Gardel** (Apollo). In this ballet Gardel became the first dancer to remove the mask, worn by dancers until this time. **Antony Tudor** used the same title for a ballet staged for the Oxford University Opera Club in 1934. As an opera-ballet it was staged by Thomas Scherman in the Philharmonic Hall, Lincoln Center, New York, in January 1965. Principal dancers, **Lupe Serrano,** Scott Douglas.

CATARINA or **La Fille du Bandit,** a ballet in three acts. Libretto and choreography, **Jules Perrot**; music, Cesare Pugni; decor, Charles Marshall. First performed in Her Majesty's Theatre, London, 3 March 1846. Principal dancers, **Lucile Grahn,** Jules Perrot. Performed at La Scala, Milan, 9 January 1847 and in St. Petersburg, 16 November 1849. Principal dancer on these occasions, **Fanny Elssler.** The story tells of a painter who wins the love of Catarina, despite his rival, a bandit lieutenant.

CECCHETTI, Enrico (1850–1928), Italian dancer and teacher. He studied with Lepri and Coppini, making his debut at La Scala, Milan in 1870, in London in 1885, and in Russia in 1887. He spent more than half of his life in Russia, became assistant second ballet master of the Imperial Theatre in 1890, and instructor at the Imperial School in 1892. His classes contained some of the most famous of the Russian dancers: **Pavlova, Fokine, Preobrajenska, Egorova, Karsavina,** and **Nijinsky.** He was ballet master for the Warsaw Government Ballet school in 1902, and in 1905 returned to Italy. However, soon he returned to Russia and opened a school there, becoming the private instructor of Pavlova, whom he accompanied on her world tour (1907–8). In 1909 he became official instructor of the **Diaghilev Ballets Russes,** and in 1918 opened a ballet school in London. Among his pupils were: **Massine, Bolm, Lopokova, de Valois, Danilova, Dolin, Lifar** and **Markova.** He returned to Italy in 1923, becoming ballet master at **Teatro alla Scala,** Milan (1925). There can be no dispute about his success as a teacher, and the influence his teaching had on the world of ballet. As a dancer he created the roles of Blue Bird and Carabosse in *Sleeping Beauty*, Charlatan in *Petrouchka* and Pantalon in *Le Carnaval*. He collapsed and died in class. *See* **Cecchetti Method.**

Cecchetti Method. After the death (1878) of **Carlo Blasis,** the teaching of ballet reverted to somewhat haphazard methods, passive and mechanical; **Enrico Cecchetti** thoroughly revised it, drawing on the delicacy and grace of the French and the acrobatic brilliance of the Italians. With this balance between **adagio** and **allegro,** Cecchetti was able to rear versatile dancers. He took the basic lesson and elaborated a series of exercises, each to serve a definite purpose and to lead logically to the next exercise in the series. These exercises assured the absolute independence of all movements of the body. In addition, Cecchetti devised exercises for each day of the week. In 1922, **Cyril Beaumont** and **Stanislas Idzikovsky** published his treatise on the dance in London, with the title *A Manual of the Theory and Practice of Classical Theatrical Dancing*. The Cecchetti Society was formed in 1922 in London and was incorporated into the Imperial Society of Teachers of Dancing in 1924. The Cecchetti Council of America was established in 1939.

CERITO or **Cerrito, Fanny** (1817–1909), Italian ballerina. She studied with **Perrot, Blasis** and **Saint-Léon** and between 1830 and 1855 danced in Italy, England, France and Russia. She is most famous for her roles in *Alma* (1842), *Ondine* (1843), *La Vivandière* which she created (1844), *Gemma*, which she choreographed (1854),

Enrico Cecchetti. Ph. Lipnitzki.

Fanny Cerito. Ph. Lipnitzki.

and *Pas de Quatre* which she danced in London with **Taglioni, Grisi** and **Grahn** (1845). She was married to Arthur Saint-Léon, and created roles in many of his ballets.

CHABUKIANY, Vakhtang (1910–   ), Russian dancer and choreographer. He studied in Leningrad and joined the Kirov Ballet in 1929, becoming premier danseur two years later. His most famous roles include Sportsman in *The Golden Age* (1931) and Jerome in *The Flames of Paris* (1932). He choreographed and created roles in *Heart of the Hills* (1938) and *Laurencia* (1939). Chabukiany enhanced the role of the male dancer in Russian ballet and introduced different executions and new movements. He toured the United States in 1934, and later became director of ballet in Tbilisi.

CHALIF, Louis H. (1876–1948), American ballet teacher, born in Russia. He studied at the Odessa Municipal Theatre ballet school and under Thomas Nijinsky. He made his debut as a child-dancer in *Excelsior* (1887). He graduated in 1893 becoming ballet master in 1897 and premier danseur in 1903. He moved to the United States in 1904, and danced with Metropolitan Opera Ballet (1904–5). In 1907 he opened the Chalif Russian Normal School of Dancing, which supplied basic dance education to teachers throughout the United States, Canada and Latin America. He wrote a number of books on dance technique.

CHAMBRE, LA, a ballet in one act. Libretto, Georges Simenon; choreography, **Roland Petit**; music, Georges Auric; decor and costumes, Bernard Buffet. First performed in the Théâtre des Champs Elysées, 1955, by **Les Ballets de Paris de Roland Petit**. Principal dancers, Veronika Mlakar, Buzz Miller. The theme is a police inspector's reconstruction of a murder in a sordid hotel room.

changement or **changement de pieds,** a spring in the air (**élévation**) from the fifth position during which the feet change their relative positions. The movement may be executed with a small or large spring.

CHANT DU ROSSIGNOL, LE, a ballet in one act, based on a fairy tale by Hans Christian Andersen. Choreography, **Léonide Massine**; music, Igor Stravinsky; decor and costumes, Henri Matisse. First performed at the Paris Opéra, 2 February 1920, by **Diaghilev**'s Ballets Russes. Principal dancers, **Tamara Karsavina, Lydia Sokolova, Stanislas Idzikowsky**. **George Balanchine** created new choreography in 1926 and presented **Alicia Markova** in the principal role. The Emperor of China is dying of grief because a mechanical nightingale has frightened

Janine Charrat. Ph. Lipnitzki.

away the real bird. However, the real nightingale returns in time to charm death away with her song. A slightly different version, with the title of *The Chinese Nightingale*, was presented at the Deutsches Museum, Munich, 7 May 1953, with choreography by Tatiana Gsovska.

CHARNLEY, Michael (1927–), British dancer and choreographer. He studied with **Kurt Jooss** and danced with Sadler's Wells Ballet and Ballets Jooss (1943–7). He was choreographer with Ballet Workshop and London's **Festival Ballet**. His works include *Bagatelle* (1951), *Symphony for Fun* (1952) and *Alice in Wonderland* (1953). He successfully fused classical with modern ballet.

CHARRAT, Janine (1924–), French ballerina and choreographer. She studied with Jeanne Ronay and **Lubov Egorova,** and at fourteen she danced in a programme of her own choreographic works. In 1940 she choreographed *Orfeo and Eurydice, Paul and Virginia* and others, which she danced in concerts with **Roland Petit** until 1944. She was ballerina with **Nouveau Ballet de Monte Carlo** (1946), dancing *Chota Roustaveli* and *Passion,* and choreographing *Cressida.* She formed her own company in 1951 (later known as Ballets de France), and choreographed *Le Massacre des Amazones, Herakles, Les Liens,* and *Les Algues,* in which she danced the title role (1953). Her company toured Europe, the United States and Japan. While preparing a second tour (1961), her dress caught fire during a television rehearsal, causing severe burns. In 1962 she became director of ballet at the Geneva Opéra, returning to the stage as dancer-choreographer in her own *Tristan and Isolde* (1963). As guest choreographer, her works included *Jeu de Cartes* for Petit's **Les Ballets des Champs- Elysées,** *Adame Miroir* for **Les Ballets de Paris de Roland Petit** (1948), *Abraxas* for Opéra Comique and Berlin Opera (1949), *Joueur de Flute* for Colon Theatre, Buenos Aires, *Les Algues* and *Jeu de Cartes* for **Béjart's** Brussels Théâtre de la Monnaie, in which she danced the leading roles. She also created the leading role in *The Seven Deadly Sins.*

CHASE, Lucia (1907–), American ballerina and director. She studied with **Mordkin, Fokine, Tudor, Vilzak** and **Nijinska,** and was ballerina with Mordkin Ballet (1938 and 1939), dancing *Giselle, La Fille Mal Gardée, The Goldfish, Trepak* and others. She financed, and was founder-director of **Ballet Theatre** (1940–5), and co-director from 1945 when it became American Ballet Theatre. She created many roles for this company including Minerva in *Judgement of Paris*, Nurse in *Romeo and Juliet*, Oldest Sister in *Pillar of Fire*, Queen in *Bluebeard*, Pallas Athena in *Helen of Troy*, and Stepmother in *Fall River Legend*. She also danced Ballerina in *Petrouchka*, Prelude in *Les Sylphides* and Cerito in *Pas de Quatre*.

chassé or **pas de chassé,** step in which one foot displaces the other, and the weight of the body is transferred to the second foot. It may be done forward, backward or sideways.

CHATTE, LA, a ballet in one act based on an Aesop fable. Libretto, Boris Kochno; choreography, **George Balanchine**; music, Henri Sauguet; decor, Naum Gabo, Antoine Pevsner. First performed in the Théâtre de Monte Carlo, 30 April 1927, by **Diaghilev**'s Ballets Russes. Principal dancers, **Olga Spessivtzeva, Serge Lifar.** The Cat was later danced by **Alice Nikitina** and **Alicia Markova.** Aphrodite tests the Cat she has turned into a Girl by tempting her with a mouse. The Girl chases the mouse and turns into a Cat again. The decor used shining Cellophane costumes and a black background.

CHAUVIRÉ, Yvette (1917–   ), French ballerina. She studied with **Boris Kniasev** and at the Paris Opéra school. She joined the **Paris Opéra Ballet** where as première danseuse étoile (1941) she created *Istar*. She first made her debut in 1937 in **Lifar's** *David Triomphant* and *Alexandre le Grand*. As ballerina with **Nouveau Ballet de Monte Carlo** (1946), she created the leading roles in *Dramma per Musica* and *Chota Roustaveli*. She returned to the Paris Opéra in 1947, continuing to make guest appearances with several companies. At the Berlin Opera she created the leading role in *Romeo and Juliet*, and danced *Giselle* with **Erik Bruhn.** With **The Royal Ballet** she danced *Giselle* and *Sleeping Beauty*; for Ballet International de la Marquese de Cuevas (1961), she danced *The Sleeping Beauty*, and was partnered by **Rudolph**

Yvette Chauviré in The Sleeping Beauty. Ph. Bernand.

Nureyev in *Giselle.* She is renowned for her interpretation of this ballet. She has also appeared in concert performances in South America and the Soviet Union, where she was partnered by **Youly Algarov.** In 1963 she was appointed director of the Paris Opéra Ballet. She is a Chevalier of the Légion d'Honneur.

CHECKMATE, a ballet in one scene with prologue, based on the game of chess. Libretto and music, Arthur Bliss; choreography, **Ninette de Valois**; decor, E. McKnight Kauffer. First performed in the Théâtre des Champs-Elysées, Paris, 15 June 1937, by the Vic-Wells Ballet. Principal dancers, **Pamela May** (Red Queen), **June Brae** (Black Queen), **Robert Helpmann** (Red King), **Harold Turner** (Red Knight), **Michael Somes, Frederick Ashton, Margot Fonteyn,** Mary Honer. Performed at Sadler's Wells

Theatre, October 1937, and staged again in Vienna and Ankara in 1964. With new designs by E. McKnight Kauffer, presented at the Royal Opera House, Covent Garden, London, 18 November 1947. The ballet uses the game of chess to symbolize life and death.

CHESWORTH, John (1930–), British dancer and choreographer. He studied at the Rambert School and joined Ballet Rambert (1952), becoming a leading dancer. His many roles with the company include 2nd Dance in *Dark Elegies*, title role in *Don Quixote*, and leading roles in *Ziggurat*, *Rag Dances* and *Solo*. He has choreographed a number of works for Ballet Rambert, including *Pawn to King 5* and *Form According*; and *Games for Five Players* for Northern Dance Theatre. He became associate director of Ballet Rambert in 1972.

CHEVALIER ET LA DAMOISELLE, LE, a ballet in two acts based on a medieval romance. Choreography, **Serge Lifar**; music, Philippe Gaubert; decor, A. M. Cassandre. First performed by **Paris Opéra Ballet,** 2 July 1941. Principal dancers, Serge Lifar, **Solange Schwartz, Roland Petit.** Revived by Paris Opéra, 8 December 1947. Principal dancers, **Alexandre Kalioujny, Yvette Chauviré.** The story tells of a Princess who is transformed into a hind each night. She gores a Knight who stabs her. This breaks the spell, and she is restored to her proper form.

CHIRIAEFF, Ludmilla (1924–), dancer, choreographer and director, born in Latvia. She studied in Berlin, and with **Fokine, Massine** and others. She danced with Colonel de Basil's Ballets Russes (1936–7), and joined the Berlin Opera Ballet (1939), becoming a soloist. After the war, she became première danseuse, choreographer and ballet mistress at Lausanne Theatre. She opened a school in Geneva (1948) and formed Les Ballets des Arts. In 1952 she moved to Montreal where she created ballets for Canadian television and subsequently formed Les Ballets

Chiriaeff (1955). This company became Les Grands Ballets Canadiens in 1956, with Chiriaeff as director and choreographer. Its reputation has been founded on her choreographic works which include *Jeu de Cartes, Les Noces, Étude* and *Concert Royal*. In 1962 she staged the first Canadian production of *La Fille Mal Gardée* for the company.

CHOPINIANA *see* **Sylphides, Les.**

CHOREARTIUM, a ballet in four movements. Choreography, **Léonide Massine**; music, Brahms (Fourth Symphony); decor, Constantine Terechkovich and Eugene Lourie. First performed at the Alhambra Theatre, London, 24 October 1933 by Colonel de Basil's **Ballet Russe de Monte Carlo.** Principal dancers, **Irina Baronova, Alexandra Danilova, Tatiana Riabouchinska,** Nina Verchinina. Thought by some to be Massine's masterpiece, the ballet is completely plotless, unlike its symphonic predecessor, **Les Présages.**

choreography, the sequence of dance patterns in a theatrical production, or the art of creating and arranging dances for a theatrical performance. The term originally meant 'dance notation'. The choreographer is responsible for co-ordinating libretto, music and dance movements. These may be his own; otherwise he works in close collaboration with composer and librettist. See illustration p. 54.

CHOTA ROUSTAVELI, a ballet in four acts based on the fairy tale by the Georgian poet Roustaveli. Libretto and choreography, **Serge Lifar**; music, Arthur Honegger, Alexander Tcherepnine, Tibor Harsanyi. First performed at Monte Carlo, 5 May 1946, by **Nouveau Ballet de Monte Carlo.** Principal dancers, **Yvette Chauviré, Janine Charrat,** Serge Lifar, **Alexandre Kalioujny.** Lifar presented the tale with dancing, music and poetry in the castle of Queen Thamar.

CHRISTENSEN, William (1902–),

American choreographer and teacher. He studied with **Michel Fokine,** and in 1932 founded his own school and company in Oregon. He became ballet master and choreographer with the San Francisco Opera Ballet (1938), and was professor of theatre ballet at the University of Utah in 1951. Utah Ballet was established the following year. For Ballet Gala, Christensen choreographed *Concerto* and *Caprice de Paris*. Among other works he has staged are *Coppélia, Swan Lake* and *The Nutcracker*.

CHUJOY, Anatole (1894–1969), American writer, critic and editor, born in Riga. He became an American citizen in 1931, and co-founded *Dance Magazine* in 1937. He edited this journal until 1941, when he

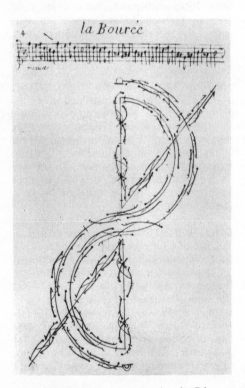

Choreography: a page by Louis Pécourt. Ph. Palais de la Découverte.

founded *Dance News*. He published several works, including *The New York City Ballet* (1953). In 1949 he published *The Dance Encyclopedia*, the first encyclopedia of ballet in the English language. An expanded and revised edition (compiled with **P. W. Manchester**) was published in New York in 1967.

CINDERELLA, many ballets have been based on the original fairy tale by Charles Perrault. A version was presented at the King's Theatre, London, 26 March 1822. Choreography, d'Albert; music, Zor; principal dancer, Mercandotti. A three act version was presented at the Maryinsky Theatre, 5 December 1893. Libretto, Lydia Pashkova; choreography, **Marius Petipa, Enrico Cecchetti, Lev Ivanov**; music, Schell; decor, G. Levogt, M. Shishkov, M. Bocharov. Principal dancers, **Pierina Legnani, Paul Gerdt**. Legnani created a sensation in this production by performing 32 fouettés, a feat which had not been seen in Russia before. On 6 January 1906, a five scene version appeared at the Empire Theatre, London; choreography, Frederick Farren; principal dancer, **Adeline Genée**. The Royal Opera House, Covent Garden, London, saw a three scene production by the Educational Ballet of Colonel de Basil. Choreography and libretto, **Michel Fokine**; music Frederic d'Erlanger; decor, Nathalie Gontcharova. Principal dancers, **Tatiana Riabouchinska, Paul Petrov**. This version had its New York première in the Fifty-First Street Theatre, 16 November 1940. In November 1945, the important three act version with libretto by Nicolai Volkov had its first performance. Choreography, Rostislav Zakharov; music, Sergei Prokofiev; decor and costumes, Peter Williams. Principal dancers, **Olga Lepeshinskaya, Mikhail Gabovich**. The same score was used at the Kirov Theatre, Leningrad, 8 April 1946, with choreography by **Konstantin Sergeyev**. Principal dancers, **Natalia Dudinskaya**, Konstantin Sergeyev. This version was presented at the Royal Opera House, Covent Garden, London, in 1963, with **Raisa Struchkova** as Cinderella. In

December 1948 Sadler's Wells Ballet took the Prokofiev score into its repertoire. Libretto and choreography, **Frederick Ashton**; decor and costumes, Jean-Denis Maclès. Principal dancers, **Moira Shearer** (Cinderella), **Michael Somes** (Prince Charming), **Robert Helpmann** and Frederick Ashton en travesti (Ugly Sisters), **Pamela May** (Fairy Godmother). A revival was presented in July 1970, by **The Royal Ballet**. Choreography, Frederick Ashton. Principal dancers, **Antoinette Sibley, Anthony Dowell**. Another version with the Prokofiev score was presented at **Teatro alla Scala,** Milan, 15 December 1955. Choreography, Alfred Rodrigues; decor, Beaurepaire. Principal dancers, **Violette Verdy,** Giulio Perugini. This score was again used for a ballet extravaganza presented at the Théâtre des Champs-Elysées, Paris, 4 December 1963, as part of the International Dance Festival. Choreography, Vaslav Orlikovsky; decor, Raymundo de Larrain. Principal dancers, **Galina Samtsova, Viktor Rona**. A new production was staged by Ben Stevenson to Prokofiev's score, 24 April 1970, for the National Ballet of Washington. Cinderella has been a popular theme for choreographers and was the first full length ballet choreographed in Britain. The Prokofiev music has eclipsed all earlier scores, having been used for all recent versions.

ciseaux or **pas ciseaux,** a movement in which the dancer springs upward from the fifth position, opening the legs to a wide second position so that body and legs resemble an inverted 'T', and closes the legs before alighting in the fifth position. The movement resembles the opening and closing of scissors. Also called écart en l'air.

City Center Joffrey Ballet *see* **Joffrey, Robert.**

CLARKE, Mary (1923–   ), British writer on ballet. She has been editor of *The Dancing Times* (1963–   ), and London correspondent of *Dance News*.

Among her published works are *The Sadler's Wells Ballet: A History and an Appreciation* (1955), and *Dancers of Mercury: The Story of the Ballet Rambert* (1962).

classical ballet, the dance technique as developed by **Carlo Blasis** at the **barre.** In this sense the term expresses the purest of lines. The term is also applied to the ballets whose structure followed the rules established by **Arthur Saint-Léon** and **Marius Petipa.** Thus the Romantic ballets *The Sleeping Beauty, The Nutcracker* and *Coppélia* are classical in form. *See* **ballet, history of.**

CLÉOPÂTRE, a ballet in one act. Libretto and choreography, **Michel Fokine**; music, Anton Arensky and others; decor, **Léon Bakst.** First produced by Fokine at the Maryinsky Theatre, St. Petersburg, 21 March 1908, with the title *Une Nuit d'Egypte*. On 2 June 1909, **Serge Diaghilev** presented it as *Cléopâtre* at the Théâtre du Châtelet, Paris. Music, Rimsky-Korsakov, Glinka, Mussourgsky. Principal dancers, **Anna Pavlova** (Ta-Hor), **Ida Rubinstein** (Cleopatra), Michel Fokine (Amoun), **Tamara Karsavina, Vaslav Nijinsky.** The mime part of Cleopatra was created for Ida Rubinstein and played by **Seraphima Astafieva** and **Lubov Tchernicheva** in London. The ballet was revived by Diaghilev in 1918 with decor by Robert and Sonia Delauney. The story tells of Amoun, a slave at the court of Cleopatra who falls in love with the queen. She makes a bargain—her love for one night in exchange for his life. He accepts.

CLUSTINE or **KHLUSTINE, Ivan** (1862–1941), Russian dancer and ballet master. He studied and danced at the Bolshoi Ballet, Moscow, becoming its premier danseur at 18 and ballet master in 1898. He left Russia in 1903 and established his own school in Paris. He was premier danseur and ballet master at Monte Carlo (1905), ballet master at the **Paris Opéra Ballet** (1909–14), choreographing *Roussalka* (1911), *Suites de Danses* (1913) and

Le Combat: Francisco Moncion. Ph. New York City Ballet.

Hansi Le Bossu (1914). He arranged a number of works for **Anna Pavlova,** and was the first Russian ballet master at the Paris Opéra after **Diaghilev** came to France.

COMBAT, LE, a ballet in one act. Choreography, **William Dollar;** music, Raffaello de Banfield; decor, Marie-Laure de Noailles. First performed at the Prince's Theatre, London, 24 February 1949, by **Les Ballets de Paris de Roland Petit.** Principal dancers, **Janine Charrat, Vladimir Skouratov.** A pas de deux derived from this was performed at the Winter Garden Theatre, New York, 6 October 1949. Principal dancers, **Colette Marchand, Milorad Miskovitch.** A slightly altered version, entitled *The Duel,* was staged by William Dollar for **New York City Ballet** at New York City Center on 24 February 1950. Costumes by Robert Stevenson. Principal dancers, William Dollar and **Francisco Moncion** (Tancredi), **Melissa Hayden** (Clorinda). *The Duel* was revived by American **Ballet Theatre** in London, 23 July 1953. Decor, Georges Wakhevitch. Principal dancers, Melissa Hayden, **John Kriza.** New York première at the Metropolitan Opera House, 27 December 1953. The ballet portrays an incident from Torquato Tasso's romantic epic *Gerusalemme Liberata.*

competitions, two very important competitions have been set up which make a major contribution to ballet. **Varna, Bulgaria,** an International Ballet Competition has been held here annually (except 1967) since 1964. An international jury was appointed under the chairmanship of **Galina Ulanova.** The competition is divided into two sections 1) for girls and boys, 15–19 years of age; 2) ballet dancers not older than 28; and three stages a) classical; b) modern or classical; c) optional. The prizes for competitors in the first section are the Special Distinction of the Youth Organization of Varna, First, Second and Third Class Distinctions. For competitors in the second section there is the Varna Summer Grand Prix, 1 gold, 2 silver and 2 bronze medals for men and for women, various 'encouragement prizes', and prizes for original choreography. **Moscow, Soviet Union,** the First Moscow International Dance Competition was held in 1969 with an international jury. There are gold, silver and bronze medals and titles of Laureat, 'encouragement prizes', diplomas of honour and prizes for accompaniment.

COMUS, a ballet in two scenes, based on the masque by John Milton. Choreography, **Robert Helpmann;** music, Henry Purcell (arranged by Constant Lambert); decor, Oliver Messel. First performed at the New Theatre, London, 14 January 1942, by Sadler's Wells Ballet. Principal dancers, Robert Helpmann (Comus), **Margot**

Fonteyn (The Lady), John Hart and David Paltenghi (Her Brothers), **Margaret Dale** (Attendant Spirit), Moyra Fraser (Sabrina). **International Ballet** presented the masque in 1946 with music by Henry Lawes (written in 1634 for the original) and George Frederick Handel; decor, Doris Zinkeisen. Principal dancers, **Mona Inglesby,** Harcourt Algeranov. The theme is the struggle between chastity and sensual pleasure in the persons of The Lady and Comus, and the ballet kept some of the characteristics of the original masque.

CON AMORE, a ballet in one act. Libretto, James Luján; choreography, **Lew Christensen**; music, Gioacchino Rossini; decor, James Brodrero. First performed at the Opera House, San Francisco, 10 March 1953, by San Francisco Ballet. Principal dancers, Sally Bailey (Captain of the Amazons), Nancy Johnson (The Lady), **Leon Danielian** (The Bandit). Presented in a revised version in the New York City Center, 9 June 1953, by **The New York City Ballet,** with principal dancers, Sally Bailey, Nancy Johnson, **Jacques d'Amboise.** The ballet remains in their repertoire and tells of a Bandit, captured by the Amazons, who prefers death to their love, and of a promiscuous Lady escaping from her husband.

CONCERTO, a plotless ballet in three scenes. Choreography, Vassili Lambrinos; music, Edvard Grieg (*Piano Concerto in A minor*); decor, Francisco Reymundo. First performed in the Festival Hall, London, 27 July 1953, by London's **Festival Ballet.** Principal dancers, **Nathalie Krassovska,** Noel Rossana, Keith Beckett.

CONCERTO, a plotless ballet in one act. Libretto and choreography, **George Skibine**; music, André Jolivet (*Concerto for Piano and Orchestra*); decor and costumes, André Delfau. First performed at the Opéra Comique, Paris, 28 March 1958. Principal dancers, **Marjorie Tallchief**, George Skibine, Michel Rayne. Staged by the Teatro Colón, Buenos Aires, in 1961.

CONCERTO, a plotless ballet in one act. Choreography, **Kenneth MacMillan**; music, Dmitri Shostakovich (*Piano Concerto No. 2*); decor, Jurgen Rose. First performed in Berlin, November 1966, by Deutsche Oper Ballet. Principal dancers, **Lynn Seymour,** Rudolf Holtz. It entered the repertoire of **The Royal Ballet,** 26 May 1967, at the Royal Opera House, Covent Garden.

CONCERTO BAROCCO, a plotless ballet in one act. Choreography, **George Balanchine**; music, Johann Sebastian Bach; decor, Eugene Berman. First performed by the **American Ballet** during their South American tour in 1941. Staged in City Center, New York, 11 October 1948, by **The New York City Ballet.** Principal dancers, **Marie-Jeanne,** Ruth Gilbert, **Francisco Moncion.** Also performed, in practice costumes, by **Ballet Russe de Monte Carlo** in the New York City Center, September 1945. Principal dancers Marie-Jeanne, **Patricia Wilde, Nicholas Magallanes.** The dance evolves from the music in the style characteristic of Balanchine's later work.

CONCURRENCE, LA, a ballet in one act. Choreography, **George Balanchine**; music, Georges Auric; decor, André Derain. First performed, 12 April 1932, by **Colonel de Basil's** Ballet Russe de Monte Carlo. Principal dancers, **Irina Baronova** and **Tamara Toumanova** (alternating in principal role), **Léon Woizikowsky** (Tatterdemalion). This is a gaily enacted fantasy telling of the antics of two rival tailors.

CONRAD, Karen (1919–), American dancer and teacher. She studied with Catherine Littlefield and **Lubov Egorova** and was principal dancer with Littlefield Ballet (1935–7), taking the leading roles in *Barn Dance*, *Sleeping Beauty* and others. In 1937 she became a soloist with Mordkin Ballet and was leading soloist when the company amalgamated with **Ballet Theatre** (1939). Her roles included Duck in *Peter and the Wolf* and French

Ballerina in *Gala Performance*. She retired in 1959.

CONSTANTIA, a plotless ballet in one scene. Choreography, **William Dollar**; music, Frederic Chopin; decor, Horace Armistead; costumes, Grace Houston. First performed in the International Theatre, New York, 31 October 1944, by **Ballet International**. Principal dancers, **Marie-Jeanne**, Yvonne Patterson, William Dollar. Revived at the Metropolitan Opera House, New York, 16 October 1946, by Original Ballet Russe. Principal dancers, **Rosella Hightower**, Yvonne Patterson, **André Eglevsky**, who performed in the revival in 1947 by Grand Ballet du Marquis de Cuevas. The ballet is an interpretation of the Chopin music which was his tribute to the young Polish singer, Constantia Gladowska.

CONTES RUSSES, a ballet in prologue and four scenes, based on Russian folk tales. Choreography, **Léonide Massine**; music, Anatole Liadov; decor, Michel Larionov. First performed in the Théâtre du Châtelet, Paris, 11 May 1917, by **Diaghilev**'s Ballets Russes. Principal dancers, **Lydia Sokolova** (Kikimora), **Stanislas Idzikowsky** (Cat), Léonide Massine (Bova Korolevich), **Lubov Tchernicheva** (Swan Princess), Nicholas Kremnev (Baba-Yaga) and later, **Bronislava Nijinska** and **Anatole Vilzak**.

contretemps, a step, danced off-beat, in which the dancer jumps from the right foot, brings the left round from behind to replace the right which then moves to the side, and the step is repeated.

COPPÉLIA or La Fille aux Yeux d'Émail, many different versions of the story by Hoffmann have been choreographed. A three act version was performed, 25 May 1870, at the Théâtre Impérial de l'Opéra in Paris. Choreography, **Saint-Léon**; music, Léo Delibes. Principal dancers, Guiseppina Bozzacchi (Swanilda), Eugénie Fiocre (Frantz). An arrangement in one act was presented, 8 November 1884, at the Empire Theatre, London. Principal dancers, Alice Holt (Swanilda), W. Warde (Dr. Coppelius). The complete ballet was produced at the Empire theatre, 14 May 1906, with **Adeline Genée** as Swanilda. This version is still in the repertoire of the **Paris Opéra Ballet** with the tradition of having a ballerina play Frantz. A version with choreography by Glaseman is in the repertoire of the Royal Danish Ballet and Swanilda has been interpreted by, among others, **Margot Lander** and **Inge Sand.** On 21 March 1933, **Nicholas Sergeyev** staged a two act version for Vic-Wells Ballet in the Sadler's Wells Theatre, London. Choreography, **Lev Ivanov, Enrico Cecchetti.** Principal dancers **Lydia Lopokova** and **Ninette de Valois** (Swanilda), Stanley Judson (Frantz), Hedley Briggs (Dr. Coppelius). In 1940 Sergeyev added the third act divertissement and decor was done by William Chappell. Principal dancers, Mary Honer, **Robert Helpmann,** Claude Newman. On 22 October 1942, **Simon Semenov** staged a

Coppélia: Inge Sand and Niels Björn Larsen. Ph. Mogens von Havens.

short version for **Ballet Theatre** in the Metropolitan Opera House, New York. Principal dancers **Irina Baronova, Anton Dolin**, Simon Semenov. The Sadler's Wells production of 4 September 1951 had decor by Loudon Sainthill and principal dancers **Elaine Fifield** and **David Blair**, and was revived, 16 January 1956, with **Svetlana Beriosova** as Swanilda. The **Royal Ballet** version of 1954 had decor by Osbert Lancaster, and **Nadia Nerina** danced the lead. The Royal Danish Ballet choreography was staged by London's **Festival Ballet** on 31 August 1956 with decor by Jean Denis Maillart. Principal dancers, **Belinda Wright** and **John Gilpin**. Another version by **Jack Carter** was staged for the same company in 1968. Principal dancers, Margot Miklosy, Dudley von Loggenburg. In August 1957 Ballet Rambert presented the ballet at Sadler's Wells Theatre, London with decor by Mstislav Doboujinsky. Principal dancers, **Violette Verdy**, Norman Dixon, **Norman Morrice**. The ballet tells the story of Swanilda, whose fiancé, Frantz, is attracted to a beautiful girl who turns out to be a doll created by Dr. Coppelius. The doctor drugs Frantz in order to transfer his soul to the doll to animate it. Swanilda has put herself in the doll's place and so rescues her fiancé. The ballet has always been extremely popular and the introduction of real people in place of the fairy tale persons usual in ballet at the time was an important innovation in Nutter's original libretto.

COQ d'OR, LE, or **The Golden Cockerel**, a ballet in three acts based on Rimsky-Korsakov's opera *The Golden Cockerel* and its source, a narrative poem by Alexander Pushkin. Libretto, V. Bielsky; choreography, **Michel Fokine**; music, Nicholas Rimsky-Korsakov; decor, Nathalie Gontcharova. First performed in the Théâtre National de l'Opéra, Paris, 21 May 1914, by **Diaghilev**'s Ballets Russes. Principal dancers, **Tamara Karsavina**, Alexis Bulgakov, **Enrico Cecchetti**. An operatic cast sang during the performance. Colonel de Basil's **Ballet Russe de Monte Carlo** revived the ballet without the singing in

1937. Principal dancers, **Irina Baronova, Tatiana Riabouchinska. Adolph Bolm** again revived the non-singing version in 1947 with Irina Baronova as the Queen. Fokine's production and Gontcharova's decor stressed the fantasy and symbolism of the fairy story. The king ignores the warning of the golden cockerel and loses his queen, his life and his kingdom.

CORALLI, Jean (Jean Coralli Peracini, 1779–1854), French dancer and choreographer. He was trained at the Paris Opéra school and made his debut in 1802. As choreographer he worked in Italy, Portugal and France (1815–25), staging *L'Union de Flore et Zéphire* (1824) and *La Statue de Venus* (1825). In 1831 he became choreographer at the Opéra, where his productions included *Le Diable Boîteux* (1836), *Giselle* (1841), with **Jules Perrot**, and *La Péri* (1843).

CORNAZANO, Antonio (*fl c* 1440), Italian writer and choreographer. He was greatly influenced by **Domenico da Piacenza** whose work he amplified, adding rules designed to give more ethereal and aesthetic qualities to the ballet, by greater extensions and longer movements. His theories were set out in *Il Libro dell'arte del danzare* (1465).

CORSAIRE, LE, a ballet in three acts based on Byron's narrative poem, *The Corsair*. Choreography, Ferdinand Albert Decombe; music, Robert Boscha. First performed at the King's Theatre, London, 29 January 1837. Principal dancers, Albert, Herminie Elssler, Pauline Duverney. Revived, 30 September 1844, in the Theatre Royal, Drury Lane, London, with Clara Webster. Another version, choreography and libretto, **Joseph Mazilier**; decor, Albert. First performed, 23 January 1856, in the Théâtre Impérial de l'Opéra, Paris. Principal dancer, **Carolina Rosati**. Russian première, Bolshoi Theatre, St. Petersburg, 24 January 1858, with **Lucien Petipa**. The role of Medora, the slave girl heroine, has been successfully danced by, among others, **Anna Pavlova, Tamara**

Karsavina, Olga Preobajenska, Alla Sizova, Margot Fonteyn. The plot of the ballet deals with the misfortunes of Medora and her pirate lover, Conrad.

COTILLON, a plotless ballet in one act. Libretto, **Boris Kochno**; choreography, **George Balanchine**; music, Emmanuel Chabrier; decor, Christian Bérard. First performed in the Théâtre de Monte Carlo, 12 April 1932, by **Colonel de Basil's** Ballet Russe. Principal dancers, Valentina Blinova, Lubov Rostova, **Tamara Toumanova, Léon Woizikowsky,** and later, **Tatiana Riabouchinska** and **Irina Baronova**. The ballet is regarded as one of the most important of Balanchine's early works.

cou-de-pied, literally the neck of the foot, that part of the leg between the calf and the ankle. In the position, sur le cou-de-pied, the heel of the working foot is placed in this position and the toe on the floor.

coupé or pas coupé, literally a cutting step in which the dancer, starting from the fifth position, rises to pointe or demi-pointe and transfers his weight from the right to the left foot. The right foot is raised sur le cou-de-pied. It can also be taken sauté.

couronne, en, literally crown, a fifth position with the arms raised above the head. The curved arms are separated by the width of the face, and frame it. Also called the fifth position en haut.

COURTING AT BURNT RANCH, THE see Rodeo.

CRANKO, John (1927–73), South African dancer and choreographer. He created his first ballet, an interpretation of Stravinsky's Soldier's Tale, at 16. For Sadler's Wells Theatre Ballet, he choreographed Tritsch-Tratsch (1946). For Sadler's Wells Ballet, he staged Bonne-Bouche (1952), The Shadow (1953) and The Prince of the Pagodas (1957). Among his productions for other companies were The

Witch (1950) for **The New York City Ballet,** La Belle Hélène (1955) for the **Paris Opéra Ballet,** Romeo and Juliet (1959) for **Teatro alla Scala,** Milan and (1964) for the National Ballet of Canada. In 1961 he was appointed director of ballet at the Würrtemberg State Opera, Stuttgart, where he staged Romeo and Juliet (1962), Présence (1968) and The Taming of the Shrew (1969). The Stuttgart Ballet made its American debut at the new Metropolitan Opera House, New York, in 1969, under his direction. In 1968 he became chief choreographer of Bayerische Staatsoper in Munich, while continuing to direct at Stuttgart. In 1969 he choreographed a new version of Daphnis and Chloë at Munich and in 1970, Poème de l'Extase at Stuttgart.

CREATION OF THE WORLD, THE, or La Création du Monde, a ballet in one act. Libretto, Blaise Cendrars; choreography, **Jean Börlin**; music, Darius Milhaud; decor, Fernand Léger. First performed in the Théâtre des Champs-Elysées, Paris, 25 October 1923, by Ballets Suédois. A new version was choreographed by **Ninette de Valois** for the **Camargo Society** in 1931 with decor by Edward Wolf. Others have been choreographed for **The New York City Ballet** by **Todd Bolender,** and by Alvin Ailey. Darius Milhaud's music introduced Negro rhythms to ballet. The story tells of three divine beings who cast spells bringing plants, animals and human beings to life.

CREATURES OF PROMETHEUS, THE, or Les Créatures de Prométhée, a ballet in two acts. Choreography, **Salvatore Vigano**; commissioned music, Ludwig van Beethoven. Originally staged in Vienna, 28 March 1801, by Jacques Rouche, and again in Milan, 1813. In 1929 **Serge Lifar** presented a similar version for the **Paris Opéra Ballet.** Principal dancers, Serge Lifar, Susanne Larcia, **Serge Peretti, Olga Spessivtseva.** This was Beethoven's only ballet music, and it inspired Lifar's first success as a choreographer. A new version was presented for the Beethoven bicentenary at Theater der Stadt Bonn, 6 June 1970, by **The Royal Ballet** (touring section). Music arranged by John Lanchbery. Choreography, **Frederick Ashton**; decor and costumes, Ottowerner Meyer. Principal dancers, Hendrik Davel, Kerrison Cooke, **Doreen Wells**. Staged at the Royal Opera House, Covent Garden, 31 October 1970, by the same company. The story tells how Prometheus steals fire from heaven in order to give life to the Mortals. Apollo helps them to create the Arts, and Death reveals grief to them.

croisé, a crossed leg position in which only one leg is fully visible to the audience. The body is placed obliquely to the line of dance. In croisé devant, the leg nearest the audience is crossed in front; in croisé derrière the leg furthest from the audience is crossed at the back.

CROQUEUSE DE DIAMANTS, LA, or **The Diamond Cruncher,** a ballet in four scenes. Libretto, **Roland Petit** and Alfred Adam; choreography, Roland Petit; music, Jean Michel Damase; verses, Raymond Querneau; decor and costumes, Georges Wakhevitch. First performed in the Marigny Theatre, Paris, 25 September 1950, by **Les Ballets de Paris de Roland Petit.** Principal dancers, **Renée Jeanmaire**, Roland Petit, **Gordon Hamilton**. Staged first in New York, 31 October 1950, at the National Theatre. The story tells of how the Delivery Boy discovers the gangster heroine's craving to eat stolen diamonds, and the gang's hideout. The ballet is in the same tradition as *Le Bal des Blanchisseuses*.

Cuba, National Ballet of, a company originally formed in 1948 by **Alicia** and **Fernando Alonso** and directed by Fernando Alonso. It was called Ballet Alicia Alonso, but was renamed in 1955 after receiving a government subsidy. The company first performed in Havana in 1948 and in 1949 it toured Latin America. During the 1950s it made regular tours of Cuba, Mexico, Central and South America, and it toured the USSR and China (1960–1). Principal dancers have included Alicia

Alonso, **Melissa Hayden, Loipa Araujo,** Josephina Mendes, **Igor Youskevitch** and Rudolfo Rodriguez. In addition to the classical ballets, the company performs original works by Alicia Alonso, Alberto Alonso, Enrique Martinez and others.

cuisse, temps de, literally a thigh step. The working foot is snatched up from the fifth position and replaced quickly. The dancer then performs a **sissonne** fermée.

CULLBERG, Birgit (1908–   ), Swedish dancer and choreographer. She returned from studying at the Jooss-Leeder School in England to form her own company in Sweden. *Héracles* was her first choreographic work. She directed the Swedish Dance Theatre (1946–7), was resident choreographer of the Royal Swedish Ballet (1952–7) and in 1960 was appointed director and choreographer of Stockholm City Theatre. Her best known productions include *Miss Julie* (1950), *Medea* (1951), *Romeo and Juliet* (1955) and *The Lady from the Sea* (1960). Her ballets have been taken into the repertoires of many companies, including American Ballet Theatre and **The New York City Ballet.** In 1970 the Cullberg Ballet, founded by her in 1967, took first prize at the Paris International Dance Festival.

CUNNINGHAM, Merce (1919–   ), American dancer and choreographer. Studied at Bennington College School of Dance and was soloist with the Martha Graham Dance Company (1939–45). He created roles in *Appalachian Spring* and *Letter to the World*. He formed his own company in 1953 and opened a dance school in New York (1959). His choreographic works include solos for himself, ballets for his own company, *Springweather and People* (1955), and experimental works using electronic sound, movements determined by chance, without apparent logical order, and improvisation. His recent works include *Place* and *Rainforest*.

CYGNE, LE *see* **Dying Swan, The.**

B   E

D

DALCROZE, Emile Jacques (1865–1950), Swiss educationist, composer and music teacher. He invented a system of musical training for his students called eurhythmics: the translation of sound into physical movement, and taught in his college, founded 1910, in Hellerau, Germany. **Diaghilev,** influenced by this method, invited **Marie Rambert** from the college to instruct his company. Her influence on **Vaslav Nijinsky** was seen in a great number of his interpretations. Today there are Dalcroze schools all over the world. Among the dancers and choreographers to be particularly influenced are **Mary Wigman** and **Kurt Jooss.** Dalcroze published, among other works, *Rhythm, Music and Education* and *Eurhythmics, Art and Education*.

DALE, Margaret (Margaret Bolan, 1922–), British dancer, choreographer and television director. She studied at the Sadler's Wells Ballet School and appeared first with the company as Child in *Le Roi Nu*. Her brilliant performance as Vilia in **Ruth Page**'s *The Merry Widow* was the turning point of her career. She danced the solos Attendant Spirit in *Comus* and Cupid in *The Prospect Before Us*. For Sadler's Wells Theatre Ballet she choreographed *The Great Detective* (1953). She joined the BBC in 1954 as ballet producer. In 1956, when the Bolshoi Ballet visited Britain, she persuaded **Galina Ulanova** to dance Act 2 of *Swan Lake* once again. Her important television productions include **Fonteyn** and **Somes** in *Sleeping Beauty* (1959) Kirov Ballet's *The Stone Flower* (1961) and **The Royal Ballet**'s *The Rake's Progress* (1961). In 1961 she staged *Giselle* for Santiago Ballet.

dance notation, a system of recording the steps and movements of a ballet. Written in its own language, like a form of shorthand, it sets down on paper the precise intention of the choreographer and makes it possible to stage revivals using earlier choreography, as well as assisting in the teaching of students. The principal names in this field are **Vladimir Stepanov, Rudolf Von Laban** and **Rudolf Benesh.** Stepanov published his system in 1892 in Paris. Von Laban's system, known as Kinetographie, is based on the movements of the body and is for the most part pictorial. The 'alphabet' includes signs for the joints and surfaces of the body, and for various movements. Benesh produced a system of dance notation in 1955.

DANCES AT A GATHERING, a plotless ballet in one act. Choreography, **Jerome Robbins**; music, Chopin; lighting, Thomas Skelton. First performed at the New York City Center, 8 May 1969, by **The New York City Ballet.** Principal dancers, **Allegra Kent,** Sara Leland, Kay Mazzo, **Patricia McBride, Violette Verdy, Anthony Blum,** John Clifford, Robert Maiorano, John Prinz, **Edward Villella.** First performed in London at the Royal Opera House, Covent Garden, 19 October 1970, by **The Royal Ballet.** Principal dancers, **Rudolph Nureyev, Anthony Dowell, Antoinette Sibley,** Monica Mason, **David Wall.** Ten dancers portray a group of people in an Arcadian landscape. Their personalities emerge through character dances.

DANIELIAN, Leon (1920–), American dancer, choreographer and teacher. He studied with **Mordkin, Fokine, Dolin, Tudor, Schwezov** and at the School of American Ballet, making his debut with Mordkin Ballet (1937). As soloist with **Ballet Theatre** (1939–41), he danced pas de trois in *Swan Lake*, and in *Lady into*

Fox, *Les Sylphides* and others. With **Colonel de Basil**'s Original Ballet Russe (1942), his repertoire included *Cimarosiana, Coq d'Or, Francesca da Rimini* and Blue Bird pas de deux. As premier danseur, and later guest artist, with **Ballet Russe de Monte Carlo** (1943–61), he danced the leading roles in the classic repertoire. He was guest artist with **Les Ballets des Champs-Elysées** (1951) and then went on tour, partnering **Yvette Chauviré**. He also toured with San Francisco Ballet during the 1950s. Between tours he choreographed *Sombreros* (1956), *Mazurka* (1958) and *España* (1962) for Ballet Russe de Monte Carlo, and later went into teaching.

DANILOVA, Alexandra (1904–), American ballerina, born in Russia. She trained at the Imperial Ballet School, joined the Soviet State Ballet at the Maryinsky Theatre and was soloist (1922–3). Touring Western Europe with **Balanchine**, she was engaged by **Diaghilev** (1924), and was ballerina with his company (1927–9). She danced the leading roles in *Firebird, La Boutique Fantasque, Apollon Musagète* and *Le Bal*, and created Fairy Queen in *The Triumph of Neptune*. She became soloist with Monte Carlo Opera Ballet (1929–30); ballerina with **Colonel de Basil**'s Ballet Russe de Monte Carlo (1933–8), creating roles in *La Gaieté Parisienne, Shadow* and *Le Beau Danube*; and prima ballerina with **Ballet Russe de Monte Carlo** (1938–53). She danced a season with Sadler's Wells Ballet (1949) and was guest artist with London's **Festival Ballet** (1951) and guest ballerina with Slavenska-Franklin Ballet (1952–3). She toured with her own company, Great Moments of Ballet (1954–6). She made her farewell appearance with Ballet Russe de Monte Carlo at The Metropolitan Opera House (1957), but followed it with a second Far East tour. Throughout her career she danced the leading roles in the classic repertoire. She staged *La Giaconda* (1959), *Gypsy Baron* (1960) and *Boris Goudonov* (1961) for the Metropolitan Opera House. She has danced in films, including *The Song of Norway*.

DANILOVA, Maria (1793–1810), Russian dancer. She became a pupil at the Imperial School of Ballet, St. Petersburg in 1801, dancing Cupid in various ballets in the following year. At 15, she danced *The Loves of Venus and Adonis* with the French dancer, Duport, as well as other ballerina roles. She graduated in 1809, but did not live to reach the official status of dancer. Considered a phenomenon in Russian ballet, she died young, but has been immortalized by contemporary Russian poets.

DANOVSKI, Oleg (1917–), Romanian dancer, choreographer and teacher, Honoured Artist. From 1942–4 he was a soloist and choreographer with the Bucharest Opera, and was chief choreographer from 1944–53. His roles included Husband in *Marriage in the Carpathians*. Among his choreographic works are *Schéhérazade, Rhapsody in Blue* (with music by George Gershwin), *The Fountain of Bakhchisarai* and *Symphonie Fantastique*.

danse abstraite, 1) dance without plot or meaning apart from movement. It may include ballet, tap dancing or modern dancing. 2) dance in which costume, colour and geometric design rather than movement are used to achieve the desired effect. This concept originated in 1925 when a German painter, Oskar Schlemmer, composed his Triadic Ballet in which yellow, pink and black seen against geometric shapes emphasized the happy, regal and fantastic moods suggested by the choreography.

DANSES CONCERTANTES, a ballet in six movements. Choreography, **George Balanchine**; music, Igor Stravinsky; decor, Eugène Berman. First performed at the New York City Center, 10 September 1944, by **Ballet Russe de Monte Carlo.** Principal dancers, **Alexandra Danilova, Leon Danielian** (later **Frederick Franklin**). A plotless ballet to this score, with choreography by **Kenneth Mac-Millan**, was staged at Sadler's Wells Theatre, 18 January 1955, by Sadler's Wells Theatre Ballet. Decor, Nicholas Georgiadis. Principal dancers, Maryon Lane, **Donald Britton**, David Poole. First performed at the Royal Opera House, Covent Garden, 13 March 1959, by **The Royal Ballet**. MacMillan also staged this version for the Royal Danish Ballet. It was this ballet which established MacMillan as a choreographer.

DANTE SONATA, a ballet in one act. Choreography, **Frederick Ashton**; music, Franz Liszt; decor, Sophie Fedorovitch. First performed at Sadler's Wells Theatre, London, 23 January 1940, by Sadler's Wells Ballet. Principal dancers, **Margot Fonteyn, Pamela May, Michael Somes, Robert Helpmann**. Inspired by the fall of Poland, it made a profound impression on its original war-time audience.

DANTON, Henry (1919–), British dancer, ballet master and teacher. He studied with **Volkova, Idzikowsky, Preo-brajenska, Gsovsky** and **Vladimirov**, dancing initially with Allied Ballet, London (1943), and **International Ballet** (1943–1944). As leading soloist with Sadler's Wells Ballet he created one of the leading roles in *Symphonic Variations*; with **Metropolitan Ballet** (1947) he was first British dancer to dance *Flower Festival at Genzano* pas de deux. He spent the 1947–8 season with **Les Ballets des Champs-Elysées**, toured Europe with **Lycette Darsonval**, the United States with **Les Ballets de Paris de Roland Petit** (1949–50) and South America with **Mia Slavenska** (1950–1). For Australian National Ballet (1951–2), he staged *The Nutcracker, Don Quixote, Swan Lake, Aurora's Wedding* and *Pas de Quatre*. For the Venezuelan National Ballet (1953–8) he staged a number of works, including *Giselle, Coppélia*, and later staged many of them for Washington (DC) Ballet. Later he became a teacher of dance in New York.

DAPHNIS AND CHLOË, a ballet in three scenes, based on an ancient Greek pastoral tale. Libretto and choreography, **Michel Fokine**; music, Maurice Ravel; decor and costumes, **Léon Bakst**. First performed at the Théâtre du Châtelet, Paris, 8 June 1912, by **Diaghilev**'s Ballets Russes. Principal dancers, **Tamara Karsavina,** (Chloë), **Vaslav Nijinsky** (Daphnis), **Adolph Bolm** (Dorkon). Revived at Theatre Royal, Drury Lane, London, 1914, by Michel Fokine. Principal dancers, Vera Fokina, Michel Fokine. Again revived by Fokine, 20 June 1921, for the **Paris Opéra Ballet**. A version by **Frederick Ashton** was presented at the Royal Opera House, Covent Garden, London, 5 April 1951, for Sadler's Wells Ballet. Decor, John Craxton. Principal dancers, **Margot Fonteyn, Michael Somes, John Field,** Alexander Grant. Versions have also been choreographed by Catherine Littlefield, **George Skibine** and **John Cranko**. The story tells of the innocent love of the shepherdess, Chloë and the goatherd, Daphnis. This was Ravel's most successful ballet score.

DARK ELEGIES, a ballet in two scenes. Libretto and choreography, **Antony Tudor**; music, Gustav Mahler (*Kinder-totenlieder*); decor, Nadia Benois. First performed at the Duchess Theatre, London, 19 February 1937, by Ballet Rambert. Principal dancers, **Agnes de Mille, Maude Lloyd, Peggy van Praagh, Antony Tudor, Hugh Laing**. Staged, 24 January 1940, by **Ballet Theatre**. Principal dancers, **Nina Stroganova,** Miriam Golden, **Lucia Chase, Antony Tudor,** Dimitri Romanov, Hugh Laing. **Nora Kaye** was a later principal dancer. American Ballet Theatre revived the work in 1965. The choreography reflects the anguish of parents after disaster has struck their village. This is the theme of the music (*Songs of the Death of Children*), from a cycle of five songs by the German poet, Friedrich Rückert.

DARRELL, Peter (1932–), British dancer, choreographer and director. He studied at the Sadler's Wells Ballet School and was an original member of the Sadler's Wells Theatre Ballet. He later joined London's **Festival Ballet**. His career is linked chiefly with Western Theatre Ballet, of which he was co-founder (1957) with Elisabeth West and chief choreographer. After the death of Elisabeth West (1962), he became sole artistic director. His ballets for this company included *The Prisoners*, *A Wedding Present*, *Mods and Rockers*, *Home* and *Sun into Darkness*. In 1970, when the company became **Scottish Theatre Ballet**, he continued as artistic director and choreographer. He staged *Giselle* (1971), and created two full-length works, *Beauty and the Beast* (1969) and *Tales of Hoffmann* (1972).

DARSONVAL, Lycette (1912–), French ballerina. She studied with **Zambelli** and **Aveline** at the Paris Opéra school. Toured North America with **Serge Lifar**, and joined **Paris Opéra Ballet** in 1935. *Giselle* was her first major role. As première danseuse étoile she created roles in *La Princesse au Jardin* (1941), *Joan von Zarissa* (1942), *Suite en Blanc* (1943), *Phèdre* (1950), *Salomé* (1955) and *Variations* (1957). She is also well-known for her interpretation of Sylvia, and as Giselle which she danced with Lifar for many years. She toured the United States and Europe with her own group. Director of the Paris Opéra Ballet school (1957–60), she founded her own teaching studio in Paris. She is a Chevalier of the Légion d'Honneur.

DAUBERVAL or **D'AUBERVAL, Jean** (Jean Bercher, 1742–1806), French dancer and choreographer. Taught by **Jean-Georges Noverre**, he made his debut at the Paris Opera (1761), became premier danseur (1770) and ballet master (1781). A contemporary of **Vestris, Allard** and **Gardel,** he danced with them extensively throughout Europe. His best known work is *La Fille Mal Gardée*, which has been in the repertoire since 1786, although his choreography for the ballet has not survived.

DAVID TRIOMPHANT, a ballet in two acts. Choreography, **Serge Lifar** ; music, Claude Debussy and Moussorgsky ; decor and costumes, Fernand Léger. First performed, 15 December 1936, at the Inauguration Gala of the Théâtre de la Cité Universitaire, Paris. Principal dancers, **Mia Slavenska,** Serge Lifar. A new version was presented by the **Paris Opéra Ballet,** at le Théâtre National de l'Opéra, 21 June 1937. Music, Rieti ; decor, Léger. Principal dancers, **Yvette Chauviré, Lycette Darsonval.** The ballet is based on episodes in the life of David of Israel from the Book of Kings.

DAYDÉ, Liane (1934–), French ballerina. She studied at the Paris Opéra school with **Aveline, Staats, Zambelli, Lifar** and **Volinine,** entering the **Paris Opéra Ballet** when 13 and becoming première danseuse étoile at 19, when she created the title role in *Blanche Neige*. In 1955 she danced Juliet in Lifar's *Romeo and Juliet*. In 1959 she left the Opéra and has toured extensively, partnered by

Jean Dauberval. Ph. M. Erlanger.

Liane Daydé. Ph. Reyna.

Michel Renault. She has been guest ballerina at Colón, Buenos Aires and La Scala, Milan; with London's **Festival Ballet** and Ballet International du Marquis de Cuevas (1961–2), where she was partnered by **Nureyev** in *The Sleeping Beauty* and also by **Serge Golovine,** with whom she appeared at Jacob's Pillow Dance Festival in 1962. As prima ballerina she toured the United States (1965) with Grand Ballet Classique de France.

DEATH AND THE MAIDEN, a ballet in one act. Choreography, **Andrée Howard**; music, Franz Schubert (variations on the song, *Der Tod und das Mädchen*). First performed at the Duchess Theatre, London, 23 February 1937, by Ballet Rambert. Principal dancer, Andrée Howard (Maiden). Andrée Howard staged the ballet in New York City Center, 1940, for **Ballet Theatre.** Principal dancers, Andrée Howard, Annabelle Lyon. A ballet using the same music was staged, 30 January 1964, by Wuppertal State Opera Ballet. Choreography, Eric Walter. A young girl encounters Death, who is surprisingly courteous.

DE BASIL, Colonel W. (Vassili Grigorievitch Voskresensky, 1888–1951), Russian ballet administrator. He began his career as assistant to Prince Zeretelli with a touring Russian opera company, and later became co-director of Ballet Russe de Monte Carlo with **René Blum** (1932). De Basil assumed complete charge of the company on Blum's retirement in 1934 (Blum left the company completely in 1936), and the name was changed to Colonel de Basil's **Ballet Russe de Monte Carlo.** In 1938 many of his dancers and choreographers left to join a new company formed by Blum and **Massine,** the Ballet Russe de Monte Carlo. Until its dissolution in 1948, de Basil continued to control his own company under the name of Original Ballet Russe.

déboulé, a series of quick, rolling half turns from one foot to the other, the feet close together, on **pointe** or demi-pointe, executed in a straight line (chaîne) or circle (en manège). The head and arms must be perfectly co-ordinated.

decor, the term for the setting of a ballet, which includes all the furniture and properties as well as the scenery, and is normally planned as a whole together with the costumes, as with any stage play. It may be a simple matter of practice costumes for the dancers, a bare stage and neutrally coloured curtains, or it may present a stylized version of a scene translated into stage terms using fixed, sometimes sloping, platforms, arches and doorways, or abstract constructions against which the costumed dancers make patterns with their movements.

Scenery for the stage originated in the Renaissance period in the palaces of Italy and France, where ballet was being developed as a spectacle for kings and courtiers. The discovery of perspective by painters made possible the illusion of space and distance behind the dancers by using painted backcloths. Meanwhile, the interest in classical architecture, as exemplified in the work of Vitruvius, resulted in the introduction of columns and arches into the design both of stages and settings. The settings designed in the 16th century by Buontalenti and Jacopo Torelli were elaborately realistic; they represented architectural façades of palaces, grottoes and other examples of classical architecture. Lighting effects, including fire, sun and moonlight, were achieved by shining lamps through coloured water in large glass containers. A feature of these settings was the use of 'transformations', in which elaborate machinery moved pieces of scenery making the change of setting a part of the performance.

The basic stage layout, with its painted scenery, including movable canvass wings, painted backcloths and solid wooden structures, became established with increasing elaboration during the Baroque period. Staging in the Romantic era which followed echoed the theatrical tendency away from architectural settings towards landscape, and developed the use of cutouts for tree borders and also transparent scenery made of gauze. This encouraged the pictorial concept of staging, which was further enhanced by the lighting of the stage area first with gas and then with electricity. It was at this point that lighting in the auditorium while a performance was in progress was finally dispensed with.

Modern scenic design for ballet began, as did so many other aspects of modern ballet, with **Diaghilev.** His genius for discovering inspired designers and co-ordinating their work with his choreographers and dancers began as early as the first season of the Ballets Russes in Paris in 1909 and 1910, when he presented *Schéhérazade, The Firebird* and *Giselle* with decors by **Bakst** and **Benois.** In the 20 years following, his productions featured designs by such artists as Larionov, Nathalie Gontcharova, Picasso, Matisse, Marie Laurencin, de Chirico, Braque and Rouault.

Since the war, specialized stage designers have tended to replace the leading artists whose work was a feature of the Diaghilev tradition, but the tendency to experiment has continued.

Marquis de Cuevas. Ph. Lipnitzki.

DE CUEVAS, George (Marquis de Piedrablanca de Guana de Cuevas, 1886–1961), American ballet impresario, born in Chile. He founded Ballet Institute (1943) and created **Ballet International,** which gave its first season under his directorship in New York in 1944. This was an artistic success and a financial disaster. De Cuevas then assumed control of the **Nouveau Ballet de Monte Carlo** in 1947, changing its name to Grand Ballet de Monte Carlo. This company attracted dancers, choreographers and designers from Europe and the United States, among whom were **Rosella Hightower, Marjorie Tallchief, William Dollar,** Ana Ricarda (Americans); Jacqueline Moreau, Denise Bourgeois, **George Skibine, Serge Golovine, Vladimir Skouratov** (French); **Margrethe Schanne** (Danish); **Svetlana Beriosova** (British). **Bronislava Nijinska** was engaged as ballet mistress, the ballet masters being **Nicholas Beriosov, William Dollar** and **John Taras.** From 1947 to 1960 the company toured the world, in 1950 joining with Ballet International to become the **Grand Ballet du Marquis de Cuevas,** and finally Ballet International du Marquis de Cuevas. The annual Paris seasons featured some of the great stars of the period: **Markova, Toumanova, Massine, Lichine** and **Bruhn**, among others. De Cuevas was instrumental in cultivating public taste for the classic repertoire, which was his great love.

dedans, en, literally inward; in a **pirouette** or a fouetté the rotating leg, arms and body turn inward towards the supporting leg.

DEEGE, Gisela (1928–), German ballerina. She studied with Gsovska, making her debut at the age of fifteen in the title role of *Romeo and Juliet* at Leipzig State Opera. As première danseuse (1947–1950) at Berlin State Opera, her principal roles included Isabeau in *Joan von Zarissa* and the lead in *Goyescas*. She toured Germany and danced with Gsovska's Berliner Ballett (1955). She became prima ballerina of Berlin Municipal Opera in 1952 and her repertoire included *The Moor of Venice, Medusa* and *Black Sun*, as well as the classic roles.

défilé du corps de ballet, a majestic, choreographic entrance of the whole corps de ballet, from pupils to stars. The backcloth is raised and the depth of the stage is further extended by the use of large mirrors. The stage is in darkness as the parade begins, and lights up gradually as the corps de ballet enter in groups, pairs and, finally, singly. Défilés are staged only on very special occasions. The Royal Ballet staged one at the Royal Opera House, Covent Garden, in 1964, in honour of Dame Ninette de Valois.

dégagé, literally disengaged, 1) a step which frees the working foot in preparation for the next step, may be executed à terre or en l'air; 2) transference of weight.

dehors, en, literally outward; in a **pirouette** or a fouetté the rotating leg, arms and body turn outward away from the supporting leg.

DE MILLE, Agnes (Mrs. Walter Prude, 1909–), American dancer and choreographer, niece of film producer, Cecil B. De Mille. Among her many teachers were **Rambert, Sokolova, Tudor** and **Stroganova.** She danced with Ballet Rambert and London Ballet, where she created Venus in *Judgment of Paris* (1938) and choreographed *Three Virgins and a Devil* (1941). As guest artist and choreographer with **Ballet Russe de Monte Carlo,** she created *Rodeo* (1942). For **Ballet Theatre** her choreographic works include her most famous work, *Fall River Legend* (1948), *Rib of Eve* (1956), *The Wind in the Mountains* and *The Four Marys* (1965). For Royal Winnipeg Ballet she staged and danced in *The Rehearsal* and created *The Bitter Weird.* She choreographed the musicals *Oklahoma* (1943), *Carousel* (1945), *Paint Your Wagon* (1951), *Brigadoon* (1947), and many others. Her publications include *Dance to the Piper* (1952), *To a Young Dancer* (1962) and *The Book of the Dance* (1963). She was the first president of the Society of Stage Directors and Choreographers, Inc. (1965) and a member of the jury at the First Moscow International Dance Competition (1969).

DEMOISELLES DE LA NUIT, LES, a ballet in one act. Libretto, Jean Anouilh; choreography, **Roland Petit**; music, Jean Françaix; decor, Léonor Fini. First performed at the Marigny Theatre, Paris, 22 May 1948, by **Les Ballets de Paris de Roland Petit.** Principal dancers, **Margot Fonteyn** (Agathe, the White Cat), Roland Petit (Young Man), **Gordon Hamilton** (Cat Baron de Grotius). Presented at the Metropolitan Opera House, New York, 13 April 1951, by **Ballet Theatre.** Principal dancers, **Colette Marchand, John Kriza,** Eric Braun. The Young Man desperately loves Agathe, who is under a spell. She becomes human but retains her feline nature and follows her cat friends over the roofs. She and the young man fall to their deaths.

DENBY, Edwin (1903–), American writer and critic, born in China. He studied

Les Demoiselles de la Nuit. Ph. Intercontinental.

ballet and worked as a dancer and choreographer until 1935. He was dance critic of the New York *Herald Tribune* (1942–5). His published works include *Looking at the Dance* (1949).

DENMARK, history of ballet in.
1771 Laurent founds a school of ballet at the Royal Theatre.
1775 Vincenéo Galeotti (Florentine) comes to Copenhagen, becoming ballet master of the Royal Theatre.
1792 Antoine Bournonville, French dancer, joins the Royal Theatre in Copenhagen, becoming its leader (1816–23).
1829 August Bournonville (born Copenhagen) becomes leading dancer and choreographer of the Danish ballet, which now emerges as one of the outstanding ballet companies. Among his dancers are **Lucile Grahn** and Juliette Price. The repertoire includes *Napoli* (1841), *Danseskolan af Konservatoriet* (1849), *Et Folkesagn* (1854) and *La Ventana* (1856).
1877 Bournonville leaves the ballet.
1894–1915 Hans Beck is ballet master of the Royal Theatre.

1932–1951 Harald Lander is ballet master of the Royal Danish Ballet. Dancers include **Margot Lander, Børge Ralov, Margrethe Schanne,** and **Toni Lander.** The repertoire includes *Études* (1948) and *Qarrtsiluni* (1942).
1949 The Royal Danish Ballet Festival is established.
1951–6, 1960–6 Niels Bjørn Larsen is director of the Royal Danish Ballet.
1966 Flemming Flindt is appointed director of the Royal Danish Ballet. He stages new productions of *Kermesse at Bruges* (1966) and *La Sylphide* (1967), and a new version of *The Miraculous Mandarin* (1967). The repertoire also includes *The Lesson* and *Le Jeune Homme à Marier.* Among the principal soloists are **Fredbjørn Bjørnsson, Kirsten Simone, Anna Laerkesen, Inge Sand, Niels Kehlet, Henning Kronstam** and **Frank Schaufuss.**
1971 The Royal Danish Ballet has a successful season at the Edinburgh International Festival. Productions include Bournonville's *Conservatoire* and *The Lifeguards of Amager*

DESCOMBEY, Michel (1930–), French premier danseur, choreographer and ballet master. He studied with **Egorova** and at the Paris Opéra school, entering the **Paris Opéra Ballet** in 1947 and becoming premier danseur in 1959. He danced mainly the character roles, including Jester in *Blanche Neige* and Eros in *Pas de Dieux.* As choreographer he has created *Les Frères Humains* (1951) for small private groups; *Fièvres, Les Baladins* and *Clairère* for Opéra Comique; and *Symphonie Concertante* for the Paris Opéra, where he became ballet master in 1962.

DESIGNS WITH STRINGS, a plotless ballet in one act. Choreography, **John Taras**; music, Tchaikovsky (*Piano Trio in A minor*); decor, George Kirsta. First performed in Edinburgh, 6 February 1948, by Metropolitan Ballet. Principal dancers, **Svetlana Beriosova, Sonia Arova, Celia Franca,** Delysia Blake, **Erik Bruhn, David Adams.** Presented in New York

City Center, 25 April 1950, by **Ballet Theatre.** Costumes, Irene Sharaff. Principal dancers, **Diana Adams, Norma Vance,** Lillian Lanese, Dorothy Scott, Erik Bruhn, Michael Lland. The choreography interprets the joy, youthfulness and wistfulness of the music. The ballet has been taken into the repertoires of many companies, including **Grand Ballet du Marquis de Cuevas** and the Royal Danish Ballet.

détourné, literally turned aside, the term for a change of direction. With the feet close together, the dancer rotates on the balls of both feet in the direction of the back foot, either making a half turn or a full turn.

DEUIL EN VINGT-QUATRE HEURES, a ballet in five scenes. Choreography, **Roland Petit**; music, Maurice Thiriet; decor and costumes, Antoni Clavé. First performed in the Théâtre de l'Empire, Paris, 17 March 1953, by **Les Ballets de Paris de Roland Petit.** Principal dancers, **Colette Marchand,** Serge Perrault, George Reich. Presented at the Broadway Theatre, New York, 19 January 1954, under the title *The Beautiful Widow.* This piquant burlesque of Paris around 1900 tells of a beautiful woman who longs for a black mourning dress and shows little concern when her husband is killed in a duel with her latest admirer. His death enables her to wear the black dress and make merry at Maxim's.

DEUX PIGEONS, LES *see* **Two Pigeons, The.**

DEUX POLICHINELLES, LES *see* **Pulcinella.**

DE VALOIS, Ninette (Edris Stannus, 1898–   ), British dancer, teacher, choreographer and director. Among her many teachers were **Edouard Espinosa** and **Enrico Cecchetti.** She was a principal dancer in a pantomime in London (1914–19) and première danseuse with the Royal Opera, Covent Garden (1919).

Dame Ninette de Valois. Ph. Royal Ballet.

In 1923 she joined **Diaghilev**'s Ballets Russes where her repertoire included solo roles in *Daphnis and Chloë, Petrouchka, La Boutique Fantasque, Les Biches* and *Les Noces.* She founded the Academy of Choreographic Art in London in 1926, and her pupils danced at the Old Vic in some of the Shakespearian productions. At the same time she choreographed works for the Abbey Theatre, Dublin, and Festival Theatre, Cambridge. Her first major success, *Les Petits Riens,* was staged at the Old Vic in 1928 for the Christmas programme. This was followed by *Danse Sacrée et Dance Profane.* In 1931 the Academy was closed and a new school founded at the rebuilt Sadler's Wells Theatre. This provided a small company which alternated between the Old Vic and the Sadler's Wells theatres and became known as Vic-Wells Ballet, subsequently Sadler's Wells Ballet, now known as **The Royal Ballet**. Her work with this company, in conjunction with that of **Marie Rambert**, effectively laid the foundations of a British national ballet. **Markova, Ashton** and **Fonteyn** were among the great dancers who joined the company during the early 1930s; also **Helpmann** and **Moira Shearer**. De Valois' choreographic works include *Job* and *La Création du Monde* for the **Camargo Society** (1931); *Bar aux Folies-Bergère* for Ballet Rambert (1934); and for Vic-Wells, *Douanes, The Haunted Ballroom, The Rake's Progress*, the dramatic *Checkmate, Orpheus and Eurydice, The Prospect Before Us, Promenade* and *Don Quixote*. She danced with the company until 1937, appearing in *Coppélia* and *Douanes*, and creating the roles Webster in *A Wedding Bouquet* and Pas de Trois in *Les Rendez-vous*. For the twenty-first anniversary of the company in 1950 she appeared off point for a single performance. She was created Dame of the British Empire in 1951 and is Chevalier of the Légion d'Honneur. Her publications include *Invitation to the Ballet* (1937) and *Come Dance With Me* (1957). She retired from her position as director of The Royal Ballet in 1963, and was appointed a Life Governor of The Royal Ballet School.

développé or **temps développé**, literally an unfolding of the leg; the thigh of the working leg is turned out and raised till it is at right angles to the body, with the toe in line with the knee cap of the supporting leg (retiré). The leg is then extended fully to the front, back or side.

DIABLE BOITEUX, LE, a ballet in three acts. Libretto, Burat de Gurgy and **Jean Coralli**; choreography, Coralli; music, Casimir Gide; decor, Feuchères, Séchan, Diéterle, Philastre, Cambon. First performed at **l'Académie Royale de Musique**, Paris, 1 June 1836. Principal dancers, Barrez (The Devil), Joseph Mazilier (Cléophas), **Fanny Elssler** (Florinda). Performed at the King's Theatre, London, 1836, under the title *The Devil on Two Sticks*. Principal dancer, Pauline Duverney (Florinda). Presented, 23 October 1839, at St. Petersburg. The Devil promotes the amorous exploits of the student, Cléophas, in repayment for his freedom. A Spanish dance, the Cachucha, made notable by Fanny Elssler, has been incorporated in many subsequent ballets.

DIAGHILEV, Serge (1872–1929), Russian ballet impresario. While a law student in St. Petersburg he associated chiefly with young artists and musicians in the city. The group included **Alexandre Benois** and **Léon Bakst**, and produced an illustrated review called *Mir Iskusstva* (World of Art) (1899). Later in the same year Diaghilev was appointed 'Official for Special Missions' at the Imperial Theatres, and was given the task of editing the 1899–1900 edition of the *Annual of the Imperial Theatres*. He also supervised productions of the opera *Sadko* and the ballet *Sylvia* at the Maryinsky Theatre. However, quarrels led to his resignation from the post in 1901. In 1906 he presented an exhibition of creative paintings in Paris, and in 1907 he organized a series of concerts of Russian music at the Paris Opéra, returning there the following year with the Russian singer Chaliapine in *Boris Godunov*. Diaghilev then made a contract with the Théâtre Châtelet for a 1909 summer season of Russian ballet in Paris. Working in conjunction with the young choreographer **Fokine**, he assembled a group of dancers including **Pavlova, Karsavina, Rubinstein, Nijinsky, Bolm** and **Mordkin**. The repertoire selected was *Les Sylphides, Cléopâtre, Le Pavillon d'Armide, Prince Igor, Le Festin* and the opera *Ivan the Terrible*. It was a great success. During the next twenty years Diaghilev drew upon the creative genius of nearly all the outstanding artists of the period, and this close collaboration of musicians, dancers, painters and choreographers brought just fame to the Russian ballet. In 1911 Diaghilev established a permanent com-

Diaghilev: drawing by Picasso. Ph. Lipnitzki.

pany, Les Ballets Russes, independent of the Imperial Theatre, which gave its first season in Rome. The original repertoire was expanded to include *Schéhérazade, The Firebird, Giselle* (1910); *Le Spectre de la Rose, Le Dieu Bleu, Narcisse, Swan Lake, Aurora and the Prince* (1911); *L'Après-midi d'un Faune, Daphnis and Chloë, Thamar* (1912); *Le Sacre du Printemps, Jeux, The Tragedy of Salome* (1913); *Le Coq d'Or, The Legend of Joseph, Papillons, Midas* (1914); *The Midnight Sun* (1915); *Til Eulenspiegel* (1916); *The Good-humoured Ladies, Contes Russes, Parade* (1917); *La Boutique Fantasque, The Three-Cornered Hat* (1919); *Le Chant du Rossignol* and the opera-ballets *Pulcinella, Le Astuzzie Femminili* (1920); *The Sleeping Beauty* (1921); *Aurora's Wedding, Le Renard* (1922); *Les Noces* (1923); *Les Biches, Les Fâcheux, Les Tentations de la*

Bergère, Le Train Bleu (1924); *Les Matelots, Zephyr and Flora, Barabaü, La Pastorale* (1925); *Jack-in-the-Box, The Triumph of Neptune* (1926); *La Chatte, Le Pas d'Acier* (1927); *Ode, Apollon Musagète, Les Dieux Mendiants* (1928); *Le Fils Prodigue* and *Le Bal* (1929). Having dismissed Nijinsky in 1913, Diaghilev was fortunate to find a gifted replacement as dancer and choreographer in **Léonide Massine.** Other dancers who joined the company later included: **Bronsilava Nijinska, Mathilda Kchessinska** (1911); **Nemtchinova, Idzikovsky, Woizikowsky, Sokolova** (1915); **Spessivtzeva** (1916); **Egorova, Lopokova,** Vladimirov (1921); **Boris Kochno** (1922); **de Valois, Dolin, Lifar** (1924); **Danilova, Markova, Balanchine** (1925). Composers who worked for the Diaghilev company included Stravinsky, Ravel, Tcherepnin, Glazunov, Prokofiev, Debussy, Auric, Satie, Milhaud and Nabokov, while the painters who provided designs for scenery and costumes included **Bakst, Benois,** Derain, Picasso, Gontcharova, Larionov, Rouault, de Chirico, Matisse and Cocteau. Diaghilev's company toured the major cities of Europe, the United States and South America, giving its last performance at Covent Garden, London, in 1929. Diaghilev's achievements were many; most significantly, he introduced Russian ballet to the Western world, and developed within his company an artistically effective combination of the elements of music, dance and painting arising out of the collaboration of the talents of the finest dancers, choreographers, painters and composers of his generation.

DIDELOT, Charles Louis (c 1765–1836), French dancer, choreographer and teacher. Initially taught by his father who was choreographer and premier danseur of the Swedish Royal Theatre, he later studied at the Paris Opéra school and with **Auguste Vestris.** He made his debut in Paris when only twelve and danced at the Paris Opéra with **Madeleine Guimard.** His first ballet, *La Méta-*

morphose, was presented at Lyons, and in 1796 his *Flore et Zéphyr* was presented in London. Ballet master and choreographer at the Imperial Ballet, St. Petersburg from 1801 to 1811, his ballets include *Apollon et Daphnis*, *Les Noces d'Or* and *Cupidon et Psyche*. In 1812 he presented *Flore et Zéphyr* in Paris. He returned to St. Petersburg in 1816. Among his other ballets were *Don Quixote*, *Paul and Virginia*, *Athis et Galathée* and *Le Prisonnier du Caucase* (1823). As head of the Imperial School he reorganized the methods of teaching ballet, and is credited with having introduced flesh-coloured tights for women.

DIEU ET LA BAYADÈRE, LE, an opera-ballet in two acts. Libretto, Augustin Eugène Scribe; choreography, **Filippo Taglioni**; music, Daniel Aubert. First performed at **L'Académie Royale de Musique**, Paris, 13 October 1830, by the **Paris Opéra Ballet**. Principal dancer, **Marie Taglioni** (Zoloe). The story, based on a Goethe ballad, tells how the Hindu dancer, Zoloe, refuses to marry a prince and is condemned to the funeral pyre. She is saved by the god, Brahma, and lives happily thereafter in the paradise of the gods.

DIEUX MENDIANTS, LES *see* **Gods Go a'Begging, The.**

DIM LUSTRE, a ballet in one act. Libretto and choreography, **Antony Tudor**; music, Richard Strauss (*Burleske for Piano and Orchestra*). First performed at the Opera House, New York, 20 October 1943, by **Ballet Theatre**. Principal dancers, **Nora Kaye, Hugh Laing, Rosella Hightower, Janet Reed, John Kriza, Antony Tudor**. Revived, 26 April 1956, at the same theatre. Principal dancers, Nora Kaye, Hugh Laing, Ruth Ann Koesun, **Sonia Arova**, Ivan Allen, Darrell Notara. Presented at the New York State Theater, 6 May 1964, by **New York City Ballet**. Principal dancers, **Patricia McBride, Edward Villella, Patricia Neary**. At a ball two people are prevented from falling in love by memories evoked by trivial incidents.

DIRTL, Willy (1931–), Austrian dancer. A pupil and dancer at Vienna State Opera Ballet, he made his debut as a child soloist in 1941 and became premier danseur in 1951. Among his roles are Albrecht in *Giselle*, Othello in *The Moor of Venice*, Joan in *Joan von Zarissa*, Prince in *Swan Lake* and Mandarin in *The Miraculous Mandarin*.

DIVERTIMENTO No. 15 or **Caracole,** an abstract ballet in one act. Choreography, **George Balanchine**; music, Mozart (*Divertimento in B flat major*); decor and costumes, Christian Bérard. First performed under the title *Caracole*, in New York City Center, 19 February 1952, by **The New York City Ballet**. Principal dancers, **Patricia Wilde, Maria Tallchief, Melissa Hayden, Diana Adams, Tanaquil LeClercq, André Eglevsky, Nicholas Magallanes, Jerome Robbins**. Revised and performed under the title *Divertimento No. 15*, 31 May 1956, at Stratford, Connecticut, and 19 December 1956, in New York City Center. Costumes, Barbara Karinska. Principal dancers, Melissa Hayden, Patricia Wilde, Yvonne Mounsey, **Diana Adams**, Barbara Milberg, **Allegra Kent**, Jonathan Watts, Nicholas Magallanes, Roy Tobias. The work is based on the 'caracole' step of the riding school. Moving in this pattern, groups of dancers correspond to sections of the orchestra in a counterpoint of steps and music.

DOLIN, Anton (Patrick Healey-Kay, 1904–), British premier danseur, choreographer and director. He studied with **Astafieva** and **Nijinska**, and made his debut in *Daphnis and Chloë* in 1923, creating the memorable role in *Le Train Bleu* the same year. He was soloist with **Diaghilev's** Ballets Russes (1924–5 and 1928–9). For his own group (1927–8), founded with **Vera Nemtchinova**, he choreographed *Rhapsody in Blue* and *Revolutionary Étude*. He helped to found **The Camargo Society** in 1930 and

Anton Dolin in Giselle. Ph. Roy Round.

with Dolin as artistic director and principal dancer until 1961. In 1962 he was director and choreographer of Rome Opera Ballet. He subsequently toured the world staging *Pas de Quatre* and *The Nutcracker*. His many publications include *Divertissement* (1930), *Ballet Go Round* (1938), *Pas de Deux: the Art of Partnering* (1949), *Alicia Markova* (1953) and *Autobiography* (1960).

DOLLAR, William (1907–), American dancer, choreographer and teacher. He studied with **Fokine, Mordkin** and **Balanchine,** among others, and from 1936 to 1944 was leading dancer with **The American Ballet,** Ballet Caravan, **Ballet Theatre** and **Ballet International.** He worked extensively as ballet master and choreographer with American Concert Ballet (1943), Ballet Society (1946), Grand Ballet de Monte Carlo (1948), Ballet International, American Ballet Theatre, **Les Ballets de Paris de Roland Petit,** Detroit City Ballet, Le Théâtre d'art du Ballet and Teatro Municipal, Rio de Janeiro. Among his works are *Constantia, Mendelssohn Concerto, Le Combat, Simple Symphony* and *Marguerite Gautier,* some of which are in the repertoire of Original Ballet Russe, American Ballet Theatre and **The New York City Ballet.** He taught extensively in South America and became a member of the staff of Ballet Theatre School.

between 1931 and 1935 he danced with it and with Vic-Wells Ballet as principal dancer or guest artist, partnering **Markova** in her first *Giselle,* and creating the role of Satan in *Job.* From 1935 to 1938 he was director and principal dancer of the Markova-Dolin Ballet. As premier danseur with **Ballet Theatre** (1939–46) he restaged *Swan Lake, Giselle,* and choreographed *Quintet, Pas de Quatre, Capriccio* and *Romantic Age.* In 1945 he re-organized Markova-Dolin Ballet, touring the United States, Mexico and South America until 1948. He has been guest artist with Original Ballet Russe (1939, 1946–7); Sadler's Wells Ballet (1948); and **Ballet Russe de Monte Carlo** (1948). The group he founded with Markova in 1949 became London's **Festival Ballet** (1950),

DOMENICO DA PIACENZA (da Ferrara, died 1462), Italian ballet master to Leonello d'Este at Ferrara where he introduced many innovations to court dancing and created new forms including the *Ballo.* His choreographic theories were based on five fundamental elements of the dance and contained precise notation for music and equally defined movements. These defined steps could be used as the basis for any dance sequence. His pupils included **Antonio Cornazzano** and **Guglielmo Ebreo.**

DONALD OF THE BURTHENS, a ballet in one act. Choreography, **Léonide**

Massine; music, Ian Whyte; decor, Robert McBride, Robert Colquhoun. First performed at the Royal Opera House, Covent Garden, London, 12 December 1951, by Sadler's Wells Ballet. Principal dancers, **Beryl Grey** (Death), **Alexander Grant** (Donald), **Leslie Edwards** (King). After promising Death never to pray, Donald the woodcutter becomes a famous doctor. He cheats Death by saving the King's life, but ironically he dies praying.

DON JUAN, a ballet in three scenes, based on the play by Molière. Choreography, **Gasparo Angiolini**; music, Gluck. First performed, 1761, in the Court Theatre, Vienna. A new version was staged at the Alhambra Theatre, London, 25 June 1936, by **René Blum**'s Ballet Russe. Libretto, Eric Allatini, **Michel Fokine**; choreography, Fokine; decor, Mariano Andreu. Principal dancers, **Anatole Vilzak** (Don Juan), Jeanette Lauret (Elvira), **André Eglevsky** (Jester). This version was also staged, 22 October 1938, in New York. Principal dancer, **Michel Panaiev** (Don Juan). In his choreography, Fokine aimed to reproduce Angiolini's idea of a dramatic pantomime. However, he placed greater emphasis on the dancing.

DON JUAN, a ballet in one act, based on Gautier's poem *La Morte Amoureuse*. Choreography, **Frederick Ashton**; music, Richard Strauss; decor, Edward Burra. First performed at the Royal Opera House, Covent Garden, London, 25 November 1948, by Sadler's Wells Ballet. Principal dancers, **Margot Fonteyn** (La Morte Amoureuse), **Moira Shearer** (Young Wife), **Robert Helpmann** (Don Juan). The work depicts Don Juan as being in love with death.

DON QUIXOTE, early ballets based on the novel by Cervantes included: *Don Quichotte chez la Duchesse*, a ballet comique by Favart. Music, Boismortier. First performed, 1743, at **L'Académie Royale de Musique,** Paris. Principal dancer, **Marie Allard.** *Don Quixote* by **Jean-Georges Noverre,** presented,

1750, in Vienna. *Les Noces de Gamache*, a ballet by Louis Milon, presented, 18 January 1801, at the Paris Opéra. *Don Quixote*, a ballet by **Paul Taglioni,** presented, 1850, in Berlin.

DON QUIXOTE, a ballet in prologue and four acts, based on the novel by Cervantes. Libretto and choreography, **Marius Petipa**; music, Leon Minkus. First performed, 26 December 1869, at the Bolshoi Theatre, Moscow. Principal dancers, Sobechanskaya, Espinosa, Gilbert. Petipa presented a five act version, 1871, in St. Petersburg. **Alexander Gorsky** presented yet another version, 1900, at the Bolshoi. A virtuoso pas de deux was introduced into the last act. Gorsky used

Don Quixote: Alla Shélest. Ph. Photo Off. Cult. Sov.

this version as the basis for his own choreography, with the same music. Decor, Vadim Ryndin. First performed, 10 February 1940, at the Bolshoi. This version is still in the Soviet repertoire. A gypsy dance was introduced into the second act. Ballet Rambert took this version into their repertoire and gave the first performance, 26 July 1962, at Sadler's Wells Theatre, London. Principal dancers, **Lucette Aldous** (Kitri), **Kenneth Bannerman** (Basilio), John Chesney (Don Quixote). A shorter version, choreographed by Laurent Navikov, was taken into the repertoire of **Anna Pavlova**. A new version based on Petipa's original with choreography by **Rudolph Nureyev** was presented by Australian Ballet in 1970. Principal dancers, Lucette Aldous, Ray Powell, **Robert Helpmann** and Rudolph Nureyev. Nureyev also staged this version for Le Nouveau Ballet de l'Opéra, Marseilles. A new version of Gorsky's 1900 production was staged at the London Coliseum in July 1970, by London's **Festival Ballet.** Choreography, Witold Borkowski; decor, Emanuele Luzzati. Principal dancers, Piers Beaumont, John Travis, **Galina Samtsova, André Prokovsky.**

DON QUIXOTE, a ballet in four scenes. Choreography, **Ninette de Valois**; music, Roberto Gerhard; decor, Edward Burra. First performed at the Royal Opera House, Covent Garden, London, 20 February 1950, by Sadler's Wells Ballet. Principal dancers, **Robert Helpmann** (Don Quixote), **Margot Fonteyn** (Dulcinea), **Alexander Grant** (Sancho Panza). Episodes from the Cervantes novel include the tilting at the windmill, of madness and death.

DON QUIXOTE, a ballet in three acts. Choreography, **George Balanchine**; music, Nicolas Nabokov; decor, Esteban Francés. First performed at the State Theater, New York, 28 May 1965, by **The New York City Ballet.** Principal dancers, **Richard Rapp** (Don Quixote), **Suzanne Farrell** (Dulcinea), Deni Lamont (Sancho Panza).

Natalia Dudinskaya in Swan Lake. Ph. Vorotgnski.

DOWELL, Anthony (1943–   ), British dancer. He studied at the Royal Ballet School and joined Covent Garden Opera Ballet while still a student. In 1962 he became a member of **The Royal Ballet,** dancing his first solo part in *Napoli* (1962). He became a principal in 1966. He has created the roles of Oberon in *The Dream* (1964), Troyte in *Enigma Variations* (1968) and The Boy in *Triad* (1972), and leading roles in *Monotones* (1965) and *Shadowplay* (1967). His repertoire has included major roles in *Romeo and Juliet, La Fête Étrange, Giselle, The Sleeping Beauty, Lilac Garden* and *Dances at a Gathering*; and he partnered **Antoinette Sibley** in *Daphnis and Chloë* during The Royal Ballet's 1970 US tour.

DROTTNEROVA, Marta (1941–   ), Czech ballerina. She was a soloist with the Ostrava Theatre company (1954–60), joining Prague National Ballet in 1961. Her roles include Katerina in *The Stone Flower* and Juliet in *Romeo and Juliet*.

DRYADE, LA *see* **Eoline.**

DUDINSKAYA, Natalia (1912–), Russian prima ballerina, Peoples' Artist of the USSR. She studied at the Petrograd ballet school and with **Vaganova,** making her debut with the Kirov Ballet in the Blue Bird pas de deux from *The Sleeping Beauty* (1931). Her repertoire included *Swan Lake*, *Giselle*, *La Bayadère*, *Flames of Paris*, *The Fountain of Bakhchisarai* and *Path of Thunder*. Her greatest role was the title role in *Laurencia*. She succeeded Vaganova as teacher of the classe de perfection, and she became principal ballet mistress of the Kirov company.

DUNCAN, Isadora (1878–1927), American dancer. Having studied ballet as a child, she developed her own theory of 'free dance', based on mimed rhythmic responses to music as opposed to formal dance steps and body movements. Her debut (1899) in Chicago was discouraging, but success in Paris (1900) led to appearances in Budapest, Berlin, Florence and elsewhere in Europe. Her first school was started in Berlin in 1904. Her visits to Russia in 1905, 1908 and 1912, aroused considerable interest and controversy; she opened a school there in 1921. She returned to the United States in 1909, 1911, 1917 and 1922. She danced barefoot, usually dressed in Grecian style loose tunics, and used music not specifically intended for dancing by Wagner, Schubert and Chopin, among others. Her style of dancing was never systematized and hence could not survive her, although there is no doubt of her influence on modern dance, especially through the innovations of Fokine. She died at Nice in a bizarre car accident; her scarf caught in the rear wheel of her car and strangled her.

DUNHAM, Katherine (1914–), American dancer, choreographer and director. She danced with Ruth Page's Martinique Ballet. She organized her own company which toured Europe and the United States. In New York (1962) she presented dancers from Africa. She is widely known for her anthropological research, especially in the Caribbean.

DUPRÉ, Louis (1697–1774), French dancer, known as 'Le Grand Dupré'. His style of dancing is regarded as the model for the danseur noble. He succeeded Blondi at the Paris Opéra and among his students were **Jean-Georges Noverre** and **Gaetan Vestris.** He danced the repertoire of his era including the ballets of Rameau, *Thésée* by Lully, *Les Fêtes Vénitiennes* and *The Loves of Mars and Venus* by Campra.

DVORAK VARIATIONS, a plotless ballet. Choreography, **Ronald Hynd**; music, Dvorak (*Symphonic Variations*, *Opus 78*); decor and costumes, Peter Docherty. First performed at the Gran Teatro del Liceo, Barcelona, 7 May 1970, by London's **Festival Ballet.** Staged at the Coliseum Theatre, London, 14 July 1970, by the same company. Principal

Isadora Duncan. Ph. R. During.

dancers, **Galina Samtsova, André Prokovsky.** The ballet consists of a suite of linked dances on a Czech folk theme.

DYING SWAN, THE or **Le Cygne,** a solo dance created by **Michel Fokine,** in 1905, for **Anna Pavlova.** Music, Saint-Saëns (*Le Cygne* from *Carnaval des Animaux*) ; costume, **Léon Bakst.** First performed, 1905, in St. Petersburg, staged by artists from the Maryinsky Theatre. The work is a pas de bourrée couru and port de bras, and its execution demands an extremely high degree of technical skill. In his choreography, Fokine put the accent on expression and Anna Pavlova effectively conveyed a sense of the loneliness of death. Other ballerinas noted for their performance of the role include **Alicia Markova, Galina Ulanova** and **Maya Plisetskaya.**

E

écart, grand, the ballet form of the splits; it is started from the fifth position. **Ciseaux** is known as écart en l'air. As the splits, the step is a feature of the can-can and is used in acrobatic dancing.

ecarté, literally separated or thrown wide apart; a position of the body in which it is at an oblique angle to the audience, and the arm and leg nearest to the audience are in the same vertical and diagonal plane as the rest of the body.

échappé or **pas échappé,** literally escaped. Sauté (as in illustration 1) from the fifth position, the dancer leaps into the air, alighting with the feet in second or fourth position. Alternatively, he may alight on **pointes** or demi-pointes in the second position. May also be executed with a **relevé** (as in illustration 2) on to the demi-pointe. The movements may be executed front, side, back or en croix.

ECK, Imre (1930–), Hungarian dancer and choreographer. In 1950 he became a soloist with the Budapest Opera company and in 1958 choreographer. He produced a series of contemporary ballets with music by Hungarian composers. These include *Variation on a Meeting*, *Miner's Ballad* and *Spider's Web*.

EDUARDOVA, Eugenia (1882–1960), Russian ballerina and teacher. She studied at the Imperial Ballet School, St. Petersburg, and danced at the Maryinsky Theatre from 1901–17, when she left Russia to dance with the **Anna Pavlova** company first in London, then Berlin. She founded a ballet school in Berlin in 1920. In 1935 she moved to Paris, and then to New York in 1947, where she continued to teach for a short time. She was particularly noted for her interpretations of demi-caractère roles

in the classical repertoire.

EDWARDS, Leslie (1916–), British dancer, ballet master and teacher. He studied with **Marie Rambert,** Craske, **Idzikovsky, Volinine, Volkova** and others. He was a member of Ballet Rambert (1935–7) and joined Vic-Wells Ballet at its inception, reaching the status of principal character dancer and mime with **The Royal Ballet.** His most celebrated roles were those he created as Magician in *Noctambules*, Charlatan in *Petrouchka*, and he has danced von Rothbart in *Swan Lake*, Catalbutte in *The Sleeping Beauty* and Hilarion in *Giselle*. He started teaching mime at The Royal Ballet in 1958. He has also danced and choreographed for television programmes. Guest director and teacher at Washington (DC) Ballet (1962). He was an example of **de Valois's** success in bringing male dancers to the fore.

EGLEVSKY, André (1917–), American dancer and teacher, born in Russia. He studied with **Egorova, Kchessinska, Volinine, Legat** and at the School of American Ballet. At fourteen he joined **Ballet Russe de Monte Carlo,** dancing leading roles in *Swan Lake*, *Les Sylphides* and *Les Présages* very soon after. He became a member of **Woizikowsky's** company (1935) and of **René Blum's** Ballets Russes de Monte Carlo (1936), where he created Young Lover in *L'Epreuve d'Amour*, and Leader of the Jesters and Leader of the Demons in *Don Juan*. He moved to the United States in 1937 and was premier danseur with **The American Ballet** (1937–8); Ballet Russe de Monte Carlo (1939–42); **Ballet Theatre** (1942–1943, 1945); and **Ballet International** (1944) where he created the title role in *Mad Tristan*, and choreographed *Senti-*

mental Colloquy. He appeared in Ballet Russe Highlights (1945) and with Original Ballet Russe (1946–7), **Grand Ballet du Marquis de Cuevas** (1947–50) and **The New York City Ballet** (1951–8). In 1958 he founded a school in Massapequa, Long Island, and also taught at the School of American Ballet. During his long career he has danced the leading roles in the classic and modern repertoires, and has partnered **Alonso, Baronova, Danilova, Hightower, Kaye, Markova** and **Toumanova.**

EGOROVA, Lubov (Princess Nikita Troubetzkoy, 1880–1972), Russian ballerina and teacher. After studying at the Imperial Ballet School, St. Petersburg, she graduated into the Maryinsky Theatre and became ballerina in 1912. She danced the classical and modern repertoire, including *Giselle* and *Les Sylphides*. She left Russia in 1917 and danced the roles of Lilac Fairy and Aurora with **Diaghilev**'s Ballets Russes (1921–3). In 1923 she opened her Paris studio, and later formed Ballets de la Jeunesse (1937) where many of her pupils made their debuts: Leskova, Moulin, Vassili and Oleg Tupine, and **Skibine**. She taught briefly in London, and staged *Aurora's Wedding* for the Royal Danish Ballet, but her life's work was her Paris studio. Her many talented students included **Solange Schwarz, Janine Charrat** and **Ethery Pagava.**

ÉLÉMENTS, LES, a ballet in one act. Libretto and choreography, **Michel Fokine**; music, J. S. Bach (*Suite for Orchestra in B minor*); decor and costumes, Dimitry Bouchène. First performed at the Coliseum Theatre, London, in 1937. Principal dancers, **Nini Theilade, Igor Youskevitch, Michel Panaiev,** Valdemar Kostenko. The ballet depicts the cycles of nature. Zephyr chases the sea waves, rain makes the flowers grow, Vulcan's fires dry them and showers hasten to cool them. The dances, sarabandes, rondos and bourrées are in an antique, stately style and include notable entrées.

élévation, a dancer's ability to jump (élévation) and perform movements in the air (*ballon*). This can enable the dancer to give the impression of flying.

ÉLÈVE DE L'AMOUR, L' *see* **Aglaë.**

ELFES, LES, a plotless ballet in one act. Choreography, **Michel Fokine**; music, Felix Mendelssohn (*Overture to a Midsummer Night's Dream*, and the second and third movements of the *Violin Concerto*); decor, Visconti; costumes, Madame Vialet. First performed in the Metropolitan Opera House, New York, 26 February 1924, by Ballet Fokine. Principal dancers, **Nana Golner,** Nina Tarakanova, Besobrasova, **Michel Panaiev.** Revived by Michel Fokine for **René Blum**'s Ballets Russes de Monte Carlo in 1937, and again by the same company in 1942. Principal dancers in 1942, **Mia Slavenska, Igor Youskevitch.** Strange, semi-human creatures of the forest arise from the mysterious vapours of mythology and their gossamer wings shiver against the sky as they play in the moonlight. This is one of Michel Fokine's many successful works.

ELSSLER, Fanny (1810–84), Austrian ballerina. She and her sister Theresa were sent by Franz Josef Haydn to study with Hershelt and later with Aumer the ballet master of the Kaernthertor Theatre, Vienna. Three years later she entered the corps de ballet at the Vienna Hoftheater, where **Filippo Taglioni** was ballet master, and in 1822 she made her debut in *La Réception d'une Jeune Nymphe à la Cour de Terpsichore*. From 1822 to 1833 her fame grew, and in 1833 she appeared at the King's Theatre, London, with **Maria Taglioni.** The contrast in their styles was striking; where Taglioni was slender and sylphlike, Elssler was more sensual and human. She was engaged by the Paris Opéra, and after studying with **Auguste Vestris,** made her debut in *La Tempête*, the success of which divided Paris audiences between Taglioni and Elssler. Théophile Gautier, poet, balletomane and ardent fan of Taglioni, compared the two dancers in his famous article : 'Mlle Taglioni is a Christian dancer . . . she flies like a spirit in the midst of transparent clouds of white muslin . . . she resembles a happy angel. Fanny is quite a pagan dancer; she reminds one of the muse Terpsichore.' Elssler realized that her success lay in **danses de caractère** and selected her repertoire accordingly, dancing *Le Diable Boiteux* (1836) and *La Gypsy* (1839). However, when Taglioni left the Opéra, Elssler inadvisedly appeared in *La Sylphide*, which was a dismal failure. In 1840 she went on a three month tour of America which was to last two years, appearing in almost every major American city, and dancing *Tarentule, La Gypsy, Natalie, La Sylphide, Le Dieu et la Bayadère, La Somnambule*, and many others; she was acclaimed everywhere. Her extended tour of America was not forgiven by the Paris

Fanny Elssler. Ph. Lipnitzki.

Opéra, and on her return to Europe she danced in all the major capitals with the exception of Paris. She retired with a great fortune in 1851.

ELSSLER, Theresa (1808–78), Austrian dancer. Trained at Kaernthertor Theatre with her sister Fanny, she frequently partnered her en travesti and staged a number of short ballets for her. When she married Prince Adalbert of Prussia, she subsequently received the title of Baroness von Barnim from King Wilhelm I of Prussia.

ELVIN, Violetta (Violetta Prokhorova, 1924–), Russian ballerina. She studied with **Vaganova** at the Bolshoi School. She moved to England in 1945 and joined Sadler's Wells Ballet, dancing Blue Bird pas de deux and Aurora in *The Sleeping Beauty*, Odette-Odile in *Swan Lake* and *Giselle*. She created Water in *Homage to the Queen* and La Favorita in *Veneziana*. In 1952 she was invited to dance at La Scala, Milan. She retired in 1956.

emboîté, literally boxed in; a series of **relevés** from one foot to the other, the dancer moving either forward or backward. May be executed on pointes. In emboîté en tournant, a 180° turn is executed by means of two emboîtés.

Empire Ballets, the popular name given to a series of over sixty ballets danced at the Empire Theatre, London, between 1887 and 1914. The total venture was artistically and commercially successful and, along with the Alhambra Ballets, did much to preserve ballet in Britain during the period, being the only ballets danced in the country. Although the name was the Empire Theatre of Varieties, the policy was to make ballet the chief attraction. Katti Lanner, as ballet mistress, directed her own national school of dancing and was able to ensure a sustained high level of technique and artistry at the Empire. Among the dancers were **Enrico Cecchetti**, Will Bishop, Malvina Cavallazzi and Emma Palladino. **Adeline Genée** made her

London debut at the Empire in 1897. *Cléopâtre*, *Orfeo* and *Faust* were among the finest productions during the early years. In 1906 *Cinderella* ran for several months and *Coppélia* was produced for Adeline Genée. *The Belle of the Ball* marked the debut of **Phyllis Bedells**. **Lydia Kyasht** and **Adolph Bolm** made their first London appearances at the Empire. There was a temporary revival of short ballets at the Empire in 1951.

enchaînement, any sequence of steps and movements which together make up a meaningful statement.

ENIGMA VARIATIONS, a ballet in one act. Libretto, Gertrude Stein; choreography, **Frederick Ashton**; music, Edward Elgar; decor and costumes, Julia Trevelyan Oman. First performed at the Royal Opera House, Covent Garden, London, 25 October 1968, by **The Royal Ballet**. Principal dancers, Derek Rencher (Elgar), **Svetlana Benosova** (Lady Elgar), **Stanley Holden**, Brian Shaw, Alexander Grant, Robert Mead, Vyvyan Lorrayne, **Anthony Dowell**, Georgina Parkinson, Desmond Doyle, **Antoinette Sibley**, Wayne Sleep, Leslie Edwards, Deanne Bergsma. The ballet depicts the friends who inspired Elgar's work and who are acknowledged in it. The composer, holding the score of his *Variations*, is surrounded by his friends, who each dance with their individual variations. In the most celebrated part of the work (*Nimrod*), A. J. Jaeger, Elgar's close friend and publisher, is joined by Elgar in a danced conversation, expressing their friendship, and then by his wife. The warlike strains of the final variations bring all the friends back to the stage, when a telegram is brought in announcing that Richter will conduct the first performance.

entrechat, a movement in which the dancer, in the air, crosses his feet as many times as possible, for example, in entrechat-quatre the feet change position four times. The number depends on his agility in the **ballon.**

ENTRE DEUX RONDES, a ballet in one act. Choreography, **Serge Lifar**; music, Marcel Samuel-Rousseau; decor and costumes, Nadine Landowsky. First performed at the Paris Opéra, 24 April 1940. Principal dancers, **Solange Schwarz,** Serge Lifar. In the Louvre Museum, after the visitors have left, the statue of a Greek god and the dancers in a painting come to life and dance in both classic and modern styles. *Entre Deux Rondes* include a series of grand pas de deux, and the total work has charm and grace.

entrée de ballet, literally an entrance. 1) a divertissement in which the dancers express that part of the total theme which has been assigned to them. 2) the beginning of the grand pas (set dance) when the danseur and the danseuse make their entrance separately or together.

ÉOLINE or **La Dryade,** a Romantic ballet in six scenes. Choreography, **Jules Perrot**; music, Cesare Pugni. First performed in Her Majesty's Theatre, London, 8 March 1845. Principal dancers, **Lucile Grahn**, Jules Perrot. Revived in St. Petersburg, 16 November 1858, with new decor and **Amalia Ferraris** dancing Eoline. The story is based on a Bohemian folk tale. Eoline's mortal life will last only as long as the life of an oak tree of which she is a wood nymph. When she is about to marry, a rejected lover sets fire to the tree and Eoline dies.

ÉPREUVE D'AMOUR, L', a ballet in one act. Libretto, **Michel Fokine** and André Derain; choreography, Michel Fokine; decor and costumes, Derain. First performed in the Théâtre de Monte Carlo, 4 April 1936, by **René Blum**'s Ballets Russes. Principal dancers, **Vera Nemtchinova** (Chung-Yang), **André Eglevsky**, **Anatole Oboukhov**, Hélène Kirsova and Jean Yazvinsky. Chung-Yang has also been danced by **Alicia Markova** and **Nathalie Krassovska**, the latter at the Metropolitan Opera House, New York, 14 October 1938. The music is believed to be by Wolfgang Mozart. A greedy Mandarin

Entre Deux Rondes: Serge Lifar and Josette Clavier. Ph. Bernand.

wishes his daughter, Chung-Yang, to marry the rich Ambassador. Her poor lover, disguised as a dragon, robs the Ambassador who realizes that it was only his money that was wanted. The money is returned and the young couple marry. Some pantomime was included in the choreography. The ballet is in the repertoire of the National Ballet of Finland, with choreography by George Gué and decor by Horvath. This version was first performed in Helsinki, 22 March 1956. Principal dancers, Rajala, Salin, Lätti.

ERDMAN, Jean, American dancer, choreographer and teacher. She studied at the School of American Ballet, with **Martha Graham,** and also Spanish, Japanese and Hawaiian dancing. She was a member of the Martha Graham company (1938–43) and guest artist (1945–6). With her own company (1944) she toured the United States. She is known for her solo roles in *The Transformation of Medusa*

(1942), *Creature on a Journey* (1943), *Ophelia* (1946), *Hamadryad* (1948), *Changing-woman* (1951), *Duet for Flute and Dancer* (1956), *Fearful Symmetry* (1957) among others. For the Vassar Experimental Theatre she choreographed *Les Mouches* (1947); for Bard Theatre *Otherman*, a ballet-play, (1954); and her work *The Coach With the Six Insides* won the 1963 Vernon Rice and Obie Awards.

ESMERALDA, LA, a ballet in three acts based on Victor Hugo's story, *The Hunchback of Notre Dame.* Libretto and choreography, **Jules Perrot**; music, Cesare Pugni; decor, W. Grieve; costumes, Madame Copère; machinery, D. Sloman. First performed at Her Majesty's Theatre, London, 9 March 1844. Principal dancers, **Carlotta Grisi** (Esmeralda), Jules Perrot (Gringoire), Antoine Coulon (Quasimodo). Monplaisir Ballet Company staged a version in New York, 18 September 1848. First performed in Russia, 2 January 1849, in St. Petersburg. Principal dancers, **Fanny Elssler,** Jules Perrot, Peter Didier. Revised by **Marius Petipa,** with his own choreography, and presented in the Imperial Theatre in 1866. Staged in Milan, Naples and Vienna in 1951. **Anton Dolin** brought the ballet to London for London's **Festival Ballet,** 14 July 1954. Principal dancers, **Nathalie Krassovska, John Gilpin,** Keith Beckett. Only the divertissement is now danced. Other ballerinas to dance Esmeralda have included **Mathilda Kchessinska, Anna Pavlova, Galina Ulanova** and **Tamara Toumanova.** The story follows Victor Hugo's novel closely, showing Quasimodo's hopeless love for the gipsy girl, Esmeralda, the plotting of the evil priest, Frollo, and Quasimodo's sacrifice of his life for Esmeralda. An earlier ballet, with choreography by Antonio Monticini, was performed at Teatro alla Scala, Milan (1839).

ESPINOSA, Edouard (1871–1950), English teacher and writer, born in Russia.

Member of a famous family of dancers and teachers, he was a co-founder of London's Royal Academy of Dancing (1920) and the British Ballet Organization (1930).

ETCHEVERY, Jean-Jacques (Marie Ernest Jean-Jacques de Peyret-Chappuis 1916–   ), French dancer and choreographer. He studied with Karpova, Ricaus and Zverev, and was premier danseur with Nouveau Ballet de Monte Carlo from 1941 to 1944, when he founded Les Ballets de l'Oiseau Bleu. As ballet master at Opéra Comique, Paris (1946–54), his choreographic works include *Le Cerf* (1944), *Printemps, Chanson Sentimentale* (1945), *La Bourée Fantasque, Le Précaution Inutile* (1946) and *La Ballade de la Geôle de Reading* (1947).

ÉTUDE, a ballet in one act. Choreography, Ludmilla Chiriaeff; music, Robert Schumann (*Scenes from Childhood*). First performed in the Comédie Canadienne Théâtre, Montreal, 12 April 1956, by Les

La Esmeralda: Fanny Elssler. Ph. Bakhruchine, Moscow.

Grands Ballets Canadiens. Principal dancers, Milenka Niderlova, Eric Hyrst. Fundamental ballet exercises are developed into dances.

ÉTUDES, a plotless ballet in one act. Choreography, **Harald Lander**; music, Karl Czerny (*Étude*, arranged by Knudage Riisager); decor, Nordgron. First performed (under name *Étude*) in Copenhagen, 15 January 1948, by the Royal Danish Ballet. Principal dancers, **Margot Lander,** Hans Brenaa, Svend Jensen. Staged by Harald Lander for the Paris Opéra, 19 November 1952 (under present name). Principal dancers, Micheline Bardin, Michel Renault, **Alexandre Kalioujny.** Again staged by Harald Lander in the 54th Street Theatre, New York, 5 October 1961, for the American Ballet Theatre. Decor, Rolf Gerard. Principal dancers, **Toni Lander,** Lupe Serrana, **Royes Fernandez.** Staged, 8 August 1955, by London's **Festival Ballet.** Principal dancers, Toni Lander, **John Gilpin, Anton Dolin.** Also staged, 4 March 1962, by Royal Danish Ballet. Principal dancers, Toni Lander, **Flemming Flindt.** This ballet of crescendo and accelerando shows the classic progression of a dancer's training, from the bar to the centre and on to the pas de deux and the tour de force.

EVDOKIMOVA, Eva (1949–), American dancer, born in Switzerland. She studied at the Munich Opera Ballet School and the Royal Ballet School, London. She joined the Royal Danish Ballet in 1966 and became soloist at the Deutsches Oper, Berlin, in 1969. She was a prizewinner at the First Moscow International Dance Competition (1969) and a Gold Medallist at Varna, Bulgaria (1970).

EVTEYEVA, Elena (1947–), Russian dancer. In 1966 she graduated from the Leningrad School of Choreography and joined the Kirov Opera and Ballet Theatre. In 1969 she made guest appearances in Japan and Hungary. She was a Silver Medallist at Varna, Bulgaria (1970).

EXCELSIOR, a spectacular ballet in twelve scenes. Choreography, Luigi Manzotti; music, Marenco; decor and costumes, Alfredo Edel. First performed at the **Teatro alla Scala,** Milan, 11 January 1881. Principal dancers, Bice Vergani, Rosina Viale, Carlo Montanari, Carlo Coppi, Achille Balbiani. Staged in Her Majesty's Theatre, London, 1885. Principal dancers, Giovanni Limido, **Enrico Cecchetti.** *Excelsior* was propaganda for science. It traced the progress of mankind, and included spectacular scenes such as the advent of the first steamboat and of wireless telegraphy, and the cutting of the Suez Canal. It ended with the union, in peace, of all nations in the world. The ballet was performed and acclaimed internationally, and was a high point in Italian choreography, but was backward looking in its aesthetic standards.

F

FAÇADE, a ballet in one act. Libretto adapted from Edith Sitwell's group of poems of that name; choreography, **Frederick Ashton**; music, William Walton; decor, John Armstrong. First performed in the Cambridge Theatre, London, 26 April 1931, by **The Camargo Society.** Principal dancers, **Pearl Argyle, Lydia Lopokova, Alicia Markova,** Frederick Ashton. Performed in the Mercury Theatre, London, 4 May 1931, by Ballet Rambert. Principal dancers, **Andrée Howard** (Milkmaid and Tango Dancer). Also staged, 8 October 1935, by Vic-Wells Ballet, with the addition of a country dance. Other dances were added in the July 1940 Vic-Wells presentation. Alicia Markova gave notable performances of the Polka with Ballet Rambert and Vic-Wells, and Frederick Ashton's Tango, notably danced by Moira Shearer, was one of his most successful creations. A revival was staged in 1970 by Frederick Ashton for **The Royal Ballet.** Principal dancers, **Antoinette Sibley, Merle Park,** Alexander Grant. The ballet is a lighthearted view of the dance. The music emphasizes the rhythm of the poetry, which was Edith Sitwell's intention.

FÂCHEUX, LES, a ballet in one act based on the Molière play. Libretto, **Boris Kochno;** choreography, **Bronislava Nijinska;** music, Georges Auric; decor, Georges Braque. First performed, 19 January 1924, by the Monte Carlo Opéra. Principal dancers, **Lubov Tchernicheva, Alice Nikitina, Léon Woizikowsky, Anatole Vilzak, Anton Dolin.** Revived in 1927 with choreography by **Léonide Massine.** Les fâcheux, street idlers and gossips, retard the love of Eraste and Orphise. The action is boisterous in places, but effectively reproduces Molière's flair for observing human nature. An early ballet by Molière, with choreography by Beauchamp, was given for Louis XIV in 1661.

FADEYECHEV, Nicolai (1933–), Russian premier danseur, Honoured Artist and Peoples' Artist of the RSFSR. He studied at the Bolshoi School (1943–52) with **Asaf Messerer,** and danced Siegfried in *Swan Lake* and Prince Désiré in *Sleeping Beauty* when he had been with the company only a short time. He partnered **Plisetskaya** and he danced with her at the Paris Opéra (1961) in *Swan Lake,* dancing the same role with **Nadia Nerina** when she was guest artist at the Bolshoi (1961). He also partnered **Galina Ulanova.** Other roles in his repertoire are Harmodius in *Spartacus* and Danila in *The Stone Flower.* He is noted for his balon and his jetés.

failli, a giving-away step. Starting from the fifth position, demi-**plié,** right foot in front, the dancer makes a straight jump in third position clinging legs together and at the last possible moment detaches the left leg outward to the left, and lands on the right foot in **fondu** and obliquely to the audience. Then he swings the left leg across to fourth position **croisé.**

FALLIS, Barbara (1924–), American dancer and teacher. She studied at the Mona Clague Ballet School and Vic-Wells Ballet School (1937–40), dancing with the company (1938–40). She joined **Ballet Theatre** (1941), and as soloist danced Waltz in *Les Sylphides,* Calliope in *Apollo,* and created the role of Grahn in *Pas de Quatre.* From 1948 to 1952 she was ballerina with Ballet Alicia Alonso, dancing in *Petrouchka, Le Spectre de la Rose* and *Giselle.* Soloist with **The New York City Ballet** (1953–8), her repertoire included *Cakewalk, Western Symphony, Nutcracker,*

Swan Lake and a role in *Pas de Dix* which she created.

FALL RIVER LEGEND, a ballet in one act. Libretto and choreography, **Agnes de Mille**; decor, Oliver Smith; costumes, Miles White; music, Morton Gould. First performed in the Metropolitan Opera House, New York, 22 April 1948, by **Ballet Theatre.** Principal dancers, **Alicia Alonso, Nora Kaye** (Lizzie Borden), **Diana Adams** (Her Mother), Peter Gladke (Her Father), Muriel Bentley, **Lucia Chase** (Stepmother), Ruth Ann Koesin (Lizzie Borden as a child), **John Kriza** (The Pastor). The story is that of Lizzie Borden of Fall River, Massachusetts, who was accused of the double murder of her father and stepmother in 1895. In the ballet she confesses and is executed. Before the execution, she relives the events leading to the crime. This is one of Agnes de Mille's best choreographic works. Nora Kaye gave a notable performance as Lizzie Borden.

FANCY FREE, a modern ballet in one act. Libretto and choreography, **Jerome Robbins**; music, Leonard Bernstein; decor, Oliver Smith; costumes, Kermit Love. First performed at the Metropolitan Opera House, New York, 18 April 1944, by **Ballet Theatre.** Principal dancers, **Janet Reed,** Muriel Bentley, Shirley Eckl (Three Young Girls), **Harold Lang, John Kriza,** Jerome Robbins (Three Sailors). The choreography includes acrobatic feats and contemporary dance hall styles alongside classic choreography.

FANFARE, a plotless ballet in one act. Choreography, **Jerome Robbins**; music, Benjamin Britten (*Young Person's Guide to the Orchestra*); decor and costumes, Irene Sharaff. Produced by **The New York City Ballet,** 2 June 1953, to celebrate the coronation of Queen Elizabeth II. Principal dancers, Yvonne Mounsey, Irene Larsson, **Jillana,** Jacques d'Amboise, Brooks Jackson, **Todd Bolender.** Also staged for the Royal Danish Ballet, 29 April 1956. In the ballet the dancers assume the roles of the instruments. The choreography

George Farmaniantz in Taras Bulba. Ph. Reyna.

brings out the individual parts and also their unity in the total orchestra. **Allegra Kent** gave a notable performance in the viola pas de deux, 12 January 1954.

FARMANIANTZ, George (1921–), Russian dancer, Honoured Artist of the RSFSR. A student at the Bolshoi School (1929–40), he appeared as Russian Doll in *Football Player* (1930). Graduating into the company in 1940, his first role was Ataman Shilo in *Taras Bulba.* He was considered one of the finest dancers of demi-caractère parts in Russia and among his roles were Basil in *Don Quixote*, Frantz in *Coppélia*, Blue Bird in *The Sleeping Beauty*, Nur-Ali in *The Fountain of Bakhchisarai*, Jester in *Swan Lake*, Philippe in *Flames of Paris* and Prince in *The Nutcracker.* He retired in 1963.

FARRELL, Suzanne (Roberta Sue Ficker, 1945–), American ballerina. She studied at the School of American Ballet, joining **The New York City Ballet** in 1961. She became soloist in 1963 after dancing in *Serenade* and *Concerto Barocco*. She created the female lead in *Arcade* (1963), *Meditation, Clarinade, Ballet Imperial*; her interpretation of Dulcinea in *Don Quixote* (1965) gained her the title of principal dancer in the company, and in 1966 she re-created Titania in the film version of *A Midsummer Night's Dream*. In 1971 she created Girl in Pink in *Nijinsky—Clown of God* for **Béjart**'s Les Ballets du XXième Siècle.

FARRON, Julia (Julia Farron-Smith, 1929–), British dancer. She studied at the Cone School and Sadler's Wells, creating Pepe the Dog in *A Wedding Bouquet* (1937) and Psyche in *Cupid and Psyche* (1939). During her career she created many character and demi-caractère roles, notably Hannah in *A Mirror for Witches*, Jocasta in *Antigone* and the Tarantella from Ashton's *Swan Lake*. Her repertoire also included *Checkmate, The Rake's Progress* and *Daphnis and Chloë*. After her retirement (1961), she created Lady Capulet in *Romeo and Juliet* (1965) and toured with **The Royal Ballet** in the United States.

FAUST, a ballet in three acts, based on Goethe's tragedy. Libretto and choreography, **Jules Perrot**; music, Panizza, Bejetti, Costa; decor, Carlo Fontana. First performed at **Teatro alla Scala**, Milan, 12 February 1848. Principal dancers, **Fanny Elssler** (Marguerite), Effisio Catte (Faust), Jules Perrot (Mephistopheles). Performed in Russia, 16 November 1854. Principal dancers, Mme. Yella, **Marius Petipa**, Jules Perrot. Perrot used only the skeleton and major characters of the Goethe story for his choreography. Performed at the Empire Theatre, London, 6 May 1895. Music, Meyer Lutz and Ernest Ford; decor and costumes, C. Wilhelm. Principal dancers, Mme. Cavallazzi, Ada Vincent, Mlle. Zanfretta.

FEDOROVA, Alexandra (1884–1972), Russian dancer and teacher. A pupil at the Imperial School, St. Petersburg, she graduated into the Maryinsky Theatre (1902) and became first soloist (1906).

After leaving Russia (1922), she was ballet mistress with the Latvian State Theatre of Opera and Ballet in Riga. In 1937 she moved to the United States where she taught in her own school until her retirement in 1965.

FEMMES DE BONNE HUMEUR, LES *see* **Good-Humoured Ladies, The.**

FENSTER, Boris (1916–61), Russian dancer and choreographer, Peoples' Artist of the RSFSR. He studied at the Leningrad Ballet School, graduating in 1936 and joining the company of the Maly Opera Theatre, Leningrad. His first choreographic work was *Ashik-Kerib* (1940). He was chief choreographer of the Maly Opera Ballet (1936–56) and the Kirov Ballet (1956–60). His works included *False Bridegroom* (1944), *Mistress into Maid* (1951) and *Taras Bulba* (1955).

FERNANDEZ, Royes (1929–), American dancer. He studied with Lelia Haller, Laurent Novikoff, **Alexandra Danilova** and Vincenzo Celli, and made his debut with **Colonel de Basil**'s Original Ballet Russe (1946–7). He was soloist with Markova-Dolin Ballet (1947–8), with Ballet Alicia Alonso (1948–50, 1952–4), and with American Ballet Theatre (1950–1953); and principal dancer and partner to **Mia Slavenska** (1951) in Mia Slavenska Ballet Variante. His roles included Siegfried in *Swan Lake*, title roles in *Le Spectre de la Rose* and *Apollo*, Albrecht in *Giselle*, Blue Bird pas de deux, and Colin in *La Fille Mal Gardée*. He was premier danseur with Borovansky Ballet in Australia (1954–6). He became premier danseur with American Ballet Theatre (1957), dancing Albrecht in *Giselle*, Prince in *Swan Lake* and male leads in *Theme and Variations* and other roles; he created Sailor in *Lady from the Sea*, Nilas in *Moon Reindeer*, one of the two male leads in *Études* and James in *La Sylphide*. He was guest artist with London's **Festival Ballet** (1962) and Australian Ballet (1964).

FERRARIS, Amalia (1830–1904), Italian

ballerina. Taught by **Carlo Blasis,** she made her debut as Queen of the Wilis in *Giselle* at the Regio Theatre, Turin, in 1844. She danced at the **Teatro alla Scala,** Milan (1846), in London (1849), and made her debut at the Paris Opéra (1856) in *Les Elfes.* There she created roles in *Marco Spada* (1857), *Sacountala* and *Faust* (1858).

FESTIN DE L'ARAIGNÉE, LE *see* Spider's Banquet, The.

Festival Ballet, London, a British company which originated out of a touring company formed by Julian Braunsweg in 1949 and headed by **Alicia Markova** and **Anton Dolin.** It became London's Festival Ballet in 1950 and after 1952 was based at the Royal Festival Hall. Since visiting Monte Carlo in 1951, it has toured widely in Europe, the Middle East, and America, engaging many well-known dancers as guest artists. The repertoire includes full-length classical ballets as well as modern works including *Études, Graduation Ball, Noir et Blanc* and *Piège de Lumière.* In 1965 **Jack Carter** became resident choreographer, and among the works he has staged for Festival Ballet are *The Witch Boy* and *The Unknown Island.* **David Adams, John Gilpin** and Shirley Graham were formerly principal dancers with the company. Recent principal dancers include **André Prokowsky, Galina Samtsova,** and Dudley von Loggenburg. **Beryl Grey** became artistic director in 1968. The company gave the first of its annual seasons at the London Coliseum (1969). After 1969 it became known as London Festival Ballet. It toured Eastern Europe in 1971.

FÊTE ÉTRANGE, LA, a ballet in two scenes based on episodes from Alain-Fournier's novel, *Le Grand Meaulnes.* Libretto, Ronald Crichton; choreography, **Andrée Howard;** music, Gabriel Fauré; decor, Sophie Federovich. First performed in the Arts Theatre, London, 23 May 1940, by London Ballet. Principal dancers, Frank Staff (The Boy), **Maude Lloyd** (The Châtelaine), David Paltenghi (The Young Nobleman). Repeated by the Ballet Rambert, 20 June 1940, with the same cast. Taken into Sadler's Wells Theatre Ballet repertoire and performed 25 March 1947. Principal dancers, Donald Britton, **June Brae,** Anthony Burke. Taken into the repertoire of **The Royal Ballet** in 1957. Pirmin Trecu made The Boy one of his best known roles. The theme is of an adolescent vision.

FEUILLET, Raoul (*c* 1675–*c* 1730), French dancer and choreographer. He studied under **Louis Pécourt** to whom he dedicated his *Chorégraphie ou l'Art d'écrire la danse par caractères, figures et signes démonstratifs* (1700). His *Recueil de Danses,* written in conjunction with André Lorin, describes in his own system of dance notation a number of dances created by Pécourt and danced at the Opéra. The *Chorégraphie* is one of the major works on dance technique of the 17th century.

FIELD, John (John Greenfield, 1921–   ), British dancer, ballet master and administrator. After a debut with Liverpool Ballet Club, he joined Sadler's Wells (1939) and became a principal dancer. His graceful style showed to advantage in classical roles: Siegfried in *Swan Lake,* Albrecht in *Giselle* and Florimund in *Sleeping Beauty.* He was appointed director of Sadler's Wells Ballet and of **The Royal Ballet** (1956) and in 1970 was co-director with **Kenneth MacMillan.** In 1970 he became director of ballet at **Teatro alla Scala.**

FIFIELD, Elaine (1931–   ), Australian dancer. She studied at Sadler's Wells and joined their Theatre Ballet in 1947, where she became principal dancer. Her repertoire included the leading roles in *Les Rendez-vous, Swan Lake* (Act 2), *The Nutcracker*; she created the title role in *Selina* and Poll in *Pineapple Poll.* In 1954 she transferred to Sadler's Wells Ballet and as ballerina (1956) danced Odette-Odile in *Swan Lake* and created the title role in *Madame Chrysanthème.* She made a few appearances with Borovansky Ballet when she returned to Australia in 1954.

FILLE AUX YEUX D'ÉMAIL, LA *see* **Coppélia.**

FILLE DE FEU, LA *see* **Alma.**

FILLE DE MARBRE, LA, a ballet in two acts. Libretto and choreography, **Arthur Saint-Léon**; music, Cesare Pugni; decor, Cambon and Thierry. First performed in the Théâtre de **l'Académie Royale de Musique,** Paris, 20 October 1847. Principal dancers, **Fanny Cerito** (La Fille), Arthur Saint-Léon (Sculptor), H. Desplaces (Prince). Staged in St. Petersburg, 1 December 1856. The Devil brings a statue to life. However, if she ever falls in love she will become a statue again. Fanny Cerito danced the principal role in a similar ballet, *Alma,* in 1842 with choreography by **Jules Perrot.** Vernoy de Saint-Georges's *The Marble Maiden,* danced at the Theatre Royal, Drury Lane, London in 1845, had a similar theme. *See also* **Alma.**

FILLE DU BANDIT, LA *see* **Catarina.**

FILLE DU DANUBE, LA, a romantic ballet in two acts. Libretto and choreography, **Filippo Taglioni**; music, Adolph Adam. First performed in the Théâtre de **l'Académie Royale de Musique,** Paris, 21 September 1836. Principal dancers, **Maria Taglioni,** Joseph Mazilier. Performed in the Theatre Royal, Drury Lane, London, 21 November 1837, and in St. Petersburg in the same year, with Maria and Filippo Taglioni in the principal parts. The story recounts the love of the Daughter of the Danube and the Baron's Squire, Rudolph.

FILLE DU PHARAON, LA, a ballet in a prologue, seven scenes and an epilogue, inspired by Théophile Gautier's novel, *Le Roman de la Momie.* Libretto, **Marius Petipa** and Vernoy de Saint-Georges; choreography, Marius Petipa; music, Cesare Pugni. First performed at the Maryinsky Theatre, St. Petersburg, 30 January 1862. Principal dancers, **Carolina Rosati** (The Mummy), Marius Petipa, **Lev Ivanov,** Nicholas Goltz. Sheltering in a pyramid, Lord Wilson and his servant, John Bull, smoke opium. In their dreams, the mummified Princess Aspicia, Pharoah's daughter, comes alive. The ballet lasted for four hours and required almost four hundred dancers. Marius Petipa choreographed *La Fille du Pharaon* for Carolina Rosati's final appearance in St. Petersburg.

FILLE MAL GARDÉE, LA, a ballet in two acts. Libretto and choreography, **Jean Dauberval.** First performed at Bordeaux in 1786 with Mlle. Théodore dancing Lise. This production was notable in that the plot dealt with French peasant life rather than with mythological and allegorical themes. First American performance in the Lafayette Theatre, New York, 31 July 1828. Revived at St. Petersburg under the title *Useless Precautions,* in 1882, by **Marius Petipa** and **Lev Ivanov.** Music, Peter Hartel. Almost all subsequent versions have been based on this one. The role of Lise was a favourite one with **Anna Pavlova,** and **Enrico Cecchetti** frequently danced Mother Simone en travesti. Revived at the Alvin Theatre, New York, 19 November 1938, by Mordkin Ballet. Choreography, **Mikhail Mordkin**; decor, Serge Soudeikine. Principal dancers, **Lucia Chase** (Lise), Dimitri Romanov (Colin), Mikhail Mordkin (Mother Simone). Re-choreographed by **Bronislava Nijinska** and performed in the New York City Center, 19 January 1940. Principal dancers, **Patricia Bowman,** Yurek Shabelevsky, Edward Caton. Restaged by **Ballet Theatre** in 1941 as *The Wayward Daughter,* and in 1942 as *Naughty Lisette.* Principal dancers, **Irina Baronova,** Dimitri Romanov, **Simon Semenov.** It has also been staged by the Robert Joffrey Ballet, and by Les Grands Ballets Canadiens. **Janet Reed, Alicia Alonso** and Lupe Serrano, among others, have played the role of Lise. This was one of the earliest comic ballets. Marriage to a rich man, arranged by her mother, is prevented by Lise and her lover. See the following entry.

FILLE MAL GARDÉE, LA, a ballet in

L'Épreuve d'Amour: performed by the Finnish Ballet. Ph. Taisto Tuomi.

two acts. Choreography, **Frederick Ashton**; music, François Hérold (arranged by John Lanchbery); decor, Osbert Lancaster. First performed in the Royal Opera House, Covent Garden, London, 28 January 1960, by **The Royal Ballet**. Principal dancers, **Nadia Nerina** (Lise), **David Blair** (Colas, the new name for Colin), **Stanley Holden** (Mother Simone), **Alexander Grant** (Alain). This was the first British ballet to use English folk dances. Lise has been danced by **Merle Park, Antoinette Sibley, Doreen Wells** and Maryon Lane. Colas has been danced by **Donald MacLeary, Christopher Gable** and Graham Usher. The story is similar to that of the earlier ballet (see previous entry).

FINLAND, history of ballet in.
1879 The Russian government builds an opera house (Alexander Theatre) in Helsingförs (Helsinki), creating a stage-supported ballet company. A ballet school is established.
1922 George Gué, choreographer and ballet master of the theatre (now called Suomen Kansallisooppera) produces *Swan Lake*. The Finnish ballet becomes professional. Among its instructors are **Legat** and **Fokine.**
1932 Alexander Saxelin becomes ballet master.
1935 Irja Koskinen, the first Finnish choreographer, stages *Scaramouche* (to Sibelius's music).
1959 A group of dancers from the Finnish National Ballet tours the US.
1963–4 Nicholas Beriosov is ballet master.
1966 Elsa Silvesteron stages *Festivo* (to Sibelius's music). The company dances in Lausanne, Bern and Stockholm. Guest choreographers have included **Skeaping, Zakharov, Cullberg, Lifar** and **Lander.**

Finnish National Ballet *see* **Finland, history of ballet in.**

FIREBIRD, THE or **L'Oiseau de Feu,** a ballet in three scenes. Libretto and

The Firebird: Nina Vyroubova and Youly Algarov. Ph. Lipnitzki.

choreography, **Michel Fokine**; music, Igor Stravinsky; decor, Alexander Golovine. First performed at the Paris Opéra, 25 June 1910, by **Diaghilev**'s Ballets Russes. Principal dancers, **Tamara Karsavina** (Firebird), Michel Fokine (Ivan Tsarevich), **Enrico Cecchetti** (Kostchei), Vera Fokina (Tsarevna). Revived in the Lyceum Theatre, London, in 1926 with new decor by Nathalie Gontcharova. Principal dancers, Felia Doubrovska, **George Balanchine**. Revived by **Colonel de Basil**'s Ballets Russes de Monte Carlo with **Alexandra Danilova** and, later, **Irina Baronova** and **Tamara Toumanova,** in the title role. Revived by Serge Grigoriev and **Lubov Tchernicheva** for the Sadler's Wells Ballet at the Edinburgh Festival, 23 August 1954. Principal dancers, **Margot Fonteyn, Michel Somes, Frederick Ashton, Svetlana Beriosova.** The title role was later taken by **Nadia Nerina** and **Annette Page** in this production. A new version

was produced at the Metropolitan Opera House, New York, 24 October 1945, by **Ballet Theatre**. Choreography, **Adolph Bolm**; decor, Marc Chagall. Principal dancers, **Alicia Markova, Anton Dolin**. Marc Chagall's decor was used for a **George Balanchine** version of the choreography staged at the New York City Center, 27 November 1949. Principal dancers, **Maria Tallchief, Francisco Moncion. Serge Lifar** choreographed still another version, at the Paris Opéra, 7 April 1954. Decor, George Wakhevitch. Principal dancers, **Nina Vyroubova, Youly Algarov.** Imprisoned by a hunter, Ivan, the Firebird regains her freedom in exchange for a magic feather with which he can summon her in time of danger. This danger threatens Ivan and his princess with the advent of the evil and apparently immortal Kostchei. Ivan summons Firebird who shows him where to find the egg containing Kostchei's life.

FISHERMAN AND HIS BRIDE, THE see **Napoli.**

Five Principles, The. On 6 July 1914, while the Ballets Russes were appearing at Drury Lane, London, **Michel Fokine** wrote a letter to *The Times*. In it he set out his five principles on which the 'new ballet' was to be based. These were: 1) The choreographer and the dancer should not form combinations of ready-made and established dance steps, but should create a new form, corresponding in each case to the subject matter of the work. 2) Dancing and mimetic gesture should be used only to enhance the dramatic content of the ballet and not as a mere divertissement or entertainment. 3) Conventional gesture is only acceptable where it is required by the style of the ballet. Otherwise mimetic gestures of the whole body are to be used. 4) The expressiveness of the individual is to be unified with that of the total configuration of all the dancers. 5) Dancing is to be allied with other art forms. It must not be the slave of music or scenic decoration, but should be in a sufficiently authoritative position to allow the musician and scenic designer complete freedom. There should result a complete whole with no single aspect having dominance.

FLAMES OF PARIS, THE or **La Flamme de Paris,** a ballet in four acts. Libretto, Nicolai Volkov and Vladimir Dmitriev; choreography, Vasily Vainonen; music, Boris Asafiev; decor, Vladimir Dmitriev. First performed at the Bolshoi Theatre, Leningrad, 7 November 1932. Principal dancers, **Olga Jordan** (Jeanne), **Galina Ulanova** (Mireille), Vakhtang Chabukiany (Jerome), **Nina Anisimova** (Thérèse). The ballet was inspired by the triumph of the people in the French Revolution. The work portrays the march on Paris and the storming of the Tuileries. The music includes contemporary street songs and the finale is a magnificent spectacle with open-air celebrations of the period.

flèche, temps de, literally the step of the arrow, so called because one leg is bent like a bow and the straight leg shoots through the arch like an arrow. From the fourth position, right leg behind, **temps levé,** the dancer executes a grande battement en cloche to the fourth position in front, bends the knee of the right leg, springs from the left leg, making a **développé** through the bent right leg, alights on the right leg en **fondu,** and closes the left foot in fifth position in front.

FLINDT, Flemming (1936–), Danish dancer and choreographer. Studied at the Royal Danish Ballet School (1946–55); entered the company and became soloist (1957). Was guest artist with London's **Festival Ballet**; danseur étoile at the **Paris Opéra Ballet,** and guest artist with **Ruth Page**'s Chicago Opera Ballet. He returned to the Royal Danish Ballet (1962) as guest artist, dancing the leading roles in *Carmen, Études* and *Graduation Ball* and others. In 1963 he danced *Flower Festival at Genzano* pas de deux, and in *La Fille Mal Gardée* and *Sylvia* with **The Royal Ballet** and was premier danseur étoile at the Paris Opéra Ballet, creating the leading male role in *Scotch Symphony*. For Danish television, he choreographed *The Lesson* (1963) and restaged it for Opéra Comique, Paris (1964); he provided choreography for the Metropolitan Opera Ballet's *Faust* (1965). In 1966, he was appointed director of the Royal Danish Ballet. For this company he choreographed his own full-length ballet, *The Three Musketeers,* and a new one-act version of *The Miraculous Mandarin* (1967). He has also staged new productions of *Kermesse at Bruges, La Sylphide,* and *The Nutcracker*. In 1972 he created *The Triumph of Death,* a dance drama.

Flames of Paris. Ph. Photo Off. Cult. Sov.

FLORE ET ZÉPHYR or **Zéphyr et Flore,** a divertissement in one act. Choreography, **Charles Louis Didelot**; music, Cesare Bossi; decor and costumes, Liparotti. First performed in the King's Theatre, London, 7 July 1796. Principal dancers, Didelot, Hilligsberg, Rose, Parisot. This ballet was credited with being Didelot's finest work. For the first time invisible wires were used to allow dancers to simulate flying. In it **Maria Taglioni** made her London debut in 1830. Zéphyr, in love with Chloris, begs Cupid to help him. Then he falls in love with Cléonise who spurns him because her life is devoted to dancing. When Chloris comes, he rejoins her.

FOKINE, Michel (1880–1942), Russian dancer, choreographer and teacher. He studied at the Imperial School, St. Petersburg, becoming a soloist at the Maryinsky Theatre in 1898. He made his debut in a **pas de quatre** in *Paquita*. He began to teach at the Imperial School in 1902 and became first soloist in 1904. He then began his great career as a choreographer. He created *The Dying Swan* for **Anna Pavlova** in 1905. For the Imperial Theatre he staged *Le Pavillon d'Armide* (1907), *Une Nuit d'Egypte* (1908, later presented by **Diaghilev** as *Cléopâtre*), *Chopiniana* (which became *Les Sylphides*), *Polovetsian Dances from Prince Igor* (1909), *Orpheus and Eurydice* (1911) and others. For the **Diaghilev** Ballets Russes he choreographed perhaps his most famous ballet, *Les Sylphides* (1909), *Schéhérazade* and *The Firebird* (1910), *Petrouchka* (1911); also *Daphnis and Chloë, Le Coq d'Or, Papillons,* and many others. Fokine left Russia in 1918, and eventually settled in the United States. Among his later works are *La Valse* (1931), *L'Epreuve d'Amour* (1936), *Les Eléménts* (1937) and *Bluebeard* (1941). He is best remembered as a teacher, reformer and innovator. *See* **Five Principles, The.**

fondu, movement in which the knee of the supporting leg is bent and the body lowered.

Margot Fonteyn in Swan Lake. Ph. Bernand.

FONTEYN, Margot (Peggy Hookham, 1919), British ballerina, Dame of the Order of the British Empire. As a child she studied under Bosutov and Goncharov in Shanghai, then with **Vera Volkova** and at Sadler's Wells Ballet School. In 1934 she made her professional debut with Vic-Wells Ballet as a Snowflake in *The Nutcracker*. This was followed a year later by a non-dancing role as the Young Master of Tregennis in *The Haunted Ballroom*. The next year she danced the lead in a revival of *Rio Grande,* her first important part. When **Markova** left the company (1935), Fonteyn was given many of her roles, becoming and remaining prima ballerina of Sadler's Wells.

In addition she created many roles in Ashton's ballets: Bride in *Le Baiser de la Fée* (1935) was her first, followed by Woman in Balldress in *Apparitions*, Flower Girl in *Nocturne*, white pas de deux in *Les Patineurs*, Julia in *Wedding Bouquet*, Girl in *Horoscope*, Bride in *The Wise Virgins*, Leader of the Children of Light in *Dante Sonata*, Una in *The Quest*, ballerina in *The Wanderer*, leading ballerina in *Symphonic Variations*, La Bolero in *Les Sirènes*, La Morte Amoureuse in *Don Juan*, ballerina in *Scènes de Ballet*, Chloë in *Daphnis and Chloë*; title role in *Sylvia*, female Tiresias in *Tiresias*, title roles in *La Péri* and *Ondine*—said to be a 'concerto for Fonteyn', first ballerina in *Birthday Offering* and Marguerite in *Marguerite and Armand* (1963) in which she was partnered by **Rudolph Nureyev**. In **Helpmann's** ballets she created Lady in *Comus*, Ophelia in *Hamlet*, and for **de Valois** she created the role of Love in *Orpheus and Eurydice* and Dulcinea in *Don Quixote*; with **Les Ballets de Paris de Roland Petit**, she created Agathe in *Les Demoiselles de la Nuit*. Since 1959 she has been guest artist with **The Royal Ballet** and has created roles in *Firebird, Petrouchka, The Three-Cornered Hat, Mam'zelle Angot, Ballet Impérial*, Macmillan's *Romeo and Juliet* (1965) and *Poème de L'Extase* (1972). She has also danced the leading roles in *Pelléas et Mélisande* (1968), and in *La Bayadère* and *Raymonda Act III* (both 1969). She is noted for the great classical repertoire including *Giselle* and *Swan Lake*, and especially *Sleeping Beauty*. Two of her greatest attributes are her 'line' and her 'musicality'. Since 1949 she appeared regularly in the United States with The Royal Ballet. On the 1963 tour she was partnered by Rudolph Nureyev. A ballerina of international fame, she is the first to be developed by a British school and company; and she has appeared as guest artist with all the major companies of Europe. She toured Australia in 1962 and Europe in 1963 with her own company. She succeeded **Adeline Genée** as President of the Royal Academy of Dancing in 1954.

FORAINS, LES, a ballet in one scene. Libretto, **Boris Kochno**; choreography, **Roland Petit**; music, Henri Sauguet; decor, Christian Bérard. First performed in the Théâtre des Champs-Elysées, Paris, 2 March 1945, by **Les Ballets des Champs-Elysées**. Principal dancers, Roland Petit, **Janine Charrat, Ethéry Pagava**. Strolling players appear in the town's square and perform amid cheering. But when the money bowl is taken round, the audience disappears. The players are presented with great sympathy.

FORNAROLI, Cia (1888–1954), Italian ballerina and teacher. She studied under **Cecchetti** at **Teatro alla Scala,** Milan and was ballerina of the Metropolitan Opera House, New York (1910–1914) and of La Scala until 1934. From 1928 to 1933 she was director of the ballet school at La Scala, but was dismissed by Mussolini. After moving to New York, she taught for a number of years in her own school. After her death, the Cia Fornaroli Collection, consisting of a large number of historic manuscripts on the dance, was donated by her husband to the Dance Collection of the New York Public Library.

fouetté en tournant, a spectacular whipping movement in which the dancer stands on one foot, whips the other leg in a circle, thus wheeling round on the supporting leg, but remaining on the same spot. Usually executed in series.

FOUNTAIN OF BAKHCHISARAI, THE, a ballet in four acts based on Alexander Pushkin's poem of the same name. Libretto, Nicolai Volkov; choreography, **Rostislav Zakharov**; music, Boris Asafiev; decor, Valentina Khodasevich. First performed at the Kirov Theatre, Leningrad, 9 September 1934. Principal dancers, **Galina Ulanova** (Maria), **Tatiana Vecheslova** (Zarema), Mikhail Dudko (Khan Guirei). The Khan loves captive princess, Maria. His wife, Zarema, is jealous and kills her. The Khan builds a Fountain of Tears in her memory. Galina Ulanova and **Maya Plisetskaya** (as

Zarema) have made this ballet one of the most notable in Russia.

FOUR TEMPERAMENTS, THE, a ballet in one act. Choreography, **George Balanchine**; music, Paul Hindemith; decor, Kurt Seligmann. First performed in Central High School of Needle Trades, New York, 20 November 1946, by Ballet Society. Principal dancers, Gisella Caccialanza, **Tanaquil LeClercq,** Mary Ellen Moylan, **Todd Bolender, Lew Christensen, William Dollar, Francisco Moncion.** A revised version was performed by **The New York City Ballet,** 25 October 1948. Principal dancers, **Maria Tallchief, Nicholas Magallanes** (Sanguine Variation), Francisco Moncion (Melancholic), Todd Bolender (Phlegmatic), Tanaquil LeClercq (Choleric). In 1951 George Balanchine dispensed with decor and costumes and the ballet was danced successfully in white practice clothes.

FOYER DE DANSE, a ballet in one act. Libretto and choreography, **Frederick Ashton**; music, Lord Berners. First performed in the Mercury Theatre, London, 9 October 1932, by Ballet Rambert. Principal dancers, **Alicia Markova** (L'Étoile), Frederick Ashton (Maître de Ballet). The ballet depicts real and imagined incidents during the rehearsal of a ballet.

FOYER DE LA DANSE, a ballet in one act suggested by the Degas painting of the same name. Libretto and choreography, **Adolph Bolm**; music, Emmanuel Chabrier; decor, Nicholas Remisov. First performed in the Eighth Street Theatre, Chicago, 27 November 1927, for Chicago Allied Arts. Principal dancers, **Ruth Page,** Adolph Bolm. The librettist tells of accidents and incidents during a rehearsal. At the Paris Opéra, the foyer de la danse was an extension of the stage where rehearsals took place and where balletomanes might gather to watch.

FRACCI, Carla (1936–), Italian ballerina. Trained at the ballet school of

Teatro alla Scala, Milan, she graduated into the company (1954), became soloist (1956) and ballerina (1958). She danced romantic roles including *Cinderella*, her first role as ballerina, *Giselle*, *La Sylphide*, *Les Sylphides* and *Pas de Quatre*. She has been guest artist with London's **Festival Ballet** (1959); Ballet Festivals, Nervi (1960, 1962); Festival of Two Worlds, Spoleto (1962); and **The Royal Ballet** (1963), for which she danced *Flower Festival at Genzano* and *Le Bal des Voleurs*; and **Ballet Theatre** (1967).

FRANCA, Celia (Celia Franks, 1921–), British dancer, director and choreographer. She won a scholarship to the Royal Academy of Dancing and also studied with **Stanislas Idzikowsky.** Her repertoire with Ballet Rambert (1936–9) included *Lilac Garden, Les Sylphides*, Blue Bird pas de deux and *Dark Elegies*. Her own first ballet, *Midas*, was choreographed for Three Arts Ballet. She appeared with Arts

Carla Fracci. Ph. Piccagliani.

Theatre Ballet (1940), **International Ballet** (1941) and joined Sadler's Wells Ballet later in 1941. Some roles from her extensive repertoire were Queen of the Wilis in *Giselle*, Dawn in *Coppélia* and Prelude in *Les Sylphides*, and she created Queen in *Hamlet*, Spider in *The Spider's Banquet* and Prostitute in *Miracle in the Gorbals*. For Sadler's Wells Theatre Ballet she choreographed *Bailemos* and *Khadra* (1947); *Dance of Salome* and *Eve of St. Agnes* for the BBC (1948–9). In 1948 she became ballet mistress and leading dancer with the new Metropolitan Ballet. As artistic director of the National Ballet of Canada (1951), she developed the new company and the National Ballet School. She has choreographed *Dance of Salome* and *L'Après-midi d'un Faun* and has staged *Les Sylphides, Giselle, Swan Lake, The Nutcracker, Polovetsian Dances from Prince Igor, Princess Aurora* and *Coppélia* for the company. She also created the ballerina role in *Offenbach in the Underworld*, and later returned as Lady Capulet in Cranko's *Romeo and Juliet* (1964).

FRANCESCA DA RIMINI, a ballet in one act based on the love story of Paolo and Francesca. Libretto, **David Lichine** and Henry Clifford; choreography, **David Lichine**; music, Tchaikovsky; decor, Oliver Messel. First performed in the Royal Opera House, Covent Garden, London, 15 July 1937, by **Colonel de Basil's Ballet Russe de Monte Carlo.** Principal dancers, **Lubov Tchernicheva** (Francesca), Peter Petrov (Paolo), Marc Platov (Malatesta), **Alexandra Danilova** (Vision of Guinevere), Roman Jasinski (Lancelot). Staged in the Metropolitan Opera House, New York, 24 October 1937. A previous version had been performed to Tchaikovsky's music at the Maryinsky Theatre, St. Petersburg in 1915. Choreography, **Michel Fokine.** The Tchaikovsky music was used for **William Dollar's** version which he staged for Le Théâtre d'Art du Ballet in 1961. Still another version was staged in Moscow in 1947. Choreography, Nicolai Kholfin; music, Boris Asafiev. The ballet follows the story closely.

FRANKIE AND JOHNNY, a ballet in one act based on the famous American ballad of the same name. Libretto, Michael Blandford; choreography, **Ruth Page** and **Bentley Stone**; music, Jerome Moross; decor, Paul Dupont. First performed in the Great Northern Theatre. Chicago, 19 June 1938, by Page-Stone Ballet. Principal dancers, Ruth Page, Bentley Stone. Revived in New York City Center, 28 February 1945 for **Ballet Russe de Monte Carlo** with the same principal dancers, and again in the Théâtre des Champs-Elysées, 1958. The story is of murder by a jealous lover.

FRANKLIN, Frederic (1914–), British dancer, teacher and choreographer. Among his teachers were **Legat** and **Egorova.** He made his professional debut in 1931 and danced with Markova-Dolin Company (1935–7); he was soloist with Massine's **Ballet Russe de Monte Carlo** (1938) and later became premier danseur and ballet master (1944). He created Baron in *Gaieté Parisienne*, Spirit of Creation in *Seventh Symphony*, Young Lover in *The Devil's Holiday* and Second Movement in *Rouge et Noir*, during the company's first two seasons. Later he also danced the leading roles in *Giselle, Swan Lake, Coppélia*, Favourite Slave in *Schéhérazade*, Gypsy Youth in *Capriccio Español*, Poet in *Night Shadow*, and created Champion Roper in *Rodeo* and the title role in *Billy Sunday*. He was renowned for his partnering of **Danilova, Markova, Slavenska, Toumanova, Baronova, Chauviré** and others. He rejoined Ballet Russe de Monte Carlo in 1954, and was director of the performing group of Washington School of Ballet (1956–60), choreographing *Étalage* and *Homage au Ballet*. During the 1961–2 seasons he staged several ballets for **Teatro alla Scala**, Milan; was artistic director to American Ballet Theatre; and choreographed *Tribute* for Ballet Russe de Monte Carlo. He was appointed director of the newly-formed National Ballet, Washington (DC), and its school (1962).

FRIS, Maria (1932–61), German prima

ballerina. She studied with **Gsovsky** and **Peretti**, dancing her first principal role, Dulcinea in *Don Quixote*, at the Berlin State Opera (1949). She danced with Weisbaden State Opera (1951–2), Ballets de France de Janine Charrat (1952–4), Municipal Opera, Frankfurt (1958–9), and toured Spain with Béjart's company (1960). She committed suicide in 1961. During her short career she danced mainly the classical repertoire.

FUGITIVE, THE, a ballet in one act. Libretto and decor, Hugh Stevenson; choreography, **Andrée Howard**. First performed in the Royal County Theatre, Bedford, 16 November 1944, by Ballet Rambert. Principal dancers, Sally Gilmour, **Walter Gore,** Joan McClelland.

FUOCO, Sofia (Maria Brambilla, 1830–1916), Italian ballerina. A pupil of **Carlo Blasis,** she made her debut at **Teatro alla Scala,** Milan (1839), and became ballerina in 1843. She created *Gisella, ossia la Willi* at its première and danced in *Pas de Quatre* with **Taglioni, Rosati** and Vente. Her Paris debut was in *Betty, ou la Jeunesse de Henry V* (1846) at Théâtre de **l'Academie Royale de Musique,** and she later danced in London, Madrid and other European cities. Her repertoire included *Il Prestigiatori* (1852), *Zuleika* (1852), *Catarina* (1853), *La Nozze di Ninetta et Nane* (1854). A very strong dancer on pointe, her nickname at the Paris Opéra was 'La Pointue'. She seemed set to rival **Elssler** and Taglioni, but faded from the public eye at the age of 28.

G

GABLE, Christopher (1940–), British dancer. A student at the Royal Ballet School, he danced with Covent Garden Opera Ballet (1956), and became premier danseur with **The Royal Ballet** where he created The Cousin in *The Invitation*, The Young Man in *The Two Pigeons* and two roles in *Images of Love*. He also danced the leading roles in *Swan Lake, Coppélia, La Bayadère* and **Cranko**'s *Card Game*. He went into films after his retirement as a dancer.

GABOVICH, Mikhail (1905–65), Russian dancer and writer, Peoples' Artist of the RSFSR. He studied at the Bolshoi school under **Alexander Gorsky**, graduating in 1924. He became one of the leading dancers of the Bolshoi company. Among his roles are Prince in *The Sleeping Beauty* and Solor in *La Bayadère*. He created Vladimir in *Prisoner of the Caucasus* (1938) and Andrei in *Taras Bulba* (1941). He was artistic director of the Moscow Ballet School (1954–8).

GAIETÉ PARISIENNE, LA, a comedy ballet in one act. Libretto, Etienne de Beaumont; choreography, **Léonide Massine**; music Jacques Offenbach (arranged by Manuel Rosenthal); decor, Etienne de Beaumont. First performed in the Théâtre de Monte Carlo, 5 April 1938, by **Ballet Russe de Monte Carlo.** Principal dancers, Nina Tarakanova, **Alexandra Danilova** (Glove-Seller), Eugenia Delarova (Flower Girl), Jeanette Lauret (La Lionne), Lubov Roudenko (Can-Can Dancer), Léonide Massine (Peruvian), **Frederic Franklin** (Baron), **Igor Youskevitch** (Officer). In the gay sparkling atmosphere of a boulevard café, the

La Gaieté Parisienne. Ph. Lido.

conceited Peruvian struts before the assembled dandies, the sophisticated Glove-Seller and the simple Flower Girl.

GALA PERFORMANCE, a comedy ballet in one act. Libretto and choreography, **Antony Tudor**; music, Serge Prokofiev; decor, Hugh Stevenson. First performed in the Toynbee Hall, London, 5 December 1938, by **London Ballet.** Principal dancers, **Peggy van Praagh, Maude Lloyd, Gerd Larsen,** Antony Tudor, **Hugh Laing.** Presented in the Arts Theatre, London, 28 June 1940 by Ballet Rambert. Principal dancers, Sally Gilmour, **Lucette Aldous,** Joan McClelland, Gillian Martlew. Presented in the Majestic Theatre, New York, 11 February 1941, by **Ballet Theatre.** Decor, Nicholas de Molas. Principal dancers, **Nora Kaye, Nana Gollner, Karen Conrad.** Antony Tudor also staged the ballet for Royal Swedish Ballet with Mariane Orlando and Bjørn Holmgren. It shows the antics of three ballerinas representing Russia, France and Italy as they compete for the applause of the audience.

GALEOTTI, Vincenzo Tomaselli (1733–1816), Italian dancer, choreographer and teacher. He studied under **Angiolini** and **Noverre,** and made his debut in Venice. He danced at the King's Theatre, London (1769–70), was ballet master at the San Moise Theatre, Venice (1770–5) and became director of the Royal Danish Ballet in 1775. Among his works were *Dido* (1777), *Les Caprices du Cupidon et du Maître de Ballet* (1786) and *Romeo and Juliet* (1811).

GARDEL, Maximilien (1741–87), French dancer and choreographer. A contemporary of **Gaetan Vestris, Dauberval** and **Noverre** at **l'Academie Royale de Musique,** he was premier danseur and choreographer at the **Paris Opéra Ballet** (1781–7). Creation of the **rond de jambe** is attributed both to Gardel and **Auguste Vestris.** His ballets for the Opéra included *Ninette à la Cour* (1778), *Le Déserteur* (1784) and *Le Coq du Village* (1787).

GARDEL, Pierre (1758–1840), French dancer and choreographer, brother of **Maximilien Gardel.** He was premier danseur at the **Paris Opéra Ballet** (1780), and chief ballet master and choreographer (1787–1827) and director of its ballet school (1799–1815). Among the works he choreographed were *Télémaque dans l'Ile de Calypso* (1791), *Psyche* (1790), *Le Jugement de Paris* and *Paul et Virginie.* His pupil, **Carlo Blasis,** acknowledged his debt to Gardel in his treatise on the dance.

gargouillade, a paddling step; during a pas de chat, the dancer introduces a **rond de jambe** en l'air with each leg.

GASKELL, Sonia (1904–   ), Dutch teacher and ballet mistress, born in Russia. She taught in Paris before moving to Holland in 1939. She formed her own group, Ballet Recital, after World War II. As director of Het Nederlands Ballet, she founded (1958) Holland's first Academy of Ballet. She became artistic director of Het Nationaal Ballet, Amsterdam.

GAVRILOV, Assen Petrov (1926–   ), Bulgarian dancer, Honoured Artist. He studied in Sofia under Anastas Petrov. In 1948 he joined Sofia National Opera as soloist. His repertoire includes the principal roles in *Swan Lake* and *The Red Poppy.* He has made many guest appearances outside Bulgaria. For a time he was director of ballet at the Sofia National Opera.

GAYANÉ, a ballet in four acts. Libretto, Konstantin Derzhavin; choreography, **Nina Anisimova**; music, Aram Khachaturian. First performed in the Opera House, Perm, 9 December 1942, by Kirov Ballet. Anisimova staged a new version at the Kirov Theatre, Leningrad, 20 February 1945. Principal dancers, Nina Anisimova, **Natalia Dudinskaya, Feya Balabina,** Nikolai Zubkovsky, **Konstantin Sergeyev.** The fourth act was revived for the Bolshoi Ballet, 19 November 1961. The theme is life on a collective farm in all its

Yekaterina Geltzer in La Bayadère. Ph. Bakhruchine, Moscow.

diversity, and the choreography employs folk dances of the region, including the Sabre Dance.

GELTZER, Yekaterina or **Catherine** (1876–1962), Russian ballerina, Peoples' Artist of the RSFSR. She studied and danced at the Bolshoi Theatre, Moscow and in 1896 went to the Imperial School to study under **Johansson** and **Petipa.** Here she was guest prima ballerina (1909–11), before returning to the Bolshoi. She danced an extensive repertoire and is best remembered in her role in *La Bayadère* and as Tao-Hoa in *The Red Poppy*.

GENÉE, Adeline (Anina Jensen, 1878–1970), Danish ballerina, Dame of the Order of the British Empire. She made her debut in 1888 and was première danseuse at the Stadttheater, Stettin (1893), the Imperial Theatre, Berlin (1895), Munich Opera (1896) and as guest at the Empire Theatre, London (1897–1907). She danced in *Les Papillons, Cinderella, Fête Galante* and *Coppélia* (the role for which she is especially remembered). She spent five seasons in the United States dancing in *Coppélia* at the Metropolitan Opera House, New York, and later visited Australia and New Zealand. She retired from dancing in 1917, but in 1932 and 1933 appeared in *The Love Song*, partnered by **Anton Dolin.** In 1920 she was elected first president of the Association of Operatic Dancing, London, which, in 1935, became the Royal Academy of Dancing and was a founder member (1930–3) of **The Camargo Society.**

GEORGI, Yvonne (1903–   ), German dancer, choreographer and ballet mistress. She was trained at the Dalcroze School, Hellerau, and studied with **Wigman** and **Gsovsky,** making her debut in 1923. She danced in recitals and concerts throughout Europe, the United States and Canada until 1939, often partnered by **Harald Kreutzberg.** She was ballet mistress and choreographer at Gera Opera, Germany (1925–6), Hanover Opera (1926–31), Amsterdam Opera (1932–4) where she founded a school, and Dusseldorf Opera (1951–4). In 1954 she returned to the Hanover Opera as ballet mistress and choreographer. She has also been guest choreographer at Berlin State Opera (1932), Vienna State Opera (1959), and at the Salzburg Festival (1959). During her career she staged most of the classic and romantic repertoire and choreographed *Orpheus and Eurydice, Electronic Ballet, Pulcinella, Symphonie Fantastique, Moor of Venice, Legend of Joseph, Petrouchka, Le Sacre du Printemps, Orpheus, Apollon Musagète, Agon, Firebird* and a number of others.

GERDT, Paul (1844–1917), Russian dancer and teacher. A student and dancer at the Imperial School, St. Petersburg, he made his debut in 1860 and became premier danseur in 1866. He continued to dance until 1916. He created the leading roles in *Kalkabrino, Cinderella, Halte de Cavalerie, The Sleeping Princess* and *The Nutcracker*, and was renowned as a partner to all the great ballerinas of the day. He taught at the Imperial School where his senior class included **Karsavina, Nijinsky** and **Fokine**, and was noted as a teacher of mime.

GEVA, Tamara (Tamara Gevergeyera, 1908–), Russian choreographer, dancer and actress. She studied at the Maryinsky Theatre School, left Russia in 1924 to work in Germany and England with the then comparatively unknown **George Balanchine** and **Alexandra Danilova.** The group was seen by **Diaghilev** and invited to join his Ballets Russes. After two years, Geva went to America, where, apart from one guest appearance with American Ballet in 1935, she concentrated on musicals, plays and films.

GIFT OF THE MAGI, a ballet in six scenes, based on a Christmas story by O. Henry. Libretto and choreography, **Simon Semenov**; music, Luke Foss; decor, Raoul Pène du Bois. First performed in the Metropolitan Opera House, New York, 15 October 1945, by **Ballet Theatre**. Principal dancers, **Nora Kaye, John Kriza**. Revived for London's **Festival Ballet**. Principal dancers, Melinda Plank, **John Gilpin**. The hero sells his watch to buy a comb for his wife's beautiful hair; ironically she has sold her hair to buy a chain for his watch.

GILPIN, John (1930–), British dancer and director. He studied at the Ripman school and with Ballet Rambert, where he became a principal dancer. He created Rabbit-Catcher in *The Sailor's Return* and danced the Blue Bird pas de deux, Peasant pas de deux, *Swan Lake* pas de trois and *Le Spectre de la Rose*. In 1949 he created the leading male role in *Le Rêve de Léonor* for **Les Ballets de Paris de Roland**

Petit. In 1950 he became principal dancer with London's **Festival Ballet,** its assistant artistic director (1959–62) and artistic director (1962–5). His large repertoire included *The Nutcracker, Giselle, Coppélia* and *Swan Lake*, and he has created the title role in *The Witch Boy*, male lead in *Études*, 2nd movement in *Bourée Fantasque* and the title role in *Peer Gynt*. He was guest artist with **The Royal Ballet** (1961, 1963) and American Ballet Theatre (1965). He is a holder of the Adeline Genée Gold Medal (1943) and the Nijinsky Prize (1959). In 1964 he was awarded the Étoile d'Or at the International Festival of Dance in Paris. He returned to dance at the 21st Birthday Gala Performance of Festival Ballet in 1971.

GISELLE, OU LES WILIS, a romantic ballet in two acts, based on a passage in Heine's *Lettres de l'Allemagne*. Libretto, Théophile Gautier, **Jean Coralli** and Vernoy de Saint-Georges; choreography, Jean Coralli and **Jules Perrot**; music, Adolphe Adam; decor and costumes, Pierre Ciceri. First performed at the Théâtre de l'**Academie Royale de Musique,** Paris, 28 June 1841, by the **Paris Opéra Ballet**. Principal dancers, **Carlotta Grisi, Lucien Petipa,** Adèle Dumilâtre. In Britain, the first performance was in 1842 with Grisi as Giselle. **Serge Diaghilev** brought his successful Ballets Russes production to London in 1911. Principal dancers, **Tamara Karsavina** and **Vaslav Nijinsky. Anna Pavlova** danced the title role in her own company's presentation in 1913. The **Camargo Society** presented at the Savoy Theatre, London, June 1932. Principal dancers, **Olga Spessivtzeva** (Giselle), **Anton Dolin** (Albrecht), **Frederick Ashton** (Hilarion), **Ninette de Valois** (Berthe). Vic-Wells staged the first all-British cast in *Giselle*, 1 January 1934, with **Alicia Markova** and Anton Dolin, in a version with choreography by **Nicholas Sergeyev. Margot Fonteyn** took over from Markova and the ballet has been in the repertoire ever since. In 1960 **The Royal Ballet** staged a version with revisions to the choreography by **Frederick**

Ashton. In France, Serge Diaghilev presented his Ballets Russes production in 1910. Principal dancers, Tamara Karsavina, Vaslav Nijinsky. Olga Spessivtzeva danced Giselle at her debut in Paris in 1924 and again in 1932 at the Paris Opéra with **Serge Lifar** as Albrecht. Lifar choreographed this version for the Opéra and it is still in use. In Russia, Antoine Titus brought a shortened version to St. Petersburg in 1842 with **Elena Andreyanova** as the heroine. Another version with some choreography by Jules Perrot was staged in 1848 with **Fanny Elssler.** In 1850 Carlotta Grisi appeared in the role in St. Petersburg. A version considerably altered by Lucien Petipa appeared in 1887 for the debut of Emma Bessonet. In the United States the first performance was on 2 January 1846, when **Mary Ann Lee** danced the title role in Boston. Anna Pavlova and **Mikhail Mordkin** danced Giselle and Albrecht in New York in 1910, and in 1937 the Mordkin Ballet presented the ballet in the Majestic Theatre, New York. Principal dancer, **Lucia Chase.** An interesting new version was first presented by the Royal Swedish Ballet in 1953, with choreography by Mary Skeaping.

Ballet dancers have always regarded *Giselle* as a touchstone of their art. All the major roles are very demanding both of dancing technique and dramatic ability. Giselle, for example, must change from the down-to-earth peasant girl who goes mad and dies on discovering the duplicity of her lover, into the unearthly wili dancing as if floating on air. Yet she must show that she retains her human love for Albrecht sufficiently strongly to defy the command to kill him. The roles of Albrecht and Hilarion also make demands on the interpretative ability of the dancers. The actual story is simple : Giselle loves Loys, who is, she thinks, a peasant like herself. He is in fact Albrecht, scion of the ruling family and engaged to a noblewoman, Bathilde. The gamekeeper, Hilarion, also in love with Giselle, unmasks Albrecht whereupon Giselle goes mad and dies. She becomes

Giselle: Jacqueline Rayet and Peter van Dijk. Ph. P.I.C.

one of the wilis, spirits of girls who die before their wedding, doomed to rise from their graves nightly to lure men to their death. The Queen commands Giselle so to lure Albrecht, but she dances with him until dawn when he gently carries her back to her grave.

GITANA, LA, a ballet in prologue and three acts. Libretto and choreography, **Filippo Taglioni**; music, Schmidt and Auber. First performed, 23 November 1838, at the Bolshoi Theatre, St. Petersburg. Principal dancers, **Maria Taglioni,** Nicholas Goltz. Staged, at Her Majesty's Theatre, London, 6 June 1839, again with Maria Taglioni. The heroine is stolen by gypsies and falls in love with a nobleman who rejects her until her true identity is discovered.

glissade, a glide along the floor, used as a connecting step. Also a step executed in preparation for travelling or jumping.

GODS GO A'BEGGING, THE or **Les Dieux Mendiants,** a ballet in one act. Libretto, **Boris Kochno**; choreography, **George Balanchine**; music, George Frederick Handel (arranged by Sir Thomas Beecham); decor, **Léon Bakst**; costumes, Juan Gris. First performed in His Majesty's Theatre, London, 16 July 1928, by **Diaghilev**'s Ballets Russes. Principal dancers, **Alexandra Danilova, Léon Woizikowsky.** A new version with choreography by **Ninette de Valois** and decor by Hugh Stevenson was staged at Sadler's Wells Theatre, London, 21 February 1936, by Sadler's Wells Ballet. Principal dancers, Elizabeth Miller, William Chappell. In 1937 **David Lichine** re-choreographed the ballet for **Colonel de Basil's Ballet Russe de Monte Carlo** with decor adapted from the Bakst original by Juan Gris. The story tells of the shepherd who gate-crashes an aristocratic picnic and is ridiculed by the guests for his wooing of the serving maid. The ridicule is effectively silenced, and the noblemen amazed when the young couple reveal their identity as gods.

GOLDEN AGE, THE, a ballet in three acts. Libretto, Ivanovsky; choreography, E. I. Kaplan and Vassily Vainonen; music Shostakovitch; decor and costumes, Khodasevich. First performed, 26 October 1930, at the Bolshoi Theatre, Moscow. Principal dancer, **Galina Ulanova** (Young Communist). The work is romantic, although inspired by the Russian Revolution.

GOLDEN COCKEREL, THE *see* **Coq d'Or, Le.**

GOLEIZOVSKY, Kasyan (1892–1970), Russian dancer and choreographer, Honoured Art Worker of the Lithuanian SSR. He studied in Moscow and St. Petersburg, joined the Maryinsky Theatre Company in 1909 and moved to the Bolshoi Ballet in 1910. He was influenced by **Michel Fokine** and **Alexander Gorsky.** As choreographer at the Bolshoi, he staged *Joseph the Handsome* (1924), *Theolinda*, versions of *Prince Igor* (1933) and *The Fountain of Bakhchisarai* (1939). He later took a teaching post at the Bolshoi School.

GOLLNER, Nana (1920–   ), American ballerina and teacher. She studied with Koslov and made her debut in *A Midsummer Night's Dream*. She was a soloist (1935–7) with American Ballet and Colonel de Basil's **Ballet Russe de Monte Carlo**; ballerina with **René Blum**'s Ballet Russe de Monte Carlo and **Ballet Theatre**; and prima ballerina (1941–3) with Original Ballet Russe. In 1947 she was guest ballerina with **International Ballet.** She danced leading roles in *Swan Lake, Giselle, Helen of Troy, Gala Performance* and *Undertow*, in which she created the role of Medusa.

GOLOVINE, Serge (1924–   ), French dancer. He studied with **Sedova** and was noticed by Ricaux. He danced with Monte Carlo Opera Ballet during the 1940s. A member of the corps de ballet of the **Paris Opéra Ballet** (1947), he left to become soloist with **Grand Ballet du Marquis**

Serge Golovine: with Nina Vyroubova. Ph. Lipnitzki.

de Cuevas (1950). His repertoire included *Spectre de la Rose*, *Les Sylphides*, *Piège de Lumière*, Black Swan and Blue Bird pas de deux, *La Sylphide* which he danced with **Markova**, and *Giselle*. When the company dissolved he organized his own group which toured Europe.

GOLOVKINA, Sophia (1915–), Russian dancer and teacher, Peoples' Artist of the RSFSR. She studied at the Bolshoi School under Victor Semyonov and **Feodor Lopukhov**, and later briefly with **Agrippina Vaganova**. She danced Tsar-Maiden in *The Humpbacked Horse*, Tao-Hoa in *The Red Poppy* and Swanilda in *Coppélia*. In 1961 she became principal of the Bolshoi Theatre School.

GOOD-HUMOURED LADIES, THE or **Les Femmes de Bonne Humeur**, a ballet in one act, based on a comedy by Carlo Goldoni. Choreography, **Léonide Massine**; music, Domenico Scarlatti (arranged by Vincenzo Tommasini); decor, **Léon Bakst**. First performed, in the Teatro

Constanza, Rome, 12 April 1917, by **Diaghilev**'s Ballets Russes. Principal dancers, Giuseppina Cecchetti (Marquise Silvestra), **Lydia Lopokova** (Mariuccia), **Lubov Tchernicheva** (Constanza), **Enrico Cecchetti** (Marquis de Luca), **Stanislas Idzikowsky** (Battista), Léonide Massine (Leonardo), Sigmund Novak (Count Rinaldo), **Léon Woizikowsky** (Niccolo). Revived for **Colonel de Basil's** Ballets Russes de Monte Carlo with **Alexandra Danilova** as Mariuccia and for **Grand Ballet du Marquis de Cuevas** with **Rosella Hightower**. Presented by Léonide Massine at the Royal Opera House, Covent Garden, London, 11 July 1962, for **The Royal Ballet**. Principal dancers, **Antoinette Sibley, Lydia Sokolova, Ronald Hynd,** Brian Shaw, Alexander Grant, **Stanley Holden**. The action is set in 18th century Venice. The ladies amuse themselves with disguises, intrigues and practical jokes.

GORE, Walter (1910–), British dancer and choreographer. A student at the Italia

Conti School, he danced with **Massine** in London, Ballet Rambert (1930–5), and Vic-Wells Ballet (1936), where he created Rake in *The Rake's Progress* and danced the Rambert repertoire. He was leading dancer and choreographer with Ballet Rambert (1939–41), his first ballet being *Paris Soir* (1939) followed by *Confessional* (1941), *Mr. Punch* (1946), *Plaisance* (1947), *Antonia* (1948) and *Variations* (1949) based on a work by Benjamin Britten; as guest artist he choreographed *La Damnée* for **Les Ballets des Champs-Elysées** (1952); *Carte Blanche* for Sadler's Wells Theatre Ballet (1953); his interpretation of *The Nutcracker* for Ballet Der Lage Landen, Holland (1956); *Eater of Darkness* for Frankfurt State Opera Ballet, where he was ballet master and chief choreographer (1957–9); *Night and Silence* for the Edinburgh International Festival (1958); *Sweet Dancer* for Ballet Rambert (1964); and *Street Games* for **Harkness Ballet** (1966). He toured Australia (1955–6) and in 1961 formed **London Ballet**. In 1965 he became ballet master with a company in Lisbon.

GORHAM, Kathleen, Australian dancer. She studied with Lorraine Norton and Leon Kellaway before joining Borovansky Ballet. After dancing with Ballet Rambert (1948), she continued her studies at the Sadler's Wells School (1949) and danced with its Theatre Ballet (1951–2). She was a soloist with **Grand Ballet du Marquis de Cuevas** (1953) returning to Borovansky Ballet (1954–9) as leading dancer. She then danced with various European companies before returning (1962) to the Australian Ballet as ballerina. Her repertoire included *Swan Lake* and *Coppélia*.

GORSKY, Alexander (1871–1924), Russian dancer and choreographer. A pupil at the Imperial School, St. Petersburg, he studied under Platon Karsavin and **Marius Petipa,** graduating in 1889, becoming soloist in 1895 and premier danseur in 1900. He taught at the Imperial School under **Paul Gerdt** (1896–1900) and in 1898 was sent to Moscow to stage

Sleeping Beauty. In 1900 he became régisseur at the Moscow Bolshoi Theatre. His first work as an independent choreographer was the restaging of *Don Quixote,* followed by *The Magic Mirror, La Fille du Pharaon* (both 1905), *Raymonda* (1908), *Salammbo* (1910), *Swan Lake, The Humpbacked Horse, Giselle* (all 1911), and as ballet master of the Bolshoi, *Le Corsaire, Notre Dame de Paris* (both 1912), *Eunice and Petronius* (1915), *La Bayadère* (1916), *Stenka Razin* (1918) and *The Nutcracker* (1919). For the coronation of George V (1911), Gorsky choreographed *The Dance Dream* at London's Alhambra Theatre. His last ballet was *The Grotto of Venus,* presented in the Bolshoi's 1923–4 season. During his career he sought to free the ballet from its stifling conventions and restore its dramatic and human appeal; to this end he unified the relationship between corps de ballet and principal dancers, thus sustaining continuous dramatic action. Much of his work is still in the Soviet repertoire.

GOVRIN, Gloria (1942–   ), American dancer. She studied at the American Ballet Academy and the School of American Ballet (1952) and became a full member of **The New York City Ballet** two years later and a soloist in 1961. Her first solo part was as Scotch Girl in *The Figure in the Carpet.* Her repertoire includes *Western Symphony, Symphony in C, The Cage, The Prodigal Son, Stars and Stripes.* She created Hippolyta in *A Midsummer Night's Dream* (1962), a leading role in *Clarinade* (1964), Danse Arabe in *The Nutcracker,* La Bonne Fée in *Harlequinade* (both 1965), and Rigaudon Flamenco and Night Spirit in *Don Quixote.*

GRADUATION BALL, THE, a ballet in one act. Libretto and choreography, **David Lichine**; music, Johann Strauss (arranged by Antal Dorati); decor, **Alexandre Benois.** First performed, in the Theatre Royal, Sydney, 28 February 1940, by **Ballet Russe de Monte Carlo.** Principal dancers, **Tatiana Riabouchinska,** David Lichine. Presented in the Fifty-First Street

Theatre, New York, 6 November 1940, with the same principals, and revived at the Metropolitan Opera House, New York, 8 October 1944, by **Ballet Theatre**, with new decor by Mstislav Doboujinsky. The Royal Danish Ballet took it into their repertoire in 1952 with **Inge Sand** and **Fredbjørn Bjørnsson** in the principal roles.

GRAEME, Joyce (Joyce Platts, 1918–), English dancer and teacher. She was a student and dancer with Vic-Wells Ballet (1936–8), soloist with **International Ballet** (1941–3) and leading soloist with Ballet Rambert (1945–8). She was director, choreographer and ballerina with Australian National Ballet (1948–51) and guest artist with London's **Festival Ballet** (1952). She taught at **Teatro alla Scala**, Milan (1955–62) and was ballet mistress at Scapina Ballet, Holland (1963–4). Her demi-caractère roles included *Giselle, La Sylphide* and *Graduation Ball*.

GRAHAM, Martha (1893–), American modern dancer and choreographer. She studied with **Ruth St. Denis** and **Ted Shawn** and danced with the Denishawn company (1916–23), making her debut in *Xochitl*. In 1925 she became a teacher at the Eastman School of Music, New York and it was there that she began to experiment with new forms of dance. With her own company she staged many new works including *Letter to the World, Punch and the Judy* (1941), *Appalachian Spring* (1944), *Errand into the Maze* (1947), *Alcestis* and *Phaedra*. Later works include *Legend of Judith, Secular Games, The Witch of Endor, Acrobats of God, Diversion of Angels*, the erotic *Part Dream, Part Real, Dancing Ground* and *Cortège of Angels*. Martha Graham's aim is to explore, in her ballets, the universal and timeless passions of men and women. She did not confine herself or her dancers within a set technique but led them in experimentation. She is regarded as the greatest exponent of the American modern dance and has been the recipient of many honours and awards.

GRAHN, Lucile (1819–1907), Danish ballerina. An international star, she is remembered for her romantic roles and classical technique. She studied at the Royal Danish Ballet School and made her debut in *Jocko, the Brazilian Ape* (1829). *Waldemar* (1835) and *La Sylphide* (1836) were created for her by Bournonville. As guest artist she danced *La Sylphide* at the **Paris Opéra Ballet**, *L'Ombre* and *Giselle* in St. Petersburg, *Pas de Quatre* with **Taglioni, Grisi** and **Cerito** in London, and throughout Germany and Austria where her repertoire included *Eoline, Catarina* and *Esmeralda*. She retired as a dancer in 1856 and taught at the Leipzig State Theatre (1858–61), and at the Munich Hofoper (1869–75). One of her most successful choreographic works was *Bacchanale* for Wagner's *Tannhäuser*.

Grand Ballet de Monte Carlo *see* **Nouveau Ballet de Monte Carlo.**

Grand Ballet du Marquis de Cuevas, a ballet company directed by the **Marquis George de Cuevas,** formed in 1950 from the **Ballet International,** and the Grand Ballet de Monte Carlo (formerly **Nouveau Ballet de Monte Carlo**). Its most notable productions included *Night Shadow* (**Balanchine**), *Idylle* (**Skibine**), and *Piège de Lumière* (**John Taras**). Among its dancers were **Rosella Hightower, Marjorie Tallchief, Jacqueline Moreau, Nina Vyroubova,** George Skibine, **Vladimir Skouratov, Serge Golovine** and **Nicholas Polajenko.** Many leading dancers appeared as guest artists. In 1958 the name changed to the Ballet International du Marquis de Cuevas (called Ballet International). The Marquis's final success was *The Sleeping Beauty*, staged by **Bronislava Nijinska** and **Robert Helpmann** in Paris (1960). After his death in 1961, his widow ran the company (Ballet International de la Marquese de Cuevas) until it split up in 1962.

Grands Ballets Canadiens, Les *see* **Canada, history of ballet in.**

GREEN TABLE, THE, a ballet in eight scenes. Libretto and choreography, **Kurt Jooss**; music, Frederick Cohen; decor, Hein Heckroth. First performed at the Théâtre des Champs-Elysées, Paris, 3 July 1932, by Ballet Jooss. Principal dancers, Kurt Jooss, Ernst Uthov, Liza Czobel. Revived by the Joffrey Ballet in 1967. The ballet is a political satire inspired by World War I. The green table is that round which politicians sit to decide the fate of men. With this ballet Jooss took first prize in a competition organized by Les Archives Internationales de la Danse, and it is probably his most successful work.

GREY, Beryl (Beryl Groom, 1927–), British ballerina. She studied under **Sergeyev, de Valois** and **Volkova** at Sadler's Wells Ballet School, entering the company in 1941. A soloist at fifteen, she danced the Lady in *Comus* and leading roles in classical ballets such as *Les Sylphides* and Odette-Odile in *Swan Lake*. In 1944 she added *Giselle* to her repertoire, and *Sleeping Beauty* in 1946. She created roles in *The Quest, Promenade, Ballet Impérial, Les Sirènes, Checkmate* and *Donald of the Burthens*. She has been a regular guest artist with the Royal Swedish Ballet. She left Sadler's Wells in 1957, and toured abroad making guest appearances with companies throughout the world. She recorded her experiences as guest artist in Russia in *Red Curtain Up* (1958), and in China in *Through the Bamboo Curtain* (1966). She was appointed artistic director of London's **Festival Ballet** in 1968, and in 1972 produced *Swan Lake* for the company.

GRIGORIEV, Serge (1883–), Russian dancer and régisseur. After dancing at the Maryinsky Theatre, St. Petersburg, he assisted in the organization of **Diaghilev's** Ballets Russes (1909), and became assistant director. He was notable as Shah Shariar in *Schéhérazade* and Russian Merchant in *Boutique Fantasque*. After the company disbanded, he joined **Colonel de Basil's Ballet Russe de Monte Carlo** as régisseur-general, remaining until 1952.

With his wife, **Lubov Tchernicheva,** he staged a revival of **Fokine's** *The Firebird* for Sadler's Wells Ballet (1954); and together they staged *Petrouchka* (1957) and *Les Sylphides*. His book, *The Diaghilev Ballet 1909–29*, is invaluable to enthusiasts.

GRIGOROVICH, Yuri (1927–), Russian dancer and choreographer, Honoured Artist of the RSFSR. He studied in Leningrad and joined the Kirov Ballet in 1946. His choreographic works include *Valse Fantaisie* (1956), a new version of *The Stone Flower* (1957, re-created 1959) and *Legend of Love* (1961). He became chief choreographer of the Bolshoi company (1964), producing new versions of *The Sleeping Beauty, The Nutcracker, Swan Lake* and *Spartacus*.

GRISI, Carlotta (1819–99), Italian ballerina. She studied ballet at the Conservatory of Music in Milan and became a member of the corps de ballet at **Teatro alla Scala** in 1829. In 1833 she met **Jules Perrot** in Naples and together they danced all over Europe. Her Paris debut (1841) was in Donizetti's opera *La Favorita* which she danced with **Lucien Petipa**. Gautier wrote *Giselle* for her and she created the role at the Paris Opéra in 1841. She also created the leading roles in *La Jolie Fille de Gand* (1842), *La Péri* (1843), *Esmeralda* (1844), *Paquita* (1845), and danced *Pas de Quatre* in London with **Taglioni, Grahn** and **Cerito** (1845). She appeared regularly in London between 1842 and 1851, and made her debut in *Giselle* in 1849 at the Imperial Theatre, St. Petersburg. She retired in 1853.

GSOVSKY, Victor (1902–), Russian dancer, choreographer and teacher. He studied in St. Petersburg and was ballet master of the Berlin State Opera (1925–8). He was ballet master of the **Paris Opéra Ballet** (1945), **Les Ballets des Champs-Elysées** (1946–7) and **Metropolitan Ballet,** London (1947–8). He trained many famous dancers, and choreographed mainly classical ballets.

GUEST, Ivor (1920–   ), British writer. Known especially for his studies of 19th century ballet, he has written *The Ballet of the Second Empire 1858–1870* (1953), *The Ballet of the Second Empire 1847–58* (1955) and *The Dancer's Heritage* (1960). In 1970 he became Chairman of the Executive Committee of the Royal Academy of Dancing, London.

GUGLIELMO EBREO (William the Jew of Pesaro), 15th century Italian dancing master, sometimes described as the first choreographer. He taught at courts in northern Italy and produced a treatise in which he laid down the qualities required in a dancer and, in a simple system of dance notation, describes some of the ballets he created. Guglielmo was a pupil of **Domenico da Ferrara** and recorded some of the ideas and theories of the latter.

GUIGNOL ET PANDORE, a ballet in one act. Libretto and choreography, **Serge Lifar**; music, André Jolivet; decor, André Dignimont. First performed at the Théâtre National de l'Opéra, 29 April 1944, by the **Paris Opéra Ballet.** Principal dancers, Susanne Lorcia, Serge Lifar, **Serge Peretti**, Marianne Ivanov. Revived in 1948 with the same principals. The ballet is a lighthearted frolic. Guignol is executed for the murder of his rival and his mother-in-law, however all the characters come to life in the end to start the cycle all over again.

GUIMARD, Marie-Madeleine (1743–1816), French ballerina. In 1758 she became a member of the corps de ballet at the Comédie Française, and was a contemporary of **Marie Allard.** She made her debut at **l'Académie Royale de Musique** in 1762 in *Les Fêtes Grecques et Romaines* becoming première danseuse noble in 1763. She slandered her rivals and led a scandalous life. Dancing many demi-caractère roles, her repertoire included *Castor et Pollux, Jason et Médée, Le Déserteur,* and her best known role in *Les Caprices de Gelatée.* She retired in 1789 but came back as one of the Three Graces in a revival of Rameau's *Talents Lyriques.*

GYPSY, LA, a ballet in three acts. Libretto, Vernoy de Saint-Georges; choreography, **Joseph Mazilier**; music, François Benoist, Ambroise Thomas; decor, Philastre, Cambon. First performed, 28 January 1839, in the Théâtre de l'Académie Royale de Musique, Paris. Principal dancer, **Fanny Elssler.** Elssler again danced the title role at Her Majesty's Theatre, London, 24 June 1839. It was in this ballet that she created the famous Cracovienne (Polish dance).

Marie-Madelaine Guimard. Ph. P.I.C.

B

H

H

HAAKON, Paul (1914–), Danish dancer. He studied at the Royal Danish Ballet and the School of American Ballet, as well as with **Fokine** and **Mordkin**, making his debut in *Harlequinade* (1927) with Fokine Ballet. He continued his studies in Spain, France, and England, and danced with the Anna Pavlova company. He was premier danseur with **The American Ballet** (1935), after which his career was in the popular theatre until 1963, when he became ballet master and instructor to the José Greco Spanish Ballet.

HALL, Fernau, Canadian dancer and writer. He studied various forms of dance and performed with Ballets Nègres and Dance Theatre. He also worked as a director. In 1958 he became ballet critic of *Ballet Today*. His published works include *Modern English Ballet* (1950).

HALLHUBER, Heino (1927–), German dancer. He studied with **Mlaker** and **Gsovsky**, making his debut in 1949 in *Don Juan* at the Munich State Opera and created Laertes in *Hamlet* (1950). His repertoire includes principal roles in the classic and modern ballets.

HALTE DE CAVALERIE, a comedy ballet in one act. Libretto and choreography, **Marius Petipa**; music, Ivan Armsheimer; decor, Levogt; costumes, Ponomarev. First performed at the Maryinsky Theatre, St. Petersburg, 2 February 1896. Principal dancers, **Pierina Legnani, Paul Gerdt.** In ascending order of rank, the officers of a cavalry regiment woo a young girl in a village where they have halted temporarily. She, however, loves a village boy.

HAMILTON, Gordon (1918–59), Australian dancer, ballet master and teacher. He studied with **Preobrajenska** and Rambert, and appeared with Anglo-Polish Ballet and Ballet Rambert. In 1940 he joined Sadler's Wells Ballet as soloist. During his six years with them he danced the character roles in *Coppélia, Sleeping Beauty, The Prospect Before Us,* and created Lepidopterist in *Promenade* and Polonius in *Hamlet.* He became ballet master and principal character dancer with **Les Ballets des Champs-Elysées** in 1946, where his repertoire included leading roles in *La Sylphide, Les Forains* and *Los Caprichos.* He returned to dance with Petit in 1949 in his **Les Ballets de Paris de Roland Petit,** where he created the male role in *La Croqueuse de Diamants.* In 1954 he became ballet master and teacher at the Vienna State Opera for which he staged classical ballets. Died while on holiday in Paris.

HAMLET, a ballet in one scene. Choreography, **Robert Helpmann**; music, Peter Tchaikovsky; decor, Leslie Hurry. First performed at the New Theatre, London, 19 May 1942, by Sadler's Wells Ballet. Principal dancers, Robert Helpmann (Hamlet), **Margot Fonteyn** (Ophelia), **Celia Franca** (Queen), David Paltenghi (King), **Gordon Hamilton** (Polonius), John Hart (Laertes), Leo Kersley (Gravedigger), **Margaret Dale** (Messenger). **Michael Somes** and David Paltenghi also danced Hamlet, and this version was revived in 1964 with **Rudolph Nureyev** in the title role.

HAMLET, a ballet in prologue and three scenes. Libretto, Tatiana Gsovska; choreography, **Victor Gsovsky**; music, Boris Blacher; decor, Helmut Jürgens. First performed, 19 November 1950, in the Bayerische Staatsoper, Munich. Principal dancers, Franz Baur (Hamlet), **Irène Skorik** (Ophelia), **Heino Hallhuber**

(Laertes), Walter Matthes (Polonius). The Berlin Stätdische Oper toured the United States with this version in 1955.

HAMLET, a ballet in three acts. Libretto, Nikolai Volkov; choreography, **Konstantin Sergeyev**; music, Nikolai Chervinsky. First performed at the Kirov Theatre, Leningrad, 12 December 1970, by the Kirov Ballet. Principal dancers, **Mikhail Barishnikov,** Valeri Panov, **Yuri Soloviev,** Sergei Vikulov.

HARANGOZO, Jules (1908–   ), Hungarian dancer, choreographer and teacher. In 1928 he became a soloist with the Budapest Opera company and was appointed choreographer in 1936. His roles included Dr. Coppelius in *Coppélia*. His choreographic works include *Romeo and Juliet*, *The Nutcracker*, *The Miraculous Mandarin*, *Coppélia* and *Schéhérazade*.

HARKARVY, Benjamin (1930–   ), American teacher, dancer and choreographer. He started his career with Brooklyn Lyric Opera, and in 1955 opened his own school in New York. From 1957–8 he was director, choreographer and ballet master of Royal Winnipeg Ballet, and in 1958 he became ballet master of Het Nederlands Ballet in The Hague. From 1959–69 he headed his own company, Het Nederlands Dans Theater, which staged many new works. He subsequently worked for **Harkness Ballet** and the Nederlands National Ballet. See also **Holland, history of ballet in.**

Harkness Ballet, an American company founded in New York in 1964, sponsored by Mrs. Rebekah Harkness. The artistic director and principal choreographer was **George Skibine**; other choreographers included **Alexandra Danilova, Vera Volkova** and Alvin Ailey. **Marjorie Tallchief** was appointed prima ballerina with **Nicholas Polajenko** as guest premier danseur. In 1968 Lawrence Rhodes was appointed artistic director, and in 1969 **Benjamin Harkarvy** became joint direc-

tor. The company's repertoire has included *The Abyss, After Eden, Feast of Ashes, Sarabande* and *Daphnis* and *Chloë*, and **Jerome Robbins'** *New York Export: Opus Jazz* was revived (1969). The Harkness Ballet has toured widely in Europe, North Africa and the United States.

HASKELL, Arnold Lionel (1903–   ), British writer and critic, Commander of the Order of the British Empire, Chevalier of the Légion d'Honneur. In 1930 he was a co-founder of **The Camargo Society** and helped to plan the Vic-Wells (later Sadler's Wells) Ballet School in 1936. He was director of the school (1947–65). He is a governor of **The Royal Ballet**, and vice-president of the Varna Competitions. He was ballet critic of *The Daily Telegraph* (1935–8) and editor (from 1947) of *Ballet Annual*; his many publications include *Ballet* (1938), *The Russian Genius in Ballet* (1963) and *Ballet Russe* (1968).

HAUNTED BALLROOM, THE, a ballet in one act. Libretto and music, Geoffrey Toye; choreography, **Ninette de Valois**; decor, Motley. First performed at Sadler's Wells Theatre, London, 3 May 1933, by Vic-Wells Ballet. Principal dancers, **Alicia Markova** (Alicia), Ursula Moreton (Ursula), **Beatrice Appleyard** (Beatrice), **Robert Helpmann** (Master of Tregennis), Freda Bamford and **Margot Fonteyn** (The Young Master), William Chappell (Player). The ghostly tale about the Masters of Tregennis who must dance until they die in the haunted ballroom.

HAYDÉE, Marcia (Marcia Pereira da Silva), Brazilian dancer. She studied with Yvonne Gamma e Silva, Yuco Lindberg and Vaslav Veltchek, and made her debut in 1953. She won a scholarship for the Sadler's Wells Ballet School (1954–5) and was soloist with **Grand Ballet du Marquis de Cuevas** (1957–61), leaving to become ballerina with the Stuttgart Ballet. She danced an outstanding *Giselle*, and created Juliet in **Cranko**'s *Romeo and Juliet* and danced it as guest artist with

National Ballet of Canada in 1964. Cranko created many ballerina roles for her.

HAYDEN, Melissa (Mildred Herman, 1923–   ), American ballerina, born in Canada. She studied with **Volkov, Vilzak, Balanchine** and **Shollar** and joined **Ballet Theatre** in 1945. Her style of dancing was competent yet lyrical. In 1950 she joined **The New York City Ballet** after a season with Ballet Alicia Alonso. From 1953–5 she danced with American Ballet Theatre but returned to The New York City Ballet. She created Profane Love in *Illuminations*, Clorinda in *The Duel*, Young Girl in *The Still Point*, title role in *Medea* and many others, and her repertoire included *Agon*, *Age of Anxiety* and *Western Symphony*. As guest artist she appeared with **Ruth Page**'s Chicago Opera Ballet, **The Royal Ballet** (1963) and Cullberg Ballet, Stockholm (1967).

HELEN OF TROY, a comedy ballet in three scenes with prologue, taken from the opera *La Belle Hélène* by Offenbach. Libretto, **David Lichine** and Antal Dorati ; choreography, **Michel Fokine** (completed by David Lichine) ; music, Jacques Offenbach (arranged by Antal Dorati) ; decor, Marcel Vertes. First performed in Palacio de Bellas Artes, Mexico City, 10 September 1942. Principal dancers, **Irina Baronova** (Helen), **André Eglevsky** (Paris), **Simon Semenov, Jerome Robbins**, Jean Hunt, Nicholas Orlov, **Sono Osato, Rosella Hightower, Lucia Chase**. It was presented with the same cast, in Detroit, 29 November 1942, and at the Metropolitan Opera House, New York, 3 April 1943, with Vera Zorina in the title role.

HELPMANN, Sir Robert (1909–   ), Australian premier danseur, choreographer and director, Commander of the Order of the British Empire. He studied with **Anna Pavlova**'s company in Australia and danced there from 1926–30. He joined Vic-Wells Ballet in 1933, continued his studies with them and was premier danseur (1934–1950). He partnered **Margot Fonteyn** throughout his career with Vic-Wells (later Sadler's Wells) Ballet. Among the many roles he created were Master of Tregennis in *The Haunted Ballroom*, Red King in *Checkmate*, Bridegroom in *A Wedding Bouquet*, White Skater in *Les Patineurs* and the title roles in *Don Juan* and *Don Quixote*. He danced leading roles in *Coppélia, Swan Lake, Les Sylphides* and *Façade*. Two of his greatest post-war successes were *Hamlet* (1942) and *Miracle in the Gorbals* (1944). He has been guest artist with Sadler's Wells Theatre Ballet and **The Royal Ballet** and toured Australia with them (1958–9). He was director and choreographer of the Royal Opera House, Covent Garden, London (1954, 1956, 1958–9). Helpmann staged *The Sleeping Beauty* with **Nijinska**'s choreography for Ballet International du Marquis de Cuevas, choreographed *Electra* for The Royal Ballet (1963), staged *Swan Lake* with **Frederick Ashton** (1963), choreographed *The Display* and *Yugen* for Australian Ballet (1964–5) and appeared as Narrator in *A Wedding Bouquet* with The Royal Ballet (1965).

HIGHTOWER, Rosella (1920–   ), American ballerina. She studied with Dorothy Perkins and was a member of **Ballet Russe de Monte Carlo** (1938–1941), a soloist and ballerina with **Ballet Theatre** (1941–5), and ballerina with **Massine**'s Ballet Russe Highlights and Original Ballet Russe (1945–6). In 1947 she joined **Nouveau Ballet de Monte Carlo** and was prima ballerina when it became Grand Ballet de Monte Carlo and later **Grand Ballet du Marquis de Cuevas** until it disbanded in 1961, dancing the great classical repertoire and leading roles in **Taras**'s *Piège de Lumière* (1952) and *Ines de Castro*, and creating Aurora in *The Sleeping Beauty* (1960). With this company she toured throughout the world, and continued to make occasional guest appearances after 1961, notably with **Sonia Arova, Erik Bruhn** and **Rudolph Nureyev** in Paris (1962) and with Les Grand Ballets Canadiens (1963). She toured North Africa and South America

Rosella Hightower. Ph. Lipnitzki.

with a group of French dancers in 1964. She choreographed *Henry VIII* for Markova-Dolin Ballet (1949), *Pleasuredrome* for Metropolitan Ballet (1949) and *Salome* (1950) and *Scaramouche* (1951) for Grand Ballet du Marquis de Cuevas. She opened a ballet studio in Cannes and was director of Le Nouveau Ballet de l'Opéra at Marseilles (1970).

HILFERDING VAN WEWEN, Franz (1710–68), Austrian ballet master and dancer. He studied with Blondi at the Paris Opéra School, was ballet master in Vienna and later in Stuttgart, where he was succeeded by **Jean-Georges Noverre,** whose **ballet d'action** was greatly influenced by his teachings. From 1758–65 he was maître de ballet at St. Petersburg, and is credited with introducing the **pirouette** and entrechat-quatre, and with greatly improving the standards of ballet at the court.

HOLDEN, Stanley (Stanley Waller, 1928–), British dancer. A student at the Bush-Davies School, he joined Sadler's Wells in 1944, and transferred to their

Theatre Ballet in 1948. As a leading character dancer he created Agnes, a Witch, in *Selina* and Pierrot in *Harlequin in April*. He taught in South Africa from 1954–1957, then returned to **The Royal Ballet** as soloist. He created Mother Simone in *La Fille Mal Gardée*, Marquis di Luca in *The Good-Humoured Ladies* and the comic Stewart-Powell in *Enigma Variations* (1968). He left The Royal Ballet in 1970.

HOLLAND, history of ballet in.
1922 Gertrud Leistikow arrives in Holland. She establishes schools in Amsterdam, Rotterdam, The Hague and Utrecht.
1934 Yvonne Georgi, as visiting artist with Hanover Opera, lays the foundations of a national ballet.
1936 Yvonne Georgi gives performances with Dutch dancers. Group forms under patronage of the Wagner Association, Amsterdam. Becomes known as Georgi Ballet.
1939 Georgi company visits the United States.
1941 Georgi Ballet becomes Opera Company of the Amsterdam Municipal Opera. Among leading dancers are **Mascha Ter Weeme,** Antony Raedt, Marie-Jeanne van der Veen, Lucas Hoving.
1945 Hans Snoek organizes the Scapino Ballet.
1946 Darja Collin organizes and directs the Opera Ballet Company attached to the re-organized Amsterdam Opera.
1947 A new company, Ballet der Lage Landen, is founded. Mascha Ter Weeme becomes artistic director.
1948 Nettie van der Valk founds Ballet Ensemble, a semi-professional group (dissolved 1951).
1958 Sonia Gaskell becomes director of Het Nederlands Ballet in The Hague. **Benjamin Harkarvy** and Karel Shook are ballet masters with Abdurahman Kumysnikov.
1959 Harkarvy resigns from Het Nederlands Ballet and organizes Het Nederlands Dans Theater. The Opera Ballet Company and Ballet der Lage Landen combine as Amsterdams Ballet, with Mascha Ter Weeme as artistic director.

1961 Amsterdams Ballet and Het Nederlands Ballet combine to form Het Nationaal Ballet, with Sonia Gaskell as artistic director and Mascha Ter Weeme in charge of Opera Ballet department. Het Nederlands Dans Theater moves its headquarters to The Hague. **Hans van Manen** becomes choreographer and artistic director. He stages many new works.

1969 Glen Tetley becomes joint artistic director of Het Nederlands Dans Theater. Het Nationaal Ballet gives a season at the Sadler's Wells Theatre, London. **Rudolph Nureyev** appears as guest artist in *Apollo* and **Rudi van Dantzig**'s *Monument for a Dead Boy*.

1970 Rudi van Dantzig becomes principal choreographer and joint director (with Robert Kaesen) of Het Nationaal Ballet. Hans van Manen resigns from Het Nederlands Dans Theater. **Jaap Flier** becomes joint artistic director. Among the many new ballets are the controversial *Mutations* and *Twice* (1970), *Variations on a Landscape* and *Grosse Flüge* (1971).

HOMAGE TO THE QUEEN, a ballet in one act. Choreography, **Frederick Ashton**; music, Malcolm Arnold; decor, Oliver Messel. First performed at the Royal Opera House, Covent Garden, London, 2 June 1953, by **The Royal Ballet**, to celebrate the coronation of Queen Elizabeth II. Principal dancers, **Margot Fonteyn** and **Michael Somes** (Air), **Nadia Nerina** and **Alexis Rassine** (Earth), **Beryl Grey** and **John Field** (Fire), **Violetta Elvin** and John Hart (Water). The theme is the homage paid to the Queen by the Four Elements.

HOROSCOPE, a ballet in one act. Choreography, **Frederick Ashton**; music, Constant Lambert; decor, Sophie Fedorovich. First performed at Sadler's Wells Theatre, London, 27 January 1938, by Sadler's Wells Ballet. Principal dancers, **Michael Somes, Margot Fonteyn, Pamela May,** Richard Ellis, **Alan Carter.** Lovers born under antagonistic signs of the Zodiac are brought together by the Moon with the help of the Gemini.

HOUSE OF BIRDS, THE, a ballet in one act based on the Grimm fairy tale, *Jorinda and Joringel.* Choreography, **Kenneth MacMillan**; music, Federico Mompou; decor, Nicolas Georgiadis. First performed at Sadler's Wells Theatre, London, 26 May 1955, by Sadler's Wells Ballet. Principal dancers, Doreen Tempest (Bird Woman), Maryon Lane and David Poole (The Lovers). Revised version presented at the Royal Opera House, Covent Garden, London, 1953, with **Christopher Gable.**

HOUSE PARTY, THE *see* **Biches, Les.**

HOWARD, Andrée Louise (1910–68), British dancer, choreographer and designer. She studied with **Rambert, Egorova, Kchessinska, Preobrajenska** and **Trefilova,** making her debut in Ashton's *Mars and Venus* (1929). As a founder member and principal choreographer of Ballet Club, her works included *Our Lady's Juggler* (1933), *Cinderella* and *Rape of the Lock* (1935), *La Fête Étrange* (1940) and *Le Spectre de la Rose.* Besides her own works, Andrée Howard's repertoire included *Dark Elegies, Bar aux Folies-Bergère, Façade* and *Les Sylphides.* She staged and danced in *Death and the Maiden* and *Lady into Fox* for **Ballet Theatre** (1940), choreographed *Twelfth Night* and *The Spider's Banquet* for Sadler's Wells Ballet (1942); *Assembly Ball* to Bizet (1946) for Sadler's Wells Theatre Ballet; *A Mirror for Witches* and *La Belle Dame Sans Merci* (1953) for **The Royal Ballet** (1959). The following year she was guest artist with The Royal Ballet, appearing as one of the Step-sisters in *Cinderella.*

HUMPBACKED HORSE, THE, a ballet in four acts based on a Russian fairy tale by P. Yershov. Choreography, **Arthur Saint-Léon**; music, Cesare Pugni. First performed at the Bolshoi Theatre, St. Petersburg, 15 December 1864, with Muravieva as the Czar-Maiden. A new three act version was first performed at the Bolshoi Theatre, Moscow, 4 March 1960. Libretto, **Vassily Vainonen** and Paval Maliarevsky;

choreography, **Alexander Radunsky**; music, Rodion Shchedrin; decor, **Boris Volkov**. Principal dancers, Alexander Radunsky (Czar), Rimina Karelskaya (Czar-Maiden), **Vladimir Vassiliev** (Ivanushka). Ivanushka falls in love with the Czar-Maiden and outwits the Czar aided by the Humpbacked Horse.

HUMPHREY, Doris (1895–1958), American dancer and choreographer. She studied at the Parker School, Chicago, joining **Ruth St. Denis** and **Ted Shawn** in 1917. In 1928 she founded a school with Charles Weidman. She attempted to move away from traditional ideas of step, music and style, seeking a basic theory of movement, universal in appeal. Her early works included *Water Study*, *Life of the Bee* and *Circular Descent*. She retired from dancing in 1945 and, for José Limón's company, staged *Day on Earth*, *Night Spell* and *Theater Piece No. 2*. In 1955 she founded the Juilliard Dance Theater in New York where she created *The Shakers*, *Song of the West* and *Decade*.

HUNDRED KISSES, THE, a ballet in one act based on a fairy tale by Hans Christian Andersen. Libretto, **Boris Kochno**; choreography, **Bronislava Nijinska**; music, Frederic d'Erlanger; decor, Jean Hugo. First performed at the Royal Opera House, Covent Garden, London, 18 July 1935, by **Colonel de Basil's Ballet Russe de Monte Carlo**. Principal dancers, **Irina Baronova, David Lichine**. Also performed at the Metropolitan Opera House, New York, 18 October 1935, with the same principals. A Princess rejects the love of the disguised Prince. She changes her mind when he offers her magic gifts. Removing his disguise he rebukes her for her haughtiness.

HUROK, Solomon (1888–　　), American impresario, born in Russia, Honorary Commander of the Order of the British Empire, Chevalier of the Légion d'Honneur. He contracted many leading international soloists and companies for American engagements, and contributed to the setting up of cultural exchanges between the United States and the Soviet Union. His autobiography was published in two volumes as *Impresario* (1946) and *S. Hurok Presents* (1953).

HYND, Ronald (1931–　), British dancer and choreographer. He studied at the Rambert School, joining Ballet Rambert (1946) and becoming soloist. In 1951 he joined the Sadler's Wells Ballet, and subsequently became soloist and principal dancer. His roles included Bridegroom in *La Fête Étrange* and Leonardo in *The Good-Humoured Ladies*. He choreographed *Le Baiser de la Fée* for Het Nederlands Ballet, and *Pasiphaë* for the Royal Ballet's Choreographic Group. In 1970 he created *Dvorak Variations* for London's **Festival Ballet**. In the same year he was appointed director of the Bavarian State Ballet, Munich.

I

ICARE, a ballet in one act, based on the Greek myth of Icarus. Libretto, choreography and drum rhythm, **Serge Lifar** (orchestrated by J. E. Szyfer); decor, P. R. Larthe. First performed, 9 July 1935, by the **Paris Opéra Ballet.** Principal dancer, Serge Lifar. The ballet consists of a solo with a very small part performed by the corps de ballet. The music is predominantly percussion and drum rhythms.

IDYLLE, a ballet in one act. Libretto, Alwyn Camble; choreography, **George Skibine**; music, François Serette; decor, Camble. First performed in the Théâtre de l'Empire, Paris, 2 January 1954, by the **Grand Ballet du Marquis de Cuevas.** Principal dancers, **Marjorie Tallchief,** George Skibine, **Vladimir Skouratov.** Later it became part of the repertoire of **Ruth Page**'s Chicago Ballet. A gay young mare is attracted away from her black stallion by a horse splendidly decked-out for the circus.

IDZIKOWSKY, Stanislas, Polish dancer and teacher. A pupil of **Cecchetti,** he made his debut with the **Empire Ballets,** later dancing with the Anna Pavlova Company, with **Lydia Lopokova,** and with **Diaghilev**'s Ballets Russes (1914–1926, 1928). He created Battista in *The Good-Humoured Ladies,* Dandy in *The Three-Cornered Hat,* Caviello in *Pulcinella,* Harlequin in *Le Carnaval* and is well-known for his Bluebird in *The Sleeping Beauty.* He was guest artist with Vic-Wells Ballet (1933) where he created the virtuoso male role in *Les Rendez-vous* in 1933. He published *A Manual of Classical Theatrical Dancing* in collaboration with **Cyril Beaumont** (1922).

Imperial Ballet *see* **Russia, history of ballet in.**

INDES GALANTES, LES, an opera-ballet. Libretto, Louis Fuzilier; music, Jean Philippe Rameau; decor, Servandoni. First performed, 23 August 1735, at l'Académie Royale, Paris. Principal dancers, **Louis Dupré,** Mlle. Rabon, Dumoulin, Le Breton, Malterre, Mariette, **Sallé,** Javellier. A completely new version was presented by the **Paris Opéra Ballet,** 18 June 1952, and retained in the repertoire. Choreography: prologue and first entrée, **Albert Aveline;** second and fourth entrées, **Serge Lifar;** third entrée, **Harald Lander.** Decor: prologue, Arbus and Jacques Dupont; first entrée, George Wakhevich; second entrée, Jean Carzou; third entrée, Fost and Moulaine; fourth entrée, Roger Chapelain-Midy. The successful combination of lavish spectacle with music and dance have made this an extremely popular production.

INGLESBY, Mona (Mona Kimberley, 1918–), British dancer. She studied with Craske, **Egorova** and **Rambert,** dancing with Ballet Club and Ballet Rambert where she created La Môme Fromage and Can-Can Dancer in *Bar aux Folies-Bergère* (1934). She was founder, director, choreographer and ballerina of **International Ballet** (1940). Her repertoire included *Coppélia, Swan Lake, Sleeping Beauty,* and she choreographed *Endymion, Everyman, Masque of Comus* and others. She retired in 1953.

International Ballet, a company founded by Mona Inglesby in London, 1940. It gave its initial performance at the Alhambra Theatre, Glasgow, 19 May 1941. After a season at the Lyric Theatre, London, the company toured Great Britain and Europe, and gave annual seasons in London. Its repertoire included many of the full-length classical ballets. Mona Inglesby was ballerina and **Celia Franca, Moira Shearer** and **Sonia Arova** danced with International Ballet early in their careers; **Nicholas Sergeyev** was ballet master. The company disbanded in 1953.

INVITATION, THE, a ballet in one act, based on two novels, *The Ripening Seed* by Colette and *House of the Angel* by Beatriz Guido. Choreography, **Kenneth MacMillan,** commissioned music, Matyas Serber; decor, Nicholas Georgiadis. First performed at the New Theatre, Oxford, 10 November 1960, by **The Royal Ballet**

(touring section). Principal dancers, **Lynn Seymour** (The Girl), **Christopher Gable** (Her Cousin), Anne Heaton (The Wife), Desmond Doyle (The Husband). The theme is of adolescent curiosity and seduction. This ballet established Lynn Seymour as a fine dramatic dancer.

ISMAILOV, Serge (1912–), Russian dancer and teacher. He studied with **Preobrajenska, Egorova, Legat, Oboukhov** and **Nijinska,** with whose company he danced in 1932. He then appeared with Les Ballets 1933, **Colonel de Basil's**

Les Indes Galantes: Liane Daydé and Michel Renault. Ph. Bernand.

Ballet Russe (1933–40), **Ballet Russe de Monte Carlo** (1943–4) and **Ballet International** (1944). His roles included Favourite Slave in *Schéhérazade*, Swineherd in *The Hundred Kisses* and Chief Cossack in *La Boutique Fantasque*. He took a teaching post in New York.

ISTOMINA, Avdotia (1799–1848), Russian ballerina. She studied under **Didelot** and danced solo parts in many of the ballets at the Imperial Theatre, St. Petersburg, before her graduation in 1815. She made her debut in *Acis and Galatea* the same year. At the peak of her career in the 1820s she became première danseuse mime. She retired in 1836.

IVANOV, Lev (1834–1901), Russian dancer, teacher and choreographer. His career was spent at the Imperial School, St. Petersburg where he was student, dancer, teacher and choreographer, as well as their régisseur-in-chief (1882) and second ballet master (1885). His creativity was overshadowed first by **Jules Perrot**, then by **Marius Petipa**, who received the credit for many of his works. He staged *La Fille Mal Gardée*, *The Enchanted Forest*, *The Haarlem Tulip*, *Cinderella* (*Act 2*) and *Sylvia*. His most important works were *The Nutcracker* and Acts 2 and 4 of *Swan Lake*. There is little doubt that his creative talent equalled Petipa's, though his fame was eclipsed by Petipa.

J

JACOBSON, Leonid Veniaminovich (1904–   ), Russian choreographer, Honoured Art Worker of the RSFSR. He was a soloist and choreographer at the Bolshoi Ballet (1933–42), moving to the Kirov Ballet in 1942. As a choreographer he staged *The Golden Age*, *Romeo and Juliet* and *Capriccio Espagñol*. In 1961 he played a major part in the setting up in Paris of the International Centre of Choreography and Culture, on the third centenary of the founding of **l'Académie Royale de Danse**, Paris.

Jacob's Pillow Dance Festival *see* **Shawn, Ted.**

JARDIN AUX LILAS, LE *see* **Lilac Garden, The.**

JEANMAIRE, Renée (1925–   ), French ballerina (also known as Zizi Jeanmaire). A pupil at the Paris Opéra school, and of **Volinine** and **Kniasev**, she joined the company in 1939, but left to give recitals in Paris, partnered by Roger Fenonjois (1944) and **Vladimir Skouratov** (1945). She also appeared with **Roland Petit**, later her husband, at the Soirées de la Danse, Sarah Bernhardt Theatre (1944), and created the leading role in *Quadrille* (1945). She was ballerina with **Nouveau Ballet de Monte Carlo** (1946), creating *Aubade*, and **Colonel de Basil**'s Original Ballet Russe (1947) where she danced in *Graduation Ball* and *The Prodigal Son*. In 1948 she joined **Les Ballets de Paris de Roland Petit** (whom she married), dancing the leading roles in *Études Symphoniques* and *Carmen*, her greatest success, which she later danced in London and New York. Since 1951 her career has been primarily in musicals, feature films and films of the ballet, notably *Black Tights*.

Jerome Robbins's Ballets: USA *see* **Robbins, Jerome.**

jeté, a jump from one foot to the other, moving either forward, backward or to the side. From the fifth position, **fondu** on the right leg, the dancer glides the left foot to the second position, springs on to the left leg and finishes with the right foot sur le **cou-de-pied.**

JEU DE CARTES *see* **Card Game.**

JEUNE HOMME ET LA MORT, LE, a ballet in two scenes. Libretto, Jean Cocteau; choreography, **Roland Petit**; music, Johann Sebastian Bach; decor, Georges Wakhevich. First performed at the Théâtre des Champs-Elysées, Paris, 25 June 1946, by **Les Ballets des Champs-Elysées**. Principal dancers, **Jean Babilée, Nathalie Philippart.** Presented at the Metropolitan Opera House, New York, 9 April 1951, with the same cast. A melodramatic tale about an artist who hangs himself on being rejected by the woman he loves. She returns as Death, and leads him to his doom.

JEUX, a ballet in one act. Choreography, **Vaslav Nijinsky**; music, Debussy; decor, **Léon Bakst.** First performed at the Théâtre des Champs-Elysées, 15 May 1913, by **Diaghilev**'s Ballets Russes. Principal dancers, **Tamara Karsavina,** Ludmila Shollar, Vaslav Nijinsky. The action revolves around a game of tennis. A ballet of the same name in one act has been based on this original. Choreography; **John Taras**; decor, Raoul Pène du Bois. First performed at the New York State Theater, 28 April 1966, by **The New York City Ballet.** Principal dancers, **Edward Villella, Allegra Kent, Melissa Hayden.** This ballet emphasizes the intrusion of a sensual element into the game.

JEUX D'ENFANTS, a ballet in one act. Libretto, **Boris Kochno**; choreography, **Léonide Massine**; music, Georges Bizet; decor, Joan Miró. First performed at the Théâtre de Monte Carlo, 14 April 1932, by **Colonel de Basil**'s Ballet Russe. Principal dancers, **'Baby Ballerinas'** **Tatiana Riabouchinska** (The Child) and **Tamara Toumanova** (The Top), **Irina Baronova, David Lichine, Léon Woizikowsky.** A revised version was choreographed and staged by **Albert Aveline,** 16 July 1941. **George Balanchine,** Barbara Milberg and **Francisco Moncion** choreographed a version for **The New York City Ballet,** performed at New York City Center, 22 November 1955, with decor by Esteban Francés. Principal dancers, **Melissa Hayden,** Roy Tobias. In a surrealist nursery the toys come to life and The Child awakens and joins them in play. At daybreak all returns to normal.

JILLANA (Jillana Zimmermann, 1936–   ), American dancer. A scholarship student at the School of American Ballet, she made her debut with Ballet Society (1948) and remained with the company when it became **The New York City Ballet** (1957), having become soloist in 1955. She danced the 1957–8 season with American Ballet Theatre, returning to The New York City Ballet in 1959 as leading soloist. She is famed for her 'line'. Her roles included Titania in *A Midsummer Night's Dream*. She created Coquette in *Night Shadow* and one of the four girls in *Liebeslieder Walzer*. She retired in 1966.

JOAN VON ZARISSA, a ballet in prologue, four scenes and an epilogue. Libretto and music, Werner Egk; choreography, Lizzie Maudrik; decor, Josef Fenneker. First performed at the Staatsoper, Berlin, 20 January 1940. Principal dancers, Ilse Meudtner, Bernhard Wosien, Rolf Jahnke. Presented, 10 July 1942, by the **Paris Opéra Ballet** with choreography by **Serge Lifar** and decor by Yves Brayer. Principal dancers, **Lycette Darsonval, Solange Schwarz, Yvette Chauviré,** Serge Lifar, **Serge Peretti.** Another version with choreography by Erika Hanka was presented at the Volksoper, Vienna, 17 September 1949, by Vienna Staatsoper Ballett. Decor, Georges Wakhevich. Tatiana Gsovska choreographed another version under the title *Juan de Zarissa*, presented, 31 October 1950, at the Teatro Colón, Buenos Aires. Decor, Hector Basaldua. Set in the late Middle Ages, the ballet tells of a Don Juan who is confronted by the ghosts of the victims of his misspent life.

JOB, a masque for dancing in eight scenes, inspired by William Blake's illustrations to the Book of Job. Libretto, Geoffrey Keynes; choreography, **Ninette de Valois**; music, Ralph Vaughan Williams; decor, Gwen Raverat. First performed at the Cambridge Theatre, London, 5 July 1931, by **The Camargo Society.** Principal dancers, **Anton Dolin** (The Devil), John McNair (Job). Performed at the Old Vic Theatre, London, 22 September 1931, by Vic-Wells Ballet and adopted into the repertoire. Revived at the Royal Opera House, Covent Garden, London, 21 May 1948, by Sadler's Wells Ballet, with new decor by John Piper and **Robert Helpmann** as The Devil. Another revival was presented, 23 April 1970, by The Royal Ballet (smaller company) at the Royal Opera House.

Jillana. Ph. New York City Ballet.

Principal dancers, Kerrison Cooke, Adrian Grater, Jean Bedells.

JOFFREY, Robert (Abdullah Jaffa Anver Bey Khan, 1930–), American dancer, choreographer and teacher. He studied at the School of American Ballet and with **Alexandra Fedorova,** and made his debut with **Les Ballets de Paris de Roland Petit** (1949–50). *Persephone*, his first ballet, was presented for the Choreographers' Workshop in 1952. The Robert Joffrey Ballet Concert, his first company, was formed in 1954. He presented both classical and creative modern works. As the Robert Joffrey Ballet, the company toured the United States (1956–64) and the USSR (1963–4). With Alexander Ewing and Gerald Arpino, Joffrey established a new company, the City Center Joffrey Ballet, and founded his own school in 1953. For the New York City Opera Company (1957–62) he choreographed the dances in a number of operas. He took a teaching post at the American Ballet Center, but returned to his post of director of the New York City Opera Company in 1965. In 1966 the City Center Joffrey Ballet became the resident ballet company at the New York City Center. For his company Joffrey created *Gamelan* (1963), and the avant garde ballet *Astarte* (1967). In 1970 he staged a revival of *Pineapple Poll*. Other ballets performed by the Joffrey Ballet have included *Nightwings, Viva Vivaldi, Arcs and Angels, Opus 65* and *Scotch Symphony*.

Joffrey Ballet, Robert *see* **Joffrey, Robert.**

JOHANSSON, Anna (1860–1917), Russian ballerina and teacher. Daughter of **Christian Johansson,** she was a pupil at

Job: performed by The Royal Ballet. Ph. Mandinian.

the Imperial School, St. Petersburg and made her debut in *Esmeralda* in 1878. She was ballerina of the Maryinsky Theatre until her retirement in 1900 when she taught at the Imperial School, teaching the classe de perfection from 1911 until her death.

JOHANSSON, Christian (1817–1903), Swedish dancer and teacher. He studied at the Royal Swedish Ballet School and with **August Bournonville,** returning to Stockholm in 1837 as premier danseur, and partnering **Maria Taglioni.** In 1841 he made his debut with the Imperial Ballet, St. Petersburg in *La Gitana*, and became its premier danseur. He spent the remainder of his life in Russia, becoming a teacher at the Imperial School in 1860. Among the great dancers of the Russian ballet, he trained **Kchessinska, Preobrajenska, Gerdt,** and many others, his daughter, Anna Johansson (1860–1917), ballerina of the Maryinsky Theatre. He retired as a dancer in 1869.

JOLIE FILLE DE GAND, LA, a romantic ballet in three acts. Choreography, François Albert; music, Adolphe Adam; decor, Ciceri, Philastre, Cambon. First performed at the Théâtre National de l'Opéra, Paris, 22 June 1842, by the **Paris Opéra Ballet.** Principal dancers, **Carlotta Grisi, Lucien Petipa,** Vera Coralli, François Albert.

JOOSS, Kurt (1901–   ), German dancer and choreographer. A pupil of **Rudolf von Laban** (1920), he became his principal dancer and assistant at the National Theatre, Mannheim. He became 'director of movement' at the Municipal Theatre, Münster. Known as Neue Tanzbühne, the dance group toured Germany (1924–6) with a Jooss repertoire. He studied in Paris and Vienna, then founded Folkwangschule für Musik, Tanz und Sprechen (1927) and Dance Theatre Studio (1928). He was ballet master at the Essen Opera (1930) when it became the official company of the Opera House. In 1933, *The Green Table*, choreographed by Jooss, was a major success. The company, called Ballets

Kurt Jooss. Ph. Enkelmann.

Jooss, left Germany at the outbreak of Nazism, toured the world, and settled in England until 1947, when it disbanded. In 1949 Jooss re-opened his school in Essen. A new company was organized (1963–4), which has danced at several annual ballet festivals in Europe. Jooss's choreographic works include *The Big City, The Prodigal Son, Seven Heroes, Pandora, Journey in the Fog, The Ghosts, Persephone* (for **Ida Rubinstein's** company) and others. His ballets use non-classical movements, minimal costumes and scenery, black backcloths and maximum lighting.

Jooss Ballet *see* **Jooss, Kurt.**

JORDAN, Olga Genrikhovna (1907–   ), Russian ballerina, choreographer and teacher, Honoured Artist of the RSFSR. She studied in Leningrad and joined the Kirov Ballet where she was a soloist from 1926–50. Her roles include Zarema in *The Fountain of Bakhchisarai*, title role in *Esmeralda* and Jeanne in *Flames of Paris.*

As a choreographer, she produced *Swan Lake* and *Italian Capriccio*. She taught in Leningrad (1939–63) and in Warsaw (1959–60). She took a teaching post in Moscow in 1963 and later returned to the Kirov Ballet. Among her pupils was **Alexandra Danilova.**

JOVITA or **Les Boucaniers,** a ballet in three scenes. Choreography, Joseph Mazilier; music, Théodore Labarre; decor, Desplechin, Thierry, Cambon. First performed at the Théâtre National de l'Opéra, 11 November 1853, by the **Paris Opéra Ballet.** Principal dancers, **Carolina Rosati,** Louis Mérante, **Lucien Petipa.**

JUDGEMENT OF PARIS, a ballet in one act. Libretto and decor, **Hugh Laing**; choreography, **Antony Tudor**; music, Kurt Weill. First performed at the Westminster Theatre, London, 15 June 1938. Principal dancers, **Agnes de Mille** (Venus), Thérèse Langfield (Juno), Charlotte Bidmead (Minerva), Antony Tudor (Client), Hugh Laing (Waiter). Presented at the Arts Theatre, London, 1 October 1940, by Ballet Rambert. Principal dancers, Sally Gilmour and Marguerite Stewart, **Gerd Larsen,** Elisabeth Schooling and **Peggy van Praagh,** Margaret Scott and Joan McClelland. Staged in the New York City Center, 23 January 1940, by **Ballet Theatre,** with decor by Lucinda Ballard. Principal dancers, Agnes de Mille, **Lucia Chase,** Viola Essen, Antony Tudor, Hugh Laing. This version of the myth is set in a French night club.

K

KALIOUJNY, Alexandre (1924–) French dancer, born in Russia. He studied with **Preobrajenska** and in 1939 won first prize at the Brussels International Dance Competition. A master of classical technique, he danced with **Nouveau Ballet de Monte Carlo** (1946) and was premier danseur étoile of the **Paris Opéra Ballet** (1947–53, 1956–61). Renowned for his roles as a warrior chief in *Chota Roustaveli* and as the Polovetsian Chief in *Polovetsian Dances from Prince Igor*, he also created the 1st movement of *Le Palais de Cristal*, and Fiancé in *Le Baiser de la Fée*. He partnered **Tamara Toumanova** at the Paris Opéra and danced with **Jeanmaire** in a revue in New York. He retired in 1961, and founded his own ballet studio in Nice.

KARELSKAYA, Rimina Klavdievna (1927–), Russian dancer, Honoured Artist of the RSFSR. She became a soloist with the Bolshoi Ballet in 1946. Her roles include Odette-Odile in *Swan Lake*, the title role in *Raymonda* and Myrtha in *Giselle*.

KARNILOVA, Maria (1920–), American dancer. She studied with **Fedorova, Fokine, Tudor,** Caton, **Dolin,** Holm, and at the Metropolitan Opera Ballet School. From 1935–7 she appeared with Victor Dandre's Opera Company, touring South America; with the Michel Fokine and **Mikhail Mordkin** companies; and with Salmaggi Opera Company. One of the first members of **Ballet Theatre** (1939–46), she soon became soloist. Her repertoire includes *Three Virgins and a Devil, Lilac Garden* and *Judgement of Paris*. From 1951–9 she made guest appearances with Metropolitan Ballet and American Ballet Theatre; at Jacob's Pillow; and with Jerome Robbins's Ballets: USA. After 1960 she turned to producing Broadway musicals.

KARSAVINA, Tamara (1885–), Russian ballerina. She studied at the Imperial School, St. Petersburg and made her debut as soloist in *Javotte* in 1902. Her repertoire included *The Awakening of Flora, The Humpbacked Horse, Swan Lake, Le Corsaire, The Sleeping Beauty, Giselle, The Nutcracker, Raymonda, La Bayadère,* and *Harlequinade.* As ballerina with **Diaghilev**'s Ballets Russes (1909–19) which she helped organize with **Fokine** and **Pavlova,** she created the principal roles in *Les Sylphides, Carnaval, Petrouchka. Le Spectre de la Rose, Firebird,*

Tamara Karsavina. Ph. Lipnitzki.

Nora Kaye in The Cage. Ph. New York City Ballet.

Street (1931), a portrait of the Maryinsky Theatre and its school. She was one of the greatest ballerinas ever known.

KAYE, Nora (Nora Koreff, 1920–), American ballerina. She studied at the School of American Ballet and the Metropolitan Opera Ballet School, appearing in the children's ballets at the Opera House (1929–35), and was a member of **The American Ballet** when it became the Opera's official company. She joined the corps of **Ballet Theatre** in 1939, became soloist, then ballerina (1942). Her repertoire included classical ballets but she dances best in modern dramatic roles. She created Hagar in *Pillar of Fire*, and Princess in *On Stage!*, and danced Caroline in *Lilac Garden*, Queen of the Wilis in *Swan Lake* and Polyhymnia in *Apollo*. In 1951 she joined **The New York City Ballet**, for which she created the outstanding role of Novice in *The Cage*. In 1954 she returned to Ballet Theatre where she created Blanche in *A Streetcar Named Desire*, Operetta Star in *Offenbach in the Underworld*, the principal role in *Fall River Legend* and the pas de deux, *Tristan*, which she danced with **Erik Bruhn** (1958). She has appeared in Japan and the USSR.

KCHESSINSKA or **KSCHESSIN-SKAYA, Mathilda** (Princess Krassinska-Romanovska, 1872–1971), Russian prima ballerina and teacher. She was the daughter of Felix Kchessinsky, a Polish character dancer at the Maryinsky Theatre. Graduating from the Imperial School, St. Petersburg (1890), she became prima ballerina assoluta in 1895 and had immense influence. Her repertoire included *Cinderella*, *La Sylphide*, *The Talisman*, *The Sleeping Beauty*, *Pharaoh's Daughter* and *The Humpbacked Horse*. She is credited with being the first Russian dancer to execute 32 fouettés. In 1911 she danced *Swan Lake* with **Diaghilev**'s Ballets Russes; in 1917 she left Russia for Paris, where she established a ballet school. At Covent Garden, London, she made her last appearance with **Ballet Russe de Monte**

Thamar, Daphnis and Chloë, Le Coq d'Or, The Three-Cornered Hat and *Pulcinella*. In 1917 she made her home in London and was vice-president of the Royal Academy of Dancing until 1955. She came out of retirement in 1930 to dance as guest artist with the newly formed Ballet Rambert, repeating many of the roles she had danced with Diaghilev's Ballets Russes, as well as *Mercury, The Crime* and her own solo *Mademoiselle de Maupin* (1931). In 1943 she staged *Le Spectre de la Rose* for Sadler's Wells Ballet, coaching **Fonteyn** in the leading role and in *The Firebird*: she assisted in the mime scenes of *La Fille Mal Gardée* (1960), as well as re-creating the role of Lise; she staged *Carnaval* for Western Theatre Ballet (1961). She has published several books including *Theatre*

Carlo (1936). Her book, *The Memoirs of Kchessinska*, was published in 1960.

KEHLET, Niels (1938–   ), Danish dancer. Trained at the Royal Danish Ballet School (1948–57), he graduated into the company and became solo dancer in 1961. His repertoire includes *Don Quixote* pas de deux, Peter in *Peter and the Wolf*, Magician in *Moon Reindeer*, one of two leading male roles in *Études*, 3rd Movement in *Symphony in C*, Joker in Cranko's *Card Game*; and he created Colas in *La Fille Mal Gardée* (1964). He was guest artist with Ballet International du Marquis de Cuevas (1961), and at Jacob's Pillow Dance Festival (1966), where he danced *Le Spectre de la Rose*.

KENT, Allegra (1938–   ), American dancer. A pupil at the School of American Ballet, she joined **The New York City Ballet** in 1953, and created her first role, 'The Unanswered Question' episode in *Ivesiana* in 1954. As ballerina (1957) her repertoire included *Swan Lake* (Act 2), *Symphony in C*, *Divertimento No. 15*, *The Cage*, **Robbins's** *L'Après-midi d'un Faune*, *Orpheus*, *Apollo* and *Agon*. She created Annie in *Seven Deadly Sins*, Sleepwalker in *La Sonnambula* and one of the leading roles in *Episodes*.

KERMESSE AT BRUGES, THE *see* **Three Gifts, The.**

KHADRA, a ballet in one act. Choreography, **Celia Franca**; music, Sibelius; decor, Honor Frost. First performed at Sadler's Wells Theatre, London, 27 May 1946, by Sadler's Wells Ballet. Principal dancers, Sheilah O'Reilly, Anne Heaton, Leo Kersley. The story is set in Persia and was suggested by Persian miniatures.

KIDD, Michael (1919–   ), American dancer, choreographer and director. He studied in New York with **Vilzak** and **Shollar**. He joined **American Ballet** in 1937 and danced for Ballet Caravan (1938–40), where he was noted for his role in *Billy the Kid*. Soloist and assistant director of Dance Players (1941–2), he joined **Ballet Theatre** (1942) and created the role of Handy Man in *On Stage!* which he choreographed (1945), and one of the four male roles in *Interplay*. He also danced *Fancy Free* and *Three Virgins and a Devil*. He left Ballet Theatre in 1947, and staged many successful musicals and films.

Kirov Ballet *see* **Russia, history of ballet in.**

Kirov Theatre of Opera and Ballet *see* **Russia, history of ballet in.**

KIROVA, Vera Lazarevna (1940–   ), Bulgarian ballerina. She studied in Sofia, becoming soloist (1958) and prima ballerina (1961) at the Sofia National Opera. Her roles include Aurora in *The Sleeping Beauty*, *Giselle* and Vida in *Legend of the Lake*. Her repertoire also includes leading roles in modern ballets.

Kirsova Ballet *see* **Australia, history of ballet in.**

KIRSTEIN, Lincoln Edward (1907–   ), American authority on dance. He organized and directed the School of American Ballet (1934), the **American Ballet** (1935); and was founder and director of Ballet Caravan (1936–41). He was founder and secretary of Ballet Society (1946), and, with **Balanchine**, helped to make **The New York City Ballet** the successful company it is today. He is author of *Fokine* (1934), *Dance* (1935), *Blast at Ballet, a Corrective for the American Audience* (1938), *Ballet Alphabet, a Primer for Beginners* (1939), and *Movement and Metaphor* (1971).

KNIASEV, Boris (1905–   ), French dancer and teacher, born in Russia. He studied with **Kasyan Goleizovsky, Mordkin** and Nelidova, leaving Russia in 1917 to become ballet master in Sofia. From 1921–32 he danced in Paris with **Olga Spessivtzeva**, whom he married. He was ballet master with Opéra Comique (1932–4), and established his own studio in Paris (1937) where his students included **Chauviré, Skouratov, Algarov** and **Jeanmaire**. He was choreographer with **Colonel de Basil's** Original Ballet Russe (1947) and with **Les Ballets de Paris de Roland Petit** (1948). His better known works include *Legend of the Birchtree* (1930). In 1953 he opened a school in Lausanne, and subsequently in Geneva and Rome, where he substituted floor exercises for the barre. He was ballet master (1967) at Colón Theatre, Buenos Aires.

KOCHNO, Boris (1903–), Russian writer. He was indispensable as secretary, friend, adviser and deputy to **Diaghilev.** For the Ballets Russes, and under the pseudonym Sobeka, he wrote the libretti for *Les Fâcheux, Zephyr and Flora, La Chatte, The Gods Go a'Begging, Ode, Le Pastorale, Le Fils Prodigue* and *Le Bal.* As artistic collaborator with Ballets Russes de Monte Carlo (1932), his libretti included *Cotillon* and *Jeux d'Enfants.* In 1933 he helped **Balanchine** found Les Ballets 1933, then returned to Ballets Russes (later Ballet Russe) until 1937. With the production of **Petit's** *Les Forains*, he helped found **Les Ballets des Champs-Elysées,** of which he was artistic director (1945–9). His libretti included *Les Forains, La Fiancée du Diable* and *Les Amours de Jupiter*. He was co-author with Maria Luz of *Le Ballet* (1954).

KOLPAKOVA, Irina (1933–), Soviet ballerina, Peoples' Artist of the RSFSR. A graduate of the Leningrad School (1951), she was a pupil of the great **Vaganova**. As ballerina with the Kirov Ballet, she has danced the title roles in *Giselle* and *Raymonda*, Maria in *The Fountains of Bakhchisarai*, Desdemona in *Othello*, Katerina in *The Stone Flower*, Shiriene in *Legend of Love*, Princess Florine in *Sleeping Beauty*, and is considered an outstanding Aurora in the same ballet. She also created Beloved in *Coast of Hope*. She danced in Paris, London and New York and was recognized as a notable exponent of the Kirov classical style.

KORRIGANE, LA, a ballet in two acts. Choreography, Louis Mérante; music, Charles Widor; decor, Lavastre, Rube, Chaperon, Lacoste. First performed at the Théâtre National de l'Opéra, 1 December 1880, at the **Paris Opéra Ballet.** Principal dancers, **Rosita Mauri,** Sanlaville, Louis Mérante. The work is a Breton version of *Giselle*. Rosita Mauri gave an outstanding performance of the waltz-mazurka, la Sabotière.

KRASSOVSKA, Nathalie (1919–), Russian ballerina, known (1936–52) as Natasha Leslie. She studied with **Preobrajenska, Legat** and at the School of American Ballet. She made her professional debut in 1932 with **Nijinska's** Ballet, was a member of Les Ballets 1933, toured South America (1934) with **Lifar** and appeared with Ballet Russe de Paris (1935). She became ballerina with **Ballet Russe de Monte Carlo** (1936–50), where her

Nathalie Krassovska. Ph. Reyna.

repertoire included *Giselle, Les Sylphides, Swan Lake, The Nutcracker,* and *The Firebird,* and with London's **Festival Ballet** (1950–5) adding *Esmeralda* and *Romeo and Juliet* to her repertoire. As guest artist she appeared with Ballet Russe de Monte Carlo, London's **Festival Ballet,** Ballet Rambert and **Grand Ballet du Marquis de Cuevas.** Latterly she took a teaching post in Dallas, Texas.

KRASSOVSKAYA, Vera (1915–), Russian dancer, historian and ballet critic. She studied at the Leningrad Choreographic School and danced (1933–41) with the Kirov Ballet. Her publications include *Leningrad Ballet* (1961), *Russian Ballet Theatre of the Second Half of the 19th Century* (1963) and *Anna Pavlova* (1964).

KREUTZBERG, Harald (1902–), German dancer, born in Czechoslovakia. A pupil of **Rudolf Von Laban** and **Mary Wigman,** he danced initially with the Hanover and Berlin Operas. With **Yvonne Georgi** and **Ruth Page** he danced in solo concerts presenting his own works, including *Aufruhr* and *Apokalyptischer Engel,* throughout the United States and Canada in the 1930s and 40s. His farewell appearances were made in Frankfurt (1959). After retiring from dancing he continued to work as a choreographer and to teach at the dance school that he ran in Berne.

KRIEGER, Victorina (1896–), Russian ballerina and journalist, Honoured Art Worker of the RSFSR. She studied at the Bolshoi Ballet School (1903–10), making her debut in 1915 as the Tsar-Maiden in *The Humpbacked Horse.* Her other roles included Kitri in *Don Quixote,* Lise in *La Fille Mal Gardée* and Swanilda in *Coppélia.* She danced in Canada with **Anna Pavlova**'s company. She went back to Russia in 1923 and toured with **Mikhail Mordkin,** returning to the Bolshoi company in 1925. In 1929 she founded the Moscow Art Theatre of Ballet. Krieger also created the roles of the Miller's Wife in

Le Tricorne and Carabosse in *The Sleeping Beauty* (1952).

KRIZA, John (1919–), American dancer. He studied with **Anton Dolin** and **Antony Tudor,** making his debut in 1939. He became leading dancer with **Ballet Theatre** where his creations included Second Sailor in *Fancy Free,* Blues pas de deux in *Interplay,* Pastor in *Fall River Legend* and Tancredi in *Le Combat.* He also danced *Los Caprichos, Winter's Eve, La Fille Mal Gardée, Helen of Troy* and *Miss Julie.* He has now retired from dancing.

KROLLER, Heinrich (1880–1930), German dancer, ballet master and choreographer. He studied at the Royal Theatre, Munich, but when refused the title of leading dancer went to Paris and worked with **Carlotta Zambelli** and **Léo Staats.** He became premier danseur of the Dresden Opera and was later ballet master at the Vienna, Berlin, Munich and Frankfurt state opera houses. He staged *La Légende de Joseph* (1921), *Don Juan* (1925), and choreographed *Schlagobers* (1924) and *Skyscrapers* (1929).

KRONSTAM, Henning (1934–), Danish dancer. A pupil of **Harald Lander** and **Vera Volkova,** he entered the Royal Danish Ballet School in 1941, and made his debut with the company as Drummer in *Graduation Ball* (1952). He became soloist in 1956, and principal dancer in 1966. His roles have included Young Poet in *Night Shadow,* Romeo in *Romeo and Juliet,* Prince Florimund in *The Sleeping Beauty*; and he created Jean in *Miss Julie* and Ballet Master in *The Lesson.* He was guest artist with **Les Ballets de Paris de Roland Petit** (1960), Ballet International du Marquis de Cuevas (1961) and **Ruth Page**'s Chicago Opera Ballet.

KSCHESSINSKAYA, Mathilda *see* **Kchessinska, Mathilda.**

KYASHT, Lydia (1885–1959), Russian dancer. She studied with **Gerdt** at the

Imperial School, St. Petersburg, and with **Pavlova** and **Karsavina.** In 1902 she made her debut at the Maryinsky Theatre, became soloist in 1908, and subsequently left Russia for England. She succeeded **Genée** as ballerina of the **Empire Ballets** (1908). She appeared with **Diaghilev's** Ballets Russes in 1919. During the 1940s she formed her own school and company, Ballet de la Jeunesse, which toured England until 1946. She wrote *Romantic Recollection* (1929).

L

LABIS, Attilio (1936–   ), French dancer. Trained by the Paris Opéra school, he became premier danseur étoile with the **Paris Opéra Ballet** (1961). He has danced *Pas de Dieux, Marines, Le Combat, Études, Swan Lake*, and has choreographed *Arcades*. After a well-received tour of the USSR (1961), he danced with the Bolshoi Ballet. In 1963 he made his American debut at Jacob's Pillow Dance Festival, and was guest artist with **The Royal Ballet** (1965).

LAC DES CYGNES, LE *see* **Swan Lake.**

LADY AND THE FOOL, THE, a ballet in one act. Libretto and choreography, **John Cranko**; music, Verdi (arranged by Charles Mackerras); decor, Richard Beer. First performed in Oxford, England, 25 February 1954, by Sadler's Wells Theatre Ballet. Principal dancers, **Patricia Miller**

Arcades by Attilio Labis. Ph. Lipnitzki.

(La Capricciosa), **Kenneth MacMillan** (Moondog), Johaar Mosaval (Bootface). Revived at the Royal Opera House, Covent Garden, London, 9 June 1955, by Sadler's Wells Ballet. Principal dancers, **Beryl Grey,** Philip Chatfield, Ray Powell. A rich girl falls in love with a clown called Moondog.

LADY OF THE CAMELLIAS, a ballet in four acts, based on the story by Alexandre Dumas. Choreography, Tatiana Gsovska; music, Henri Sauguet; decor, Jean Ponelle. First performed, 29 September 1957, by the Berliner Ballett. Principal dancers, **Yvette Chauviré,** Gert Reinholm. Revived, 1960, for the **Paris Opéra Ballet.** Principal dancers, **Yvette Chauviré,**

George Skibine. It was also presented by **Anton Dolin** in Mexico and New York.

LAERKESEN, Anna (1942–   ), Danish ballerina. She was trained by Edith Feifere Frandsen, entered the Royal Danish Ballet School in 1959 and made her debut later that year. For the Royal Danish Ballet she danced *Graduation Ball, Solitaire* and *Lady from the Sea.* After her outstanding Juliet in **Ashton**'s *Romeo and Juliet* (1963), she became soloist (1964) and principal dancer (1966), and danced the principal roles in *Swan Lake, La Sylphide, Moon Reindeer,* and *The Three Musketeers.* She toured the United States as soloist with **Inge Sand**'s group in 1961, and in 1964 made a study visit to the Bolshoi Ballet, Moscow. In 1971 she danced a season with Eliot Feld's American Ballet Company.

LAFON, Madeleine (1924–67), French dancer. She studied with **Alexandre Volinine** and at the Paris Opéra school where she became première danseuse étoile in 1952. She danced her entire career with the **Paris Opéra Ballet,** except for occasional guest appearances. The principal ballets from her repertoire were Chimère in *Les Mirages, Suite en Blanc, Coppélia* and *Études.*

LAINE, Doris (1931–   ), Finnish ballerina. After studying in Helsinki, Moscow and London, she joined the National Ballet of Finland in 1947, became soloist in 1952, ballerina in 1956 and prima ballerina. Her extensive repertoire includes *Swan Lake, Giselle, Cinderella, Coppélia, Romeo and Juliet, The Sleeping Beauty, The Firebird* and *Don Quixote.* In 1960 she was guest artist with the Bolshoi Ballet, Moscow. In 1963 she created the title role in *Esmeralda.*

LAING, Hugh (1911–   ), British dancer, born in Barbados, West Indies. He studied with Craske, **Rambert** and **Preobrajenska,** and was soloist with Ballet Club (1932) and **Tudor**'s **London Ballet** (1938). He created the leading roles in Tudor's ballets including *The Planets, The*

Madelaine Lafon. Ph. Liseg.

Descent of Hebe, Lilac Garden and *Judgement of Paris.* For **Ballet Theatre** (1939–50) he created roles in *Pillar of Fire, Romeo and Juliet, Aleko* and *Undertow.* With **The New York City Ballet** (1950) he created roles in *La Gloire, The Miraculous Mandarin* and others. His interpretation of *Prodigal Son* was noteworthy.

LANDER, Harald (1905–71), Danish dancer, choreographer, director, ballet master and teacher. A pupil of **Bournonville,** he was trained by the Royal Danish School (1913–23). He graduated into the company and made his debut as Spanish dancer in *Far from Denmark* (1925). He studied in America with **Fokine,** Ivan

Tarasov and Juan de Baucaire (1926–7), and in Mexico in 1929. He returned to the Royal Danish Ballet (1929) as leading dancer, and was ballet master (1932–51). Dancing until 1945, his roles included Don Alvarez in *Far from Denmark.* He choreographed *Gaucho* (1931), *Bolero* (1934), *Anna-Anna* (1936), *La Valse* (1940), *Études* (1948) and *Aubade* (1951), and he carefully revived and preserved the **Bournonville** repertoire. For the **Paris Opéra Ballet** (1952) he choreographed *Les Fleurs* from *Les Indes Galantes,* became ballet master (1953) and director of the Ballet School (1959–63). He also choreographed *Hop-Frog* (1953), *Printemps à Vienne* (1956), *Les Rendezvous* (1·961) and restaged *Études,* and *La Valse.* He has been guest choreographer with London's **Festival Ballet,** Ballet International du Marquis de Cuevas, **Teatro alla Scala,** Milan, American Ballet Theatre and Nederlands Nationaal Ballet.

LANDER, Margot (Margot Florentz-Gerhardt, 1910–61), Danish ballerina, wife (1931–50) of **Harald Lander.** A pupil and dancer with the Royal Danish Ballet, she made her debut in the Eskimo dance in *Far From Denmark.* In 1931 she became soloist with the company, and extended her studies with **Egorova** and **Volinine.** She was the first Danish dancer to receive the title prima ballerina (1942). She danced leading roles in the works of **August Bournonville** and of her husband; and the classic repertoire, especially *Napoli, Coppélia, Swan Lake, Giselle,* and the comediènne role in *The Sorcerer's Apprentice.*

LANDER, Toni (Toni Pihl Petersen, 1931–   ), Danish ballerina, wife (until 1965) of **Harald Lander.** She studied at the Royal Danish Ballet School and danced her first solo in *The Life-Guard Corps on Amager* (1947), while ·still a pupil. She graduated in 1948 and became ballerina in 1950, creating the leading role in *Études* shortly after. She was guest artist with Original Ballet Russe (1951–2), soloist with **Grand Ballet du Marquis de**

Cuevas (1953) ; has toured with London's **Festival Ballet** (1954–9) ; and been guest artist (1962), and ballerina with American Ballet Theatre (1960–1, 1963). Her repertoire included *Miss Julie, Napoli* (1954), *Bluebeard, Le Rendez-vous Manqué* and *Grand Pas-Glazounov*. On her return to Denmark in 1962 she re-created *Études*. In 1964 she danced the title role in Lander's successful *La Sylphide* with American Ballet Theatre.

LANDET or **LANDE, Jean-Baptiste** (died 1748), French dancer and ballet master. He was ballet master to the Swedish king (1727), went to Russia as a dancer in 1734 and became the ballet master of a school for poor children (1735). His work impressed the Empress Anne whom he petitioned to found an Academy of Dancing (1737). In 1738 the Imperial Theatre School, St. Petersburg, was founded in his charge, and the first graduation occurred in 1743. He was succeeded on his death by Rinaldo Fuseno, his assistant from 1742.

LANG, Harold, American dancer. He studied with **William Christensen,** dancing his first major role with San Francisco Ballet. From 1941–3 he danced with **Ballet Russe de Monte Carlo,** where his roles included mainly character roles such as Melon Seller and Snob in *La Boutique Fantasque*. With **Ballet Theatre** (1943–5) he danced *Bluebeard*, First Cadet in *Graduation Ball*, Faun in *Helen of Troy* and Gypsy in *Aleko*. His creations included First Sailor in **Jerome Robbins's** *Fancy Free*. Since 1946 he has made occasional guest appearances with **The New York City Ballet** and American Ballet Theatre, but has otherwise devoted his time to musicals.

LANGAGE DES FLEURS, LE *see* Adelaide.

LAPAURI, Alexander (1926–), Russian dancer and choreographer, Honoured Artist of the RSFSR. He studied at the Bolshoi School (1935–44) and joined the Bolshoi company. He is especially famous for his acrobatic dancing skill in such roles as Khan Guirei in *The Fountain of Bakhchisarai*, Paris in *Romeo and Juliet* and Don Fernando in *Laurencia*. His choreographic works include *Song of the Woods* (1960) and *Lieutenant Kije* (1963). With his wife, **Raisa Struchkova,** he has toured extensively outside the Soviet Union.

LARSEN, Gerd (1921–), Norwegian dancer. She studied with Craske and **Tudor,** making her debut with **London Ballet,** where she created French Ballerina in *Gala Performance* (1938). She has danced with Ballet Rambert, **International Ballet** (1941), and Sadler's Wells (now **The Royal Ballet**) (1944), becoming soloist in 1954. After 1956 she taught the company's classes, and performed leading mime roles such as Demeter in *Persephone* and Nurse in *Romeo and Juliet* (1965).

LARSEN, Niels Bjørn (1913–), Danish dancer and choreographer. He studied at the Royal Danish Ballet School (1920–9), and became a dancer with the company in 1933. After four years with the Trudi Schoop Comic Ballet (1935–7) and guest appearances abroad, he rejoined the Royal Danish Ballet and became soloist (1942). His imaginative roles included Angelok in *Qarrtsiluni*, Madge in *La Sylphide* and Vidrik in *A Folk Tale* ; and he created figures such as Gurn in *La Sylphide* and Tybalt in *Romeo and Juliet*. He was artistic director of the Royal Danish Ballet (1951–6, 1960–6), and choreographed *Drift, Til Eulenspiegel, Peter and the Wolf, Wild West* and others. In 1956 he became director of the Tivoli Pantomime Theatre. He has appeared as guest artist in Britain and the United States.

LAURENCIA, a ballet in three acts, based on the tragic drama *Fuente Ovejuna* by Lope de Vega. Libretto, Yevgeny Mandelberg ; choreography, **Vakhtang Chabukiany** ; music, Alexander Krein ; decor, Simon Virsaladze. First performed at the

Kirov Theatre, Leningrad, 22 March 1939. Principal dancers, **Natalia Dudinskaya** (Laurencia), Vakhtang Chabukiany (Frondozo). The pas de six from *Laurencia* was staged for **The Royal Ballet**, 24 March 1965, by **Rudolph Nureyev**. Principal dancers, Rudolph Nureyev, **Christopher Gable**, Graham Usher, **Nadia Nerina, Antoinette Sibley, Merle Park**. The action depicts a revolt in a fifteenth-century Spanish village, led by a young peasant girl.

LAVROVSKY, Leonid M. (Leonid Ivanoff, 1905–67), Russian dancer and choreographer, Peoples' Artist of the RSFSR. He studied under Andrianov and Ponomaryov at the Imperial School, St. Petersburg, graduating in 1922. With the Kirov Ballet he danced the leading male roles in *Swan Lake, Raymonda, Cléopâtre* and *Les Sylphides* and Fascist in *The Golden Age*. He made his choreographic debut (1930) with a suite of dances, followed by a piece to Tchaikovsky's *The Seasons* (1931), *Fadette*, his first full-length ballet (1934), and *Katerina* (1935), all composed for student performances. *Fadette* was re-created for the Maly Opera Theatre, Leningrad, where Lavrovsky was artistic director (1934–8). He choreographed new versions of *La Fille Mal Gardée* (1937) and *Prisoner of the Caucasus* (1938). From 1937–41 he was artistic director of the Kirov, creating his own version of *Romeo and Juliet* (1940) with music by Prokofiev. He was artistic director and choreographer of the Bolshoi Ballet from 1944 until 1956, then again in 1960. His revival of *Giselle* for its Russian centenary was met with great success in London. Other works were his versions of *The Stone Flower* (1952), a new version of *The Red Poppy* (1957), *Paganini* (1960), *Night City* and *Pages of Life* (1961). In 1964 he was made director of the Moscow Academic Choreographic School (formerly Moscow Bolshoi School of Ballet). Mikhail Lavrovsky is his son.

LAZAROV, Ichko (1937–), Bulgarian dancer, Honoured Artist. He studied with **Assen Gavrilov** and became premier danseur with Sofia National Opera. His repertoire includes leading roles in *Swan Lake, The Sleeping Beauty* and *Giselle*. He has made many guest appearances abroad, and was a prizewinner at the First International Competition in Varna (1964).

LECLERCQ, Tanaquil (1929–), American dancer, born in France. She won a scholarship in 1941 to study at the School of American Ballet, and then went to the Ballet Society Fellowship in 1946. She danced with Ballet Society, and continued as ballerina when it became **The New York City Ballet**. Her repertoire included **Robbins's** *Piper*, and Praying Mantis in *The Cage*. Among her creations were Choleric Variation in *The Four Temperaments*, 2nd movement in *Bourrée Fantasque*, Young Girl in *La Valse*, 4th movement in *Western Symphony* and Girl in Robbins's *Afternoon of a Faun*. In 1956 her career ended when she was struck down with poliomyelitis while on tour in Denmark. She married Balanchine (1956).

LEE, Mary Ann (1823–99), American ballerina. She studied in Philadelphia under P. H. Hazard of the **Paris Opéra Ballet**, making her debut as Fatima in *The Maid of Cashmere* (1837), which she danced in New York in 1839. In 1840 she studied with **Fanny Elssler's** partner, James Sylvain, learning most of Elssler's spectacular character solos. In 1844 she went to Paris to study with **Jean Coralli** at the Paris Opéra school, and returned to America the following year to dance *Giselle, La Fille du Danube* and *Jolie Fille de Gand*. She was the first American Giselle (in 1846) ; her partner was George Washington Smith.

LEGAT, Nicholas (1869–1937), Russian dancer and teacher. He was a student at the Imperial School, St. Petersburg, under **Christian Johansson**, whom he succeeded as teacher of the classe de perfection (1903), having graduated in 1888. Among his students at the Imperial School were **Fokine, Nijinsky, Bolm,**

Karsavina, Pavlova, Preobrajenska, Kyasht, Vaganova and **Kchessinska.** He left Russia in 1914, and in 1923 was instructor to **Diaghilev's** Ballets Russes where he taught **Danilova** and **Lifar.** In 1929 he and his wife opened a ballet school in England, which she continued after his death. He trained Ana Roje, **Alan Carter, André Eglevsky** and **Moira Shearer.** His published works include *Russky Balet (The Russian Ballet)* and *The Story of the Russian School.*

LEGAT, Serge (1875–1905), Russian dancer and teacher, brother of **Nicholas Legat.** He graduated from the Imperial School, St. Petersburg (1894), and was considered a promising figure both as dancer and teacher in Russian ballet. It is thought that his suicide was precipitated by his relationship with his common-law wife, Maria Petipa, the choreographer's daughter; other sources attribute it to the authoritarian regime of the Imperial Theatres.

LEGEND OF JOSEPH, THE, a ballet in one act, based on the biblical story of Joseph and Potiphar's wife. Libretto, Hugo von Hofmannsthal, Count Harry Kessler; choreography, **Michel Fokine**; music, Richard Strauss; decor, Jose Maria Sert; costumes, **Léon Bakst.** First performed at the Théâtre National de l'Opéra, Paris, 14 May 1914, by **Diaghilev's** Ballets Russes. Principal dancers, **Léonide Massine** (Joseph), Maria Kusnetzova, Vera Fokine, Alexis Bulgakov. Massine played his first major role in this production. Another version was presented at **Teatro alla Scala,** Milan, 1952, by Margaret Wallman.

LEGNANI, Pierina (1863–1923), Italian ballerina assoluta. She studied with Biretta at **Teatro alla Scala,** Milan, and made her debut there. After dancing in Paris, Madrid and London, she rose to fame after her debut at the Maryinsky Theatre (1893) in *Cinderella,* as it was the first time in the history of the Imperial Ballet that 32 fouettés were performed. She was engaged as guest artist, and remained in St. Petersburg until 1901. Her great success made Russian dancers more interested in technique. In 1895 she created Odette-Odile in *Swan Lake.* She also danced in *Coppélia, The Humpbacked Horse, Swan Lake, Bluebeard, Camargo* and *Raymonda.* After leaving Russia she danced in Italy, France and in some of the **Alhambra Ballets,** London. She and **Kchessinska** were the only dancers to receive the title of prima ballerina assoluta from the Maryinsky Theatre.

LEPESHINSKAYA, Olga Vassilievna (1916–), Soviet ballerina, Peoples' Artist of the USSR. She entered the Bolshoi School in 1925, where she studied under **Tikhomirov**; she danced Cupid in *Don Quixote* (1926), Masha in *The Nutcracker* (1932) and graduated in 1933. As a member of the company she created Suok, the Circus Dancer, in *Three Fat Men* (1935) and danced in *Svetlana, The Sleeping Beauty, La Fille Mal Gardée, Flames of Paris, The Red Poppy* and *Don Quixote.* She has appeared widely abroad.

LE PICQ, Charles (1749–1806), French dancer and ballet master. A pupil of **Noverre,** he made his debut at Stuttgart in 1766. In 1783, he danced in *Apollon et les Muses* for the **Paris Opéra Ballet,** a role he repeated at the King's Theatre, London (1785). In 1785 Noverre invited him to Paris where he partnered **Madeleine Guimard** in *Les Caprices de Galatée.* From 1786–98 he was choreographer and ballet master at the Imperial Ballet, St. Petersburg. For Catherine the Great he choreographed *Didon Abandonnée* (1792) and *Amour et Psyché* (1794).

LESLIE, Natasha *see* **Krassovska, Nathalie.**

LESTER, Keith (1904–), British dancer, choreographer and ballet master. He studied with **Serafima Astafieva, Nicholas Legat** and **Anton Dolin,** and made his debut in London (1923) in **Fokine's** dances from *Hassan.* He partnered **Lydia Kyasht** and continued his studies with **Tamara Karsavina**. He danced at Colón Theatre, Buenos Aires, with **Olga Spessivtzeva**; and with **Ida Rubinstein**'s company in Paris (1934). As a dancer and choreographer with the Markova-Dolin Company (1935), his works were *David* (1935) and *Death in Adagio, Pas de Quatre* and *Bach Suite No. 2 in B Minor* (all 1936). He choreographed for Open Air Theatre, Regent's Park (1937), and the **London Ballet** (1939); he formed the Arts Theatre Ballet (1939–40), and staged a number of works for Ballet Guild (1941). He became ballet master and choreographer of the Windmill Theatre, London (1945). He later became a teacher at the Royal Ballet School, London.

LEVINSON, André (1887–1933), Russian writer and ballet critic. He went to Paris after the Russian revolution and pioneered dance criticism there. He was considered to be the first dance critic in France. Among his published works are *La Vie de Noverre* (1925), *Anna Pavlova* (1928) and *Les Visages de la Danse* (1933).

LICHINE, David (David Lichtenstein, 1910–72), Russian dancer, choreographer and teacher. He studied in Paris with **Egorova** and **Nijinska**, making his debut with **Ida Rubinstein**'s company (1928), and later dancing with the **Pavlova** company. He joined **Colonel de Basil**'s Ballets Russes de Monte Carlo (1932), and remained when the company became Original Ballet Russe. During his nine years with the company, he created Hero in *Les Présages*, King of the Dandies in *Le Beau Danube*, Traveller in *Jeux d'Enfants*, title roles in *Protée* and his own version of *The Prodigal Son* and many others. His choreographic works include *Nocturne* (1933), *Les Imaginaires* (1934), *Le Pavillon* (1936), *Francesca da Rimini* (1937), *Protée* (1938), *Graduation Ball* (1940), and *The Nutcracker* (1957) for London's **Festival Ballet**, which is now a film. He has been guest choreographer at **Teatro**

alla **Scala**, Milan, and with **Ballets des Champs-Elysées**. He formed his own group, Los Angeles Ballet Theatre, in California. He was married to the ballerina **Tatiana Riabouchinska**.

LICIU, Irinel, Romanian ballerina, Honoured Artist. She studied with **Mikhail Gabovich** and **Oleg Danovski**, and became a ballerina with the Bucharest Opera company in 1943. Her repertoire included principal roles in *The Scarlet Poppy*, *The Fountain of Bakhchisarai*, *Swan Lake* and *Romeo and Juliet*. She has been a guest artist in many European countries, and in Egypt.

LIDO, Serge, French ballet photographer, born in Russia. He published a series of collections of his photographs under the title *Ballet* (1950–60), with text by his wife **Irène Lidova**. Earlier collections include *Danse* (1947) and *Danse No. 2* (1948).

LIDOVA, Irène, French writer and ballet critic, born in Russia. In 1944, at the Sarah Bernhardt Théâtre, Paris, she founded Soirées de la Danse. She was also a founder of **Les Ballets des Champs-Elysées**. Among her written works is *17 Visages de la Danse Française* (1953). She has worked on several photographic publications with her husband, ballet photographer **Serge Lido**.

LIEBESLIEDER WALTZER, a romantic ballet in one act. Choreography, **George Balanchine**; music, Brahms (*Liebeslieder Waltzer*); decor, David Hays; costumes, Barbara Karinska. First performed in New York City Center, 22 November 1960, by **The New York City Ballet**. Principal dancers, **Diana Adams**, Bill Carter, **Melissa Hayden**, Jonathan Watts, **Violette Verdy, Nicholas Magallanes**. The waltzes begin in Victorian splendour and decorum, but the dancers are carried away by the music and rhythm.

LIEPA, Maris (1930–), Russian dancer, born in Latvia, Peoples' Artist of the RSFSR. Trained at the Riga Choreographic School (1945–53) and at the Moscow School under Nicolai Tarasov, he danced in Riga (1955–6) and was soloist of Ballet of the Stanislavsky and Nemirovich-Danchenko Theatre, Moscow, where he worked with **Vladimir Bourmeister**. In 1961 he made his debut with the Bolshoi Ballet in *The Path of Thunder* and became leading male dancer. He danced the classic repertoire, and the title role in *Spartacus*. In 1962 he toured the United States with the company.

LIFAR, Serge (1905–), Russian dancer and choreographer. He studied at the State School, Kiev, was introduced to **Diaghilev**'s Ballets Russes by **Nijinska** in 1923, and became premier danseur in 1925. He created the title role in *The Prodigal Son* (1929), and the same year saw his first choreographic attempt, *Le Renard*. From 1930–44 he was ballet master and premier danseur at the **Paris Opéra Ballet**. The works he choreographed for the Opéra include *Prométhée* (1929), *Bacchus et Ariadne* (1931), *Alexandre le Grand* (1937), *Joan de Zarissa* (1942), and many others. He was artistic director and choreographer for **Nouveau Ballet de Monte Carlo** (1944–6), where his works included *Dramma per Musica* and *Chota Roustavelli*. He returned to the Paris Opéra in 1947 as choreographer, ballet master and dancer; among the works of this period were *Le Chevalier et la Damoiselle*, *Mirages* (1947), *Blanche-Neige* (1951), *Les Noces Fantastiques*, *Romeo and Juliet* (1955) and *Daphnis and Chloë* (1958). He danced the classic repertoire and retired as a performer in 1956, having often partnered **Yvette Chauviré**. He did much to revitalize ballet at the Paris Opéra until his retirement (1959), and many of his works remain in the current repertoire. As guest choreographer he created *The Moor of Venice* for Netherlands Ballet (1960), *Bonaparte at Nice* for London's **Festival Ballet** (1960), *Pique Dame* for Monte Carlo Opéra (1960) and *Phèdre* for Teatro Colón, Buenos Aires. In 1962 he was invited to return as choreographer to the Paris Opéra by Georges Auric. His company included internationally famous names such as **Youly Algarov, Vladimir Skouratov, Yvette Chauviré** and **Liane Daydé**. His publications include *La Danse* and *Serge de Diaghilev*.

LILAC GARDEN, THE or **Le Jardin aux Lilas,** a ballet in one act. Libretto, Hugh Stevenson, **Antony Tudor**; choreography, Antony Tudor; music, Ernst Chausson (*Poème*); decor, Hugh Stevenson. First performed at the Mercury Theatre, London, 26 January 1936, by Ballet Rambert. Principal dancers, **Maude Lloyd** (Caroline), **Peggy van Praagh** (An Episode from the Past of the Man She Must Marry), **Hugh Laing** (Her Lover), Antony Tudor (The Man She Must Marry)

Serge Lifar in Les Indes Galantes. Ph. Lipnitzki.

Lilac Garden: Tanaquil LeClercq and Antony Tudor in New York City Ballet production. Ph. New York City Ballet.

Also staged in New York, 15 January 1940, for **Ballet Theatre**. Principal dancers, Viola Essen, **Karen Conrad**, Antony Tudor, **Hugh Laing**. Staged in New York City Center, 27 November 1951, by **The New York City Ballet**. Principal dancers, Antony Tudor, **Nora Kaye, Tanaquil LeClercq,** Hugh Laing. Since 1954 the ballet has been in the repertoire of the National Ballet of Canada. It was staged on 12 November 1968 by Antony Tudor for **The Royal Ballet**. Principal dancers, **Antoinette Sibley, Anthony Dowell**. The story is of a girl forced into a marriage of convenience.

LINDEN, Anya (1933–   ), English dancer. She studied under Theodore Koslov in the USA, and at the Sadler's Wells School. In 1951 she joined Sadler's Wells (now **Royal**) **Ballet**, and became soloist (1954) and ballerina (1958). She created Poor

Girl in *Noctambules*, leading role in *Agon* and title role in *Antigone*. She also danced the classic ballerina repertoire as well as Bride in *La Fête Étrange* and The Wife in *The Invitation*.

LIVRY, Emma (1842–62), French ballerina. She was taught by **Maria Taglioni** and made her debut at the **Paris Opéra Ballet** in *La Sylphide* in 1858. In 1860 she created the leading role in *Le Papillon* which Taglioni had staged for her. In 1862, during a rehearsal of *La Muette de Portici*, her costume caught fire and she died from burns several months later.

LLOYD, Maude, South African dancer and ballet critic. She studied with **Marie Rambert** and was première danseuse of the Rambert company from 1936–40. She also danced with Markova-Dolin Ballet and **London Ballet**. Among the roles she created were Caroline in *The Lilac Garden* and Italian Ballerina in *Gala Performance*. As a ballet critic she and her journalist husband Nigel Gosling write jointly, under the pseudonym of Alexander Bland.

London Ballet, The, a company founded in 1938 by **Antony Tudor**. At first it performed jointly with **Agnes de Mille**. The repertoire included works by Tudor; and *Pas des Déesses, The Seasons* and *La Fête Étrange*. Among its dancers were **Hugh Laing, Peggy van Praagh, Maude Lloyd** and **Gerd Larsen**. At the outbreak of World War II the company joined with Ballet Rambert for a short time, but was disbanded in 1941.

LOPOKOVA or **LOPOUKHOVA, Lydia** (1891–   ), Russian dancer. A graduate of the Imperial School, St. Petersburg (1909), she left Russia in 1910 with **Diaghilev**'s Ballets Russes with whom she danced until 1926. She created Mariuccia in *The Good-Humoured Ladies*, Acrobat in *Parade*, Can-Can Dancer in *La Boutique Fantasque* (1919), Street Dancer in *Le Beau Danube*, a role she also danced with Soirées de Paris (1924), and she danced the leading roles in *Carnaval*,

Le Loup: Violette Verdy and Roland Petit.
Ph. Lipnitzki.

Petrouchka and *The Sleeping Beauty*. In 1931 she created the Milkmaid in *Façade* for **The Camargo Society** and danced Swanilda in *Coppélia* for Vic-Wells Ballet (1933).

LOPUKHOV, Feodor (1886–   ), Russian dancer and choreographer, Peoples' Artist of the RSFSR, brother of **Lydia Lopokova**. He studied at the Imperial School, St. Petersburg (1896–1905) and in Moscow (1907–9). He travelled to Paris and, with **Pavlova**'s company, to the United States. He was chief choreographer at the Kirov Theatre, Leningrad (1922–30; 1944–7; 1955–8) and was director of ballet at the Maly Opera Theatre, Leningrad. Among his best known works are *The Firebird* (1921), *Ice Maiden* (1927), *Taras*

Bulba (1940) and a revival of *Swan Lake* (1945). He has been a leading classical choreographer, and has encouraged and influenced **Yuri Grigorovich.**

LOUP, LE, a ballet in one act. Libretto, Jean Anouilh, Georges Neveux; choreography, **Roland Petit**; music, Henri Dutileux; decor and costumes, Jean Carzou. First performed at the Théâtre de l'Empire, Paris, 17 March 1953, by **Les Ballets de Paris de Roland Petit.** Principal dancers, **Violette Verdy** (Bride), Roland Petit (The Wolf), **Claire Sombert** (The Gypsy), George Reich (Husband). When the bridegroom absconds with a gypsy girl, his bride, believing he has been turned into a wolf, falls in love with the animal.

LUBITZ, Monika (1943–   ), East German dancer. Graduated from the State Ballet School, Berlin (1965) and went on to study in Leningrad. She had joined Leipzig Opera as soloist in 1964 and in 1969 she was accorded the title of prima ballerina. In 1970 she joined Komische Oper, Berlin. Her repertoire includes the principal roles in *Swan Lake, Cinderella, The Nutcracker* and *The Stone Flower.*

LUDLOW, Conrad (1935–   ), American dancer. He studied with Willam, Harold and Lew **Christensen** at the San Francisco School of Ballet, graduating into the San Francisco Ballet. His first creation was Student in *Con Amore* (1953). He became principal dancer in 1955, and created Paris in *Masque of Beauty and the Shepherd* and Death in *Tarot* (both 1955), and Hunter in *The Dryad* (1956). He became principal dancer with San Francisco Opera Ballet (1956), joined **The New York City Ballet** in 1957, and, after military service in Japan and Korea, rejoined in 1959. He dances a large repertoire including *Liebeslieder Walzer* (1960), *Episodes* and *Stars and Stripes*. He created Titania's Cavalier and leading male dancer in Act 2 pas de deux of *A Midsummer Night's Dream* (1961).

LULLY, Jean Baptiste (Giovanni Batista

Lulli, 1632–87), Florentine musician, composer and dancer. He organized court entertainments for Louis XIV, and appeared with the King in many ballets. In 1635 he danced in *Ballet de la Nuit*. He was largely responsible for l'**Académie Royale de Musique,** of which he was director, stage manager and conductor (1672). Conceiving ballet as being linked with singing, he collaborated with designer Bérain, dancer **Charles Beauchamp** and the poets Racine, Molière and Benserade. His works included *Le Mariage Forcé, Cadmus et Hermione, Proserpine, Isis, Le Triomphe de l'Amour* (1681) and *Le Temple de la Paix* (1685).

M

MCBRIDE, Patricia, American ballerina. She studied with Ruth Vernon, at Dance Circle New York, and at the School of American Ballet. She danced with the André Eglevsky Ballet Company (1958) and joined **The New York City Ballet** in 1959. She became soloist the following year and ballerina in 1961 at the age of 18. Her roles include Girl in Robbins's *L'Après-midi d'un Faune*, Sleepwalker in *La Sonnambula*, 3rd movement in *Symphony in C* and 2nd movement in *Western Symphony*. She has created Hermia in *A Midsummer Night's Dream*, Columbine in *Harlequinade*, and, with **Edward Villella,** dances a number of pas de deux including **Balanchine's** *Tarantella* (1964) and *Jewels*. She has been guest artist with Washington Ballet (1960).

MACDONALD, Brian (1928–), Canadian dancer, choreographer and teacher. He studied with Gerald Crevier and Elizabeth Leese, and was a founder member of National Ballet of Canada. He studied in New York, the Soviet Union and Europe (1962) and staged *Time Out of Mind* for the Robert Joffrey Ballet the same year. For Norwegian Ballet he staged *Hymn* (*Prothalamion*) and was director of Swedish Royal Ballet (1964–5). In the repertoire of the Royal Winnipeg Ballet are his works *The Darkling, Les Whoops-de-Doo, A Court Occasion* and *Prothalamion*. The same company presented his *Rose Latulippe* at the Shakespeare Festival Theatre (1966), the title role being danced by Macdonald's wife, Annette Weidershein-Paul. He became director of the **Harkness Ballet** in June 1967.

MACLEARY, Donald (1937–), British dancer, born in Scotland. He studied with Sheila Ross (1950–1) and at the Sadler's Wells School (1951), entering their Theatre Ballet in 1954 and becoming soloist in 1955. He then joined Sadler's Wells Ballet and became a principal dancer with **The Royal Ballet,** and regular partner to **Svetlana Beriosova** (1959). He has created Bridegroom in *Le Baiser de la Fée* (1960), Principal in *Symphony* (1961), and the male lead in *Diversions*, and has partnered **Fonteyn** in *Cinderella*. He has danced Romeo in **MacMillan's** *Romeo and Juliet*, The Lover in *The Lilac Garden* (1968), Friday's Child in *Jazz Calendar* (1969) and Jean de Brienne in *Raymonda*.

MACMILLAN, Kenneth (1930–), British dancer and choreographer. He studied at the Sadler's Wells School, joining its Theatre Ballet in 1946 and transferring to Sadler's Wells Ballet in 1948, where he danced the Florestan and His Sisters pas de trois in *The Sleeping Beauty* and pas de trois in *Ballet Impérial*. He returned to Sadler's Wells Theatre Ballet (1952), making his choreographic debut with *Somnambulism* (1953). In 1955 he choreographed *Danses Concertantes* and *The House of Birds*. For **The Royal Ballet** he staged *Noctambules* (1956), *Agon* (1958), *Le Baiser de la Fée* (1960), *The Invitation* (with **Lynn Seymour**) and *Diversions* (1961), *The Rite of Spring* (1962), *Symphony* (1963) and *Song of the Earth* (1965). *Romeo and Juliet* (1965) was his first full-length ballet. For American Ballet Theatre he choreographed *Journey* and *Winter's Eve* (1957); for the Royal Danish Ballet *The Burrow, Danses Concertantes* and *Solitaire* (1961); he was guest choreographer with Stuttgart Opera Ballet (1965), where he also staged *Miss Julie* (1970); and resident choreographer with The Royal Ballet (1965–6). In 1966 he became resident choreographer with the German Opera Ballet, West Berlin, where he has staged *Valse Nobles* and *Concerto*

(1966), *Olympiade* (1968), and created *Cain and Abel* (1968). He became joint director of The Royal Ballet in 1970, and for them staged *Anastasia* (1971) and *Triad* (1972).

MAD TRISTAN *see* **Tristan Fou.**

MADAME CHRYSANTHÈME, a ballet in one act, based on the novel by Pierre Loti. Choreography, **Frederick Ashton;** music, Alan Rawsthorne; decor, Isabel Lambert. First performed at the Royal Opera House, Covent Garden, London, 1 April 1955, by Sadler's Wells Ballet. Principal dancers, **Elaine Fifield** (Chrysanthème), Alexander Grant (Pierre), Ray Powell (Marriage Broker). Pierre, a sailor on shore leave in Japan, marries Chrysanthème. For her, it is no more than a 'port' wedding.

MAGALLANES, Nicholas, American dancer, born in Mexico. A pupil at the School of American Ballet, he made his professional debut in *A Thousand Times Neigh* (1940). With Ballet Society he danced the first American performance of *Symphony in C.* He was soloist with Ballet Caravan for their 1941 South American tour, and danced with Littlefield Ballet in 1942. From 1943–6 he danced with **Ballet Russe de Monte Carlo,** rising from the corps de ballet to leading dancer. Here he created the roles Poet in *Night Shadow,* Cléonte in *Le Bourgeois Gentilhomme* and danced in *Concerto Barocco* (1945). He joined Ballet Society in 1946 and remained as principal dancer when it became **The New York City Ballet** in 1948. From his enormous repertoire are the creations in **Balanchine**'s *Orpheus* (1948) and 2nd movement in *Western Symphony;* and he is noted for his dancing in **Ashton**'s *Illuminations* and *Bourée Fantasque* in **Robbins**'s *La Cage* (1951).

MAGIC FLUTE, THE, a ballet in one act. Libretto and choreography, **Lev Ivanov;** music, Riccardo Drigo. First performed, 22 March 1893, by the Imperial Ballet School, St. Petersburg, and presented at the Maryinsky Theatre, 23 April 1893. Principal dancers, **Michel Fokine** (Luke), **Agrippina Vaganova, Serge Legat.** The ballet was taken into her company's repertoire by **Anna Pavlova.** Pavlova took the part of Lise, with **Alexandre Volinine** (Luke) and **Enrico Cecchetti** (Marquis). Lise and Luke are village lovers. Lise's mother favours her engagement to the Marquis. Oberon gives Luke the magic flute which makes everyone dance and Luke persuades Lise's mother to consent to their marriage. This work is in no way connected with the opera by Mozart.

MAKAROVA, Maria (1885–   ), Russian ballet teacher, Honoured Artist of the RSFSR. She studied at the Imperial School, St. Petersburg and joined the Maryinsky Theatre. In 1936 she became teacher at the Kiev Theatre and in 1955 was appointed ballet mistress of Ballet Rio de Janeiro, Brazil.

Nicholas Magallanes in The Cage. Ph. New York City Ballet.

MAKAROVA, Natalia Romanovna (1940–), Russian ballerina. She studied in Leningrad, joining the Kirov company in 1959. Her repertoire includes many of the classical roles. She was a Gold Medallist at Varna (1965). In 1970, during the London season of the Kirov Ballet, she elected to remain when the company left for Holland, and later that year joined American Ballet Theatre. She was awarded the Pavlova Prize (1970).

MAM'ZELLE ANGOT, a ballet in three scenes. Libretto and choreography, **Léonide Massine**; music, Charles Lecocq (from his comic opera, *La Fille de Madame Angot*); decor, Mstislav Doboujinsky. First performed at the Metropolitan Opera House, New York, 10 October 1943, by **Ballet Theatre**. Principal dancers, **Nora Kaye, Janet Reed** (Mam'zelle Angot), **André Eglevsky** (Artist), **Rosella Hightower** (Aristocrat), **Simon Semenov** (Official). Performed at the Royal Opera House, Covent Garden, London, 26 November 1947, by Sadler's Wells Ballet. Decor, André Derain. Principal dancers, **Margot Fonteyn, Nadia Nerina,** Alexander Grant, **Michael Somes, Moira Shearer,** Franklin White. The work is a confusing but jovial love story.

MANCHESTER, P. W., American editor and critic, born in Britain. She was ballet critic of *Theatre World* (1941–3) and founder-editor of *Ballet Today* (1946). In 1951 she moved to the United States and became managing editor of *Dance News*. Among her published works is *Vic-Wells: A Ballet Progress* (1942). With **Anatole Chujoy,** she compiled and edited *The Dance Encyclopedia* (1967 edition).

MARCHAND, Colette (1925–), French dancer. She studied with **Gsovsky** and **Volinine**; and at the Paris Opéra school, dancing with the **Paris Opéra Ballet** until 1946. She was ballerina with the **Metropolitan Ballet,** England (1947). As leading dancer with **Les Ballets de Paris de Roland Petit** (1948), she created the leading roles in

L'Oeuf à la Coque and *Le Combat* (1949), and danced Agathe in *Les Demoiselles de la Nuit*. In 1953 she created the leading roles in *Deuil en 24 Heures, Ciné-Bijou* and *Lady in the Ice*. She toured with **Milorad Miskovitch** during the 1950s. Nicknamed 'Legs' by the Americans, she was chosen to play leading role in the film *Moulin Rouge* (1953). Guest artist in London (1960).

MARIE-JEANNE (Marie-Jeanne Pelus, 1920–), American dancer and teacher. She entered the School of American Ballet in 1934 and was a member of Ballet Caravan (1937–40). As guest artist with **Ballet Russe de Monte Carlo** (1941), she danced *Serenade*, and with **The American Ballet** South American tour the same year she created the leading roles in *Concerto Barocco* and *Ballet Impérial*. In 1942 she danced with Original Ballet Russe, and in 1944 created the leading roles in *Constantia* and *Colloque Sentimental* for Ballet International du Marquis de Cuevas. As ballerina with Ballet Russe de Monte Carlo (1945–7), her repertoire included *Concerto Barocco, Ballet Impérial, Le Baiser de la Fée, Les Sylphides* and *Night Shadow*. With Ballet Society (1948), she created Nymph in *Triumph of Bacchus and Ariadne*. She then joined **Grand Ballet du Marquis de Cuevas** and took up teaching on her retirement in 1954.

MARIÉS DE LA TOUR EIFFEL, LES, a surrealistic ballet in one act. Libretto, Jean Cocteau; choreography, **Jan Börlin**; music, G. Tailleferre, Georges Auric, Arthur Honegger, Darius Milhaud, Francis Poulenc; decor, Irène Lagut; costumes, Jean Hugo. First performed at the Théâtre des Champs-Elysées, Paris, 18 June 1921, by Ballet Suèdois. Principal dancer, **Carina Ari.** On the first platform of the Eiffel Tower, a photographer raises his camera and there appear, in turn, an ostrich, a bathing belle and a lion. The work is intended as a satire on the narrow-mindedness of the bourgeoisie; it is vulgar and audacious, yet evokes the atmosphere of the years following World War 1.

MARKOVA, Alicia (Lilian Alicia Marks, 1910–   ), British prima ballerina, Dame of the Order of the British Empire. She studied with **Astafieva, Legat, Cecchetti** and Celli, and made her debut with **Diaghilev's** Ballets Russes in *Aurora's Wedding*. Dancing with this company (1925–9), she won great acclaim dancing the title role in *Le Rossignol* (1926) and Blue Bird pas de deux in *Aurora's Wedding*. Her graceful, poetical style resembled that of Taglioni. With Ballet Rambert, she created the leading roles in *La Péri, Foyer de Danse, Bar aux Folies-Bergère*; with **The Camargo Society** she created Polka in *Façade*. From 1931–3 she danced with Vic-Wells Ballet and was prima ballerina (1933–5). She created the Ballerina role in Ashton's *Les Rendez-vous* (1933), Betrayed Girl in *The Rake's Progress* in 1935, and was the first English ballerina to dance Giselle and Odette-Odile. She was prima ballerina and co-founder of the Markova-Dolin Company (1935–8) and ballerina with the

Alicia Markova. Ph. Maurice Seymour.

Blum-Massine **Ballet Russe de Monte Carlo** (1938–41), where she created the 3rd movement – Sky in *Seventh Symphony*. She danced leading roles in **Massine's** *Rouge et Noir* and *L'Étrange Farandole*, and title role in *Giselle*. While ballerina with **Ballet Theatre** (1941–4, 1945–6), she created Zemphire in *Aleko*, Juliet in **Tudor's** *Romeo and Juliet* and the title role in *Firebird*. From 1944–5 she was with Seven Lively Arts Revue; she toured the United States, Canada, Mexico and the Philippines with a new Markova-Dolin company (1945–6, 1947, 1947–8). When she was guest artist with Original Ballet Russe (1946–7) she created the title role in *Camille*. In 1948 she danced *Giselle, Swan Lake* and her first *Sleeping Beauty* as guest artist with Sadler's Wells Ballet. Later in the same year she was guest artist with **Ballet Russe de Monte Carlo.** She toured South Africa with **Anton Dolin** in 1949, and together they founded London's **Festival Ballet** with Markova as prima ballerina (1950–1). After leaving Festival Ballet, toured all over the world as guest artist with **Grand Ballet du Marquis de Cuevas** (1955), **Ruth Page's** Chicago Opera Ballet (1955–6), Metropolitan Opera House, New York, the Royal Danish Ballet, **Teatro alla Scala,** Milan and Teatro Municipal, Rio de Janeiro. She made her final appearance in 1962 with Festival Ballet, dancing in *L'Après-midi d'un Faune* partnered by **Milorad Miskovitch**; officially retired in January 1963 and became director of the Metropolitan Opera Ballet. She retired from the Metropolitan in 1970 and took a teaching post at Cincinatti University, Ohio. She has written a book entitled *Giselle and I.*

MARTIN, John (1893–   ), American writer and dance critic. He was dance editor and critic of *The New York Times* (1927–62), and lectured on dance history and criticism (1930–45). An early supporter of modern dance, his published works include *The Modern Dance* (1933) and *World Book of Modern Ballet* (1952). In 1965 he was appointed lecturer on dance at the University of California.

Maryinsky Theatre *see* **Russia, history of ballet in.**

MASSACRE DES AMAZONS, a ballet in one act. Libretto and choreography, **Janine Charrat**; music, Ivan Semenov; decor, Jean Bazaire. First performed at the Théâtre Municipal, Grenoble, France, 1952, by Janine Charrat's company. Principal dancers, Janine Charrat, René Bon, Vladimir Oukhtomsky, Tania Ouspenska, Annik Tassigny. A herd of wild horses are attacked and slaughtered by hunting Amazons. One white horse revives some of his companions and they attack the Amazons. The horse bears away the body of the Amazon who had tried to tame him.

MASSINE, Léonide (Leonid Fedorovitch Miassine, 1896–   ), Russian choreographer and dancer. A graduate of the Imperial School, Moscow (1912), he studied under Domashov and **Nicholas Legat,** and with **Cecchetti** when he joined the **Diaghilev** company (1914–20). With Diaghilev's Ballets Russes, he made his debut in *The Legend of Joseph* (1914). and his choreographic debut with *Soleil de Nuit* (1915). He was choreographer, dancer and artistic director of **Ballet Russe de Monte Carlo** (1932–

1941), and **Ballet Theatre** (1941–4); he organized Ballet Russe Highlights (1945-6); was guest choreographer with **Ballet International**; Sadler's Wells Ballet; the Royal Danish Ballet; **Teatro alla Scala** and Opéra Comique (1947–51); Ballet Européens (1960) and **The Royal Ballet** (1962). His most famous ballets include *The Good-Humoured Ladies, Contes Russe* (1917), *La Boutique Fantasque, The Three-Cornered Hat* (1919), *Le Sacre du Printemps, Les Fâcheux* (1924), *La Belle Hélène* (1932), *Les Présages* and *Choreartium* (1933), *Le Bal* (1935), *Aleko* (1942), *La Valse* (1950) and *The Fall of the House of Usher* (1955). He also choreographed dances for a number of films, including *Red Shoes* (1948), and film versions were made of a number of his ballets including *Capriccio Espagñol* and *Gaieté Parisienne.* In 1966 he joined the newly founded **Ballets de Monte Carlo** as choreographer and artistic director. See illustration p. 146.

MATELOTS, LES, a ballet in five scenes. Libretto, Boris Kochno; choreography, **Léonide Massine**; music, Georges Auric; decor, Pedro Pruna. First performed at the Théâtre Gaîté-Lyrique, Paris, 17 June 1925, by **Diaghilev's** Ballets Russes.

Massacre of the Amazons. Ph. Lipnitzki.

Léonide Massine. Ph. Lipnitzki.

Principal dancers, **Serge Lifar, Vera Nemtchinova, Léon Woizikowsky, Lydia Sokolova.** Presented at the Coliseum Theatre, London, 25 June 1925. Revived, 14 September 1946, by Ballets for America. Decor, Eugene Dunkel. Principal dancers, Tatiana Grantzeva, Galina Razoumova, Yurek Shabelevsky, **Paul Petrov.** A sailor and his friends disguise themselves to test the fidelity of the sailor's fiancée.

MAURI, Rosita (1849–1923), Spanish dancer. She made her debut in 1866 and was principal dancer at Teatro Principal, Barcelona (1868). Her debut at the Paris Opéra (1878) was in the opera *Polyeucte.* As danseuse étoile with the **Paris Opéra Ballet** she created the leading role in *La Korrigane*, which Mérante choreographed for her (1880). She also created Gourouli in *Les Deux Pigeons* (1886), her most famous role. She danced at the Opéra until 1907.

MAXIMOVA, Yekaterina (1939–), Russian ballerina. She studied at the Bolshoi Theatre School (1949–58) and danced the adagio from *Sleeping Beauty* and 2nd pas de deux from *Giselle* for her graduation performance. During her first season with the Bolshoi (1958–9) she created Katerina in *The Stone Flower*. **Ulanova** coached her for *Giselle* (1960) and she danced Waltz and Prelude in *Chopiniana*, Jeanne in *Flames of Paris* and in *The Nutcracker*. During the Bolshoi's 1966 American visit she was acclaimed for her Kitri in *Don Quixote*, partnered by her husband **Vladimir Vassiliev.** In 1969 she danced *Giselle* and *Swan Lake* in London.

MAY, Pamela (1917–), British ballerina and teacher, born in Trinidad. A graduate of the Sadler's Wells School, she made her debut in the pas de trois in *Swan Lake* (1934) with Vic-Wells Ballet, dancing under the name Doris May. With the company until 1953, she rose from soloist to ballerina. Among the roles she created were Girl in Brown in *Les Patineurs*, Lover in *The Wanderer*. She danced Odette-Odile in *Swan Lake*, Lilac Fairy, Aurora and Blue Bird in *Sleeping Beauty* and Rich Girl in *Nocturne*. She is also noted for her role in **Ashton's** *Symphonic Variations* (1946). As guest artist with **The Royal Ballet,** she has appeared in the mime role Princess Mother in *Swan Lake* and Bathilde in *Giselle*. She has been guest artist with **Teatro alla Scala,** Milan, and has taught at the Royal Ballet School.

MAZILIER, Joseph (Guilio Mazarini, 1797–1868), French dancer and choreographer. He made his debut in Paris (1822). He joined the **Paris Opéra Ballet,** where he became first character dancer (1833) and ballet master and choreographer (1839). Among his choreographic works are *La Gypsy* (1839), *Le Diable à Quatre* (1845), *Paquita* (1846), *Vert-Vert* (1851) and *Le Corsaire* (1856). Mazilier was not recognized in his lifetime, but *Paquita* and *Le Corsaire* still survive, although much altered.

MEDEA AND JASON, a ballet-pantomime. Choreography, **Jean-Georges Noverre**; music, Rodolphe. First performed at Stuttgart, 11 February 1763. Principal dancers, Nency, **Gaetan Vestris**

It was in this production that Vestris was the first dancer in the history of ballet to appear unmasked.

MESSERER, Asaf (1903–), Russian premier danseur and teacher, Peoples' Artist of the RSFSR. He was a pupil of **Mikhail Mordkin** and danced in the Theatre of Working Youth, Moscow. He entered the senior class at the Bolshoi School in 1920 and graduated in 1921. He replaced mime with expressive acting in his first important role, Siegfried in *Swan Lake* (1922). The undisputed premier danseur noble of the Bolshoi, he added many new steps to the male dancer's repertoire. He danced the principal male roles in the Bolshoi's entire repertoire, including *The Red Poppy, Flames of Paris, The Fountain of Bakhchisarai* and *Cinderella*. A teacher at the Bolshoi School after 1923, he began to teach the classe de perfection in 1942, and was considered the most important teacher there. He retired from the stage in 1954. In 1924 he choreographed *The Battle of Toys* and *Schumanniana* for Victorina Krieger Art Ballet. His 4th Act of *Swan Lake* is now in the Bolshoi's repertoire. He was one of the first Soviet dancers to tour outside the Soviet Union, partnering his wife **Irina Tikhomirnova.** For the Budapest Opera he choreographed *Swan Lake* (1952), and in 1960 was invited to Brussels to establish a school at the Théâtre Royal de la Monnaie. He was ballet master for the Bolshoi's foreign tours in 1956, 1958 and 1962, and choreographed *School of Ballet* for the last tour.

Metropolitan Ballet, a company formed in London in 1947 by Leon Hepner. **Victor Gsovsky** was ballet master and choreographer. It was re-organized after its first season, with **Nicholas Beriosov** as régisseur and **Celia Franca** as ballet mistress. Among its dancers were **Svetlana Beriosova, Colette Marchand** and **Erik Bruhn ; Sonia Arova, David Adams** and **Henry Danton** also made appearances. For this company **John Taras** created *Designs with Strings* (1948). The Metropolitan Ballet was disbanded in 1948.

MILLER, Patricia (1927–), South African ballerina and teacher. She joined South African Ballet (1941) and Cape Town Ballet Club. In 1947 she went to London to study at Sadler's Wells School, and became a principal dancer with Sadler's Wells Theatre Ballet. She created Columbine in *Harlequin in April* and La Capricciosa in *The Lady and the Fool.* She visited South Africa in 1953 and 1954 with Sadler's Wells Ballet, and returned there in 1956 to set up a school in Cape Town.

MILLOSS, Aurel (Aurel Milloss de Miholy or Aurel von Milloss, 1906–), Hungarian dancer, choreographer and director, a naturalized Italian citizen. A pupil at École Blasis, Belgrade, he also studied with **Laban, Wigman** and **Gsovsky,** making his debut in 1929. He succeeded **Harald Kreutzberg** as premier danseur at the Berlin Opera where he staged *Gaukelei.* He danced in Augsburg and Düsseldorf, and was guest premier danseur with Budapest Opera (1933–5), National Hungarian Theatre, Budapest (1936–8), and San Carlo Opera, Naples (1936). He succeeded **Boris Romanov** as choreographer and ballet master at Teatro Reale, Rome (1938), and from 1939–41 staged works for the Florence, Venice, and other European Festivals. He spent the 1942–3 season at **Teatro alla Scala,** Milan, where he staged his version of *The Miraculous Mandarin.* Toscanini invited him to re-organize the ballet company at La Scala in 1946, where he remained until 1950. He spent two seasons with Rome Opera (1951–2) and re-organized the ballet companies of São Paulo and Rio de Janeiro (1953, 1954). He returned to South America in 1958. In 1959 he became ballet director of Cologne Opera where he separated the opera from the ballet in 1962. He was director of ballet at the State Opera, Vienna (1963–6) and became choreographer with Teatro dell' Opera, Rome. He has choreographed *Jeu de Cartes, Marsyas* and *Mystères de Bartók* (1951), and re-choreographed *Pulcinella,*

Petrouchka, Coppélia, The Prodigal Son, Firebird and *Le Sacre du Printemps*.

MIRACULOUS MANDARIN, THE, a dramatic dance pantomime in one act, based on a story by Melchior Lengyel. Libretto, Béla Bartók; choreography, Hans Strobach; music, Bartók. First performed, 28 November 1926, in Cologne, but banned on the grounds of immorality. The ban was imposed for the same reasons in 1927 in Prague, and in 1945 in Budapest. A revised version was given in Budapest in 1956, and is still performed there. Aurel Millos staged a new version (1942), at **Teâtro alla Scala,** Milan. A version was presented in New York City Center, 6 September 1951, by **The New York City Ballet.** Choreography, **Todd Bolen-** der; decor, Alvin Colt. Another version was presented in Edinburgh, 27 August 1956, by Sadler's Wells Ballet. Choreography, Alfred Rodrigues; decor, Georges Wakhevich. Principal dancers, **Elaine Fifield, Michael Somes.** The ballet was staged in Paris, 1958, by Ballet de France de Janine Charrat, and in Moscow, 1961, by the Bolshoi Ballet (under the title *The Night City*). A new version was staged at the Royal Theatre, Copenhagen, 19 June 1967, by the Royal Danish Ballet. Choreography, **Flemming Flindt.** Principal dancers, Flemming Flindt, Vivi Flindt. A prostitute attracts victims for gangsters who rob and murder them. The Mandarin falls victim but miraculously resists death for long enough to force the gangsters to flee in panic, and to forgive the prostitute.

Milorad Miskovitch and Claire Sombert in Prometheus. Ph. S. Lido.

MIRROR FOR WITCHES, A, a ballet in prologue and five scenes, based on a novel by Esther Forbes. Choreography, **Andrée Howard**; music, Dennis Aplvor; decor, Norman Adams; costumes, Andrée Howard, Norman Adams. First performed at the Royal Opera House, Covent Garden, London, 4 March 1952, by Sadler's Wells Ballet. Principal dancers, Anne Heaton (Doll), **Julia Farron** (Hannah), **Leslie Edwards** (Bilby), John Hart (Stranger), Philip Chatfield (Titus). In 17th century New England, a jealous wife engineers a charge of witchcraft against the young girl whom her husband has adopted.

MISKOVITCH, Milorad (1928–), Yugoslav dancer. He studied under **Kirsanova, Kniasev** and **Preobrajenska,** and at the dance school of the Belgrade Opera, where he made his debut. He was soloist with **Les Ballets des Champs-Elysées, International Ballet** and Original Ballet Russe (1947), and **Grand Ballet du Marquis de Cuevas** (1948). With **Les Ballets de Paris de Roland Petit** he danced in *Le Combat, Le Beau Danube* and *Adame Miroir.* He was leading dancer with Ballets Janine Charrat and guest artist with London's **Festival Ballet** (1952). In 1954 he partnered **Markova** in recitals, and in 1956 founded his own company, of which he was premier danseur and created the title role in *Promethée.* In 1961 he was guest artist with **Ruth Page's** Chicago Opera Ballet. He partnered Markova in *L'Après-midi d'un Faune* (1962), her final appearance before retirement, with Festival Ballet.

MISS JULIE, a ballet in one act, based on the play by Strindberg. Libretto, Allan Fredericia; choreography, **Birgit Cullberg**; music, Ture Rangström; decor, Fredericia. First performed at the Riksteatern, Stockholm, 1 March 1950, by the Royal Swedish Ballet. Principal dancers, Elsa-Marianne von Rosen, Julius Mengarelli. This version was presented in London in 1951. A revised version was taken into the repertoire of American Ballet Theatre and performed at the Metropolitan

Miss Julie. Ph. Taisto Tuomi.

Opera House, New York, 18 September 1958. Principal dancers, **Violette Verdy, Erik Bruhn.** The ballet is also in the repertoire of the Royal Danish Ballet. Another version was staged by **Kenneth MacMillan** for the Stuttgart Opera Ballet, 8 March 1970. Music, Andrzej Panufnik. Principal dancer, **Marcia Haydée.**

MITCHELL, Arthur (1934–), American dancer. A graduate of the High School of Performing Arts, he won a scholarship to the School of American Ballet, made his debut in *Western Symphony* (1955), and joined **The New York City Ballet** in 1956, becoming soloist in 1959. He has created Unicorn in *The Unicorn, the Gorgon and the Manticore,* pas de deux in *Agon,* male lead in *Ebony Concerto.* He is noted for his outstanding Puck in *A Midsummer Night's Dream.* He danced at Spoleto's Festival of Two Worlds (1960, 1961); created the title role in *Othello* in Munich and was guest artist with Stuttgart Ballet where he danced Mercutio in **Cranko's** *Romeo and Juliet* (1963). He founded his own company, the Haarlem Dance Company.

MLAKAR, Pino (1907–   ), German dancer and choreographer, born in Yugoslavia. A student of **Rudolf von Laban** and Yelena Poliakova, he made his debut in Darmstadt in 1929 and was soloist at Dessau in 1930. For his *Un Amour du Moyen Age* he won the Bronze Medal in Les Archives Internationales de la Danse competition, Paris (1932). It was later presented at Stadttheater, Zurich, where he was principal dancer and choreographer (1935–8). His other works included *The Devil in the Village* (1935), *Prometheus* (1937), *Jeu de Cartes* and *Til Eulenspiegel*. For the State Opera, Munich, where he was danseur étoile and choreographer (1939–1943), his works included *Damina* and *La Fée des Poupées*. For Prinz Regenttheatre, Munich, he choreographed *Tragedy of Salome*, *Bolero* and *Turandot*. For Ljubljana Opera he created *Kolo Symphone* and *The Little Ballerina*. Mlakar choreographed most of his ballets with his wife Pia.

MLAKAR, Veronika (1935–   ), Yugoslav dancer, born in Switzerland, daughter of Pia and **Pino Mlakar**. She studied with her mother, and at the Sadler's Wells School, the School of American Ballet and the Ballet Theatre School. In 1947 she made her debut in *Ljubljana* and danced Swanilda in *Coppélia* (1951) with the Munich State Opera Ballet. In 1955 she joined **Les Ballets de Paris de Roland Petit**; danced a season with **Milorad Miskovitch**'s company; and joined **Ruth Page**'s Chicago Opera Ballet (1957) and Jerome Robbins's Ballets: USA (1961). In 1964 she joined American Ballet Theatre, and became soloist, dancing Mother of the Groom in *Les Noces*, Hagar in *Pillar of Fire* (1966), and title roles in *Moon Reindeer* (1966) and *Miss Julie* (1967).

MOISEYEV, Igor (1906–   ), Russian choreographer and dancer, Peoples' Artist of the USSR. Initially he studied privately, then entered the Bolshoi School in 1921 and made his debut in 1924. He also studied under **Tikhomirov**. As soloist with the Bolshoi (1925), he danced both classic and demi-caractère roles including *Sailor's Dance*, *The Partisans*, Slave in *La Bayadère*, Phoenix Bird in *The Red Flower*, and title role in the marvellously comic *Football Player* which he choreographed in 1930. Dances set to Prokofiev's *The Love of Three Oranges* established him as a choreographer; *Salammbo* was his first major work (1932), followed by *Three Fat Men*. In 1936 he was invited to head the choreographic department of the Folk Art Theatre. In 1937 the State Folk Dance Ensemble was founded and Moiseyev became its director. Today company dancers are trained in classic and character dance at either the Bolshoi Theatre School or its National Dance Department, which Moiseyev heads. He has choreographed numerous folk ballets, and the Ensemble has toured Europe.

MOISEYEVA, Olga (1928–   ), Russian ballerina, Honoured Artist of the RSFSR. She studied with **Agrippina Vaganova** in Leningrad and danced the leading role in *Nikia* (1949) with the Kirov Ballet. She became ballerina in 1953. Among her roles are Odette-Odile in *Swan Lake*, the title role in *Gayané* and Kitri in *Don Quixote*. She toured with the Kirov in Britain, France, the United States and Canada during the 1960s.

MONAHAN, James Henry Francis (1912–   ), English writer and critic, Commander of the Order of the British Empire. He was ballet critic of *The [Manchester] Guardian*. Among his published works is *Fonteyn: Study of the Ballerina in Her Setting* (1958). He is currently working with the BBC.

MONCION, Francisco, American dancer, born in the Dominican Republic. A pupil at the School of American Ballet, he made his debut with New Opera Company (1942) in **Balanchine**'s *Imperial*. As soloist with **Ballet International** (1944) he created the title roles in *Sebastian* and *Mad Tristan*. He joined Ballet Society (1946) and remained with the company when it became

The New York City Ballet. He created the leading roles in *La Valse, Divertimento* (1947), *L'Après-midi d'un Faune* (1953), *Prodigal Son*, and in his own work *Pastorale* (1957). During his career he partnered **Maria Tallchief, Nora Kaye** and **Tanaquil LeClercq.**

MONOTONES I AND II, plotless ballets in one act with choreography by **Frederick Ashton.** *Monotones II* was the first. Music, Satie (*Trois Gnossiennes*). First performed at the Royal Opera House, Covent Garden, 24 March 1965, by **The Royal Ballet.** Principal dancers, Vyvyan Lorrayne, **Anthony Dowell,** Robert Mead. A trio of dancers group together, separate into solos and duets, and rejoin. *Monotones I* followed a year later. Music, Satie (*Trois Gymnopédies*). First performed at The Royal Opera House, Covent Garden, 25 April 1966, by The Royal Ballet. Principal dancers, **Antoinette Sibley,** Georgina Parkinson, Brian Shaw. The casting of *Monotones II* is reversed by using two women and one man.

MORDKIN, Mikhail (1881–1944), Russian dancer, choreographer and teacher. A graduate of the Imperial School of Ballet, Moscow, he was premier danseur (1900) and ballet master at the Bolshoi Theatre, Moscow. In 1909 he danced with the **Diaghilev** Ballets Russes, but left to partner **Pavlova** at the **Paris Opéra Ballet.** He and Pavlova were then invited to appear at the Metropolitan Opera House (1910) in New York. Their outstanding performance led to a tour of the United States during 1910 and 1911. Mordkin subsequently returned to Russia, where he organized European and American tours with a company which included **Yeka-tarina Geltzer, Julia Sedova, Lydia Lopokova** and **Alexandre Volinine.** He then became ballet master at the Bolshoi Theatre, Moscow. He returned to the United States in 1923, formed his own company which appeared in the Greenwich Village Follies, New York (1924), and toured America with the company (1925–1926). His dancers included **Vera Nem-** tchinova, Xenia Makletzova and Hilda Butsova. Mordkin then opened his own school in New York, also teaching in Philadelphia, and re-organized his company. In 1938 the Mordkin Ballet became a professional company, and in 1939 it was re-organized into **Ballet Theatre,** later American Ballet Theatre. Mordkin then returned to teaching. Ballets he staged for his own company included *Giselle*, a revival of *La Fille Mal Gardée* (1939) and *Trepak*.

Mordkin Ballet *see* **Mordkin, Mikhail.**

MOREAU, Jacqueline (1926–), French dancer. She studied with Nora Kiss and at the Paris Opéra school, with whose company she made her debut in *La Nuit Ensorcelée*. She became première danseuse of the **Paris Opéra Ballet** in 1948, joined **Les Ballets des Champs-Elysées** as leading dancer in 1951 and was ballerina with **Grand Ballet du Marquis de Cuevas** (1952–9). Her repertoire included *Serenade, Pas de Quatre, Les Sylphides, Apollo* and *Giselle*.

Jacqueline Moreau: with Nicholas Pola-jenko. Ph. Lipnitzki.

MORRICE, Norman (1931–   ), British dancer and choreographer, born in Mexico. He studied at the Royal Academy of Dancing, London, and at the Rambert school. He joined Ballet Rambert company in 1953, dancing Dr. Coppelius in *Coppélia*, James in *La Sylphide* and Poet in *Night Shadow*. His first choreographic work *Two Brothers* (1958), was followed by the obscure *Tribute* (1965), *The Realms of Choice* (1965), *Hazard* (1967), *1-2-3* (1968), and *Blind-sight* (1969). He became associate director of the new avant-garde Ballet Rambert in 1966.

MOTTE, Claire (1937–   ), French dancer. She studied at the Paris Opéra school and with Yves Brieux. She became première danseuse of the **Paris Opéra Ballet** in 1955 and étoile in 1961 dancing mainly the classical repertoire. Her roles include *Chemin de Lumière*, *Les Sylphides*, *Giselle*, both title role and Queen of the Wilis and Odette-Odile in *Swan Lake*.

MUSIL, Karl (1939–   ), Austrian dancer. Having studied with Willy Fränzl and at the ballet school of the Vienna State Opera, he entered the company in 1953 and became soloist in 1958. His repertoire includes leading roles in *Giselle*, *Black Swan* and *Don Quixote* pas de deux, *Paquita* pas de trois and Siegfried in Nureyev's *Swan Lake* (1964). As guest artist with London's **Festival Ballet** (1963), he alternated with John Gilpin in *Peer Gynt*. He was guest artist with **Ballet Russe de Monte Carlo,** Stuttgart Opera Ballet, **Janine Charrat's** company at the International Ballet Festival (1964) and with **Ruth Page's** Chicago Opera Ballet (1965). In June 1967 he partnered **Beriosova** with **The Royal Ballet,** dancing in *Swan Lake* and *Giselle*.

MUTE WIFE, THE, a ballet in one act, based on *The Man Who Married a Dumb Wife* by Anatole France. Choreography, Antonia Cobos; music, Vittorio Rieti; decor, Rico Lebrun. First performed at the International Theatre, New York, 22 November 1944, by **Ballet International.** Principal dancers, Antonia Cobos (Wife), **Francisco Moncion** (Husband), **Serge Ismailov** (Doctor). A short version was staged at the Metropolitan Opera House, New York, October 1946, by Original Ballet Russe. Principal dancers, Antonia Cobos, **George Skibine, Francisco Moncion.** Performed at the Metropolitan Opera House, New York, 16 September 1949, by **Ballet Russe de Monte Carlo.** Choreography (revised), Antonia Cobos; music, Scarlatti. Principal dancers, Nina Novak, **Leon Danielian,** Robert Lindgren. The husband calls on the doctor to restore his wife's speech. But she chatters so much that he then asks the doctor to stop his hearing. The chattering is simulated by the dancer playing castanets.

N

NAÏAD AND THE FISHERMAN, THE
see **Ondine, ou la Naïade.**

NAPOLI or **The Fisherman and his Bride,** a ballet in three acts. Choreography, **August Bournonville**; music, Paulli, Helsted, Gade. First performed at the Royal Theatre, Copenhagen, 29 March 1842, by the Royal Danish Ballet. Principal dancer, August Bournonville. A one-act version by Giovanni Pratesi was presented at the Alhambra Theatre, London in 1900, with music by George Byng. **Harald Lander** staged it as a one-act ballet, 30 August 1954, for London's **Festival Ballet.** Decor, Osbert Lancaster. Principal dancers, **Toni Lander** (Bride), **Oleg Briansky** (Bridegroom). **Erik Bruhn** staged the third act divertissement at the Royal Opera House, Covent Garden, London, 3 May 1962, for **The Royal Ballet.** The story is of the tribulations of lovers. It is one of Denmark's most popular ballets, includes many theatrical devices and notable mime and crowd scenes, and ends with a spectacular Tarantella.

Nationaal Ballet, Het *see* **Holland, history of ballet in.**

National Ballet of Canada *see* **Canada, history of ballet in.**

National Ballet of Cuba *see* **Cuba, National Ballet of.**

NAUTÉOS, a ballet in three acts. Choreography, **Serge Lifar**; music, Leleu; decor, Brayer. Originally prepared for **Nouveau Ballet de Monte Carlo,** it was first performed, in a shortened version, 12 July 1954, by the **Paris Opéra Ballet.** Principal dancers, **Yvette Chauviré, Madelaine Lafon, Michel Renault.** The story is of a water nymph and a shipwrecked sailor. See illustration p. 154.

Nederlands Ballet, Het *see* **Holland, history of ballet in.**

NEARY, Patricia (1942–), American dancer. She studied with Georges Milenov, Thomas Armour, at the National Ballet

Napoli: performed by the London Festival Ballet Ph. Lipnitzki.

Nautéos by Serge Lifar. Ph. Lipnitzki.

School, Toronto, Canada, and the School of American Ballet. In 1962 she danced the leading roles in *Apollo, Orpheus* and *Agon* at the Stravinsky Festival in Hamburg. Later that year she joined **The New York City Ballet** as soloist where her repertoire includes Polyhymnia in *Apollo*, Dewdrop in *The Nutcracker*, Leader of Bacchantes in *Orpheus*, pas de neuf in *Swan Lake*, Hippolyta in *A Midsummer Night's Dream*, and roles in *Raymonda, Episodes, Dim Lustre* and *La Valse*.

NEGRI, Cesare (born 1530), Italian dancer, choreographer and dancing master. He danced and taught at various courts throughout Europe, producing *Grand Masquerade* in 1564, in which he symbolized human emotions. Over forty of his pupils were placed in the courts of Europe. His autobiographical treatise *Le Grazie d'Amore*, later retitled *Nuove Inventioni di Balli* (1604), laid the foundation of the classical ballet. Divided into three parts, it consists of fifty-five technical rules, which are lessons in themselves, and discusses dances such as balli, brandi and pavanes.

NEMECEK, Irji (1924–   ), Czech dancer, choreographer and teacher. He studied with **Vanya Psota** and danced with the Prague National Ballet from 1939–51. In 1957 he became artistic director of Prague National Ballet. His roles included Franz in *Coppélia* and Romeo in *Romeo and Juliet*. As a choreographer he has staged over thirty ballets including *Othello* and *Romeo and Juliet*. He later took a teaching post at Prague Academy of Art.

NEMTCHINOVA, Vera (1903–   ), Russian ballerina and teacher. She was first taught by Lydia Nelidova and had been studying with Elisabeth Anderson when she was discovered by **Serge Grigoriev**, régisseur-general of **Diaghilev**'s Ballets Russes. He engaged her for the corps de ballet where she made her debut in 1915 in *Les Sylphides*. She became first soloist, then ballerina (1924), creating the leading female roles in *Les Biches* (1924), *Les Tentations de la Bergère* (1924) and *Les Matelots* (1925), having previously created Queen of Hearts in *La Boutique Fantasque* in 1919. She also danced in *Swan Lake, Rhapsody in Blue* and *Pulcinella*. Nemtchinova-Dolin Ballet was formed (1927), gave short seasons at the Stoll Theatre, London, and toured Britain (1927–8). In 1929 she toured with her own company, and in 1930 toured Argentina with **Léo Staats**'s Ballet Franco-Russe. She was guest ballerina in Riga; became prima ballerina of Lithuanian State Ballet (1931–1935), and ballerina with **René Blum's Ballet Russe de Monte Carlo** (1936), creating the leading role in *L'Epreuve d'Amour*. She was guest artist with **Colonel de Basil's** company at Covent Garden, London (1938), staying with the company when it became Original Ballet Russe for its tour of Australia and the United States (1939). She danced Aurora in *Sleeping Beauty* for **Ballet Theatre** (1943), and for San Francisco Russian Opera and Ballet (1946). She later took a teaching post in New York.

NERINA, Nadia (Nadine Judd, 1927–), South African dancer. She studied with Eileen Keogan and Dorothea MacNair in South Africa, won many competitions, and toured the country from 1942–5, when she left to study at the Rambert School. She later studied with Elsa Brunelleschi and at Sadler's Wells School, joining the newly-formed Theatre Ballet in 1946 and creating the Circus Dancer in *Mardi Gras*. She was transferred to Sadler's Wells Ballet in 1947, became ballerina in 1952 and created Spring Fairy in *Cinderella*. She danced *Homage to the Queen* and *Birthday Offering*, the title roles in *Elektra* and *La Fille Mal Gardée* which was considered her greatest role. She also danced the leading roles in the classic repertoire. Famed for her athletic style and demi-caractère interpretations she has toured widely, appearing with great success with the Bolshoi and Kirov companies. In 1965 she created the solo part in the *Laurencia* pas de six for **The Royal Ballet**, and the leading role in *Home* for Western Theatre Ballet. She retired in 1968.

Netherlands, The, history of ballet in *see* **Holland, history of ballet in.**

New York City Ballet, The, a company founded by **Lincoln Kirstein** and **George Balanchine.** The origins of The New York City Ballet go back to 1946, when Kirstein and Balanchine formed Ballet Society. The Society produced many ballets by Balanchine, including *The Four Temperaments, Concerto Barocco, Orpheus* and *Symphony in C*. After a season at the New York City Center in 1948, the company was invited to become its resident company, The New York City Ballet (with Balanchine as artistic director). The company toured widely after 1950, beginning with a successful London season at Covent Garden and visiting Europe, Japan and Australia (1958), and the Soviet Union. In 1964 it moved into the newly-built New York State Theater. Many ballets were added to its repertoire, including new works, notably by Balanchine, **Antony Tudor** and **Jerome Robbins** (associate artistic director 1949–63). Principal dancers have included **Suzanne Farrell, Melissa Hayden, Jillana, Patricia McBride, Mimi Paul, Violette Verdy, Jacques d'Amboise, Conrad Ludlow, Nicholas Magallanes, Arthur Mitchell, Francisco Moncion, André Prokovsky** and **Edward Villella.** The New York City Ballet has developed an American ballet style largely due to the direction of Balanchine.

NEW YORK EXPORT: OPUS JAZZ, an abstract ballet in three movements. Choreography, **Jerome Robbins**; music, Robert Prince; decor, Ben Shahn. First performed at the Festival of Two Worlds, Spoleto, Italy, 8 June 1958, by Jerome Robbins's Ballets: USA. Staged at the Alvin Theatre, New York, 4 September 1958, by the same company. Principal dancers, Patricia Dunn, Jay Norman, Wilma Curley, John Jones. Revived by Robbins at Brooklyn Academy of Music, 6 November 1969, for the **Harkness Ballet.**

NIGHT AND SILENCE, a ballet in one act. Choreography, **Walter Gore**; music, J. S. Bach (arranged by Charles Mackerras); decor, Ronald Wilson. First performed at the Empire Theatre, Edinburgh, 25 August 1958, by Edinburgh International Ballet. Principal dancers, Paula Hinton, David Poole. Revived at Sadler's Wells Theatre, London, 20 July 1961, by Ballet Rambert. Principal dancers, Paula Hinton, Walter Gore. It was taken into the repertoire of Walter Gore's London Ballet. A man's jealousy is aroused at the sight of his lover carrying a bouquet.

NIGHT SHADOW or **La Sonnambula,** a ballet in one act. Libretto, Vittorio Rieti; choreography, **George Balanchine**; music, Rieti; decor, Dorothea Tanning. First performed in New York City Center, 27 February 1946, by **Ballet Russe de Monte Carlo.** Principal dancers, **Alexandra Danilova** (Sleepwalker), **Nicholas Magallanes** (Poet), **Maria Tallchief** (Coquette), Michel Katcharov (Baron). Performed at the Cambridge Theatre, London, 26 August 1948, by **Grand Ballet du Marquis de Cuevas.** Decor, Jean Robier, André Delfau. Principal dancers, **Margrethe Schanne, Henning Kronstam,** Mona Vangsaa. Staged in New York City Center, 6 January 1960, by **The New York City Ballet.** Decor, Esteban Francés; costumes, André Levasseur. Principal dancers, **Allegra Kent, Erik Bruhn,** Nicholas Magallanes, **Jillana, John Taras** (Baron). Performed by Ballet Rambert, 18 July 1961, and taken into the repertoire. Decor, Alix Stone. Principal dancers, June Sandbrook, **Norman Morrice.** The Coquette, the Baron's mistress, is jealous when she sees the Baron's wife in a sleepwalking dance with the Poet. She betrays them and the Baron kills the Poet.

NIJINSKA, Bronislava (1891–1972), Russian dancer, choreographer, teacher and ballet mistress, sister of **Vaslav Nijinsky.** She graduated from the Imperial School, St. Petersburg (1908) into the corps de ballet of the Maryinsky Theatre, making her debut as one of the four cygnets in *Swan Lake,* later dancing Dew in *Awakening of Flora,* and one of the Precious Stones variations in Act 3 of *Sleeping Beauty.* In 1909 she joined **Diaghilev's** Ballets Russes, dancing her first major role as Papillon in *Carnaval*

(1910). She resigned from the Imperial Theatres in 1911 and returned to Diaghilev. Her repertoire included Street Dancer in *Petrouchka,* Bacchante in *Narcisse* (1911), Ballerina in *Petrouchka* (1912) and Polovetsian Girl in *Prince Igor.* In 1914 she danced with Nijinsky's company in London. She was ballerina of Prince Oldenbourg's Opera (1914–15) and of the Kiev Opera (1915–18). She founded a school in Kiev, but left Russia after the Revolution, in 1921, to rejoin Diaghilev's company. She arranged some new numbers for *The Sleeping Beauty* (1921), her first serious attempt at choreography, which was presented at the Alhambra Theatre, London in 1921. For the Diaghilev company her choreographic works include *Le Mavra* (1922), *Les Noces* (1923), *Les Biches* and *Le Train Bleu* (1924). For **Ida Rubinstein** (1928–9) she choreographed *Nocturne,*

Bronislava Nijinska in Petrouchka. Ph. Lipnitzki.

La Bien-Aimée, Bolero, Le Baiser de la Fée and *La Valse*. She was ballet mistress of the Opéra Russe à Paris (1930–1) and established Théâtre de Danse, Paris (1932) where she revived her successful ballets and staged her own version of *Hamlet*. For **Colonel de Basil's Ballet Russe de Monte Carlo** she choreographed *Les Cent Baisers* (1935), *Danses Slaves et Tziganes*, and revived *Les Noces* (1936); for Markova-Dolin company she revived *Les Biches* and *La Bien-Aimée*. In 1938 she returned to America and founded her own school in Hollywood. For some years she was ballet mistress with Grand Ballet du Marquis de Cuevas for whom she re-staged several ballets, including a considerably altered version of *The Sleeping Beauty*, which was presented in Paris (1960). Nijinska recently spent several seasons as ballet mistress at Teatro Colón, Buenos Aires.

NIJINSKY, Vaslav Fomich (1890–1950), Russian dancer and choreographer. He entered the Imperial School of Ballet, St. Petersburg (1900), and made his debut at the **Maryinsky** in 1908. He then met **Serge Diaghilev,** who was greatly impressed by his technique and acting ability. Diaghilev's subsequent plans for the Ballets Russes were formulated around Nijinsky as premier danseur. In May 1909, the company made its first appearance in Paris with Nijinsky dancing the **Fokine** ballets *Le Pavillon d'Armide, Les Sylphides, Prince Igor* and *Cléopâtre*. *Schéhérazade, Giselle* and *Carnaval* were added to the repertoire in 1910. The company's success was spectacular. After Nijinsky returned to Russia, he resigned from the Maryinsky Theatre (1911) as result of a disagreement over wearing improper dress in *Giselle*. Supported by Diaghilev, **Benois** and others, he resigned, thus enabling Diaghilev to build a permanent company based in Western Europe. In 1911 he danced *Le Spectre de la Rose* and *Petrouchka*, and in 1912 he choreographed *The Afternoon of a Faun*, his first attempt at choreography. This was followed by the ill-received *Le Sacre du Printemps* and *Jeux* (1913).

Vaslav Nijinsky. Ph. Lipnitzki.

During a tour of South America (1913), Nijinsky married Romola de Pulszky, and soon after was dismissed from the company for refusing, without excuse, to dance *Carnaval*. He rejoined the company in 1916 after a disastrous attempt to organize his own group (1914), and after two years spent as a civilian prisoner of war in Austria-Hungary. After a 1916 tour of the United States, he organized his own troupe for which he choreographed *Til Eulenspiegel*. His company did not achieve success. He then toured again for Diaghilev in South America, but it was his last professional engagement. He settled in Switzerland after his return from the South American tour, and there suffered mental illness until the end of his life. He died in 1950 in London. In 1953 his body was re-interred in the Montmartre cemetery, Paris. The enormous fame of the strange, inarticulate little man with the Mongolian features is astounding in view of the fact that his entire professional career lasted only nine years, during two of which he was unable to dance. However, published material about Nijinsky indicates clearly that his **élévation** and **ballon** were unsurpassed by any other dancer of his time.

NIJINSKY—CLOWN OF GOD, a ballet in two parts. Choreography, **Maurice Béjart**; music, Pierre Henry (including a sequence from Tchaikovsky's *Pathétique Symphony*); costumes, Joëlle Roustan and Roger Bernard. First performed at the Forest National Auditorium, Brussels, 8 October 1971, by Les Ballets du XXième Siècle. Principal dancers, Jorge Donn (Nijinsky), Paolo Bortoluzzi (The Rose), **Suzanne Farrell**. Presented at the London Coliseum, 3 May 1972, by the same company. The first part of the ballet evokes the Nijinsky of the Ballets Russes, while the second part is dedicated to him as the Clown of God.

NIKITINA, Alice (1909–), Russian dancer. She studied with **Preobrajenska, Egorova, Legat** and **Cecchetti**, making her debut with the Ljubljana Opera Ballet, Yugoslavia, later dancing with the Romantic Theatre of **Boris Romanov**. From 1923–9 she was ballerina with **Diaghilev's** Ballets Russes where she created the leading roles in *Zéphyr et Flore* (1925), *La Chatte* (1927) and *Ode* (1928).

NOBILISSIMA VISIONE or **Noble Vision** or **Saint Francis**, a ballet in five scenes. Libretto, **Léonide Massine**, Paul Hindemith; choreography, Massine; music, Hindemith; decor, Pavel Tchelichev. First performed at the Theatre Royal, Drury Lane, London, 21 July 1938, by **Ballet Russe de Monte Carlo**. Principal dancers, Léonide Massine (Saint Francis), **Nini Theilade**, Jeannette Lauret, Lubov Rustova, **Frederic Franklin, Simon Semenov**. The ballet deals with the life of Saint Francis. *Saint Francis* is the title given to this work in the United States.

NOCES, LES, a ballet in four scenes. Choreography, **Bronislava Nijinska**; words and music, Igor Stravinsky; decor and costumes, Nathalie Gontcharova. First performed at Théâtre Gaîté-Lyrique, Paris, 14 June 1923, by **Diaghilev's** Ballets Russes. Principal dancers, Felia Doubrovska (Bride), Nicholas Semonov (Bridegroom). Revived by Nijinska for **Colonel de Basil's Ballet Russe de Monte Carlo**, for its 1936 American tour. A version was also staged by **Ludmilla Chiriaeff** for Les Grands Ballets Canadiens. Revived by Nijinska at the Royal Opera House, Covent Garden, London, 23 March 1966, for **The Royal Ballet**. Principal dancer, **Svetlana Beriosova**. The ballet is considered one of the most important of the 20th century. It portrays the esoteric rites and customs of a traditional Russian peasant wedding of the pre-revolutionary period. There is intricate ceremonial dancing accompanied by hypnotic chanting. Although the theme was a nationalistic one, its treatment was considered revolutionary for its time. Another version in one act with new choreography was created by **Jerome Robbins**. Decor, Oliver Smith; costumes, Patricia Zipprodt. First performed at New York State Theater, 30 March 1965, by American Ballet Theatre. Principal dancers, Erin Martin, William Glassman. This ballet was presented for American Ballet Theatre's 25th Anniversary Season.

NOCES FANTASTIQUES, LES, a ballet in two acts. Choreography, **Serge Lifar**; music, Marcel Delannoy; decor, Roger Chastel; costumes, André Levasseur. First performed, 9 February 1955, by the **Paris Opéra Ballet**. Principal dancers, **Nina Vyroubova** (Fiancée), **Claude Bessy** (Océanide), Peter van Dijk (Captain). The shipwrecked captain is saved from drowning by Océanide, Queen of the Sea. Remembering his fiancée, the captain rejects Océanide's love and she casts him back into the sea, where he drowns. His ghost sails his phantom ship, bringing his fiancée to a ghostly wedding under the sea.

NOCTURNE, a ballet in one act. Libretto, Edward Sackville-West; choreography, **Frederick Ashton**; music, Delius (*Paris*); decor, Sophie Fedorovich. First performed at Sadler's Wells Theatre, London, 10 November 1936, by Vic-Wells Ballet. Principal dancers, **Margot Fonteyn** (Poor Girl), **June Brae** (Rich Girl), **Robert Helpmann** (Young Man), Frederick Ashton (Spectator). The ballet is about the wistfulness of the Poor Girl as she watches the fashionable world arrive at a ball. She attracts, but cannot keep the Young Man, and is comforted by the Spectator.

NOIR ET BLANC *see* **Suite en Blanc.**

Northern Dance Theatre, a company based in the North-West of England, founded by Laverne Meyer in 1969. It held its inaugural performance at the University Theatre, Manchester, 28 November 1969, and gave its first London season at The Place in 1970. With Meyer as artistic director, the company presents a wide range of dance works both by new and established choreographers. Its repertoire includes works by Frank Staff, Laverne Meyer, **Peter Darrell, Walter Gore** and John Chesworth. Although a regional company aiming to promote local talent, Northern Dance Theatre has also toured nationally.

Les Noces: Jean Pierre Bonnefous and Nanon Thibon. Ph. Bernand.

NORWAY, history of ballet in.
1948 First performance, in Oslo, by Ny Norsk Ballett (Norwegian Ballet) created by Gerd Kjølaas and Louise Browne.
1950 Première, in Oslo, of Norsk Opera-selskap (Norwegian Opera Company), first native permanent operatic company.
1950s Norwegian Ballet merges with Norsk Operaselskap.
1957 Foundation of Den Norske Opera A/S, a permanent institution for the twin arts of opera and ballet.
1958 First ballet performance, at Hamar, by the Norwegian Opera Company.
1960s H. Algeranoff is first director of ballet. Succeeded by Joan Harris and later **Sonia Arova.**
1965 Joan Harris is appointed head of the Opera's new School of Ballet.
1972 Anne Borg becomes director of the Norwegian Ballet. *Daphnis and Chloë*, *Medusa* (**Cullberg**) and *Mythical Hunters* (**Tetley**) are staged.

Norwegian Ballet *see* **Norway, history of ballet in.**

notation *see* **dance notation.**

Nouveau Ballet de Monte Carlo, a ballet company formed in Monte Carlo in 1942. It was sponsored by Prince Louis II of Monaco and directed by Marcel Sablon. **Serge Lifar** became artistic director in 1946, and among its dancers were **Yvette Chauviré, Renée Jeanmaire, Youly Algarov, Janine Charrat** and **Vladimir Skouratov.** The **Marquis George de Cuevas** became its director in 1947, changing its name to Grand Ballet de Monto Carlo. In 1950 the company was incorporated with **Ballet International** to form the **Grand Ballet du Marquis de Cuevas.**

NOVERRE, Jean-Georges (1727–1810), French choreographer, dancer and writer. A pupil of **Louis Dupré** at the **Paris Opéra Ballet** and of the dancer-choreographer Martel, he made a modest debut in 1743 at the Court of Fontaine-bleau. His first ballet, *Les Fêtes Chinoises*

(1749), was presented at the Opéra Comique, where he was dancer and ballet master. From 1755–7 he worked on a revival of mime with Garrick at Drury Lane Theatre, London. His *Lettres sur la Danse et sur les Ballets* was published in 1760. He advocated unity of design and a logical progression from introduction to climax, and the elimination not only of unnecessary gestures but of masks, wigs and cumber-some costumes. He lived to see these last reforms take place. His ideas were worked out at the Württemberg Ducal Theatre where he was ballet master (1760). From 1767–74 he worked with Gluck in Vienna. They produced *Iphigénie en Tauris* (1774). Having been dancing master to Marie Antoinette in Vienna, he succeeded **Gaetan Vestris** as ballet master at the Paris Opéra in 1776. He returned to England at the outbreak of the French Revolution and presented his ballets at the King's Theatre, London (1782, 1788–9). Although he choreographed over 150 ballets, none has survived; his major works were *La Toilette de Venus*, *Médée et Jason* and *Les Horaces*. He edited a new edition of his *Lettres* and his libretti, and was writing a *Dictionary of Ballet* at the time of his death. He trained **Marie Allard, Marie Sallé** and **La Guimard.**

NUREYEV, Rudolph (1938–   ), Russian dancer and choreographer. Initially he studied privately and danced with amateur groups and with the Ufa Opera Ballet. He entered the Leningrad Ballet School in 1955, studied with Alexander Pushkin and was accepted into the Kirov Ballet Company as a soloist in 1958. He danced leading roles in *La Bayadère*, *Le Corsaire*, *Don Quixote* and *Taras Bulba*. He resisted being recalled to Russia, remaining in France when the company was making its Paris-London-New York tour (1961). He danced Prince and Blue Bird in *Sleeping Beauty* with great success for **Grand Ballet du Marquis de Cuevas** and made his London debut at the Royal Academy of Dancing Gala (1961), partnering **Rosella Hightower.** He appeared on US television with **Sonia Arova,** and with **Ruth**

Rudolph Nureyev in The Sleeping Beauty.
Ph. Bernand.

companies. Several choreographers have created roles specially for Nureyev, notably **Ashton** (Armand in *Marguerite and Armand* and Friday's Child in *Jazz Calendar*), **MacMillan** (Romeo in *Romeo and Juliet*), **Roland Petit** (Adam in *Paradise Lost* and Pelléas in *Pelléas et Mélisande*) and **Rudi van Dantzig** (The Traveller in *The Ropes of Time*). He staged *Raymonda* and danced Jean de Brienne with the touring section of The Royal Ballet, at the 1964 Festival of Two Worlds, Spoleto, and he staged the same production for Australian Ballet (1965). In addition, he has staged *Le Corsaire* pas de deux, Kingdom of Shades act of *La Bayadère* and *Laurencia* pas de six for The Royal Ballet, as well as choreographing a new Polonaise and Mazurka for *Swan Lake* (1965) and a full-length version of *The Nutcracker* (1968). He danced the leading male roles in his own works and created Warrior Chief in the revival of *Polovetsian Dances from Prince Igor*. For the Vienna State Opera Ballet he staged *Swan Lake*, dancing the première with Fonteyn, and the full-length *Don Quixote* (1966), which he also produced for Australian Ballet (1970) and for Le Nouveau Ballet de l'Opéra, Marseilles.

Page's Chicago Opera Ballet (1962). He made his debut at Covent Garden as guest artist with **The Royal Ballet**, 21 February 1962, partnering **Margot Fonteyn** in *Giselle*. Their immediate, riveting empathy has lasted ever since. Nureyev's fantastic career had begun. In 1963 he danced with The Royal Ballet, partnering Fonteyn in *Le Corsaire* pas de deux, *Les Sylphides*, *Swan Lake* and *Marguerite and Armand*, and became a permanent guest artist, together with Fonteyn and **Pamela May**, dancing the London season and the American tours. He has danced the classical repertoire in addition to leading roles in *Hamlet*, *Petrouchka*, *Song of the Earth*, *Apollo*, *Field Figures*, **Jerome Robbins**'s *L'Après-midi d'un Faune* and *Dances at a Gathering*. He also dances frequently with small groups or as guest artist with other

NUTCRACKER, THE or **Casse-Noisette**, a ballet, based on a tale by Hoffmann. Libretto and choreography, **Lev Ivanov**; music, Peter Tchaikovsky; decor, Bocharov and Ivanov. First performed, 18 December 1892, at the Maryinsky Theatre, St. Petersburg. Principal dancers, Antoinette dell'Era (Sugar Plum Fairy), **Paul Gerdt** (Prince). Revived by **Nicholas Sergeyev**, with the title *Casse-Noisette*, at Sadler's Wells Theatre, London, 30 January 1934, for Vic-Wells Ballet. Principal dancers, **Alicia Markova** (Sugar Plum Fairy), **Harold Turner** (Prince). Mary Honer, **Margot Fonteyn, Nadia Nerina** and **Robert Helpmann** have danced the principal roles. The ballet has been taken into the repertoires of Markova-Dolin Ballet, **Ballet Russe de Monte Carlo**, National Ballet of Canada and Ballet Rambert. **Nicholas Beriosov** staged a revival, 1950, for London's **Festival Ballet**. Principal dancers, Alicia Markova, **Anton Dolin**. A new version was presented, 24 December 1957, at the Festival Hall, London, by **Alexandre Benois**. Choreography, **David Lichine**. Principal dancers, **Nathalie Krassovska, John Gilpin**. **Frederick Ashton** staged the second act for Sadler's Wells Theatre Ballet; and in 1968 **Rudolph Nureyev** also mounted a version presented by **The Royal Ballet** at The Royal Opera House, Covent Garden. At her Christmas party, Clara is given a nutcracker. That night she dreams of a battle between her toy soldiers and some mice. The Nutcracker challenges the King of the Mice but has to be rescued by Clara. He changes into a prince and together they travel through the land of the Snowflakes to the Kingdom of Sweets and the Sugar Plum Fairy's home. A pas de deux by the Prince and the Sugar Plum Fairy from the Ivanov production has become a popular divertissement.

NUTCRACKER, THE, a ballet in three acts and epilogue. Libretto and choreography, **Vassily Vainonen**; decor, Nicolas Seleznyov. First performed, 18 February 1934, at the Kirov Theatre, Leningrad. Principal dancers, **Galina Ulanova, Konstantin Sergeyev**. Presented, 28 April 1938, at the Bolshoi Theatre, Moscow. Decor, Vladimir Dimitriev.

NUTCRACKER, THE, a ballet in two acts. Choreography, **George Balanchine**; decor, Horace Armistead; costumes, Barbara Karinska. First performed in New York City Center, February 1954, by **The New York City Ballet**. Principal dancers, **Maria Tallchief** (Sugar Plum Fairy), **Nicholas Magallanes** (Prince). This version is a popular New York Christmas event. Another version by George Balanchine was presented at New York State Theater, 11 December 1964.

NYMPHE DE DIANE, LA *see* Sylvia.

Ny Norsk Ballett *see* **Norway, history of ballet in.**

O

OBOUKHOV, Anatole (1895–1962), Russian dancer and teacher. A graduate of the Imperial School, St. Petersburg, he remained with the Maryinsky Theatre until 1920, having become premier danseur in 1917. His roles included Siegfried in *Swan Lake*, an outstanding Albrecht in *Giselle* and Prince in *The Sleeping Beauty*. In 1913 he partnered **Pavlova** in her final appearance in Russia. After leaving Russia in 1920 he was premier danseur at Opera Royal, Bucharest (1920–2) and was then with Romanoff's Romantic Theatre, Berlin (1922–8). As guest artist at **Teatro alla Scala**, Milan, he danced *Petrouchka* and with the **Nemtchinova-Dolin** ballet he appeared in Paris and London (1928–9). In 1930 he was guest artist with Riga State Ballet, Latvia. With Ballet Russe de Monte Carlo (1936–8), he created the role Ambassador in *L'Épreuve d'Amour* in 1936. In 1939 he toured Australia as ballet master with Original Ballet Russe and toured the United States with the same company in 1940. He took a teaching post with the School of American Ballet (1940) at **Balanchine's** invitation, remaining there until his death. The first time the *Don Quixote* pas de deux was seen in the United States was when he staged it for **Ballet Theatre** (1944). He was famed for his batterie and soaring jetés. He taught Vaslav Nijinsky.

ODE, a ballet in two acts. Choreography, **Léonide Massine** ; music, Nicholas Nabokov; decor, Pavel Tchelichev. First performed at the Théâtre Sarah Bernhardt, Paris, 6 June 1928, by **Diaghilev's** Ballets Russes. Principal dancer, **Serge Lifar**.

OEDIPUS AND THE SPHINX or **La Rencontre,** a ballet in one act. Libretto, Boris Kochno; choreography, **David Lichine**; music, Henri Sauguet; decor,

Christian Bérard. First performed at the Théâtre des Champs-Elysées, Paris, 8 November 1948, by **Les Ballets des Champs-Elysées**. Principal dancers, Leslie Caron (Sphinx), **Jean Babilée** (Oedipus). Leslie Caron was only sixteen years old, but gave a remarkable performance. As the Sphinx, she lay on a trapeze-like structure, high above the stage, while Jean Babilée leaped and danced around her. At the end, she plunged downward and hung from a ladder by one foot. Under the title *The Sphinx*, the ballet was staged at the Metropolitan Opera House, New York, 21 April 1955. Principal dancers, **Nora Kaye, Igor Youskevitch.** The Sphinx destroys humans who cannot solve her riddles. For the common good, Oedipus destroys the Sphinx. In the decor of the original production, the inter-play of light and colour was used to create the mythical atmosphere.

OEUF À LA COQUE, L', a ballet. Libretto and choreography, **Roland Petit**; music, Thiriet; decor, Giovanni Lepri. First performed in the Princess Theatre, London, 16 February 1949, by **Les Ballets de Paris de Roland Petit**. Principal dancers, **Colette Marchand, Renée Jeanmaire, Nina Vyroubova**, Roland Petit. The action is burlesque in character and is set in a kitchen.

OISEAU DE FEU, L' *see* **Firebird, The.**

OMBRE, L' or **Pas de l'Ombre, Le,** a ballet in three acts. Libretto and choreography, **Filippo Taglioni**; music, Wilhelm Maurer; decor, Fedorov, Serkov, Shenian, Roller, Mathieu. First performed at the Bolshoi Theatre, St. Petersburg, 10 December 1839. Principal dancers, **Maria Taglioni**, Antonio Guerra. A version in two acts with decor by W. Grieve and with

Maria Taglioni again in the principal role, was staged in Her Majesty's Theatre, London, 18 June 1840. Another version, *Le Pas de l'Ombre*, was presented in Paris in June 1844. L'Ombre (Spirit) of a murdered woman returns to dance with her mourning lover. The ballet was choreographed by Filippo Taglioni to exhibit the ethereal quality of his daughter Maria's dancing.

ONDINE, a romantic ballet in three acts. Choreography, **Frederick Ashton**; music, H. W. Henze; decor, Lisa de Nobile. First performed at the Royal Opera House, Covent Garden, London, 27 October 1958, by **The Royal Ballet**. Principal dancers **Margot Fonteyn** (Ondine), **Michael Somes** (Palemon), **Julia Farron** (Berta), **Alexander Grant** (Tirrenio). Ondine was one of Margot Fonteyn's great creations. Another version was first performed in the Opera House, Munich, 25 January 1959. Choreography, **Alan Carter**; decor, von Gugel. Principal dancers, Dulce Anaya, Franz Baur, Inge Bertl, **Heino Hallhuber**. A new version in two acts was first performed in West Berlin, 22 September 1959, by the Städtische Oper. Choreography, Tatiana Gsovska; decor, Werner Schachteli. Principal dancers, Judith Dornys, Wolfgang Leistner, Suse Preiser, Manfred Taubert. Frederick Ashton's version was filmed in 1959. Ondine, a water sprite, entices Palemon from his lover, Berta. They are re-united, but on their wedding day, Ondine reappears, protected by Tirrenio, King of the Sea. Palemon kisses her, well knowing it means he will die, and she carries him away to live with her under the sea. Inspired by **Ondine, ou la Naïade.**

ONDINE, OU LA NAÏADE or **The Naïad and the Fisherman**, a romantic ballet in six scenes. Libretto and choreography, **Jules Perrot** and **Fanny Cerito**; music, Cesare Pugni; decor, William Griève. First performed at Her Majesty's Theatre, London, 22 June 1843. Principal dancers, Fanny Cerito (Ondine), Jules Perrot (Matteo the Fisherman). In this ballet Fanny Cerito danced with her shadow the *pas de l'ombre* which became one of her most famous solos. Staged at St. Petersburg, 11 February 1851, with the title, *The Naïad and the Fisherman*. Principal dancer, **Carlotta Grisi**. On the wedding day of Matteo and Giannina, the Naïad, Ondine, who loves Matteo, lures Giannina under the water and takes her place; but she is unable to live on earth and is soon on the point of death. Hydrola, Queen of the Water, who had warned her of this risk, re-unites Giannina and Matteo and takes Ondine back under the sea. **Ondine** was inspired by this ballet.

ON STAGE! a ballet in one act. Libretto, Michael and Mary Kidd; choreography, **Michael Kidd**; music, Norma dello Joio; decor, Oliver Smith; costumes, Alvin Colt. First performed in Boston, Massachusetts, 4 October 1945, at the Metropolitan Opera House, New York, 9 October 1945, by **Ballet Theatre**. Principal dancers, Michael Kidd (Handyman), **Janet Reed**, Alicia Alonso (Girl), **Nora Kaye** (Princess), **John Kriza** (Hero). Failing in her ballet audition, the shy Girl is comforted by the Handyman and dances for him alone. But she is observed by those in authority, and her dancing is so beautiful that she is engaged there and then.

Original Ballet Russe *see* **Ballet Russe de Monte Carlo.**

ORLANDO, Mariane (1934–), Swedish ballerina. She studied at the Royal Swedish Ballet School, with Lilian Karina, and at the Sadler's Wells Ballet School. In 1948 she joined the Royal Swedish Ballet. She became ballerina in 1953, and was their youngest dancer to assume this title. For her debut as ballerina she danced Odette-Odile in *Swan Lake* (1953). She danced in Russia (1959), and furthered her studies at the Leningrad Kirov School (1960). She was guest artist with American Ballet Theatre (1961–2). She dances the classical repertoire, including *Giselle* and *Medea*. She created the role of Hagar in *Pillar of Fire*.

Orpheus: Maria Tallchief. Ph. New York City Ballet.

look at her, and he must resist or lose her) and the other between Orpheus and the Dark Angel which is marked by great tenderness.

ORPHEUS AND EURYDICE, a ballet in two acts based on the 1762 opera, *Orpheo ed Euridice*, composed by Christoph Willibald Ritter von Gluck for a libretto by Ranieri di Calzabigi. Choreography, **Ninette de Valois**; music, Gluck; decor, Sophie Fedorovich. First performed at the New Theatre, London, 28 May 1941, by Sadler's Wells Ballet. Principal dancers, **Pamela May** (Eurydice), **Robert Helpmann** (Orpheus), **Margot Fonteyn** (Amor), Mary Honer (Leader of the Furies). The action of the ballet follows closely that of the opera. *See also* **Orpheus.**

OROSZ, Adele (1938–), Hungarian ballerina. She became a soloist with the Budapest Opera company in 1958. Her roles include Swanilda in *Coppélia*, the title role in *Giselle*, Odette-Odile in *Swan Lake* and Juliet in *Romeo and Juliet*.

ORPHEUS, a narrative ballet in three scenes, retelling the Orpheus-Eurydice story. Choreography, **George Balanchine**; music, Igor Stravinsky; decor and costumes, Isamu Noguchi. First performed in New York City Center, 28 April 1948, by Ballet Society. Principal dancers, **Nicholas Magallanes** (Orpheus), **Maria Tallchief** (Eurydice), **Francisco Moncion** (Dark Angel), Herbert Bliss (Apollo), Edward Bigelow (Pluto), **Tanaquil LeClercq** (Leader of the Bacchantes). Also danced by the same cast for **The New York City Ballet** when Ballet Society took that name, 11 October 1948. This ballet is notable in that George Balanchine and Igor Stravinsky collaborated closely from the inception. It contains two famous pas de deux, one danced by Orpheus and Eurydice (in which she implores him to

Othello: Rosella Hightower and Nicholas Polajenko in Grand Ballet du Marquis de Cuevas production. Ph. Lipnitzki.

OSATO, Sono (1919–   ), American dancer and actress. She studied with **Adolph Bolm,** Bernice Holmes and **Egorova,** and joined **Colonel de Basil's** Ballet Russe de Monte Carlo in 1934. As soloist she created one of the Nymphs in *Protée*, Barman's Assistant in *Union Pacific* and Siren in *Prodigal Son* (1939). She left the company in 1940 to join **Ballet Theatre** where she created Rosaline in **Tudor's** *Romeo and Juliet* and Lover-in-Experience in *Pillar of Fire*, and danced many solo roles. In 1949 she danced with Experimental Theatre.

OSIPENKO, Alla (1932–   ), Russian ballerina, Peoples' Artist of the RSFSR. She studied in Leningrad and joined the Kirov Theatre in 1950, becoming ballerina in 1954. She created Mistress of the Copper Mountain in *The Stone Flower*. Her other roles include Lilac Fairy in *The Sleeping Beauty*, Queen of the Ball in *The Bronze Horseman*, Odette-Odile in *Swan Lake* and Sari in *Path of Thunder*. She has danced in Paris and London.

OTHELLO, a ballet in four acts. Libretto and choreography, **Vakhtang Chabukiany**; music, Alexei Machavariani; decor, Simon Virsaladze. First performed at the Paliashvili Theatre of Opera and Ballet, Tiflis, 29 November 1957. Principal dancers, Vera Zigvadze (Desdemona), Vakhtang Chabukiany (Othello). Repeated at the Kirov Theatre, Leningrad, 24 March 1960. The action follows Shakespeare's play closely. See illustration p. 165.

ouvert, any open position or movement.

P

PAGANINI, a ballet in one act, based on the gossip which surrounded Niccolà Paganini, the Italian violin virtuoso, during his lifetime. Libretto, **Michel Fokine** and Sergei Rachmaninov; choreography, Michel Fokine; music, Sergei Rachmaninov (*Rhapsody on a Theme by Paganini*); decor, Sergei Soudeikine. First performed at the Royal Opera House, Covent Garden, London, 30 June 1939, by **Colonel de Basil's Ballet Russe de Monte Carlo.** Principal dancers, Dmitri Rostov (Paganini), **Irina Baronova** (Divine Genius), **Tatiana Riabouchinska** (Florentine Beauty), Tamara Grigorieva (Guile), **Paul Petrov** (Florentine Youth). Divine Genius rescues Paginini from Gossip, Scandal and Guile, and brings him immortality. A completely new version, showing Paginini creating violin music of extraordinary technical skill, with libretto and choreography by **Leonid Lavrovsky,** and decor by Vadim Rydin, was first performed at the Bolshoi Theatre, Moscow, 7 April 1960. Principal dancers, Yaroslav Sekh, Marina Kondratieva.

Ethéry Pagava. Ph. Reyna.

PAGAVA, Ethéry (1932–   ), French dancer. She studied with **Egorova** and was a child dancer with **Roland Petit's** and **Janine Charrat's** groups. Soloist with **Les Ballets des Champs-Elysées** (1945), she danced the little acrobat in *Les Forains*, and Ganymede in *Les Amours de Jupiter* (1946). With **Le Grand Ballet du Marquis de Cuevas,** which she joined in 1948, she created Sleepwalker in *Night Shadow*, and danced Juliet in *Tragedy in Verona* (1950)

PAGE, Annette (1932–   ), British dancer. A student at the Sadler's Wells School (1945), she joined their Theatre Ballet (1950), became soloist (1954), transferred to Sadler's Wells Ballet (1955) and became ballerina with **The Royal Ballet** (1959). She has danced the title role and Peasant pas de deux in *Giselle*, Aurora and Blue Bird pas de deux in *The Sleeping Beauty*, Odette-Odile in *Swan Lake*, The Lady in *The Lady and the Fool*, Lise in *La Fille Mal Gardée* and Blue Skater in *Les Patineurs*. She was guest artist with National Ballet Ireland (1960), and toured Australia with **Fonteyn's** concert group in 1962. She left The Royal Ballet during the 1966/7 season.

PAGE, Ruth (1903–   ), American dancer, choreographer and director. She trained with **Ivan Clustine, Adolph Bolm** and **Enrico Cecchetti.** She toured South America with **Pavlova,** and in 1919 created the title role in *The Birthday of the Infanta* in Chicago. After dancing with Bolm in London she became première danseuse with Chicago Allied Arts (1924–

1927), dancing with **Diaghilev**'s Ballets Russes (1925), and Metropolitan Opera Ballet (1926–8). She appeared in Moscow (1930), gave solo performances throughout America (1930–5), and toured the Orient with **Harald Kreutzberg** (1932–1934). She was première danseuse and ballet director of the Chicago Grand Opera Company from 1934–7. She toured with **Bentley Stone**, and in 1938 they formed a company, choreographing many works including *Frankie and Johnny*, *The Bells* and *Billy Sunday*, all of which were restaged for **Ballet Russe de Monte Carlo** (1945–8). She was director of Chicago Opera Ballet (1944–7). For **Les Ballets des Champs-Elysées** she choreographed *Revanche* and *Impromptu au Bois* (1951); for London's **Festival Ballet**, Vilia (*The Merry Widow*) (1953); and for Chicago Lyric Opera, *Susanne and the Barber* and *El Amor Brujo* (1955). In 1955 she formed Chicago Opera Ballet.

During the first season she staged *The Merry Widow*, *Il Ballo delle Ingrate* and her masterpiece, *Revanche* (1957). Principal dancers were **Alicia Markova, Sonia Arova** and **Oleg Briansky**. Among the ballets choreographed by Ruth Page have been *Camille*, *Die Fledermaus* and *Carmen* (1959). In 1962 **Nureyev** made his US debut with the company, in *Don Quixote* pas de deux, and also danced in *Polovetsian Dances from Prince Igor*, staged by Ruth Page for the Chicago Lyric Opera. In 1966 the company was renamed Ruth Page's International Ballet. Her controversial style frequently shocked audiences with its daring realism.

PALAIS DE CRISTAL, LE or **Symphony in C**, a plotless ballet in four movements. Choreography, **George Balanchine**; music, Georges Bizet (*Symphony in C*); decor, Leonor Fini. First performed at the Paris Opéra, 28 July 1947, by the **Paris Opéra Ballet**. Principal dancers, **Tamara Toumanova, Lycette Darsonval, Alexandre Kalioujny**. Performed at New York City Center, without decor, and under the title, *Symphony in C*, 22 March 1948, by Ballet Society. Principal dancers, **Maria Tallchief, Tanaquil LeClercq, Nicholas Magallanes, Francisco Moncion**. Taken into the repertoire of the Royal Danish Ballet in 1953. The choreography evoked effectively the freshness of Bizet's allegro movement and the romanticism of his adagio movement.

PANAIEV, Michel (1913–　), Russian dancer, choreographer and teacher. He studied at the Royal Opera, Belgrade, State Theatre, Zurich, and with **Legat, Egorova**, and at the School of American Ballet. He made his debut in Belgrade. He was soloist with **René Blum**'s **Ballet Russe de Monte Carlo** and Original Ballet Russe (1940–1), dancing the leading roles in *Swan Lake*, *Coppélia*, *L'Épreuve d'Amour* and *Les Sylphides*. He danced with San Francisco Opera and Ballet Musicale, before founding his own school and company, Los Angeles Civic Ballet.

Ruth Page. Ph. Reyna.

PAPLINSKI, Eugene (1908–), Polish dancer and choreographer. He studied at the Warsaw Ballet School, becoming a soloist with the Warsaw Bolshoi company. He later worked as a choreographer in different parts of Poland. In 1954 he founded the Ensemble of Polish Dancing and was artistic director and choreographer until 1960.

PAQUITA, a ballet in two acts. Libretto, Paul Foucher and Joseph Mazilier; choreography, **Joseph Mazilier**; music, Edward Deldevez; decor, Philastre, Cambon, Diéterle, Séchan, Despléchin. First performed at the Théâtre de l'Académie Royale de Musique, Paris, 1 April 1846. Principal dancers, **Carlotta Grisi** (Paquita), **Lucien Petipa**. Performed in the Theatre Royal, Drury Lane, London, 3 June 1846, with Carlotta Grisi again dancing Paquita. A version, revised by· **Marius Petipa,** was performed at the Bolshoi Theatre, St. Petersburg, September 1847. Music, Leon Minkus. It is still in the repertoires of Russian ballet companies, and was successfully revived by the Kirov Ballet (1970). **Alexandra Danilova** staged a one-act version for **Ballet Russe de Monte Carlo** at the Metropolitan Opera House, New York, 20 September 1949. Principal dancers, **Alexandra Danilova** (Paquita), Oleg Tupine. A pas de trois from this ballet has become a favourite divertissement in the repertoire of **The New York City Ballet.** Divertissements from the complete ballet have also been staged by **Nureyev** (1964) and by Casenave for London's **Festival Ballet** (1967). Paquita, a Spanish gypsy dancer, loves Lucien, a scion of French nobility but, of course, cannot marry him. However, it eventually transpires that she, too, is an aristocrat, and is able to marry Lucien after all.

PARADE, a ballet in one act. Libretto, Jean Cocteau, choreography, **Léonide Massine**; music, Eric Satie; decor, Pablo Picasso. First performed at the Théâtre du Châtelet, Paris, 18 May 1917, by **Diaghilev's** Ballets Russes. Principal dancers, Léonide Massine, **Léon Woizikowsky, Lydia Lopokova.** Circus performers parade through the town to attract an audience and are later seen in the circus arena. The bitter-sweet music (including sounds from typewriter and siren) and the cubist decor were considered too avant-garde in 1917.

Paris Opéra Ballet, the French national company, an outgrowth of the Théâtre National de l'Opéra (formerly **L'Académie Royal de Musique,** 1671–1871). It was considered the leading company of Western Europe during the 18th and early 19th centuries, with **Noverre** and **Dauberval** among its choreographers. Its dancers included **Marie Camargo, Marie Sallé, Louis Dupré,** the Vestris, the Gardels, Louis Duport; and in the 19th century **Maria Taglioni, Fanny Elssler, Carlotta Grisi, Fanny Cerito, Jules Perrot** and **Lucien Petipa.** *La Sylphide* and *Giselle,* the great Romantic ballets, were premièred at the Paris Opéra. After a disappointing spell, the company was revitalized in the 20th century by Jacques Rouché, director of the Paris Opéra, who engaged **Michel Fokine, Anna Pavlova, Olga Spessivtzeva** and **Bronislava Nijinska** as guest artists. He engaged **Serge Lifar** as director after 1929; he was succeeded by **George Skibine** in 1958. Its dancers have included **Yvette Chauviré, Roland Petit, Renée Jeanmaire** and **Jean Babilée, Claire Motte** and **Attilio Labis.** The company danced in New York (1948), London (1954) and Moscow (1958). Yvette Chauviré was director 1963–70. In 1970, **Roland Petit** was appointed dance director but resigned in the same year and was replaced by **Claude Bessy.**

PARK, Merle (1937–), South African dancer. She studied with Betty Lamb at the Elmhurst School, England, joined Sadler's Wells Ballet (1954) and became soloist with **The Royal Ballet** in 1958. Her roles have included Lise in *La Fille Mal Gardée,* Blue Bird pas de deux and Aurora in *The Sleeping Beauty,* Juliet in *Romeo* *and Juliet.* She danced in *Les Biches*, and created one of the solo parts in *Laurencia* pas de six (1965). By 1970 she was a principal in the Royal Ballet and *Giselle* is considered one of her strongest roles.

PARLIC, Dimitri (1919–), Yugoslav dancer and choreographer, born in Greece. He studied with **Olga Preobrajenska** and joined Belgrade National Ballet in 1938, becoming principal dancer in 1941 and choreographer in 1949. He was ballet master and choreographer with the Vienna State Opera Ballet (1958–61) and with Teatro dell'Opera, Rome (1963–6). Among his works are *Coppélia, Macedonian Tale, Symphony in C, El Amor Brujo* and *The Miraculous Mandarin.*

pas ballotté *see* **ballotté.**

PAS D'ACIER, LE, a ballet in one act. Choreography, **Léonide Massine**; music, Serge Prokofiev; decor, Georges Jakoulov. First performed at the Théâtre Sarah Bernhardt, Paris, 8 June 1927, by **Diaghilev's** Ballets Russes. Principal dancers, Felia Doubrovska, **Lubov Tchernicheva, Alice Nikitina, Serge Lifar, Léonide Massine.** Serge Prokofiev intended his music and ballet to glorify the new concept of labour and machinery in the USSR. The score was strident, and the movement followed the rhythm of mechanical devices in the factory. In the finale, the decor moved. Wheels turned, pistons rose and fell. The ballet was received coldly in Paris, and more so in London a month later.

pas de deux, any dance for two or a dance comprising (i) **adagio** (a dance of love performed by the ballerina and her partner), (ii) **variations** (solos by both), (iii) the coda (solos by both after which they dance together as a finale).

PAS DE L'OMBRE, LE *see* **Ombre, L'.**

PAS DE QUATRE, LE, a divertissement, choreographed by **Jules Perrot** for the four greatest ballerinas of the time, **Maria Taglioni, Carlotta Grisi, Fanny Cerito** and **Lucile Grahn.** Music, Cesare Pugni. First performed at Her Majesty's Theatre, London, 12 July 1845. There were only four presentations that year, and two in the same theatre in 1847, when **Carolina Rosati** replaced Lucile Grahn. The divertissement was regarded as the most outstanding ballet event of that time. Describing it, *The Illustrated London News* of 19 July 1845 wrote of the 'dignity, repose and exquisite grace' of Maria Taglioni and Lucile Grahn, of the 'charming archness and twinkling steps' of Carlotta Grisi, and the 'wonderful flying leaps and revolving bounds' of Fanny Cerito. The spectacle was recorded in a lithograph by A. E. Chalon which captured the grace of the dancing. Cyril Beaumont found Cesare Pugni's original score in the British Museum in London in the 1930s, and it was orchestrated by Leighton Lucas for new choreography by **Keith Lester.** The costumes were after A. E. Chalon. This new version was performed by the Markova-Dolin Company in 1936. Principal dancers, Molly Lake, Diana Gould,

Le Pas de Quatre: left to right, Rosella Hightower, Denise Bourgeois, Jacqueline Moreau and Alicia Markova. Ph. Lipnitzki.

Kathleen Crofton, Prudence Hyman. The same version was staged by **Ballet Theatre** at the Royal Opera House, Covent Garden, London, 26 August 1946, and at the Broadway Theatre, New York, 8 October 1946. Principal dancers, **Alicia Alonso** (Taglioni), **Nora Kaye** (Grisi), Barbara Fallis (Grahn), **Lucia Chase** (Cerito). **Anton Dolin** choreographed another version, again using Cesare Pugni's music (but orchestrated by Paul Bowles). First performed at the Majestic Theatre, New York, 26 February 1941, by Ballet Theatre. Principal dancers, **Nana Gollner, Nina Stroganova,** Alicia Alonso, Katherine Sergava. Presented at the 44th Street Theatre, New York, November 1941, by Ballet Theatre. Principal dancers, **Alicia Markova, Nora Kaye, Irina Baronova,** Annabelle Lyon. Anton Dolin also staged the divertissement for **Ballet Russe de Monte Carlo** at the Metropolitan Opera House, New York, 18 September 1948. Principal dancers, **Mia Slavenska,** Alicia Markova, **Nathalie Krassovska, Alexandra Danilova.** There was a revival, 21 May 1961, by London's **Festival Ballet.** Principal dancers, Alicia Markova, **Tatiana Riabouchinska,** Paula Hinton, Noel Rossana.

passé, movement in which the working foot passes the supporting leg either forward or back.

passepied, a 17th century French dance.

PATINEURS, LES, a skating suite de danse. Choreography, **Frederick Ashton**; music, Giacomo Meyerbeer (from his operas, *La Prophète* and *L'Étoile du Nord*); decor, William Chappell. First performed at the Sadler's Wells Theatre, London, 16 February 1937, by Vic-Wells Ballet. Principal dancers, **Margot Fonteyn,** Mary Honer, **Robert Helpmann, Harold Turner** (Blue Skater), **Pamela May, June Brae,** Elizabeth Miller. Brian Shaw and Graham Usher also danced the Blue Skater part which Harold Turner had made famous. Another notable feature was the series of fouettés danced by Mary Honer.

Taken into the repertoire of **Ballet Theatre** with decor by Cecil Beaton and first performed at the Broadway Theatre, New York, 2 October 1946. Principal dancers, **John Kriza, Nora Kaye, Hugh Laing.** The ballet is based on ice-skating movements. The Blue Skater performs a series of pirouettes as the curtain falls.

PAUL, Mimi (1943–), American dancer. She studied with Lisa Gardiner, Mary Day, **Frederick Franklin** and **Boris Kniasev,** and at the School of American Ballet. She danced *The Chinese Nightingale* (1957) and *Ondine* (1959) with Washington Ballet (1955–60). Her first solo roles with **The New York City Ballet,** which she joined in 1961, were 2nd movement in *Symphony in C*, Symphony Section in *Episodes*, 5th and 6th Waltzes in *La Valse*, and leader of the pas de neuf in Act 2 of *Swan Lake* (1962). In 1963 she danced her first leading role in *Bugaku*. In 1965 she danced with the company at Covent Garden. She later joined American Ballet Theatre.

PAVILLON D'ARMIDE, LE, a ballet in one act, based on Théophile Gautier's story, *Omphale*. Libretto, **Alexandre Benois**; choreography, **Michel Fokine**; music, Nicholas Tcherepnin; decor, **Benois.** First performed at the Maryinsky Theatre, St. Petersburg, 25 November 1907. Principal dancers, **Anna Pavlova, Vaslav Nijinsky, Paul Gerdt.** Presented by **Serge Diaghilev** on the first night of the first season of the Ballets Russes in the Théâtre du Châtelet, Paris, 19 May 1909. Principal dancers, Vera Karalli, Vaslav Nijinsky, **Tamara Karsavina, Mikhail Mordkin.**

PAVLOVA, Anna (1891–1931), Russian ballerina. A student of the Imperial School of Ballet, St. Petersburg, (1891–9) under **Paul Gerdt, Christian Johannson,** Oblakhov and Vasem. She danced in the Pas des Aimées in *The Daughter of Pharaoh* before her graduation. She became a coryphée (1899), second soloist (1902), first soloist (1903), ballerina

(1905) and prima ballerina (1906). During the regular seasons at the Maryinsky Theatre (until 1913) her repertoire included *Swan Lake, La Bayadère, Harlequinade, The Magic Flute, The Seasons, Don Quixote, Giselle, Le Corsaire, Paquita, Raymonda, La Source, Esmeralda, The Sleeping Beauty, The Talisman, Chopiniana, The Dying Swan, Les Preludes* and *Gavotte*. She danced in Stockholm, Copenhagen, Prague, Berlin, Leipzig, and Vienna (1907, 1908), with **Diaghilev**'s Ballets Russes in Paris (1909), and in New York (1910). She made her London debut in 1910, formed a troupe of primarily English dancers (1914), and established her permanent residence at Ivy House, London. During World War 1 she toured North and South America, and from 1919–1931 she danced all over the world, except

Anna Pavlova. Ph. Lipnitzki.

in Russia. She was seen by millions, some of whom had never seen ballet before. Her partners included **Fokine,** Paul Gerdt, Samuel Andrianov and **Nicholas Legat** (Maryinsky Theatre); **Fokine, Nijinsky** and Theodore Koslov (Diaghilev's Ballets Russes); **Adolph Bolm,** Nicholas Legat, **Mikhail Mordkin,** Laurent Novikov, **Vladimir Tikhomirov, Alexander Volinine** and Pierre Vladimirov (her own company). After leaving the Maryinsky Theatre, **Ceccetti** was her teacher until his death (1928). She was conservative and traditional in her choice of choreography, decor, costumes and music, and had no use for the changes in ballet effected by Fokine and Diaghilev. Famous in her repertoire were *Gavotte, Autumn Leaves, The Dying Swan* (created for her by Fokine), *Giselle* and *Les Sylphides* (she created the chief role).

PÉCOURT or **PÉCOUR, Louis Guillaume** (1655–1729), French dancer. A demi-caractère dancer, he first appeared at the **Paris Opéra Ballet** in 1672 in *Cadmus*, and danced the leading roles in the works of **Lully** and **Pierre-Louis Beauchamp,** whom he succeeded at the Opéra (1687). He created dances for Louis XIV and introduced some variety into ballets. He retired in 1703, but continued to work with his ballet until his death. Two of his pupils were Blondi and **Balon.**

PERCIVAL, John (1927–), English ballet critic. He started writing for *Dance and Dancers* in 1950 and became associate editor. He became ballet critic of *The Times* in 1965, and is London correspondent of *Dance Magazine* (New York) and European dance correspondent of the *New York Times*. His publications include *Antony Tudor* (1963), *Modern Ballet* (1970), *The World of Diaghilev* (1971) and *Experimental Dance* (1971).

PERETTI, Serge (1910–), French dancer, ballet master and teacher. He studied and danced at the **Paris Opéra Ballet** where he was the first male dancer

30 September 1843, with the same principal dancers. Presented at St. Petersburg, 1 February 1844, with Elena Andreyanova dancing La Péri. Carlotta Grisi's dancing was acclaimed in London. The intricate plot was based on a Persian legend, and was the troubled but happily-ending love story of La Péri and Achmet in scenes of Arabian Nights splendour. A new one-act version was first performed at the Royal Opera House, Covent Garden, London, 15 February 1956, by Sadler's Wells Ballet. Choreography, **Frederick Ashton**; music, Paul Dukas; decor, Ivor Hitchens; costumes, André Levasseur. Principal dancers, **Margot Fonteyn** (La Péri), **Michael Somes** (Iskender). At the gate of Paradise, Iskender steals the flower of immortality from La Péri, who immediately becomes old. Because of his love for her, however, he returns it. She regains her youth, but he becomes old and mortal. This was Frederick Ashton's second version of *La Péri*. His first version was performed at the Mercury Theatre, London, 16 February 1931, by Ballet Rambert. Decor, William Chappell. Principal dancers, **Alicia Markova, Frederick Ashton**. Restaged at the Mercury Theatre, 13 March 1938. Decor, Nadia Benois. Principal dancers, Deborah Dering, Frank Staff. Yet another early version was performed, 20 June 1921, by the Paris Opéra Ballet. Choreography, Ivan Clustine; music, Paul Dukas; decor, Piot. Principal dancer, **Anna Pavlova**.

PERROT, Jules Joseph (1810–92), French dancer and choreographer. He studied with **Auguste Vestris** and **Salvatore Vigano** and made his debut with the **Paris Opéra Ballet** (1830) after appearing throughout the provinces as a circus pantomimist and clown. He was considered one of the great male dancers of all time; he was so successful that **Maria Taglioni**, jealous, refused to appear with him, thus forcing him to leave the Opéra in 1835. He danced throughout Europe in his own ballets including *The Naïad and the Fisherman, Caterina, Esmeralda, La Filleule des Fées, Gazelda, The*

Serge Peretti. Ph. Lipnitzki.

to be given the title étoile (1941). His repertoire included *The Creatures of Prometheus, Giselle, Salade, La Vie de Polichinelle, Oriane et le Prince d'Amour, Le Chevalier et la Damoiselle, Joan de Zarissa* and *Le Tambourin*. As ballet master (1944) he produced *The Call of the Mountain* (1945). After his retirement he became a teacher at the Paris Opéra school.

PÉRI, LA, a ballet in two acts. Libretto, Théophile Gautier; choreography, **Jean Coralli**; music, Norbert Burgmüller; decor, Séchan, Diéterle, Despléchin, Philastre, Cambon. First performed at the Théâtre de l'Académie Royale de Musique, Paris, 17 July 1843, by the **Paris Opéra Ballet.** Principal dancers, **Carlotta Grisi** (La Péri), **Lucien Petipa** (Achmet). Repeated at the Theatre Royal, Drury Lane, London,

Wilful Wife and *Faust*. In 1833 he met the young **Carlotta Grisi**, became her teacher and later married her. At the Paris Opéra, where she was invited in 1841, they received an overwhelming welcome, but he was unable to secure a permanent position. At Her Majesty's Theatre, London, he restaged *Giselle* and created *Alma, Ondine, Eoline, Lalla Rookh, Le Jugement de Paris, Les Éléments, Les Quatre Saisons* and *Pas de Quatre*. Dancer, choreographer, ballet master and artistic leader at the Imperial Theatre, St. Petersburg (1848–1859), he restaged his previous works and created eight new ballets. He was forced to leave Russia because of his political views and returned to a greatly changed Europe; his attempts to regain fame were not successful. He died virtually forgotten.

Jules Perrot. Ph. Lipnitzki.

PERSEPHONE, a ballet in three scenes. Libretto, Igor Stravinsky and André Gide; choreography, **Frederick Ashton**; music, Igor Stravinsky; decor, Nico Ghika. First performed at the Royal Opera House, Covent Garden, London, 12 December 1962, by **The Royal Ballet**. Principal dancers, **Svetlana Beriosova** (Persephone), Keith Rosson (Pluto), **Alexander Grant** (Mercury). The work was part of the world celebration of Igor Stravinsky's eightieth birthday, but is seldom danced because Gide's poem has to be spoken and it is not easy to find a dancer who can recite the lines.

PETER AND THE WOLF, a ballet in one act to Serge Prokofiev's symphonic tale for orchestra of the same name. Choreography, Frank Staff; decor, Guy Sheppard. First performed at the Arts Theatre, Cambridge, 1 May 1940, by Ballet Rambert. Principal dancers, Helen Ashley (Peter), Lee Kersley (Wolf), **Celia Franca** (Bird), Sally Gilmour (Duck), **Walter Gore** (Cat). Another version was first performed in New York, 13 January 1940, by **Ballet Theatre**. Principal dancers, Eugene Loring (Peter), **William Dollar** (Wolf), Viola Essen (Bird), **Karen Conrad** (Duck), **Nina Stroganova** (Cat). Another version was staged by Elizabeth West in 1957 for Western Theatre Ballet. The story, told by a narrator, is that of Peter who, heedless of Grandfather's warning, sets out to find and capture the dangerous Wolf that has been terrorizing the neighbourhood. He is aided by his friends the Cat, the Duck and the Bird. Serge Prokofiev's music was composed to introduce the instruments of the orchestra to children. Grandfather is portrayed by the bassoon, Peter by the strings, the Bird by the flute, the Cat by the clarinet and the Wolf by the horn.

PETIPA, Jean Antoine (1796–1855), French dancer, choreographer and teacher, the father of **Lucien** and **Marius Petipa**. He made his debut in Marseilles and danced in Paris, Bordeaux, Madrid and Brussels, where he was ballet master for twelve years. From 1848 until his death he taught at the Imperial School, St. Petersburg.

PETIPA, Joseph Lucien (1815–98), French dancer and choreographer. He studied with his father Jean Antoine Petipa and made his debut in Brussels. He partnered **Fanny Elssler** in *La Sylphide* for his debut at the **Paris Opéra Ballet** (1840), and created Albrecht in *Giselle* (1841), and the leading male roles in *La Péri* and *La Jolie Fille de Gand*, partnering **Grisi**. He was ballet master at the Paris Opéra (1865) and choreographed *Namouna* (1882). His other creations include *Sakountala* and *Graziosa* (1861).

PETIPA, Marius (1819–1910), French dancer and choreographer. Trained by his father, he made his debut at Nantes (1838), and danced in Brussels, the United States, with **Grisi** at Comédie Française (1840); with **Fanny Elssler** at the Paris Opéra (1841) and at Bordeaux and Madrid (1842–5). He went to Russia in 1847, became instructor at the Imperial School in 1854, and ballet master at the Imperial Theatre, St. Petersburg (1860). He revived *Paquita* in which he made his debut and was considered an outstanding dancer and partner. His first original work for the Imperial Theatre was *A Marriage During Regency* (1858), followed by *The Paris Market* and *The Blue Dahlia* (1859). After the presentation of *The Daughter of Pharaoh* he became choreographer-in-chief in place of **Perrot** (1862). He toured Europe with his wife, Maria Sourovshchikova (1859–60). He created 54 new works, revived 17, and arranged the dances for 34 operas. The Soviet repertoire rests mainly on his work, his masterpieces being *Don Quixote, Camargo, La Bayadère, The Sleeping Beauty* (1890), *The Nutcracker* (1892), *Raymonda, Harlequinade*, and his revivals of *Paquita, Giselle, Le Corsaire, Coppélia, La Sylphide, Swan Lake* with Ivanov, and *The Humpbacked Horse*. His work *The Magic Mirror* was a failure and he retired in 1904. His *Memoirs* were published in 1906, and he remains the greatest single figure in Russian ballet.

PETIT, Roland (1924–   ), French dancer and choreographer. He studied with Lifar, then at the Paris Opéra school with Gustave Ricaux, became a member of the corps de ballet (1939) and danced his first major role in *L'Amour Sorcier* (1943). During the war years he gave concert performances with **Janine Charrat**. *Orphée* and *Rêve d'Amour* were his first choreographic successes. He left the **Paris Opéra Ballet** in 1944 and presented *Soirées de la Danse* with **Irène Lidova**. *Les Forains* was his first major success, and led to the founding of **Les Ballets des Champs-Elysées** (1945–7) with **Boris Kochno**, of which he was choreographer, ballet master and principal dancer. His works including *Les Rendez-vous, La Fiancée du Diable, Les Amours de Jupiter, Le Jeune Homme et la Mort* and *Le Bal des Blanchisseuses* were well received. In 1948 he founded **Les Ballets de Paris de Roland Petit**. For the première of *Les Demoiselles de la Nuit*, the principal role was danced by **Margot Fonteyn**. *L'Oeuf à la Coque, Carmen* and *La Croqueuse de Diamants* followed. In 1952 he toured the United States and Europe, and was choreographer in Hollywood. With the re-organization of Les Ballets de Paris de Roland Petit (1953), he choreographed *Le Loup, Deuil en 24 Heures, Ciné-Bijou, La Dame dans la Lune, Rose des Vents* and *Cyrano de Bergerac*. He has staged *Ballabile* for Sadler's Wells (1950) and *La Chaloupée, Carmen* and *Cyrano de Bergerac* for the Royal Danish Ballet. Other works include *Notre Dame de Paris* (1965), *Turangalila* (1968), *L'Éloge de la Folie* (1966), *Paradise Lost* (1967) for Nureyev and Fonteyn and *Pelléas et Mélisande* (1969). In 1970 he was appointed director of the **Paris Opéra Ballet**, but resigned in the same year. He became director of Le Nouveau Ballet de l'Opéra at Marseilles. See illustration p. 176.

PETROUCHKA, a ballet in four scenes. Libretto, Igor Stravinsky and Alexandre Benois; choreography, **Michel Fokine**; music, Igor Stravinsky; decor, Alexandre Benois. First performed at the Théâtre du

Roland Petit: Le Bal des Blanchisseuses. Ph. Lipnitzki.

Châtelet, Paris, 13 June 1911, by **Diaghilev**'s Ballets Russes. Principal dancers, **Vaslav Nijinsky** (Petrouchka), **Tamara Karsavina** (Ballerina), Alexandre Orlov (Moor), **Enrico Cecchetti** (Charlatan). Restaged for Original Ballet Russe in New York, 21 November 1940, by Michel Fokine. Principal dancers, Yurek Lazowski (Petrouchka), **Tamara Toumanova** (Ballerina), **Alberto Alonso** (Moor), Marian Ladré (Charlatan). Presented in New York, 8 October 1942, by **Ballet Theatre.** Principal dancers, **Irina Baronova** (Ballerina), Yurek Lazowski (Petrouchka), Richard Reed (Moor), **Simon Semenov** (Charlatan). Revived by **Nicholas Beriosov** for London's **Festival Ballet,** 1950, with **Anton Dolin** dancing Petrouchka. Revived for **The Royal Ballet** at the Royal Opera House, Covent Garden, London, 26 March 1957, by **Serge Grigoriev.** Principal dancers, **Alexander Grant** (Petrouchka), **Margot Fonteyn** (Ballerina), Peter Clegg (Moor). Revived at New York City Center, 12 March 1970, by City Center Joffrey Ballet. Choreography, Léonide Massine. Principal dancer, Edward Verso. The title role has also been danced by **Léonide Massine, Leon Woizikowsky. Stanislas Idizikowsky,** Yurek

Shabelevsky. At a fair in St. Petersburg, the Charlatan's puppet, Petrouchka is seen to be in love with another puppet, the Ballerina. She flouts him and favours the Moor who ultimately kills Petrouchka. The Charlatan shows the frightened audience that Petrouchka is only a stuffed puppet which he proceeds to drag away. But the soul of the dead Petrouchka appears to curse his master. This ballet has always been controversial both for Igor Stravinsky's music and for the underlying meaning of the story. Was it intended to be a typically Russian view of the lives of the poor and downtrodden people under the despotic Czarist regimes? Was Petrouchka intended to portray a soul struggling to find itself? Whatever the interpretation, and several are possible, Igor Stravinsky, Michel Fokine, Vaslav Nijinsky and Tamara Karsavina together gave the ballet a tremendous impact upon audiences and this impact was maintained by later dancers. Igor Stravinsky, Michel Fokine and Alexandre Benois were in perfect partnership and harmony in the production, and public acclaim has been such that *Petrouchka* has been taken into the repertoires of most major ballet companies and is a lasting tribute to Diaghilev.

PETROV, Paul (Paul Eilif Eilhelm Petersen), Danish dancer and teacher. He studied with Katja Lindhart and made his debut in a concert performance with Violet Fischer in 1930. As premier danseur with **Colonel de Basil's Ballet Russe de Monte Carlo** and Original Ballet Russe (1932–43), he danced most of the classical roles, and created Florentine Youth in *Paganini* (1936) and Paolo Malatesta in *Francesca da Rimini* (1937). He was premier danseur with **Ballet Theatre** (1943–5), and **International Ballet** (1947), and toured North and South America with **Nana Gollner** (1948). He later became a teacher in California.

PHÈDRE, a ballet in one act based on the Racine poem. Libretto, Jean Cocteau; choreography, **Serge Lifar**; music, Georges Auric; decor, Cocteau. First performed at the Paris Opéra, 14 June 1950, by **Paris Opéra Ballet**. Principal dancers, **Tamara Toumanova** (Phèdre), Serge Lifar (Hippolyte), **Lycette Darsonval** (Oenone),. **Liane Daydé** (Aricie), Roger Ritz (Thesée). The story is similar to that of Joseph and Potiphar's wife with psychological overtones brought out, largely in tableaux vivantes in a small temple erected mid-stage. The action is partly mimed. Georges Auric's music reflects the tumult of the tragedy.

Petrouchka: performed by The Royal Ballet. Ph. Anthony Crickmay.

PHILIPPART, Nathalie, French dancer. After studying with **Lubov Egorova,** she joined **Irène Lidova**'s Soirées de la Danse (1944). From 1945–8 she was a principal dancer with **Les Ballets des Champs-Elysées,** dancing in *Jeu de Cartes, Les Amours de Jupiter* and as the girl in Cocteau's *Le Jeune Homme et la Mort,* which was a masterpiece. She danced Psyche in *L'Amour et son Amour,* choreographed by her husband, **Jean Babilée** (1948), and appeared with him as guest artist with American Ballet Theatre (1951).

PIED PIPER, a ballet in one act. Choreography, **Jerome Robbins**; music, Aaron Copland (*Clarinet Concerto*). First performed in New York City Center, 4 December 1951, by **The New York City Ballet.** Principal dancers, Jerome Robbins, Janet Reed, Tanaquil LeClercq, Jillana, Nicholas Magallanes, Todd Bolender, Herbert Bliss. The clarinet player at one side of the stage (which is fully open to the back wall) practises a tune to which the dancers improvise steps.

PIÈGE DE LUMIÈRE, a ballet in one act.

Piège de Lumière: Rosella Hightower and Vladimir Skouratov. Ph. Eric Betting.

Libretto, Philippe Hériat; choreography, **John Taras**; music, Jean-Michel Damase; decor, Felix Labisse; costumes, André Levasseur. First performed at the Théâtre de l'Empire, Paris, 23 December 1952, by **Grand Ballet du Marquis de Cuevas.** Principal dancers, **Rosella Hightower** (Morphide), **Serge Golovine** (Iphias), **Vladimir Skouratov** (Prisoner). Revived at New York State Theater, 1 October 1964, by John Taras for **The New York City Ballet.** Principal dancers, **Maria Tallchief, Arthur Mitchell, André Prokovsky.** Presented by London's **Festival Ballet,** 22 April 1969, at Teatro la Fenice, Venice. Principal dancers, **Galina Samtsova, André Prokovsky.** A fantasy on escaped convicts encamped in a forest. To amuse themselves they try to capture the exotic butterflies in a light-trap. One captures the beautiful Morphide but the Iphias, to save her, covers the Prisoner with his pollen. The Iphias dies and the Prisoner goes insane, imagining himself to have been changed into an Iphias.

PIERROT LUNAIRE, a ballet in one act. Choreography, **Glen Tetley**; music, Arnold Schoenberg; decor, Reuben Ter-Arutunian. First performed at the New York School of Fashion Design, 5 May 1962, by Glen Tetley and Company. Principal dancers, Christopher Bruce, Sandra Craig, Jonathan Taylor. Staged at the Richmond Theatre, Richmond, Surrey, 26 January 1967, by Ballet Rambert. Principal dancers, Peter Curtis, Patricia Rianne, Bob Smith. The ballet consists of a setting of *Three Times Seven,* poems by Albert Giraud in German translation, and includes a vocal soloist. Pierrot, the white clown of innocence and Brighella, the dark clown of experience, are portrayed in a series of situations with Columbine, the eternal feminine.

PILLAR OF FIRE, a ballet in one act. Libretto and choreography, **Antony Tudor**; music, Arnold Schoenberg (*Verklärte Nacht*); decor, Jo Mielziner. First performed at the Metropolitan Opera House, New York, 8 April 1942, by **Ballet**

Theatre. Principal dancers, **Nora Kaye** (Hagar), **Lucia Chase** (Elder Sister), Annabelle Lyon (Younger Sister), Antony Tudor (Friend), **Hugh Laing** (Young Man). Restaged for the **Royal Swedish Ballet,** 30 December 1962, by Antony Tudor. Principal dancers, Mariane Orlando, Conny Borg, Verner Klavsen. Revived at New York State Theater, 1966, by American Ballet Theatre. Principal dancers, **Sallie Wilson, Veronika Mlaker** (Hagar), Bruce Marks, Gayle Young. Danced by the same cast on a Russian tour, 1966. Hagar fears that she has lost her lover, the Friend, to her foolish Young Sister, and is afraid she will become a spinster like her Elder Sister. In desperation, she throws herself into an affair with the Young Man from the house opposite. She suffers in consequence, but eventually the Friend returns to her, bringing happiness. Nora Kaye achieved great success dancing the role of Hagar, and consequently became ballerina.

PINEAPPLE POLL, a ballet in one act, based on W. S. Gilbert's poem, *The Bumboat Woman's Story.* Choreography, **John Cranko**; music, Arthur Sullivan (from *The Mikado, Trial by Jury, The Sorcerer, Patience, The Gondoliers, Cox and Box, Pirates of Penzance, Ruddigore, Princess Ida, Yeomen of the Guard*) arranged by Charles Mackerras; decor, Osbert Lancaster. First performed at Sadler's Wells Theatre, London, 13 March 1951, by Sadler's Wells Theatre Ballet. Principal dancers, **Elaine Fifield** (Poll), **David Blair** (Captain Belaye), David Poole (Jasper). Taken into the repertoires of the National Ballet of Canada and of the Australian Ballet. Revived by David Blair at the New York City Center, 25 February 1970, by City Center Joffrey Ballet. Principal dancers, Rebecca Wright, Chanthel Arthur (Poll), Burton Taylor, Edward Verso (Belaye). The wives of Portsmouth have been captivated by the handsome Captain Belaye and want to sign on as crew of his ship. But he had got married that morning. Jasper consoles one of the ladies, Pineapple Poll.

piqué, a picked-up step.

pirouette, a turning on one foot, impelled by a swing of the arms. The most common is the pirouette en dehors (executed towards the working leg). Others are pirouette en dedans (towards the supporting leg), and pirouette sur le **cou-de-pied.** In a grande pirouette, the working leg is in an open position, eg **attitude, arabesque** or second.

plié, bending the knees. Properly executed pliés are fundamental to ballet movements, especially turns and jumps. In demi-plié the heels are kept firmly on the ground. In grande plié they are raised so that the greatest bend can be achieved, except in second and fourth opposite first positions.

PLISETSKAYA, Maya (1925–), Russian prima ballerina, Honoured Artist of the USSR. A student at the Bolshoi School (1934–43), she danced Breadcrumb Fairy in *The Sleeping Beauty* (1936), Pussy in *Baby Stork* (1937) and Grand Pas in *Paquita* (1941). During the war years she danced many solos before graduation and before her first official season had danced

Maya Plisetskaya, prima ballerina of the Bolshoi Ballet. Ph. Lipnitzki.

at least 20 important roles. During her first season she studied in **Vaganova**'s classe de perfection when she visited the Bolshoi for one year, and was rehearsed as Mazurka in *Chopiniana*, Lilac Fairy in *The Sleeping Beauty* and Masha in *The Nutcracker*. For her ballerina examination (1945) she danced *Raymonda*, and in 1947 danced a dramatic Odette-Odile in *Swan Lake*, which has since been considered to be her most famous role. Her repertoire includes Kitri in *Don Quixote*, Myrtha in *Giselle*, Czar-Maiden in *The Humpbacked Horse*, Zarema in *The Fountain of Bakhchisaral*, title role in *Laurencia*, and in 1961, after five years work on the role, she danced Juliet in *Romeo and Juliet*. She has danced in Britain, Czechoslovakia, Hungary, India, Germany, the United States (as prima ballerina of the Bolshoi Ballet, 1966), Canada, France, and London (1969).

pointe, position of the dancer in which she rises up on the point of her toes and executes movements without a heel or any other part of the foot touching the ground. The use of the pointe gives the dancer the appearance of having no weight and of being so light that she becomes air-borne. It is not used by male dancers. The advent of dancing on the points at the beginning of the 18th century was the result of the development of technique and also of the evolution of the heel-less slipper. No one individual can be credited with the invention of the technique; it was introduced and made indispensable by the great ballerinas of the day, the Russian **Istomina,** the French Gosselin, the Italian Amalia Brugnoli and most effectively by **Maria Taglioni** in *La Sylphide* at the Paris Opéra (1832). The use of the pointe became the symbol of romantic ballet.

poisson, temps de, literally fish movement, a step in which the dancer leaps off the ground with legs held tightly together and body curving sideways, and lands on the right foot.

Poker Game *see* **Card Game.**

POLAJENKO,   Nicholas   (1932–   ), American dancer. He studied with Shollar and **Vilzak,** making his debut with the Ottawa Ballet Company in 1947, partnering **Svetlana Beriosova** in *The Nutcracker* and *Les Sylphides*. In 1948 he joined **Metropolitan Ballet,** London, then **Les Ballets des Champs-Elysées** the same year. He danced with **Les Ballets de Paris de Roland Petit,** toured the United States and joined Metropolitan Opera when Petit's company dissolved. He was with London's **Festival Ballet** (1954–5) and was principal dancer with **Ballet International du Marquis de Cuevas** (1956–62). He danced with **George Skibine**'s company and was principal dancer with **Harkness Ballet** (1965) at Cannes.

POLOVETSIAN   DANCES   FROM PRINCE IGOR or **Prince Igor,** a plotless ballet in one act. Choreography, **Michel Fokine**; music, Alexander Borodin (from Act 2 of the Borodin-Rimsky Korsakov opera, *Prince Igor*); decor, Nicholas Roerich. First performed at the Théâtre du Châtelet, Paris, 18 May 1909, by **Diaghilev**'s Ballets Russes. Principal dancers, Sophie Federova (Polovetsian Girl), Yelena Smirnova (Polovetsian Woman), **Adolph Bolm** (Polovetsian Warrior Chief). Revived by **Serge Grigoriev** and **Lubov Tchernicheva** for **The Royal Ballet,** 24 March 1965, with **Rudolph Nureyev** as the Chief. This ballet is in the repertoires of many leading companies. There is spectacular wild dancing (originally included in the opera), with which, in the second act, the Chief wishes to entertain his noble prisoners of war. The dances are of Tartar origin. The work helped greatly to raise the status of the male dancer in Western Europe. Before this, many male parts had been danced by women en travestie.

POPA, Magdalena (1941–   ), Romanian ballerina. She studied in Leningrad and in 1961 became a soloist in Bucharest. Her roles include Pastushka in *Symphonie Fantastique* and *Giselle*.

PORTER, Andrew (1928–), ballet critic born in South Africa. He has written for *The Financial Times* since 1953, and is a member of the Music Advisory Panel (and ballet subcommittee) of the Arts Council of Great Britain. His publications include "Frederick Ashton 1960–70" in *About the House* (1970).

PREOBRAJENSKA, Olga (1871–1962), French prima ballerina and teacher, born in Russia. Considered the greatest dancer of her time, she graduated from the Imperial School, St. Petersburg, in 1889 and became prima ballerina at the Maryinsky Theatre in 1898. During her 25 years with the Imperial Ballet, she danced mainly the classical roles with outstanding skill, including *Coppélia, Paquita, The Nutcracker, Esmeralda, The Fairy Doll, Talisman, The Sleeping Beauty, Raymonda, The Seasons, Harlequinade, Giselle* and *La Sylphide*. She received two gold medals from the Ministry of the Court. During her dancing career in Russia she appeared at **Teatro alla Scala**, Milan (1904), the Paris Opéra (1909),

Olga Preobrajenska as The White Cat in The Sleeping Beauty. Ph. Bakhruchine, Moscow.

Royal Opera House, Covent Garden, London (1910), with **Diaghilev** at Monte Carlo, and taught at the State School of Ballet, Leningrad (1917–21). She toured Europe and America, and spent three years in Berlin and then settled in Paris (1923) where she opened her own school. Her pupils included **Irina Baronova, Tamara Toumanova, Igor Youskevitch, George Skibine, Milorad Miskovitch** and **Agrippina Vaganova.**

PRÉSAGES, LES, a symphonic ballet in four parts. Libretto and choreography, **Léonide Massine**; music, Tchaikovsky (*Fifth Symphony*); decor, André Masson. First performed at the Théâtre de Monte Carlo, 13 April 1933, by **Colonel de Basil's Ballet Russe de Monte Carlo.** Principal dancers, Nina Verchinina (Action), **Irina Baronova** (Passion), **Tatiana Riabouchinska** (Frivolity), **David Lichine** (The Hero), **Léon Woizikowsky** (Fate). Presented at the Alhambra Theatre, London, July 1933. Man is presented in his struggle with his Fate, with Temptation and Frivolity. Fate urges him to self-destruction, but reason and love prevail and peace is restored. This was Léonide Massine's first symphonic ballet and it aroused opposition from the music purists who maintained that the music should be heard alone without the distractions of dance and decor. Colonel de Basil gave one presentation in London without the decor and in practice costumes, but the critics clamoured for the decor and costumes to be restored. The choreography is marked by symbolic power befitting, and closely following, the theme of Tchaikovsky's music.

PRÉVOST, Françoise (1680–1741), French dancer. The daughter of the régisseur of the **Paris Opéra Ballet,** she made her first appearance in 1699, later gaining success in the ballet *Atys*. In 1708 she appeared with Blondi in a work based on an episode in Corneille's *Les Horaces*. She followed Mlle. Subligny as première danseuse at the Paris Opéra and also taught at **L'Académie Royale de Danse.**

Among her students were **Marie Camargo** and **Marie Sallé.**

PRINCE IGOR *see* **Polovetsian Dances from Prince Igor.**

PRINCE OF THE PAGODAS, a ballet in three acts. Libretto and choreography, **John Cranko**; music, Benjamin Britten; decor, John Piper; costumes, Desmond Heeley. First performed at the Royal Opera House, Covent Garden, London, 1 January 1957, by **The Royal Ballet.** Principal dancers, **Svetlana Beriosova** (Princess Belle Rose), **Julia Farron** (Princess Belle Épine), **David Blair** (Salamander Prince), **Leslie Edwards** (Emperor of the Middle Kingdom), Ray Powell (Dwarf), **Anya Linden** (Moon), Maryon Lane and Brian Shaw (Fire). A new version was first performed at Munich State Opera, 17 March 1958. Choreography, **Alan Carter**; decor, Fabius Gugel. The fairy story plot relates how the Princess Belle Épine usurps a kingdom. Under a spell, the Prince is a salamander until the Princess Belle Rose releases him by falling in love with him. He thereupon vanquishes the evil Belle Épine, restores the King and succeeds in marrying Belle Rose.

PRINCESS AURORA *see* **Aurora's Wedding.**

PRODIGAL SON, THE, a narrative ballet in one act, based on the St. Luke parable. Libretto, Boris Kochno; choreography, **George Balanchine**; music, Serge Prokofiev; decor and costumes, Georges Rouault. First performed at the Théâtre Sarah Bernhardt, Paris, 21 May 1929, by **Diaghilev's** Ballets Russes. Principal dancers, **Serge Lifar** (Prodigal Son), Felia Doubrovska (Siren), Michael Federov (Father). Revived for **The New York City Ballet** in New York City Center, 23 February 1950. Principal dancers, **Jerome Robbins** (Prodigal Son), **Maria Tallchief** (Siren), Michael Arshansky (Father). In this retelling of the Bible story in dance, George Balanchine drew on gymnasts and acrobats to enhance his symbolic and

The Prodigal Son: Serge Lifar and Felia Doubrovska. Ph. Lipnitzki.

expressionist choreography. Tenderness and depravity were depicted with startling realism, and the simple, clear story is seen through Russian eyes. George Balanchine found inspiration for his role of the Prodigal Son in his own artistic life. The title role has also been danced successfully by **Francisco Moncion, Hugh Laing** and **Edward Villella.** The Siren role has been danced by Yvonne Mounsey and **Diana Adams. David Lichine** produced a new version to Serge Prokofiev's music for Original Ballet Russe in 1939, when it was first performed in Sydney. Principal dancers, David Lichine (Prodigal Son), **Sono Osato** (Siren).

PRODIGAL SON, THE, a ballet in two acts. Libretto and choreography, **Kurt Jooss**; music, F. A. Cohen; decor, Hein Heckroth. First produced in Amsterdam, 1933, and re-presented (decor, Dimitri Bouchene) in England in 1939 in a double-bill with *The Green Table*. The dramatic re-enactment of the story made much use of acrobatic movement and mime.

PRODIGAL SON, THE, a ballet in four scenes. Choreography, Ivo Cramér; music, Hugo Alfvén; decor, Rune Linstrom. First performed, 1957, by the Royal Swedish Ballet. Principal dancers, Bjørn Holmgren (Prodigal Son), Teddy Rhodin (False Prophet), Elsa-Marianne von Rosen (Arabian Queen), Julius Mangarelli (Father), Anne-Marie Lagerborg (Mother). The ballet is inspired by some early biblical paintings by Dalarna farmers.

PROKOVSKY, André (1939–   ), French dancer. He studied with **Egorova**, Nora Kiss, **Serge Peretti** and Nicholas Zverev. He won a medal at the World Festival of youth in Moscow (1947) and made his debut in 1954 with the Comédie-Française. In 1956 he danced with **Janine Charrat's** company and became soloist with **Les Ballets de Paris de Roland Petit**. He was leading dancer with London's **Festival Ballet** in 1958 and a year later became premier danseur with **Ballet International du Marquis de Cuevas**. He joined **The New York City Ballet** as leading soloist in 1963, making his debut as 1st Movement of *Symphony in C*. His repertoire included *Swan Lake*, (Act 2), *Raymonda Variations*, and he created leading roles in *The Chase*, *Piège de Lumière* and *Irish Fantasy*. In 1964 he toured with Stars of French Ballet, which was headed by **Rosella Hightower** and **Liane Daydé**. In 1966 he left The New York City Ballet and in 1967 rejoined the Festival Ballet as principal dancer, partnering **Galina Samtsova**. The same year he was awarded the Nijinsky Prize. His major roles include Siegfried in *Swan Lake*, Florimund in *The Sleeping Beauty*, Prince in *The Nutcracker*, and Albrecht in *Giselle*. He has also danced leading roles in *Beatrix* (1966), *Dvorak Variations* (1970), *Études* and *The Unknown Island* (1970). In 1972 he founded New London Ballet with **Galina Samtsova**.

PROMENADE, a ballet divertissement in one act. Choreography, **Ninette de Valois**; music, Josef Haydn; decor, Hugh Stevenson. First performed at the King's Theatre, Edinburgh, 25 October 1943, by Sadler's Wells Ballet. Principal dancers, **Margot Fonteyn, Beryl Grey, Gordon Hamilton, Moira Shearer.**

PROSPECT BEFORE US, THE, a ballet in seven scenes, adapted from *Seven Years of the King's Theatre* by John Eber. Libretto and choreography, **Ninette de Valois**; music, William Boyce (sonatas and symphonies arranged by Constant Lambert); decor (based on a Thomas Rowlandson print), Roger Furse. First performed at Sadler's Wells Theatre, London, 4 July 1940, by Vic-Wells Ballet. Principal dancers, **Robert Helpmann,** Claude Newman, **Pamela May, Frederick Ashton**, Mary Honer. Stanley Holden danced Robert Helpmann's role in a Sadler's Wells Theatre Ballet revival. The ballet depicts the rivalry between the King's Theatre and the Panthéon in 1789. The managers steal each other's dancers, when the theatres burn down. One manager gives up and takes to drink. Ninette de Valois arranged a ballet within a ballet for this work.

PSOTA, Vanya (1908–52), Czech dancer, choreographer and teacher. He danced with Prague National Theatre company (1923–6), in Brno (1927–32) and with **Ballet Russe de Monte Carlo** (1933–6). He was artistic director of Brno Ballet (1937–52). His roles included Blackamoor and Korrehidor. His choreographic works include *Romeo and Juliet* (1938), *Slavonica* (1941) and *Treason* (1944).

PULCINELLA, a ballet in one act, based on an old Italian comedy, *The Four Pulcinellas*. Choreography, **Léonide Massine**; music, Igor Stravinsky and Giambattista Pergolesi; decor, Pablo Picasso. First performed at the Théâtre National de l'Opéra, Paris, 15 May 1920, by **Diaghilev's** Ballets Russes. Principal dancers, Léonide Massine (Pulcinella), **Tamara Karsavina** (Pimpinella), **Vera Nemtchinova, Lubov Tchernicheva, Enrico Cecchetti, Stanislas Idzikowsky.** Revived at the Coliseum, London, 1935, by

Léon Woizikowsky, with himself in the title role and under the title, *Les Deux Polichinelles*. Pulcinella was a commedia dell'arte character. The story tells of his love affair with Pimpinella and of his trick to escape death at the hands of his rivals. The ballet ends in a general charivari with much noise and excitement. Serge Diaghilev found the scores of several unknown tarantellas in Italy and gave them to Igor Stravinsky to adapt for this ballet.

PYGMALION, a classical ballet. Choreography, **Marie Sallé.** First performed at Covent Garden, London, 14 February 1734. Marie Sallé danced the role of Galatea. For this ballet she abandoned the heavy, restricting, frilled costume, powdered hair and mask which were de rigueur at the time, and danced in a plain, muslin dress, with her hair loose and uncovered. A ballet of the same name was produced by **Angiolini** in Russia in 1772.

Q

QARRTSILUNI, a ballet in one act. Libretto, **Harald Lander** and Knudaage Riisager; choreography, Harald Lander; music, Knudaage Riisager; decor, Svend Johansen. First performed at the Royal Theatre, Copenhagen, 21 February 1942, by the Royal Danish Ballet. Principal dancer, **Niels Bjørn Larsen** (Sorcerer). Revived 1960 at the Paris Opéra with new decor by Bernard Daydé. Principal dancer, **Michel Descombey** (Sorcerer). Knudaage Riisager's music was inspired by the Eskimo legend of the resurrection of the spring sun after the darkness of winter.

QUATRE SAISONS, LES, a romantic divertissement in one act. Libretto and choreography, **Jules Perrot.** First performed, 13 June 1848, at Her Majesty's Theatre, London. Principal dancers, **Carlotta Grisi** (Summer), **Carolina Rosati** (Autumn), **Fanny Cerito** (Spring), **Maria Taglioni** (Winter). A new version, based on **Petipa**'s divertissement in Verdi's Opera, *The Sicilian Vespers*, was produced at Her Majesty's Theatre, London, 16 May 1856.

QUEST, THE, a ballet in five scenes, based on *The Faerie Queene* by Edmund Spenser. Libretto, Doris Langley Moore; choreography, **Frederick Ashton**; music, William Walton; decor, John Piper. First performed at the New Theatre, London, 6 April 1943, by Sadler's Wells Ballet. Principal dancers, **Margot Fonteyn** (Una), **Robert Helpmann** (St. George), **Leslie Edwards** (Archimago), **Celia Franca** (Servant), **Beryl Grey** (Duessa), **Moira Shearer** (Pride).

R

raccourci, a movement in which the toe of the working leg returns along the line of the movement executed.

RADICE, Attilia (1913–), Italian dancer and teacher. She studied at **Teatro alla Scala,** Milan and became prima ballerina there, and at Teatro dell'Opera, Rome, dancing mainly the classical repertoire. In 1958 she became director of the Rome Opera ballet school.

RADUNSKY, Alexander (1912–), Russian dancer and choreographer, Honoured Artist of the RSFSR, Honoured Art Worker of the RSFSR. He studied at the Bolshoi school, joining the Bolshoi company in 1930. He danced the title role in *Don Quixote* and Lord Capulet in *Romeo and Juliet.* He is especially renowned in mime. His choreographic works include *Svetlana* (1939), *Swan Lake* (1956) and *The Humpbacked Horse* (1960). In 1962 he became chief choreographer of the Soviet Army Song and Dance Ensemble on his retirement from dancing. .

The Rake's Progress: performed by The Royal Ballet. Ph. Dominic.

RAKE'S PROGRESS, THE, a ballet in six scenes, inspired by paintings by William Hogarth. Libretto, Gavin Gordon; choreography, **Ninette de Valois**; music, Gordon; decor, Rex Whistler. First performed at Sadler's Wells Theatre, London, 20 May 1935, by Vic-Wells Ballet. Principal dancers, **Walter Gore, Robert Helpmann** (The Rake), **Alicia Markova** (Betrayed Girl), Aline Phillips (Her Mother), Ursula Moreton (Dancer), Joy Newton (Street Singer), **Harold Turner** (Music Master). **The Royal Ballet** successfully presented the ballet on a tour of Russia. It tells of a young man's downfall in the city, of his remorse, insanity and death after squandering his inheritance. Deserted by fairweather friends, he dies in the forgiving arms of the girl he has betrayed. A version with music by Stravinsky was performed at the International Festival in Venice in 1951.

Dame Marie Rambert. Ph. Reyna.

RALOV, Borge (Leo Sylvester Ralov, 1908–), Danish dancer and choreographer. A pupil of **Legat** and **Idzikowski**, he graduated from the Royal Danish Ballet School in 1927, became solo dancer in 1933, instructor in 1934 and first solo dancer in 1942. He danced the classical repertoire, the Bournonville ballets including *The Kermesse at Bruges*, and a number of modern ballets. His *Petrouchka* was outstanding, and he was the frequent partner of **Margot Lander**. His choreographic works include *The Widow in the Mirror* (1934), *Twelve for the Mail Coach* (1942), and *The Courtesan* (1953). He retired as a dancer in 1957 to teach at the Royal Danish Ballet School.

RAMBERT, Marie (Myriam Ramberg, 1888–), English teacher, producer and director born in Poland, Dame of the Order of the British Empire. She was a pupil of **Jacques Dalcroze** and **Enrico Cecchetti,** and was a member of the **Diaghilev** Ballets Russes (1912–13). In 1920 she opened a ballet school, and in 1926 she produced her first ballet, *A Tragedy of Fashion*, by **Frederick Ashton.** The first season of the Ballet Rambert was in 1930, when The Rambert Dancers gave their own public performance at the Lyric Theatre, Hammersmith. Later that year, the Ballet Club was founded at the Mercury Theatre, which was also the home of the ballet school. This was the first permanent English company and ballet school, and it trained such people as **Pearl Argyle, Andrée Howard, Frederick Ashton, Harold Turner** and **Antony Tudor.** Mme. Rambert also played a part (with **Ninette de Valois**) in the founding of **The Camargo Society** (1930). In 1940 the Ballet Rambert joined the London Ballet, forming the Rambert-London Ballet. The company was disbanded in 1941, but in 1943 the Ballet Rambert was re-established. The company toured extensively after World War II, and grew steadily under Mme. Rambert's expert eye. With her remarkable ability to recognize and develop talent, she did a great deal to further ballet in England. Among her discoveries (besides those already mentioned) were **Walter Gore, Sally Gilmour, Celia Franca, Lucette Aldous** and **Norman Morrice.** The company expanded its repertoire greatly by producing many new works by its own choreographers. It also staged *La Sylphide* (1960) and revived **Gorsky**'s *Don Quixote*. Mme. Rambert was awarded the Legion of Honour (1957). In 1966 the company was re-organized and made smaller, with Marie Rambert and Norman Morrice as joint directors. The 'new' company, while preserving the best of the old repertoire, has been primarily concerned with the promotion of new works by contemporary choreographers. The current repertoire includes works by leading choreographers such as **Glen Tetley**, Norman Morrice, **Anna Sokolow, John Chesworth** and Christopher Bruce. The company also presented a programme, *Dance for New Dimensions*, (1972), created specially for 'open' stages.

RAMEAU, Pierre, 18th century French dancing master. He was dancing master to Elizabeth Farnese, second wife of Philip V of Spain. In 1725 he wrote *The Dancing Master*, the best source of 18th century dance technique. Primarily a guide to social dancing, it contains rules for dance and engravings of the various postures, and has had a considerable influence on theatrical dancing. Rameau believed that everyone should be skilled in the dance because it makes them graceful and covers up body defects. He emphasized the importance of the five absolute posture positions, which he attributed to **Beauchamp**. They were, however, mentioned in Arbeau's *Orchésographie* (1588).

RAPP, Richard, American dancer. He studied with Adele Artinian, Ann Barzel and at the School of American Ballet. He joined **The New York City Ballet** in 1958, became soloist in 1961, and dances the company's large repertoire. He created the title role in Balanchine's *Don Quixote* (1965).

RASSINE, Alexis (1919–   ), South African dancer, born in Lithuania. He studied in Cape Town and later with **Preobrajenska, Volkova** and **Idzikowsky,** making his debut in *Bal Tabarin*. He danced with Ballet Rambert (1938), Ballets

Trois Arts (1939–42), and was soloist with Anglo-Polish Ballet (1940). In 1942 he joined Sadler's Wells Ballet and became premier danseur. He danced Albrecht in *Giselle*, Blue Bird pas de deux in *The Sleeping Beauty*, Franz in *Coppélia*, the title role in *Le Spectre de la Rose*, and created pas de trois in *Promenade*, Sansloy in *The Quest*, Lover in *Miracle in the Gorbals* and Spirit of the Earth in *Homage to the Queen*. Partnering **Nadia Nerina** he toured South Africa (1952, 1955) ; he also partnered **Yvette Chauviré** at Covent Garden (1958).

RAYMONDA, a ballet in three acts. Libretto, **Marius Petipa** and Lydia Pashkova ; choreography, Marius Petipa ; music, Alexander Glazunov ; decor, Allegri, Ivanov, Lambini. First performed at the Maryinsky Theatre, St. Petersburg, 19 January 1898. Principal dancers, **Pierina Legnani** (Raymonda), **Olga Preobrajenska, Paul Gerdt.** The work is still in the repertoire of the Soviet ballet. Revived by **Alexandra Danilova** and **George Balanchine** for **Ballet Russe de Monte Carlo,** with decor and costumes by **Alexandre Benois.** First performed at **The New York City Center,** 12 March 1946, with Alexandra Danilova as Raymonda. Revived in 1964, with choreography by Rudolph Nureyev, by **The Royal Ballet** (touring section) at the Spoleto Festival of Two Worlds. In 1965 Nureyev staged his version, slightly amended for the Australian Ballet. Act III only was performed at The Royal Opera House, Covent Garden, 16 July 1966 by The Royal Ballet. Principal dancers, **Doreen Wells, David Wall.** The story tells of the love of Raymonda and Jean de Brienne in medieval Hungary. The Saracen knight Abderahman attempts to kidnap her, but she is rescued by the White Lady, and de Brienne kills the Saracen in a duel and marries his lady.

RAYMONDA VARIATIONS or **Valses et Variations,** an abstract ballet in one act. Choreography, **George Balanchine** ; music, Alexander Glazunov ; decor, Horace

Armistead. First performed in the New York City Center, 7 December 1961, by **The New York City Ballet**. Principal dancers, **Patricia Wilde, Jacques d'-Amboise**. The ballet comprises an ensemble waltz, pas de deux for ballerina and principal dancer, nine variations and a finale.

RED FLOWER, THE *see* Red Poppy, The.

RED POPPY, THE, a ballet in three acts. Libretto, **Vassily Tikhomirov** and Mikhail Kurilko; choreography, Vassily Tikhomirov and Lev Lashchilin; music, Reingold Glière; decor, Mikhail Kurilko. First performed at the Bolshoi Theatre, Moscow, 14 June 1927, by the Bolshoi Ballet. Principal dancers, **Yekaterina Geltzer** (Tao Hoa), Alexei Bulgakov (Captain). In 1949 a new version was presented in Moscow with choreography by **Leonid Lavrovsky**. Principal dancers, **Galina Ulanova, Olga Lepeshinskaya, Mikhail Gabovich**, Yuri Kondratov. Lavrovsky choreographed a considerably altered version with the title *The Red Flower*. First performed, 24 November 1957, at the Bolshoi Theatre, Moscow. Another version with choreography by Alexei Andreyev was first performed, 2 May 1958, at the Kirov Theatre, Leningrad. The Chinese dancer, Tao Hoa, falls in love with the Soviet captain and refuses to poison him at the command of her manager. She then gives her life to save him from being shot and dies with the red flower, symbol of his love, in her hands.

REED, Janet (1916–), American dancer and ballet mistress. After studying with **Willam Christensen** she was première danseuse of San Francisco Opera Ballet (1937–41), dancing Swanilda in *Coppélia* and Odette-Odile in *Swan Lake*, the first full-length version staged by an American company. With **Ballet Theatre** (1943–6), she created Second Girl in *Fancy Free*, and danced in *Gala Performance, Pillar of Fire* and *Graduation Ball*. She joined **The New York City Ballet** in 1949, dancing

an extensive repertoire and creating new roles. She was ballet mistress of The New York City Ballet (1959–64) and in 1965 took a teaching post at Bard College.

relevé, snatch to **pointe** or demi-pointe from flat-footed position.

RENARD, LE, a ballet in one act. Choreography, **Bronislava Nijinska**; music, Igor Stravinsky; decor, Michel Larinov. First performed at the Paris Opéra, 18 May 1922, by **Diaghilev**'s Ballets Russes. Principal dancers, Bronislava Nijinska, **Stanislas Idzikowsky**. A new version was choreographed by **Serge Lifar** for the same company. First performed, 21 May 1929, at the Théâtre Sarah Bernhardt, Paris. Another version was commissioned for the Edinburgh Festival Society and staged by Alfred Rodrigues with decor by Arthur Boyd. Performed at the Empire Theatre, Edinburgh, 4 September 1961, by Western Theatre Ballet. Principal dancers, Suzanne Musitz, Dennis Griffith, Oliver Symons, Peter Cazalet. A new ballet-burlesque in one act with chorus to the same music was choreographed by **George Balanchine**. Decor, Esteban Francés. First performed in the Hunter College Playhouse, New York, 13 January 1947, by Ballet Society. Principal dancers, Lew Christensen, Fred Danieli, **John Taras, Todd Bolender**. Both ballets are based on the fable of the Fox and the Rooster, in which the bird just manages to outwit his enemy.

RENAULT, Michel (1927–), French dancer. He trained at the Paris Opéra school, where he studied with Gustave Ricaux and **Serge Peretti**, and, at 18, was the **Paris Opéra Ballet**'s youngest premier danseur étoile. He danced many of **Lifar**'s ballets, and created leading roles in *Les Mirages* and *Le Palais de Cristal*; and danced *Le Chevalier et la Damoiselle*, *Études*, *La Belle Hélène*, *Giselle*, *Apollon Musagète* and *Romeo and Juliet*. In 1959 he left the company and made a number of guest appearances on tour with **Liane Daydé**.

RENCONTRE, LA *see* **Oedipus and the Sphinx.**

RENDEZ-VOUS, LES, a ballet in one act. Choreography, **Frederick Ashton**; music, François Auber; decor, William Chappell. First performed at Sadler's Wells Theatre, 5 December 1933, by Sadler's Wells Ballet. Principal dancers, **Alicia Markova, Margot Fonteyn, Stanislas Idzikowsky** and **Harold Turner, Ninette de Valois, Robert Helpmann.** Revived, 26 December 1947, by Sadler's Wells Theatre Ballet, with **Elaine Fifield** and Michael Boulton as principal dancers. Young couples meet and flirt in a park.

RENÉ, Natalia Petrovna (1907–), Russian ballet critic and historian. She studied ballet and modern dance, and after working in journalism, began writing on ballet in 1943. Her published works include *Maya Plisetskaya* (1956) and *English Ballet* (1959). She worked on *Agrippina Vaganova* (1958), and on the Russian edition of Fokine's memoirs (1962); and her *Era of the Russian Ballet 1770–1965* (1966) is the outstanding work on the subject. Under the pseudonym Natalia Roslavleva she wrote for *Ballet Today* (1946–50). She has contributed to *Dancing Times* and *Dance and Dancers.* She is president of the ballet section of the USSR-UK Friendship Society.

REYNA, Ferdinand (1899–1969), French historian and ballet critic. He founded the International Festival of the Dance (1919) at Nervi in northern Italy. His published works include *Les Origines du Ballet* (1955) and *A Concise History of Ballet* (1964). In 1961 he founded the International Critics Association of the Ballet.

RHODES, Lawrence (1939–), American dancer and choreographer. After studying dance in Detroit with Violette Armand, he joined the corps de ballet of **Ballet Russe de Monte Carlo.** In 1960 he joined the Robert Joffrey Ballet, where he danced leading roles in *Time Out of Mind, Partita for Four* and *Palace.* In 1964 he joined the **Harkness Ballet,** and became joint director in 1970. His style and technique are considered to be that of **August Bournonville.**

RIABOUCHINSKA, Tatiana (1917–), Russian ballerina. She studied with **Preobrajenska** and **Kchessinska,** making her debut with the revue Chauve-Souris, Paris, when she was fifteen. As one of the **baby ballerinas** with **Colonel de Basil'**s Ballet Russe de Monte Carlo (1932–41) she created Frivolity in *Les Présages,* Butterfly in *Carnaval,* Child in *Jeux d'Enfants,* Florentine Beauty in *Paganini,* Junior Girl in *Graduation Ball,* and the title roles in *Coq d'Or* and *Cinderella.* Her repertoire also included *Les Sylphides, Concurrence; Carnaval* and *Choreartium.* She was guest artist with her husband, **David Lichine,** at London's **Festival Ballet, Ballet Theatre** (1944), Original Ballet Russe (1947), **Les Ballets des Champs-Elysées** (1948), and **Grand Ballet du Marquis de Cuevas** (1950). She later took a teaching post in California.

RIABYNKINA, Yelena (1941–), Russian ballerina. She studied at the Bolshoi School (1950–9) under Vera Vassilieva, making her debut as Odette-Odile in *Swan Lake* (1959). Her studies were continued with Yelizaveta Gerdt when she became a member of the company. Her repertoire includes Queen of the Ball in *The Bronze Horseman,* title role in *Raymonda,* Czar-Maiden in *The Humpbacked Horse,* Kitri in *Don Quixote* and Phyrgia in *Spartacus.* She has danced in Europe, China and the United States.

RICARDA, Ana, American dancer and choreographer. After studying in Washington, New York and Europe, she danced with the Markova-Dolin Ballet and was ballerina with the **Grand Ballet du Marquis de Cuevas.** She was guest artist with London's **Festival Ballet** in 1951. Her choreographic works include *Del Amor y de la Muerte* (1949), *Doña Ines de Castro* and *La Tertulia* (1952).

RICHARDSON, Philip J. S. (1875–1963), English editor and writer. Co-founder and Director (1910–57) of *The Dancing Times.* Co-founder (1920) of the Association of Operatic Dancing of Great Britain, now the Royal Academy of Dancing. Co-founder (1929) with **Arnold Haskell** of **The Camargo Society.** Awarded OBE (1952).

RINALDI, Antonio, 18th century Italian dancer and choreographer. In 1733 he danced in Venice and London under the name of Fossan. Invited to Russia (1735), he produced *The Force of Love and Hate* (1736), *False Nino* (1737) and *Ataxerxes* (1738) at the Imperial Theatre, St. Petersburg. He fled Russia and danced with **La Barberina** at **L'Académie Royale de Musique,** Paris, appearing in *Zaide, Reine de Grenade* and *Momus Amoureux* (1739). **Landet** invited him back to Russia where he choreographed and danced in the ballets for the operas *Seleuco* and *Cupid and Psyche* (1744).

RINALDO AND ARMIDA, a ballet in one act, based on a poem by Torquato Tasso. Choreography, **Frederick Ashton** ; music, Malcolm Arnold ; decor, Peter Rice. First performed at the Royal Opera House, Covent Garden, London, 6 January 1955, by Sadler's Wells Ballet. Principal dancers, **Svetlana Beriosova** (Armida), **Michael Somes** (Rinaldo), **Julia Farron** (Sibilla), **Ronald Hynd** (Gandolfo). The ballet tells of Armida, who, bewitched, entices men to their deaths. She falls in love with Rinaldo but saves him with a kiss, knowing that it will mean her own death.

RITE OF SPRING, THE or **Le Sacre du Printemps,** a ballet in two scenes. Libretto and decor, Nicholas Roerich ; choreography, **Vaslav Nijinsky** ; music, Igor Stravinsky. First performed at the Théâtre des Champs-Elysées, Paris, 29 May 1913, by **Diaghilev**'s Ballets Russes. Principal dancer, Maria Piltz. **Léonide Massine** revived the ballet with his own choreography, October 1920. Principal dancer, **Lydia Sokolova.** On 11 April 1930,

The Rite of Spring. Ph. Roy Round.

Léonide Massine and **Martha Graham** staged this version in Philadelphia, and Massine staged it for Royal Swedish Ballet, 30 May 1956. A new version with considerable alterations to libretto and choreography was staged by **Maurice Béjart** at the Théâtre Royale de la Monnaie, Brussels, December 1959. Principal dancers, **Tania Bari,** Germinal Casado. On 8 May 1962, a version with choreography by **Kenneth MacMillan** was presented at the Royal Opera House, Covent Garden, London. Principal dancer, Monica Mason. This version was given in the Metropolitan Opera House, New York, 8 May 1963. On 24 June 1964, a version with choreography by **Vladimir Vassiliev** and Natalia Kasatkina was presented in Moscow by the Bolshoi Ballet. The theme is the fertility ritual of a primitive tribe when a young girl is worshipped and then sacrificed. Stravinsky's music is difficult, but matches the ballet's theme of primitive vigour. The dancers had difficulty with the original choreography which owed much to the eurhythmic theories of **Jacques Dalcroze**, and Diaghilev asked **Marie Rambert** to assist in unravelling the complex rhythms and steps.

ROBBINS, Jerome (1918–   ), American choreographer and dancer. He studied ballet with **Antony Tudor**, Eugene Loring, Ella Daganova and Helene Platova ; he also studied modern, Spanish, Oriental, and interpretative dance. He danced with **Ballet Theatre** (1940–8). Rising from the corps de ballet to soloist with Ballet Theatre, he created leading roles in *Romeo and Juliet, Helen of Troy, Bluebeard* and *Aleko,* and danced the title role in *Petrouchka.* His choreographic works included *Fancy Free, Pied Piper, Interplay* and *Facsimile.* As associate artistic director of **The New York City Ballet** (1949–73) he produced ten works including *Age of Anxiety, Jones Beach* (with **Balanchine**), *The Cage, Ballade* and *L'Après-midi d'un Faune.* In his works, essentially classical ingredients are expressed in a contemporary idiom. He has choreographed many musicals, notably *West Side Story* (1962), for which he won two Oscars, and *Fiddler on the Roof* (1964). In 1964 he was made Chevalier de l'Ordre des Arts et Lettres by the French government. In 1965 his *Les Noces* was a major success at the American Ballet Theatre's 25th anniversary, and in 1966 the National Council of the Arts agreed to support his proposed project, The American Lyric Theatre Workshop. After several years Robbins returned to ballet. As ballet master with The New York

The Cage by Jerome Robbins. Ph. New York City Ballet.

City Ballet he has created *Dances at a Gathering* (1969), *Goldberg Variations* (1971) and *Watermill* (1972).

Robert Joffrey Ballet *see* **Joffrey, Robert.**

RODEO or *The Courting at Burnt Ranch*, a ballet in two scenes. Libretto and choreography, **Agnes de Mille**; music, Aaron Copland; decor, Oliver Smith; costumes, Kermit Love. First performed at the Metropolitan Opera House, New York, 16 October 1942, by **Ballet Russe de Monte Carlo**. Principal dancers, Milada Mladova (Rancher's Daughter), Agnes de Mille, Lubov Roudenko, Dorothy Etheridge (Cowgirl), **Frederic Franklin** (Champion Roper), Casimir Kokitch (Head Wrangler). Revived for American Ballet Theatre in 1950 with **John Kriza** and Allyn McLerie. At a Saturday night dance on a ranch in the American South-West, the Cowgirl in her boots and jeans is the only wallflower. She slips away and changes into a pretty dress and, on her return, all the men are at her feet. The ballet made use of a square dance with hand-clapping by dancers and orchestra.

RODHAM, Robert (1939–), American dancer and choreographer. After study with Barbara Weisberger and Virginia Williams, he entered the School of American Ballet. He joined **The New York City Ballet** in 1960, and became soloist in 1963. Puck in *A Midsummer Night's Dream* is considered his best role, but he also danced *Agon, La Valse, Arcade* and *Pas de Dix*. He choreographed *Ballade* (1963) in Detroit.

ROI NU, LE, a ballet based on a Hans Andersen fairy tale. Choreography, **Serge Lifar**; music, Jean Françaix; decor, Pruna. First performed at the Théâtre National de l'Opéra, 15 June 1936, by the **Paris Opéra Ballet**. Principal dancers, Serge Lifar, **Yvette Chauviré**. A new version with choreography by **Ninette de Valois** and decor by Hedley Briggs was first performed, 7 April 1938, by Sadler's Wells Ballet. Principal dancers, **Pearl Argyle, Robert Helpmann.**

ROMANOV, Boris (1891–1957), Russian dancer and choreographer. He graduated from the Imperial School, St. Petersburg, into the Maryinsky Theatre (1909), dancing concurrently with **Diaghilev**'s Ballets Russes (1910–14), where he choreographed *The Tragedy of Salome* (1912). For the **Paris Opéra Ballet** he staged dances for Stravinsky's *The Nightingale* (1913). He made his choreographic debut at the Maryinsky Theatre (1914) and staged dances for operas until 1917. In 1921 he left Russia and went to Germany where along with his wife, Helen Smirnova, he founded Romantic Theatre, a small travelling company, which toured for some years in Germany, France, Spain and England. He was choreographer for **Teatro alla Scala,** Milan (1925); Teatro del Opera, Rome; Metropolitan Opera House, New York (1938–41, 1942, 1945–50) and other major companies. He staged ballets for **Ballet International** (1944) and for **Ballet Russe de Monte Carlo** (1956), and taught at the School of Ballet Repertory.

romantic ballet, term for the type of ballet introduced during the Romantic period. It represented a fundamentally different approach from anything that had gone before. The idea of representing a dream world and fairy tales brought about the development of new techniques, especially for the ballerina, who rose on her toes for the first time in an attempt to represent ethereality and 'other-worldliness'. Music and decor were carefully planned to portray character and atmosphere, and the standard white costume was adopted for the ballerina. There was a temporary decline in the importance of the male dancer. The poet, Théophile Gautier (1811–72), gave considerable impetus to the movement in his writings and with his work on the libretto of the most famous romantic ballet of all, *Giselle* (1841), which successfully fused all the romantic elements.

ROMEO AND JULIET. Many ballets have been inspired by Shakespeare's tragedy. The earliest had choreography by **Vincenzo Galeotti** and music by Schall. First performed, 2 April 1811, by the Royal Danish Ballet Company in Copenhagen. Principal dancers, Anna Margrethe Schall, **Antoine Bournonville.** A version in one act was presented, 4 May 1926, by the **Diaghilev** Ballets Russes in Monte Carlo. Choreography, **Bronislava Nijinska** and **George Balanchine**; music, Constant Lambert; decor, Joan Miró and Max Ernst. Principal dancers, **Tamara Karsavina, Serge Lifar.** This ballet is about two dancers rehearsing a ballet on the Romeo and Juliet theme. The Shakespeare plot translated into dance idiom provided a three act version: libretto, **Leonid Lavrovsky,** Serge Prokofiev and Sergei Radlov; choreography, Leonid Lavrovsky; music, Serge Prokofiev; decor, Peter Williams. Principal dancers, **Galina Ulanova, Konstantin Sergeyev.** First per-

formed, 11 January 1940, at the Kirov Theatre, Leningrad, and restaged in 1946. A version in one act, with choreography by Serge Lifar and music, Peter Tchaikovsky, was originally produced for **Nouveau Ballet de Monte Carlo** in 1946 and restaged by the **Paris Opéra Ballet,** 13 April 1949. Principal dancers **Yvette Chauviré,** Serge Lifar. Lifar also choreographed a version in two acts to music by Prokofiev for the Opéra, presented 28 December 1955. Principal dancers, **Liane Daydé, Michel Renault.** The Prokofiev music was also used by **Frederick Ashton** for the version he choreographed for the Royal Danish Ballet. First performed, 19 May 1955, at the Royal Theatre, Copenhagen. Principal dancers, Mona Vangsaa, **Henning Kronstam. Kenneth MacMillan** also used it for his three act version, with decor by Nicholas Georgiadis. First performed, 9 February 1965, in the Royal Opera House, Covent Garden, London. Principal dancers, **Margot Fonteyn,**

Romeo and Juliet: Anna Laerkesen and Ole Fatum. Ph. Reyna.

Lynn Seymour and Antoinette Sibley (Juliet), Rudolph Nureyev, Christopher Gable, Donald MacLeary and Anthony Dowell (Romeo). This version concentrated on the fate of the two young lovers. A one act ballet, choreography, Antony Tudor; music, Frederick Delius (arranged by Antal Dorati); decor, Eugene Berman, was first performed at the Metropolitan Opera House, New York, 6 April 1943, by Ballet Theatre. Principal dancers, Alicia Markova, Nora Kaye and Alicia Alonso (Juliet), Hugh Laing and John Kriza (Romeo), Antony Tudor (Tybalt). This was staged, 30 December 1962, for Royal Swedish Ballet. Principal dancers, Berit Skold, Conny Borg.

RONA, Victor (1936–   ), Hungarian dancer and teacher. He studied in Budapest and Leningrad, becoming a soloist with the Budapest Opera in 1955. As well as classical roles, his repertoire includes *The Miraculous Mandarin* and *The Wooden Prince*.

Carolina Rosati. Ph. Lipnitzki.

rond de jambe, movement in which the leg describes the shape of 'D' à terre, and en l'air from the knee to the toe only.

ROSATI, Carolina (1826–1905), Italian ballerina. She studied with Carlo Blasis and made her debut in Verona. She danced in London (1847–58), at the Paris Opéra (1853–9) and was guest artist at the Imperial Theatre, St. Petersburg (1859–1861), where she created the principal role in *Pharaoh's Daughter*. For the Paris Opéra Ballet she created Medora in *Le Corsaire* (1856), and the principal roles in *La Sonnambula* and *Marco Spada* (1857). She also danced in Paul Taglioni's *Corali*, *Les Patineurs*, *Thea* and *Les Éléments*. She retired in 1862.

ROSEN, Heiné, German choreographer and ballet master. He studied with Rudolph von Laban, Jooss and Gsovsky, dancing with Ballet Jooss during its world tours. In 1953 he was ballet master at the State Opera, Munich, where he worked with Jean Cocteau on *The Lady and the Unicorn*, which was subsequently staged in Berlin, Paris, Buenos Aires and America. Other works include *L'Indifférent*, *Le Bourgeois Gentilhomme*, *Cantique du Cirque*. He revised *The Legend of Joseph*, *Joan von Zarissa* and others for the Bavarian State Opera, where he became ballet master in 1959. He has also made several ballet films, including *Homage to Fanny Elssler*.

ROSLAVLEVA, Natalia *see* RENÉ, Natalia Petrovna.

Royal Ballet, The, a British company, formerly known as the Sadler's Wells Ballet. It was directed by Ninette de Valois until her retirement in 1963, when she was succeeded by Frederick Ashton. The roots of The Royal Ballet reach back to 1926, when de Valois founded the Academy of Choreographic Art. Her pupils danced frequently at the Old Vic Theatre, and their success led to the founding of a ballet school at the rebuilt Sadler's Wells Theatre in 1931. The group alternated between the Old Vic and the Sadler's Wells theatres, and became known as the Vic-Wells Ballet. The company grew rapidly, engaging such dancers as **Alicia Markova, Anton Dolin, Robert Helpmann, Pamela May, June Brae, Harold Turner** and **Michael Somes**. The repertoire included *The Haunted Ballroom* (1934), *The Rake's Progress* (1935) and *Checkmate* (1937) by de Valois, and *Apparitions* (1935), *Nocturne* (1936) and *Les Patineurs* (1937) by Frederick Ashton. The company toured extensively during World War II, and in 1946 it moved to the Royal Opera House, Covent Garden. Many works were produced during this period, among them Ashton's *Symphonic Variations* (1946) and revivals of *La Boutique Fantasque* and *Le Tricorne* by **Léonide Massine**. Promising choreographers included **Kenneth MacMillan** and **John Cranko**. A second company, the Sadler's Wells Opera (later Theatre) Ballet, was formed in 1946. In 1956 the two companies were joined to form The Royal Ballet, although the company was still divided into two sections, the Opera House section (headed by **Margot Fonteyn**) and the touring section. The 1960s were a period of great activity. Ashton staged a new version of *La Fille Mal Gardée* (1960) and **Bronislava Nijinska** revived *Les Noces* (1968). In 1964 Kenneth MacMillan created a new version of *Romeo and Juliet*, with Margot Fonteyn in the role of Juliet. New ballets included Ashton's *The Dream* (1964), *Monotones* (1965) and *Enigma Variations* (1968); **Antony Tudor**'s *Shadowplay* (1967); and **Rudi van Danzig**'s *The Ropes of Time* (1970). Principal dancers are **Svetlana Berisiova, Merle Park, Antoinette Sibley, Lynn Seymour, Anthony Dowell** and **David Wall**. Margot Fonteyn appeared frequently as guest artist after 1959. Frederick Ashton retired from the directorship in 1970, and was replaced by joint directors Kenneth MacMillan and **John Field**. In the same year the Royal Ballet underwent reorganization, whereby the touring company was merged with the Opera House section, and the number of dancers reduced. Since the first tour of the USA in 1949, which established it as an international company, The Royal Ballet has made frequent visits to America. Its 1972 New York season was its 13th US visit.

Royal Danish Ballet *see* **Denmark, history of ballet in.**

Royal Swedish Ballet *see* **Sweden, history of ballet in.**

Royal Winnipeg Ballet *see* **Canada, history of ballet in.**

RUBINSTEIN, Ida (1885–1960), Russian dancer. She studied with **Fokine** and made her debut dancing in a solo called *Salome* (1909). Her sensational debut was with **Diaghilev**'s Ballet Russe in the title role of *Cléopâtre* (1909), which she created, dancing with **Pavlova, Karsavina** and **Nijinsky**. She created Zobeide in *Schéhérazade*, commissioned Ravel to create the music for *Bolero*. She danced with Diaghilev's company from 1909–15, and in 1911 commissioned Debussy to compose music for a mystery play *The Martyrdom of Saint Sebastian*, in which she danced the title role. She also created *Diane de Poitiers, La Valse* and *Bolero*. In 1928 she formed her own company for which Nijinsky, **Massine, Jooss,** Guerra and **Fokine** all choreographed works. She was a generous patron to poets, composers and painters. Her last appearance was in Paris in 1928 in *Orphée*. She retired in 1930; her company disbanded in 1935.

RUSSIA, history of ballet in.
1682–1725 Peter the Great rules Russia. During his reign a public theatre is built in Moscow, and dancing is encouraged.
1727 The first ballet performances are given at St. Petersburg.
1738 The Imperial Theatre School is founded by the Empress Anne. **Jean-Baptiste Landet** is director.
1783 The Bolshoi Theatre, St. Petersburg, is opened. All ballet performances are given here until 1880.

1791 Charles Le Picq dances at the Taurida Palace in a performance he staged himself for Catherine II.

1801 Charles Louis Didelot is appointed principal dancer, choreographer, and director of the Imperial School, St. Petersburg.

1825 The Imperial Theatre, Moscow, later to become the Bolshoi Theatre, is opened.

1829 Didelot retires.

1837–42 Marie Taglioni dances in Russia.

1825–55 Nicholas I rules Russia. Ballet thrives under his reign. Dancers of this period include **Elena Andreyanova** and **Christian Johannson.**

1847 Marius Petipa arrives in St. Petersburg and becomes premier danseur.

1848 Jules Perrot arrives in St. Petersburg and becomes dancer and choreographer of the Imperial Theatre.

1862 Petipa is appointed chief choreographer (replacing Perrot) after the success of his ballet *La Fille du Pharaon.*

1869 *Don Quixote* is first produced at the Bolshoi Theatre, Moscow.

1877 *La Bayadère* is first produced at the Maryinsky Theatre, St. Petersburg.

1889 The Maryinsky Theatre replaces the Imperial Theatre, St. Petersburg, as the home of all official ballet performances.

1890 *The Sleeping Beauty* is first produced at the Maryinsky Theatre, St. Petersburg.

1895 A second version of *Swan Lake* is produced at the Maryinsky Theatre, St. Petersburg.

1896 Alexander Gorsky is appointed ballet master at the Maryinsky Theatre.

1898 *Raymonda* is first produced at the Maryinsky Theatre. **Michel Fokine** graduates from the Imperial School of Ballet and joins the company of the Maryinsky Theatre as soloist.

1903 Petipa retires from the Imperial Theatre.

1905 Fokine produces *The Dying Swan* (created for **Pavlova**).

1907 Fokine stages *Le Pavillon d'Armide.*

1908 Serge Diaghilev invites Fokine to stage ballets for the 1909 Paris season of the Russian ballet. Fokine's *Eunice* and *Chopiniana* are staged for the Imperial Theatre.

1909 Fokine's *Polovetsian Dances from Prince Igor* and *Egyptian Nights* are among the ballets staged for the Imperial Theatre.

1909–14 Fokine works in France.

1911 Fokine's *Orpheus and Euridice* is staged for the Imperial Theatre.

1912 Gorsky is appointed ballet master of the Bolshoi Theatre, Moscow.

1914 Fokine returns to Russia.

1917 Fokine's *Stenka Razin* is staged for the post-revolutionary State Theatre. The Maryinsky Theatre is renamed the State Academic Theatre of Opera and Ballet.

1918 Fokine leaves Russia for the last time.

1921 Agrippina Vaganova teaches at the Leningrad Choreographic School (formerly the Maryinsky). Among her pupils are **Marina Semyonova, Natalia Dudinskaya, Galina Ulanova,** and **Irina Kolpakova.**

1933 Vaganova stages a new version of *Swan Lake.* New heroic ballets of the 1930s include *The Fountain of Bakhchisarai, Romeo and Juliet, Flames of Paris* and *Laurencia.*

1935 The State Academic Theatre of Opera and Ballet (formerly the Maryinsky Theatre) is called the Kirov Theatre of Opera and Ballet.

1944 Ulanova is transferred to the Bolshoi Ballet in Moscow.

1946–51 Vaganova teaches at the Leningrad Conservatory. Her pupils include **Konstantin Sergeyev** and **Vakhtang Chabukiany.**

1957 Yuri Grigorovitch stages *The Stone Flower* at the Kirov Theatre.

1958 Rudolph Nureyev joins the Kirov Ballet as soloist.

1959 Ulanova becomes ballet mistress of the Bolshoi Theatre. Among her pupils is **Yekaterina Maximova.**

1961 The Kirov Ballet visits London for the first time with Konstantin Sergeyev as director. Dancers include Irina Kolpakova, **Alla Sizova** and **Yuri Soloviev.** Rudolph Nureyev leaves the Kirov (while on tour) and remains in France.

1962 Ulanova retires from the stage but continues teaching. **Maya Plisetskaya**

becomes prima ballerina of the Bolshoi Ballet.

1966 The Kirov company visits London for the second time. Dancers include **Natalia Makarova** and **Sergei Vikulov**.

1969 The Bolshoi Ballet visits London. Dancers include Yekaterina Maximova, **Vladimir Vassiliev, Natalia Bessmertnova, Raisa Struchkova, Mikhail Lavrovsky** and **Maris Liepa**.

1970 The third Kirov season in London, includes *La Bayadère*, *Coppélia*, *Swan Lake* and *The Nutcracker*. Dancers include **Mikhail Barishnikov** and **Yuri Soloviev**. Natalia Makarova leaves the Kirov Ballet while on tour and remains in London. Konstantin Sergeyev stages a new version of *Hamlet*, for the Kirov Ballet. The Kirov Ballet retains much of the style of the old Imperial Ballet, while the Bolshoi exemplifies a more florid Soviet style. Apart from these, there are 34 ballet companies in 31 cities of the Soviet Union, and 20 state choreographic schools.

S

SABIROVA, Malika, Russian dancer. She studied (1952–61) in Leningrad and has danced the principal roles in *Giselle, Don Quixote, Chopiniana, Daphnis and Chloë.* She has made guest appearances in England, Italy, India, Canada and Japan. She was a Gold Medallist at the First Moscow International Dance Competition (1969).

SACHS, Curt (1881–1959), German dance historian. He moved to the United States, becoming Professor of Music at the Graduate School of Liberal Arts, New York. His best known work on dance is *Eine Weltgeschichte des Tanzes* (1933, *A World History of Dance,* 1937).

SACRE DU PRINTEMPS, LE *see* **Rite of Spring.**

Sadler's Wells Ballet *see* **Royal Ballet, The.**

ST. DENIS, Ruth (1877–1968), American dancer, choreographer and teacher. Her first ballet *Radha* (1906) was based on a Hindu theme, and was followed by *The Incense* and *The Cobras.* She made a successful tour of Europe (1906–9), adding *The Nautch* and *Yogi* to her repertoire. Returning to America she produced *Egypta* (1909), presented a Japanese ballet *O-Mika* and appeared in vaudeville until she met and married **Ted Shawn** (1914). Together they established the Denishawn schools and company, but in 1932 she and Shawn separated and the company came to an end. St. Denis continued to create religious works in support of her Society of Spiritual Arts. In 1940 she opened the School of Natya, New York, with La Méri, revived her earlier works; and in 1960 and 1961 returned to Adelphi College to head a department combining arts and religion. In her eighties she still continued to perform, teach, film and lecture in New York, and appeared as narrator and dancer in *Incense* for Boston Arts Festival (1961), 55 years after her debut in the same role. She wrote *Ruth St. Denis: An Unfinished Life* (1939). Although her work was little known outside America, she was a great influence on Martha Graham.

SAINT FRANCIS *see* **Nobilissima Visione.**

Arthur Saint-Léon. Ph. Lipnitzki.

SAINT-LÉON, Arthur Michel (*c* 1815–1870), French dancer, choreographer and violinist. He made his professional debut at fourteen in Munich, dancing and playing the violin. From 1833–59 he toured Europe; in Milan he met and married **Fanny Cerito**. He was choreographer at the **Paris Opéra Ballet** (1847–52) and ballet master (1863–70). His first choreographic work, *La Fille de Marbre*, was created for Cerito's Paris debut in 1847. Other works created for the Opéra were *La Vivandière* (1844) and *Stella* (1850). In 1850, Cerito and Saint-Léon separated; he became ballet master of the Imperial Theatre, St. Petersburg (1859–67) and created *Mariquita* (1860), *The Nymphs and the Satyr* (1861), *The Humpbacked Horse*, created while working in Russia in 1866 and his last work *The Goldfish* (1867) which was a failure. For the Paris Opéra he staged *La Source* (1866) and his last but greatest work, *Coppélia* (1870). He worked in all the European capitals except Milan, usually staging his ballets under different names. His book *La Sténochorégraphie ou l'art d'écrire promptement la danse* (1852) tries to evolve a system of dance notation. See illustration p. 199.

SALADE, a ballet with sung and spoken words, based on the style of Italian comedy. Choreography, **Léonide Massine**; music, Darius Milhaud; decor, Georges Braque. First performed at the Théâtre de la Cigale, Paris, 1924, at a Soirée de Paris de Comte Etienne de Beaumont. Another version, with the same music, was performed, 13 February, by the **Paris Opéra Ballet**. Choreography, **Serge Lifar**; decor, André Derain. Principal dancers, Suzanne Lorcia, **Serge Peretti**, Serge Lifar.

SALLÉ, Marie (1707–56), French ballerina. She danced in London as early as 1716, and made her debut with the **Paris Opéra Ballet** in 1721 in *Les Fêtes Vénitiennes*. She was in London (1725–7) dancing *Love's Last Shift* and *Les Caractères de la Danse*. Later at the Paris Opéra, she was outstanding in *Les Amours des Dieux*. In 1734, Sallé created a precedent by adopting a simplified dress without panniers in a version of *Pygmalion*, in which she also wore her hair loose and abandoned the traditional mask.

SAMTSOVA, Galina (Galina Ursuliak, 1937–   ), Russian dancer. She graduated

Marie Sallé. Ph. P.I.C.

from the Kiev Choreography School into the Kiev Opera and Ballet Theatre, and graduated dancing the Wedding Scene from *Laurencia*. Her repertoire with the company included *Swan Lake* pas de trois, Queen of the Wilis in *Giselle*, and Snowflake pas de deux in *Song of the Forest*. In 1961 she joined National Ballet of Canada, and the same year danced Blue Bird and Black Swan pas de deux at Jacob's Pillow Dance Festival. She created the title role in *Cinderella* at the International Dance Festival (1963) in Paris. In 1964 she joined London's **Festival Ballet** as ballerina and became prima ballerina. Her leading roles have included Odette-Odile in *Swan Lake*, Aurora in *The Sleeping Beauty*, Kitri in *Don Quixote*, Snow-Sugar Fairy in *The Nutcracker*, *Dvorak Variations* (1970), Sleepwalker in *Night Shadow*, *Petrouchka*, *Phaedra*, *Piège de Lumière* and *The Unknown Island* (1970). With **Prokovsky**, in 1972, she founded the New London Ballet.

SAND, Inge (1928–), Danish dancer, Knight of the Order of Dannebrog. She studied in Copenhagen, Paris, London and New York, and made her debut at the Royal Theatre, Copenhagen in 1945 as the butterfly in Harald Lander's *Spring*. Became soloist with the Royal Danish Ballet in 1950 and danced with Original Ballet Russe (1951–2). She has toured Europe, the United States and South America. Her repertoire includes leading roles in *Swan Lake*, *Night Shadow*, *Coppélia*, *Graduation Ball*, *The Lesson*, *Carmen*, Bartók's *Sonata for Three*, *The Kermesse at Bruges* and *Le Jeune Homme à Marier*. In 1966 she was appointed assistant ballet mistress at the Royal Danish Ballet.

SANGALLI, Rita (1851–1909), Italian ballerina. She studied at **Teatro alla Scala**, Milan, under Augusto Hus, and danced in Italy, London and New York, where she created the principal role in *The Black Crook* (1866). She appeared with the **Paris Opéra Ballet** in 1872 in *La Source*, and created roles in *Sylvia* (1876), *Yedda* (1879) and *Namouna* (1882).

Scala, Teatro alla, an opera house in Milan, Italy, opened in 1778. **Carlo Blasis** became director of its Imperial Dancing Academy in 1837, and greatly influenced classical dance during the 19th century. **Enrico Cecchetti** became ballet master in 1925. Directors of the school include **Cia Fornaroli** (1929–33), and **Vera Volkova** (1950–2). Esmée Bulnes became director of the school and the company in 1954, but after 1962 devoted herself entirely to the school. The company has no permanent choreographer. Its repertoire includes classical ballets, and works have been staged by **George Balanchine**, **Léonide Massine** and **Frederick Ashton**. A revival of Rudolph Nureyev's *Sleeping Beauty* was presented in 1970.

SCARLET SCISSORS, THE *see* **Tragedy of Fashion, A.**

SCÈNES DE BALLET, a ballet in one act. Choreography, **Frederick Ashton**; music, Stravinsky; decor, André Beaurepaire. First performed at the Royal Opera House, Covent Garden, London, 11 February 1948, by Sadler's Wells Ballet. Principal dancers, **Margot Fonteyn, Michael Somes**. The music was originally composed for a revue, *Seven Lively Arts*, presented, 1944 and 1945, at the Ziegfeld Theatre, New York. **Anton Dolin** choreographed a ballet for the revue.

SCHANNE, **Margrethe** (1921–), Danish dancer. She studied at the Royal Danish Ballet School (1930–41) and become a soloist with the company in 1943. She danced the leading roles in *Les Sylphides*, *Petrouchka*, *Swan Lake*, *Giselle*, *Pas de Quatre* and *Medea*. As guest artist she appeared with **Les Ballets des Champs-Elysées** (1946), Ballet International du Marquis de Cuevas (1955), and toured South Africa (1958) and the United States (1965). Her last appearance was in *La Sylphide*, considered her major role, 1966.

SCHAUFUSS, Frank (1921–), Danish

dancer. He entered the Royal Danish Ballet School in 1931, and also studied in London and Paris. He joined the company in 1941 and became soloist (1949). His repertoire includes leading roles in *Swan Lake, Romeo and Juliet, Miss Julie, Night Shadow, Napoli, Coppélia* and *The Three Musketeers*. He has also choreographed works such as *Idolon* (1952), *Opus 13* (1958) and *Garden Party* (1963). He was director of the Royal Danish Ballet (1956–1958). He has made guest appearances with **Metropolitan Ballet, Les Ballets de Paris de Roland Petit, Grand Ballet du Marquis de Cuevas** and the National Ballet of Canada.

SCHÉHÉRAZADE, a dramatic ballet in one act, based on a tale in *The One Thousand and One Nights*. Libretto, **Alexandre Benois**; choreography, **Michel Fokine**; music, Rimsky-Korsakov; decor and costumes, **Léon Bakst**. First performed at the Paris Opéra, 4 June 1910, by **Diaghilev**'s Ballets Russes. Principal dancers, **Ida Rubinstein** (Zobeide), **Vaslav Nijinsky** (Favourite Slave), **Enrico Cecchetti** (Chief Eunuch). A major controversy arose; critics argued that the libretto and the choreography departed from the declared intention of the composer. Bakst's decor consisted for the most part of masses of brilliant colour, and the overall effect was exotic and sensuous. *Schéhérazade* was one of the most sensational of the Diaghilev productions and was taken into the repertoires of the **Paris Opéra Ballet** and London's **Festival Ballet.**

SCHILLING, Tom (1928–   ), East German dancer and choreographer. He was a soloist in Dresden (1946–52) and Leipzig, choreographer in Weimar (1953–6) and artistic director in Dresden. His choreographic works include *Swan Lake, Abraxas, Gayane, Flames of Paris* and *The Stone Flower*.

SCHORER, Suki (Suzanne Schorer), American dancer. A pupil and dancer with the San Francisco Ballet, she danced Clara in Lew Christensen's *The Nutcracker*. In 1953 she went to Italy and danced *Comus;* then toured the Far and Middle East and South America with the company. She joined **The New York City Ballet** in 1959, becoming soloist in 1963. She created roles in *Donizetti Variations* and *Raymonda Variations*, Leading Fairy in *A Midsummer Night's Dream* and Pierrette in *Harlequinade*, and danced Blackamoor in *La Sonnambula* and 3rd movement in *Symphony in C*.

SCHULZ, Klaus (1934–   ), East German dancer and teacher. In 1952 he became soloist at Komische Oper, Berlin, and in 1956 first soloist at the German State Opera. He later became director and ballet master.

SCHWARZ, Solange (1910–   ), French ballerina. A member of a famous family of

Solange Schwarz. Ph. Lipnitzki.

dancers and teachers, she was a student of the Paris Opéra school, made her debut at the Opéra Comique (1933), then returned to the **Paris Opéra Ballet** (1937) where she was première danseuse étoile (1940–1945). She danced character and classical roles and was outstanding as *Coppélia*. Her repertoire also included *Les Sylphides*, *Entre deux Ronds*, *Suite en Blanc* (1943), *Sylvia* and *Alexandre le Grand* and **Lifar**'s two masterpieces, *Le Chevalier et La Damoiselle* and *Joan de Zarissa*. As guest artist with **Les Ballets des Champs-Elysées** (1946), she danced *La Forêt* and *Concert de Danses*. She was première danseuse étoile with **Grand Ballet de Monte Carlo** (1947) and with Opéra Comique (1949–51). Earlier in her career she had danced at the Royal Opera House, Covent Garden, in the coronation celebrations of George VI.

SCHWEZOV, Igor (1904–   ), Russian dancer, choreographer and teacher. He was a soloist with **Ballet Russe de Monte Carlo** (1931). His roles include *Prince Igor*, *Carnaval* and *Firebird*. He toured France and Italy with **Nijinska**'s company (1932) and was assistant choreographer during the company's Monte Carlo season (1936–7). He taught in London (1937–9), was soloist with Original Ballet Russe (1939–40), choreographer with the New Opera Company, New York (1941), and in 1945 he was appointed director of ballet, choreographer and dancer at the Municipal Theatre, Rio de Janeiro. Among the works he staged were *Swan Lake*, *Les Sylphides*, *Eternal Struggle* and *The Red Poppy*. In 1949 he opened up his own dance studio in New York. His company toured South America in 1953. From 1956–62 Schwezov taught at Ballet Theatre School. His autobiography (published 1935) was called *Borzoi*.

Scottish Theatre Ballet is the national ballet company of Scotland. Originally Western Theatre Ballet, the company has been based in Glasgow since 1970. The repertoire includes both classical ballets and contemporary dance works, ranging from ballets by **August Bournonville** to works by **Jack Carter, Peter Darrell, Flemming Flindt, Walter Gore, Kenneth MacMillan** and Laverne Meyer. Unique to this company are two full-length ballets by Peter Darrell: *Beauty and the Beast* (1969) and *Tales of Hoffmann* (1972). Scottish Theatre Ballet is also closely involved in dance education in Scotland.

SCUOLA DI BALLO, a ballet in one act, based on the comedy by Carlo Goldoni. Libretto and choreography, **Léonide Massine**; music, Luigi Boccherini (arranged by Jean Françaix); decor and costumes, Comte Etienne de Beaumont. First performed in Paris, 1924, at a Soirée de Comte Etienne de Beaumont. Staged at the Théâtre de Monte Carlo, 25 April 1933, by **Colonel de Basil**'s **Ballet Russe de Monte Carlo**. Principal dancers, **Irina Baronova, Tatiana Riabouchinska, André Eglevsky,** Léonide Massine, **Léon Woizikowsky.** The ballet satirizes intrigue in the dancing profession.

SEBASTIAN, a ballet in three scenes. Libretto, Gian Carlo Menotti; choreography, Edward Caton; music, Menotti; decor and costumes, Oliver Smith, Milena. First performed at the International Theatre, New York, 31 October 1944, by **Ballet International**. Principal dancers, **Francisco Moncion** (Sebastian), Viola Essen (Courtesan), Kari Karnakoski (Prince). Revived at the Metropolitan Opera House, New York, 13 October 1946, by Original Ballet Russe. Principal dancers, Francisco Moncion, **Rosella Hightower, George Skibine.** Revived, 1947, by Grand Ballet de Monte Carlo. Principal dancer, George Skibine (Sebastian). A new version, with choreography by **Agnes de Mille,** was performed only once, 27 May 1957, by American Ballet Theatre. Principal dancers, **John Kriza,** Lupe Serrano. John Butler created another version for Nederlands Dans Theater (1963), revived (1967) by **Harkness Ballet.** Sebastian, a Moorish slave, secretly loves a Courtesan who, in turn, is loved by a Prince. The Prince's outraged sisters try to kill the Courtesan by stabbing her wax image. Sebastian, to save her, stands in place of the image, and is himself murdered. The Prince goes off with the Courtesan.

SEDOVA, Julia (1880–1970), Russian ballerina and teacher. She studied at the Imperial School, St. Petersburg, making her debut at the Maryinsky Theatre in 1898. She appeared in *Le Corsaire, Don Quixote, The Sleeping Beauty* and *The Nutcracker,* among other ballets. She resigned from the Imperial Theatres in 1911 and made guest appearances in Europe and the United States, returning to St. Petersburg in 1914. She later moved to France where she taught in Nice and Cannes.

SEMENOV, Simon (1908–   ), Latvian dancer and choreographer. He studied with **Fedorova, Messerer, Tikhomirov,** Reinhardt, **Preobrajenska, Egorova** and **Fokine,** and was soloist with Riga National Opera, Latvia (1922–30). He appeared in Reinhardt's productions in Vienna and Paris (1930), and from 1937–1945 danced with Woizikowsky's company, **René Blum's Ballet Russe de Monte Carlo,** Ballet Russe de Monte Carlo, **Ballet Theatre** and **Ballet International.** His roles included Slave and Saracen in *Raymonda,* Dr. Coppelius in *Coppélia,* Chief Eunuch in *Schéhérazade,* and Charlatan in *Petrouchka.* His choreographic works included *Memories* (1944) and *Gift of the Magi* for **Ballet Theatre** (1945) and San Francisco Ballet (1949). For London's **Festival Ballet** he created *Rhapsody, Debut* and *Hebrew Chant* (1957). He opened a dance school in California in 1947, then in 1954 opened one in Connecticut. He has appeared as guest artist with several international companies.

SEMYONOVA, Marina (1908–   ), Soviet ballerina and teacher, Peoples' Artist of the RSFSR. She was trained by **Vaganova** at the Leningrad Ballet School (1919–25), and danced Nymph of the Stream in *La Source* for her graduation.

Her debut at the Kirov was as Aurora in *The Sleeping Beauty,* and she was promoted to ballerina during her first season. Coached by Vaganova, her first dramatic role was Nikia in *La Bayadère,* and her greatest role is considered to be Odette-Odile in *Swan Lake.* In 1930 she became prima ballerina at the Bolshoi, where her repertoire included the classical roles including *The Sleeping Beauty, Swan Lake, Raymonda* and *Cinderella.* For the 1935–6 season at the **Paris Opéra Ballet** she danced *Giselle* with **Lifar.** She retired from dancing in 1955, and became coach to the dancers at the Bolshoi Ballet, and instructor at the Moscow Choreographic School. She was a formative influence on Soviet ballet and was noted for the technical skill of her dancing.

SERGEYEV, Konstantin (1910–   ), Russian premier danseur and choreographer, Peoples' Artist of the USSR. He studied with Victor Semyonov at the Leningrad Ballet School (1924–8), and was a pupil of **Vaganova.** He was premier danseur with Kchessinsky's travelling ballet company, dancing mainly the classical repertoire including Siegfried in *Swan Lake.* He graduated into the Kirov Ballet in 1930, making his debut as Young Coolie in *The Red Poppy,* a propagandist work. Later that year he joined the Leningrad Academic Theatre of Opera and Ballet and became premier danseur and partner to **Ulanova.** Among his creations were Vaslav in *The Fountain of Bakhchisarai* (1934), Romeo in *Romeo and Juliet* (1940), and Prince in his own version of *Cinderella.* He revived Petipa's *Raymonda* (1948), *Swan Lake* (1950) and *The Sleeping Beauty* (1952), and was director of the Kirov Ballet (1951–6), resuming the post in 1960. When Ulanova left the Kirov he partnered his wife, **Natalia Dudinskaya,** and toured extensively in Eastern Europe and China. He partnered **Nadia Nerina** in *Giselle* during the Kirov season (1960–1). In 1970 he staged a new full-length ballet, *Hamlet,* for the Kirov company. He is a holder of the Lenin Prize (1970).

SERGEYEV, Nicholas (1876–1951), Russian dancer and ballet master. A graduate of the Imperial School, St. Petersburg (1894), he became premier danseur in 1904 and régisseur-general in 1914 before leaving Russia in 1918. He is considered to have done more for the preservation of the classical ballet than any other dancer or ballet master. He kept voluminous notes in Stepanov notation while at the Maryinsky Theatre. For **Diaghilev**'s Ballets Russes he revived *The Sleeping Beauty* (1921); and he brought authentic versions of *The Nutcracker* and *Swan Lake* (1934, 1943), *Giselle* (1935), *Coppélia* (1933 and 1940) to Sadler's Wells. For **International Ballet** (1947–8) he staged these same works; for **Ballet Russe de Monte Carlo** he staged *Giselle* (1938), and for **Colonel de Basil**'s company, *The Nutcracker*.

SEVENTH SYMPHONY, THE, a ballet in four movements. Libretto and choreography, **Léonide Massine**; music, Beethoven (*Seventh Symphony in A major*); decor and costumes, Christian Bérard. First performed at the Théâtre de Monte Carlo, 5 May 1938, by **Colonel de Basil's Ballet Russe de Monte Carlo**. Principal dancers, **Alicia Markova**, Jeannette Lauret, **Nini Theilade, Rosella Hightower, Frederic Franklin, Igor Youskevitch**. The theme of the ballet is creation (vivace movement), earth (allegretto), sky (presto), bacchanale and destruction. Each movement is complete in itself, but they are all linked by the idea of the life story of the human race, from creation through joy and sin to destruction.

SEVENTH SYMPHONY, a plotless ballet in one act. Libretto and choreography, **Igor Belsky**; music, Shostakovich (*Seventh Symphony*, the *Leningrad*). First performed, 4 April 1961, at the Kirov Theatre, Leningrad. Principal dancers, **Yuri Soloviev** (Youth), **Alla Sizova** (Girl). The ballet deals with youth's resistance to the enemy and was inspired by the siege of Leningrad during the Second World War.

SEYMOUR, Lynn (Lynn Springbett, 1939–), Canadian dancer. She studied in Vancouver with Jepson and Svetlanov, danced successfully at the 1953 Canadian Ballet Festival and the following year became a pupil at Sadler's Wells Ballet School. She danced with Covent Garden Opera Ballet (1956), joined **The Royal Ballet** (1957) and became a soloist in 1958. As a principal dancer, she created Young Lover in *The Burrow*, Bride in *Baiser de la Fée*, The Girl in *The Invitation* (1960) and Girl in **Ashton**'s *Les Deux Pigeons*. The role of Juliet was created for her in **MacMillan**'s *Romeo and Juliet* (1965), although the première was danced by **Fonteyn**. Her repertoire includes leading roles in *Giselle, Swan Lake, Danses Concertantes, Symphony, La Bayadère* and *Dances at a Gathering*. In 1966 she joined the Deutsche Oper Ballet, Berlin, continuing her artistic collaboration with MacMillan and creating the title role in his *Anastasia* (1971) for The Royal Ballet, which she rejoined in 1970.

SHADOWPLAY, a ballet in one act. Libretto and choreography, **Antony Tudor**; music, Charles Koechlin; decor, Michael Annals. First performed at the Royal Opera House, Covent Garden, 25 January 1967, by **The Royal Ballet**. Principal dancers, **Anthony Dowell** (Boy), Derek Rencher (Terrestrial), **Merle Park** (Celestial). The ballet is inspired by Kipling's *Jungle Book*. It shows a boy setting out in search of knowledge and wisdom, and struggling to overcome a number of forces represented by character dancers.

SHAWN, Ted (1891–1972), American dancer and choreographer. He studied theology, then turned to dance. In 1914 he met and married **Ruth St. Denis** and together they founded the Denishawn school and dancers. He pioneered modern dance, and was inspired by primitive dance, classical ballet, Oriental, American Indian, Folk and ethnic dances. Traditional ballet music was rejected; he concentrated on Bach, Beethoven and Mozart, and experimented with contemporary French and American music. Denishawn presented religious and philosophical ballets for churches and theatres, and toured the world until St. Denis and Shawn split up in 1931. Shawn's all male company of dancers (1933–40) removed a great deal of the prejudice against male dancers in America, and he himself continued to dance well into his seventies. He made a solo tour of Australia in 1947. His own creations and new roles created for him by Myra Kinch include *Sound of Darkness* and *A Waltz is a Waltz, is a Waltz*. From 1941–6 Shawn organized an annual summer school and dance festival at Jacob's Pillow Farm in Massachusetts, and built the Ted Shawn Theatre. In 1948 he returned to direct Jacob's Pillow Dance Festival. The company toured all over America and throughout the world, gaining international fame with the varied styles of dancing, and for the new as well as established dancers who were members. Shawn imported dancers from The Royal Danish Ballet, The National Ballet of Canada, Ballet Rambert and other companies for the ten week festival. Shawn contributed much to American dance with this festival, and he gave demonstrations and lectures right up to the time of his death. He created many works including *Job*, *Xochitl*, *Cuadro Flamenco* and *Feather of the Dawn*, and he danced solos in *Invocation to the Thunderbird*, *Death of Adonis*, *Prometheus Bound* and many others. His publications include *Ruth St. Denis: Pioneer and Prophet*, *The American Ballet* and *Fundamentals of a Dance Education*. His teachings made a widespread educational and artistic impression on American dance; **Martha Graham** was particularly influenced; other pupils included Jack Cole and **Doris Humphrey**.

SHEARER, Moira (Moira Shearer King, 1926–), British ballerina. She studied in Rhodesia (1932), with **Legat** (1936), at Sadler's Wells Ballet School (1940), and with **Preobrajenska**, making her debut as a member of **International Ballet** in 1941. In 1942 she rejoined Sadler's Wells

Ballet School and was ballerina of the Sadler's Wells Ballet (1944–52), gaining recognition as Pride in *The Quest*. Her repertoire included the classic ballets *Swan Lake*, *Sleeping Beauty*, *Giselle* and *Coppélia*, and she created Lover in *Miracle in the Gorbals*, pas de trois in *Promenade*, Young Wife in *Don Juan*, and danced *La Boutique Fantasque* (1948–9 season) with **Massine**. She also danced White Skater in *Les Patineurs*, First Ballerina in *Ballet Impérial* and one of three ballerinas in **Ashton**'s *Symphonic Variations* (1946). She danced as guest artist with **Les Ballets de Paris de Roland Petit**, returned to **The Royal Ballet** as guest artist and danced Titania in *A Midsummer Night's Dream* at the Edinburgh Festival (1954). She later toured the US with the same production. She starred in the films *The Red Shoes* (1948) and *The Tales of Hoffmann* (1950).

SHÉLEST, Alla (1919–), Russian ballerina and teacher, Peoples' Artist of the RSFSR. She studied in Leningrad (1927–1937), joining the Kirov Ballet and dancing Girl-Swan in *Swan Lake*. Her other roles include Zarema in *The Fountain of Bakhchisarai*, Juliet in *Romeo and Juliet*, Myrtha in *Giselle* and Czar-Maiden in *The Humpbacked Horse*.

SIBLEY, Antoinette (1939–), British dancer. She studied at the Arts Educational School (1949), and at the Royal Ballet School, entering **The Royal Ballet** in 1956, becoming soloist in 1959 and principal dancer in 1960. Roles she created include Mary Stone in *Jabez and the Devil*, Ballerina in *Les Rendez-vous*, Lise in *La Fille Mal Gardée*, Titania in *The Dream* and leading roles in *Monotones* (1966), *Enigma Variations* (1968) and *Triad* (1972). Her repertoire has also included Blue Bird pas de deux in *The Sleeping Beauty*, Columbine in *Harlequin in April*, Juliet in *Romeo and Juliet* and Clara in *The Nutcracker*; and she has danced leading roles in *Song of the Earth* (1966), **Ashton**'s *Cinderella* (1967), *The Lilac Garden* (1968), *Daphnis and Chloë* (1969) and in *Façade* and *Dances at a Gathering* (both 1970).

sickling, a fault in which the foot turns over and the leg assumes the shape of a sickle.

SIFNIOS, Dusanka or **Duska** (1934–), Yugoslav ballerina. She studied with Kirsanova and **Lavrovsky**, and at the Royal Ballet School, London. She became prima ballerina of the Belgrade National Ballet. Her roles include *Giselle*, Girl in *The Miraculous Mandarin*, Eurydice in *Orpheus* and Juliet in *Romeo and Juliet*. In 1960 she was ballerina with Miskovitch Ballet and Ballet Européen.

SIMON, Victoria (1939–), American dancer. She studied at the High School of Performing Arts, New York, at the School of American Ballet, the American Ballet Center and the Ballet Theatre School. At 14 she danced in Balanchine's première of *The Nutcracker* and became a permanent member of **The New York City Ballet** in 1958. In 1963 she became soloist after dancing her first important solo role, First Variation in *Raymonda Variations* (1961). Her other roles include Third Waltz Variation in *La Valse*, Pastorale interludes in *La Sonnambula*, pas de quatre and pas de neuf in Act 2 of *Swan Lake* and solo role in *Donizetti Variations*, which she staged for City Center Joffrey Ballet in 1966.

SIMONE, Kirsten (1934–), Danish ballerina. Trained at the Royal Danish Ballet School (1947–52), and became soloist with the company in 1956. She danced the leading roles in *Et Folkesagn*, *The Nutcracker, Night Shadow, Konservatoriet, La Sylphide, Apollo, The Sleeping Beauty, Harlequinade, Miss Julie, Carmen, Blood Wedding, Cyrano de Bergerac, Medea, Don Quixote* pas de deux, *Les Sylphides, Giselle, Swan Lake, Dances Concertantes, Pas de Quatre, Romeo and Juliet* and *The Wolf*. She toured the United States in 1965. In 1966 she became principal dancer of the Royal

Danish Ballet. She has appeared as guest artist with many European and American companies, and has toured with **Ruth Page**'s International Ballet in the United States.

sissonne, pas de, literally a scissor-like movement, a step which begins with a demi-plié, after which the dancer leaps into the air opening the legs in fourth position and alighting again in fifth position. It may be performed travelling forwards, backwards, sideways and en tournant.

SIZOVA, Alla (1939–), Russian ballerina. She studied in Leningrad, graduating into the Kirov Ballet in 1958 and becoming ballerina. Her roles include Masha in *The Nutcracker*, Nikia in *La Bayadère* and Katerina in *The Stone Flower*. She danced Aurora in *The Sleeping Beauty* in London (1961) and New York.

SKEAPING, Mary, British choreographer, teacher and director. She studied with Novikov, **Cecchetti, Trefilova, Egorova** and Craske, and later toured with the **Pavlova** (1925–31) and Nemtchinova-Dolin companies. During the Second World War she taught in South Africa. She directed the ballet sequences of the film *The Little Ballerina* (1947), and was ballet mistress of the Sadler's Wells Ballet (1948–1951). Among the classical ballets she has staged are *Swan Lake* and *Giselle* (1953), *Les Sylphides* and *Le Spectre de la Rose* (1957) for the Royal Swedish Ballet, of which she became director in 1953. Her historical ballets at the Drottningholm Court Theatre have also been notable, for example, *Cupid Out of His Humour* (1956) and *Atis and Camilla* (1965). After lecturing and teaching in South America, she returned to Sweden in 1964 and revived her production of *The Sleeping Beauty* (1965).

SKIBINE, George (1920–), American dancer and choreographer, born in Russia. He studied with **Preobrajenska, Egorova, Vilzak, Oboukhov** and **Lifar.** Engaged by **Massine** for the **Ballet Russe**

de Monte Carlo (1938), he made his debut in *Seventh Symphony*. He danced with Original Ballet Russe (1940) in Australia, and with **Ballet Theatre** (1941), dancing *Les Sylphides*, *Bluebeard*, *La Fille Mal Gardée* and *Aleko*. He returned to the ballet after World War II as a member of the Markova-Dolin group. From 1947–55 he danced with **Grand Ballet du Marquis de Cuevas**. His repertoire included *Les Biches*, *Del Amor y de la Muerte*, *Sebastian*, the principal role in *Night Shadow* and *Giselle*. As choreographer he staged *Tragedy in Verona* (1948), *Annabel Lee* and *Prisoner of the Caucasus* (1951), *Idylle* (1954) and *Romeo and Juliet* (1955). With **Ruth Page**'s Chicago Opera Ballet he toured the United States (1956), dancing *Merry Widow*, *Camille* and *Revenge*. Later the same year he became premier danseur étoile of the **Paris Opéra Ballet**. Partnering his wife, ballerina **Marjorie Tallchief**, he danced *Giselle*, *Firebird*, *Phèdre*, *Suite en Blanc* and many other works. In 1958 he became ballet master of the Paris Opéra Ballet, where he choreographed *Isoline* and *Atlantide* (1958), *Daphnis and Chloë*, *Les Fâcheuses*, *Rencontres* and *Conte Cruel* (1959) and *Pastorale* (1961). For Opéra Comique he choreographed *Concerto* (1958); and for Buenos Aires, *Metamorphoses* and *Concerto* (1961). He resigned as ballet master of the Paris Opéra Ballet in 1962, and toured Europe with a small group. From 1964–6 he was choreographer and artistic director of **Harkness Ballet**. Ballet Théâtre Contemporain, a company formed in 1968, perform many of his later works.

SKORIK, Irène (1928–), French dancer. She studied with **Zambelli, Preobrajenska, Gsovsky** and Yves Brieux, making her debut in 1942 with **Egorova**'s Ballet Russe. As ballerina with **Les Ballets des Champs-Elysées** (1945–50) she created roles in *Les Forains*, *Jeu de Cartes*, *La Fiancée du Diable*, *Les Amours de Jupiter* and *La Sylphide*. She joined the Munich State Opera Ballet in 1950 and was ballerina there for several years,

Irène Skorik. Ph. Rudolf Betz.

dancing the principal roles in *Cinderella*, *La Sylphide*, *Swan Lake*, *Giselle* and *Coppélia*. As guest artist she danced with Tatiana Gsovska's Berlin Ballet; Strasbourg Opera; **Milorad Miskovitch**'s companies (1957–60); Het Nederlands Ballet; Basel Opera, Switzerland (1961–2) where she danced *Daphnis and Chloë*, *Prince of the Pagodas* and others. Appeared with London's **Festival Ballet** in 1963.

SKOURATOV, Vladimir (1923–), French dancer. He studied with **Preobrajenska** and **Kniasev**. He partnered **Renée Jeanmaire** in *Aubade* and *Chota Roustaveli* with **Nouveau Ballet de Monte Carlo** (1946), was soloist with **Colonel de Basil**'s Original Ballet Russe (1947), and premier danseur with **Les Ballets de Paris de Roland Petit** (1947), partnering **Yvette Chauviré** and **Janine Charrat**. He created *Que le Diable l'Emporte* and danced the leading roles in *L'Oeuf à la Coque* and *La Femme et son Ombre*. He danced with **Les Ballets des Champs-Elysées** (1951), and was principal dancer with **Grand Ballet du**

Marquis de Cuevas (1952) performing most of the repertoire, notably *Piège de Lumière* and *Prisoner of the Caucasus*. In 1958 he created one of the leading roles in Françoise Sagan's *Le Rendez-vous Manqué*. He was guest artist with London's **Festival Ballet,** Nice Opera and the Royal Swedish Ballet.

SLAVENSKA, Mia (Mia Corak, 1916–), Yugoslav ballerina, choreographer and teacher. She studied with **Nijinska** in Paris, and Vincenzo Celli in New York, making her debut in 1921 at the Zagreb National Opera House. She joined this company in 1923 and became soloist in 1931. After becoming ballerina in 1933, she danced with Nijinska's company and made concert tours of Europe and North Africa (1936). She won first prize at Dance Olympiad, Berlin and Plaque d'Honneur, France (1936), dancing with **Kreutzberg** and **Wigman.** She was ballerina with the Massine-Blum **Ballet Russe de Monte Carlo** (1938–42) and she toured the United States, Canada and South America with her own Slavenska Ballet Variante (1947–52). She formed the Slavenska-Franklin Ballet in 1952 and danced the role of Blanche in their famous production, *A Streetcar Named Desire*. The company toured the United States, Canada and Japan in 1953. She was guest artist with London's **Festival Ballet** (1952) and prima ballerina with Metropolitan Opera Ballet (1955–6). Although she has staged a number of ballets for her own company, Slavenska is best known for her interpretation of the classic roles, including *Giselle, Coppélia* and *Swan Lake*.

SLAVSKA, Olga (Olga Slavska-Lipshinska, 1915–), Polish ballerina and teacher. She was a soloist with the Warsaw Bolshoi company (1932–7) and the Polish Ballet (1937–9). In 1938 she won a gold medal at the Warsaw Dancing Competition. Her roles include Swanilda in *Coppélia* and Bride in *Song of the Earth*. She later became director of the Poznan Ballet School in western Poland.

SLEEPING BEAUTY, THE or **La Belle au Bois Dormant,** a ballet in three acts, based on the fairy tale by Charles Perrault. Libretto and choreography, **Marius Petipa**; music, Peter Tchaikovsky; decor and costumes, Ivan Vsevolojsky. First performed, 15 January 1890, at the Maryinsky Theatre, St. Petersburg. Principal dancers, **Carlotta Brianza** (Princess Aurora), **Paul Gerdt** (Prince Charming), **Enrico Cecchetti** (Carabosse), Maria Petipa (Lilac Fairy). Revived with minor changes to the libretto and choreography, 5 January 1922, to mark Cecchetti's fifty years on the stage. He danced his original part of Carabosse. Revived as *The Sleeping Princess*, by **Nicholas Sergeyev** at the Alhambra Theatre, London, 2 November 1921, for the **Diaghilev** Ballets Russes. Choreography, Marius Petipa, **Bronislava Nijinska**; decor, **Léon Bakst.** Principal dancers, **Olga Spessivtzeva, Lubov Egorova, Lydia Lopokova, Vera Trefilova** (Princess Aurora), Pierre Vladimirov (Prince Charming), Carlotta Brianza (Carabosse), **Bronislava Nijinska** (Lilac Fairy), **Stanislas Idzikowsky,** Lydia Lopokova (Blue Birds). This version was revived, again as *The Sleeping Princess*, at Sadler's Wells Theatre, London, 2 February 1939, by Vic-Wells Ballet. Decor, Nadia Benois. Principal dancers, **Margot Fonteyn** (Princess Aurora), **Robert Helpmann** (Prince Charming), **June Brae** (Lilac Fairy), John Greenwood (Carabosse), Mary Honer and **Harold Turner** (Blue Birds). In 1939 a version based on the Vic-Wells production was produced by the Royal Swedish Ballet. Choreography, **Mary Skeaping**; decor, Gamlin. Principal dancers, Elsa-Mariane von Rosen (Aurora),

Bjørn Holmgren (Prince Charming), Anne-Marie Lagerborg (Lilac Fairy), **Gerd Anderssen** and Bengt Anderssen (Blue Birds). Revived as *The Sleeping Beauty* at the Royal Opera House, Covent Garden, London, 20 February 1946, by Sadler's Wells Ballet. Decor, Oliver Messel. Principal dancers, Margot Fonteyn (Aurora), **Beryl Grey** (Lilac Fairy), Robert Helpmann (Carabosse), **Pamela May** and **Alexis Rassine** (Blue Birds). **Ashton** choreographed a new Garland Waltz for Act I, and a new Florestan and His Sisters for Act 3. **Ninette de Valois** choreographed a new Three Ivans. This version was presented, October 1949, at the Metropolitan Opera House, New York. Revived, as *The Sleeping Princess*, by Nicholas Sergeyev and presented, May 1948, by **International Ballet**. Principal dancers, **Mona Inglesby** (Aurora), Ernest Hewill (Prince Charming), Herida May (Lilac Fairy). A new version was performed at the Théâtre des Champs-Elysées, Paris, 27 October 1960, by **Grand Ballet du Marquis de Cuevas**. Choreography, Bronislava Nijinska, Robert Helpmann; decor, R. de Larrain. Principal dancers, **Rosella Hightower, Nicholas Polajenko**. A new production of Petipa's ballet was staged by **Jack Carter** in 1968 for London's **Festival Ballet**, with **Galina Samtsova** in the title role. Another version was presented at the Royal Opera House, Covent Garden, 17 December 1968, by **The Royal Ballet**. Choreography, **Peter Wright** and Frederick Ashton; decor, Henry Bardon, Lila de Nobili, Dobujinsky. *See also* **Aurora's Wedding**, a divertissement from the last act.

The Sleeping Beauty: Rudolph Nureyev. Ph. Bernand.

Swan Lake: performed by The Royal Ballet. Ph. Roger Houston.

SLEEPING PRINCESS, THE *see* **Sleeping Beauty, The.**

SMITH, Lois, Canadian ballerina, wife of **David Adams.** She became prima ballerina with National Ballet of Canada (1951). Her repertoire included Odette-Odile in *Swan Lake*, the title role in *Giselle*, Swanilda in *Coppélia* and Caroline in *The Lilac Garden*. She created Electra in *House of Atreus* (1964).

SOIR DE FÊTE, a ballet. Choreography, Léo Staats; music, Delibes. First performed, 30 June 1925, by the **Paris Opéra Ballet.** Principal dancer, **Olga Spessivtzeva.** The work is marked by a suite of classical entrées. It is one of the most frequently performed at the Opéra.

SOKOLOVA, Lydia (Hilda Munnings, 1896–   ), British ballerina and choreographer. A pupil at Stedman's Academy, she made her professional debut in *Alice in Wonderland* in 1910. She studied with **Pavlova** and **Mordkin** and joined Mordkin's Imperial Ballet group for the 1911 United States tour. From 1913–29 she danced with **Diaghilev** Ballets Russes, becoming principal character dancer, and was the first British dancer in the company. She created Kikimora in *Contes Russes*, Tarantella Dancer in *La Boutique Fantasque*, Goddess in **Balanchine**'s enthusiastically received *Triumph of Neptune* (1926), and danced *Columbine, Carnaval, Le Train Bleu, Les Biches* and *The Sleeping Beauty*. Her knowledge of music was an asset in her role of Chosen Maiden in

Le Sacre du Printemps, considered her greatest role. In 1935 she danced briefly with Woizikowsky's company. When teaching in England, she re-created Marquise Silvestra in *The Good-Humoured Ladies* for **The Royal Ballet** (1962). She is the author of *Dancing for Diaghilev* (1961).

SOKOLOW, Anna (1915–), American modern dancer, choreographer and teacher. She studied with **Martha Graham** and Louis Horst, and at the Metropolitan Opera Ballet School. She was a member of Martha Graham's company from 1930–9, and formed her own dance group in 1934, staging her own works. In 1939 she was invited to perform in Mexico City, and subsequently founded a modern dance group there. At this time she danced several remarkable solos, including *Lament for the Death of a Bullfighter* and *Mama Beautiful*. She has frequently returned to Mexico to train dancers and choreograph works for ballet and opera. In 1954 her company was re-organized. They performed modern works, often with weird decor and lighting and sound effects. She staged *Rooms* and *Opus '58* for Het Nederlands Dans Theater (1959); *Deserts* for Ballet Rambert (1967). She has also choreographed for theatre, television and opera. In 1962 she went to Israel to form a group of actor-dancers. She continues to teach in the US and abroad.

SOLOVIEV, Yuri (1940–), Russian dancer. Trained at the Leningrad Ballet School (1949–58), his first important role at the Kirov Ballet was Blue Bird pas de deux in *The Sleeping Beauty* in which his performance was considered to be outstanding. Consequently, he was given more important roles including Andrei in *Taras Bulba*, a completely new pas de deux in *Giselle*, pas de trois in *Swan Lake*, Danila in *The Stone Flower*, Frondozo in *Laurencia*, and in 1961 he created Youth in *Seventh Symphony*. As a leading soloist with the company, he has toured London, the United States and Canada, dancing the leading roles with a notably graceful and elegant technique.

SOMBERT, Claire (1935–), French ballerina. She studied with Yves Brieux, making her debut in 1950. She danced with Ballets Janine Charrat, **Les Ballets de Paris de Roland Petit**, Ballets Jean Babilée and **Milorad Miskovitch**'s company. Her repertoire includes Young Gypsy in *Le Loup* (1953), *Le Jeune Homme et la Mort*, *Prometheus* and Lisa in *Queen of Spades* (1960). She danced in London (1961) and, partnered by Michel Bruel, in New York (1966).

SOMES, Michael (1917–), British premier danseur and director. A member of the corps de ballet of Sadler's Wells Ballet (1937), he attracted attention with his great jump and ballon in *Les Patineurs*, and as Guy in *A Wedding Bouquet*. His first creation was Young Man in *Horoscope* (1938), followed by Pan in *Cupid and Psyche*, Monseigneur in *Harlequin in the Street*, Bridegroom in *The Wise Virgins*, Leader, Children of Light, in *Dante Sonata* and Young Lover in *The Wanderer*. He returned to the company in 1945 after the war, and created Florestan in *The Sleeping Beauty* and one of the three leading male dancers in *Symphonic Variations* (1946). In 1950 he succeeded **Helpmann** as partner to **Fonteyn** and after 1951 created Prince in *Cinderella*, Daphnis in *Daphnis and Chloë*, Rinaldo in *Rinaldo and Armida*, and leading roles in *Ballet Impérial*, *Scènes de Ballet*, *Homage to the Queen* and *Birthday Offering* for the twenty-fifth anniversary of Sadler's Wells (1956). He also danced in *Miracle in the Gorbals* and *Hamlet*. He retired as a dancer in 1961, but continued to dance roles involving mime and acting. He created Capulet in MacMillan's *Romeo and Juliet* in 1965. He was awarded the CBE in 1959 and is one of the company's principals and repetiteurs.

SONNAMBULA, LA *see* **Night Shadow.**

soubresaut, literally a sudden jump, a movement in which the dancer leaps off the ground with the feet fully pointed in fifth position, the right foot in front, and lands again in the same position, having arched the body while in the air.

SOURCE, LA, a ballet in three acts. Libretto, Charles Nuitter, **Arthur Saint-Léon**; choreography, Saint-Léon; music, Leon Minkus, Léo Delibes; decor, Depléchin, Rube, Lavastre, Chapéron. First performed at the Théâtre Impérial de l'Opéra, Paris, 12 November 1866, by the **Paris Opéra Ballet.** Principal dancers, Guglielmina Salvioni (Naila), **Louis Mérante** (Djemil). Performed in St. Petersburg, December 1902, at a benefit for **Olga Preobrajenska.** A new version by **Agrippina Vaganova** was performed, 13 January 1916, in St. Petersburg. The story, of Persian origin, is of love, magic and sacrifice.

soutenu, term meaning held or sustained, used especially of a complete turn on full or demi-pointe.

SOUTH AFRICA, history of ballet in, Dulcie Howes founded the University Ballet Club in Cape Town (1934), and later Cecily Robinson and Yvonne Blake formed the Cape Town Ballet Club. The tours of the University Ballet Club prompted the foundation of the Festival Ballet Societies of Pretoria and Johannesburg. Outstanding South African dancers and choreographers include **John Cranko,** Maryon Lane, **Patricia Miller, Nadia Nerina** and **Alexis Rassine.**

SPARTACUS, a ballet in four acts. Libretto, Nicholai Volkov; choreography, **Léonide Jacobson**; music, Aram Khachaturian; decor, Valentina Khodasevich. First performed, 27 December 1956, at the Kirov Theatre, Leningrad. Principal dancers, Inna Zubkovskaya (Phrygia), Askold Makarov (Spartacus). A new version was choreographed by **Igor Moiseyev,** with the same music. Decor, Alexander Konstantinovsky. First performed, 11 March 1958, by the Bolshoi Ballet. Léonide Jacobson choreographed another version, in three acts. Presented at the Metropolitan Opera House, New York, September 1962, by the Bolshoi Ballet. Principal dancers, Dmitri Begak (Spartacus), **Maya Plisetskaya** (Phrygia). A new version was produced by **Grigorovich,** 1968, for the Bolshoi Ballet. The ballet is based on Plutarch's account of the revolt of the Roman slaves in 73 BC.

SPECTRE DE LA ROSE, LE, a ballet in one act. Libretto, Louis Vaudoyer; choreography, **Michel Fokine**; music, Carl Maria von Weber (*Invitation to the Dance*); decor and costumes, **Léon Bakst.** First performed at the Théâtre de Monte Carlo, 19 April 1911, by **Diaghilev's** Ballets Russes. Principal dancers, **Tamara Karsavina, Vaslav Nijinsky.** A young girl fondles a rose which an admirer has given her, then falls asleep. In her dream, the Spirit of the Rose leaps through her window (the **élévation** which made Nijinsky famous), dances around her, then gently draws her into the romantic pas de deux which constitutes the main part of the ballet. The artistry of the two original principal dancers remains outstanding. The dancers' technique, the music, decor and choreography were all in perfect harmony.

SPESSIVTZEVA, Olga (1895–   ), Russian ballerina. A graduate of the Imperial School, St. Petersburg (1913), she became ballerina of the Maryinsky Theatre in 1918, and danced the principal roles in *Giselle, Esmeralda, The Nutcracker, The Sleeping Beauty* and *Swan Lake.* She was the greatest Romantic ballerina of her era. In 1916 she took Karsavina's place when **Diaghilev's** Ballets Russes toured the United States, dancing *Le Spectre de la Rose* with **Nijinsky**; she returned to the Maryinsky in 1917. Diaghilev invited her to dance Aurora in the London production of *The Sleeping Beauty* (1921). She left Russia in 1923 and danced with Teatro Colón, Buenos Aires (1923). She was première danseuse étoile of the **Paris Opéra Ballet** (1924–32) with whom she danced *Soir de Fête,* and she made guest appearances with Diaghilev's company, dancing *La Chatte* (1927) and Act 2 of

Swan Lake (1929). In 1930 she danced *Giselle* with **The Camargo Society,** partnered by **Dolin.** In 1932, when **Fokine** was ballet master at Teatro Colón, she danced there for six months; and was ballerina with the Victor Dandré-Alexander Levitov company (**Pavlova**'s former company) for its Australian tour (1934), when she was partnered by **Vilzak.** She settled in the United States in 1939 but suffered mental illness for many years. Anton Dolin has written her biography, *The Sleeping Ballerina.*

SPIDER'S BANQUET, THE, a ballet in one act. Choreography, **Andrée Howard**; music, Albert Roussel, composed for the original ballet pantomime, *Le Festin de l'Araignée* (1913), with choreography by **Léo Staats**; decor, Michael Ayrton. First performed at the New Theatre, London, 20 June 1944, by Sadler's Wells Ballet. Principal dancer **Celia Franca** (The Spider). The Spider sits in her web awaiting her prey. With the assistance of other insects, praying mantises escape and kill the Spider.

STAATS, Léo (1877–1952), French dancer, choreographer and ballet master. He studied with **Louis Mérante** and made his debut at the **Paris Opéra Ballet** in 1887, aged ten, choreographing his first work when he was sixteen. From 1909–36 he was ballet master at the Opéra where he choreographed *Cydalise et le Chèvre-pied* (1923), *Les Abeilles, La Péri* and *Herodiade*, and revived many other works. *Javotte* is notable among the roles he danced. He was artistic director of Théâtre des Arts (1910–14); and was commissioned (1933) to create the dances in Berlioz's *Faust* at Covent Garden for the Royal Academy of Dancing, England. Until his death he taught in his own studio.

STAFF, Frank (1918–71), British dancer and choreographer, born in South Africa. He studied with Helen Webb and Marie Lloyd, **Marie Rambert** and **Antony Tudor** for Ballet Rambert (1933–45). His repertoire included Faun in *L'Après-midi*

d'un Faune, Lover in *The Lilac Garden* and Blue Bird pas de deux. He also created the role of Boy in *La Fête Étrange*. During this period he danced seasons with Vic-Wells Ballet, for which he created Cupid in *Cupid and Psyche*, and appeared with London Ballet. He choreographed a number of works for Ballet Rambert. His choreographic works include *Czernyana* (1939), *Enigma Variations* and *Peter and the Wolf* (1940); and *The Lovers' Gallery* (1947) and *Fanciulla delle Rose* (1948) for Metropolitan Ballet.

State Academic Theatre of Opera and Ballet *see* **Russia, history of ballet in.**

STEPANOV, Vladimir (1866–96), Russian dancer. In 1892 he published a system of **dance notation** in collaboration with **Gorsky,** called *Alphabet des Mouvements du Corps Humain*. This system was adopted by the Imperial School, St. Petersburg, in 1893 and the Bolshoi Theatre, Moscow, in 1895. The system ceased to be used after Stepanov's death.

STONE, Bentley, American dancer, choreographer and teacher. After appearing in concerts with Margaret Severn he was soloist with Chicago Civic Opera Ballet (1930–2), premier danseur with the Chicago Grand Opera Ballet (1933) and Opera Intime (1934) and premier danseur and ballet director of Century of Progress Ballet (1934). He was premier danseur and co-choreographer with the Chicago City Opera (1935–7); with Ballet Rambert in London (1937); with Page-Stone Ballet which he founded with **Ruth Page** (1938–1941); and was guest artist with **Ballet Russe de Monte Carlo** (1945). He danced the principal roles in *Le Spectre de la Rose, Les Sylphides, Death and the Maiden* and many other works. His choreographic works include *Les Préludes, Rhapsody in Blue* (1934), *Mercure, Casey at the Bat* (1939), *Les Enfants Perdus* (1951), *The Wall* (1956), *Les Biches* (1961); and with Ruth Page he choreographed a number of works, including *An American in Paris, Frankie and Johnny*

The Stone Flower: performed by the Finnish Ballet. Ph. Taisto Tuomi.

and *Zephyr and Flora*. He became a teacher at the Stone-Camryn School, Chicago, and has appeared with Ruth Page's Chicago Opera Ballet as guest artist, touring all over the world.

STONE FLOWER, THE, a ballet in three acts, based on a folk tale from the Ural Mountains, *The Malachite Casket*. Libretto, Mira Mendelssohn-Prokofieva, **Leonid Lavrovsky**; choreography, Lavrovsky; music, Prokofiev. First performed, 1954, at the Bolshoi Theatre, Moscow. Principal dancers, **Galina Ulanova, Maya Plisetskaya,** Vladimir Preobrazhensky, **Alexei Yermolayev.** A new version was staged by **Yuri Grigorovich**, 25 April 1957, at the Kirov Theatre, Leningrad. Restaged by Lavrovsky, 7 March 1959, in Moscow, and presented in New York, 5 May 1959, by the Bolshoi Ballet. Principal dancers, Maya Plisetskaya, Nina Trimofeyeva (Mistress of the Copper Mountain), **Vladimir Vassiliev** (Danila, The Stone Cutter), Marina Kondratieva, **Yekaterina Maximova** (Katerina), Vladimir Levashev (Bailiff).

STROGANOVA, Nina (Nina Rigmor Strom), Danish dancer and teacher. She studied first with Jenny Moller, then later with **Preobrajenska, Shollar, Vilzak, Nijinska** and **Mordkin.** She danced with Opéra Comique (1936), Mordkin Ballet and **Ballet Russe de Monte Carlo** (1937), **Ballet Theatre** (1940) and Original Ballet Russe (1942–7, 1951–2). Her repertoire included leading roles in *Swan Lake, Les Sylphides, Le Spectre de la Rose, Les Présages, Le Beau Danube Pas de Quatre* and *Giselle*, in which she danced both title role and Queen of the Wilis. As guest ballerina with the Royal Danish Ballet (1950) she was the first Danish dancer trained outside the Royal Theatre to appear with the company. She took up a teaching post in New York in 1947 and has danced with her husband, Vladimir Dokoudovsky, at Jacob's Pillow Dance Festival.

STRUCHKOVA, Raïsa (1925–   ), Russian ballerina, Honoured Artist of the USSR. She studied with Elizabeth Gerdt, and was a student at the Bolshoi Ballet School (1935–44). She created the title role in *Baby Stork* (1937–8). For her graduation performance she danced White and Black Swan pas de deux from *Swan Lake*. Lise in *La Fille Mal Gardée* was her first major role at the Bolshoi, where she later became ballerina. Her repertoire included the title role in Prokofiev's *Cinderella*, Maria in *The Fountain of Bakhchisarai* (1948), Parasha in *The Bronze Horseman*, Jeanne in *Flames of Paris* (1951), Odette-Odile in *Swan Lake*, Aurora in *The Sleeping Beauty*, Tao Hoa in *The Red Flower*, Juliet in *Romeo and Juliet* and Katerina in *The Stone Flower*. She is renowned for her Bacchante in 'Walpurgis Night' from *Faust*. With her husband, **Alexander Lapauri**, she has toured extensively in Europe, North and South America, and the Soviet Union.

Raisa Struchkova, ballerina of the Bolshoi Theatre, Moscow. Ph. Reyna.

SUBLIGNY, Marie-Thérèse de (1666–1736), French dancer. One of the first professional women dancers at the **Paris Opéra Ballet**, she succeeded La Fontaine as première danseuse in 1690, and danced *Le Triomphe de l'Amour* and other works by **Lully**. She was also the first professional ballerina to be seen in England (London, 1700–2). She retired in 1707.

SUITE DE DANSES, a ballet. Choreography, **Ivan Clustine**; music, Chopin. First performed, 23 June 1913, by the **Paris Opéra Ballet**. Remade, 1931, by **Albert Aveline**. Principal dancers, **Serge Lifar, Olga Spessivtzeva**. The work was inspired by *Les Sylphides*.

SUITE EN BLANC, a themeless **ballet blanc**, without decor and danced in practice clothes. Choreography, **Serge Lifar**; music, Edouard Lalo (from *Namouna*). First performed at the Paris Opéra, 23 July 1943, by the **Paris Opéra Ballet**. Principal dancers, **Yvette Chauviré, Solange Schwarz, Lycette Darsonval**, Serge Lifar, René Fenonjois. Restaged by Lifar, as *Noir et Blanc*, 1946, for **Nouveau Ballet de Monte Carlo**. The work consists of ten choreographic studies designed to demonstrate the technical and expressive qualities of the company. This is one of Lifar's best known ballets.

SUMNER, Carol (1940–   ), American dancer. She studied with Eileen O'Connor (1953), and while at the School of American Ballet was an apprentice member of **The New York City Ballet**, where she became soloist in 1963. She danced Sacred Love in *Les Illuminations*, Marzipan Shepherdess in *The Nutcracker*, Leader of 1st Regiment in *Stars and Stripes*, 1st pas de trois in *Agon*, Prince's Bride in *The Firebird*, 3rd Waltz in *La Valse*, Young Girl in *Souvenirs*, and created 4th Variation in *Raymonda Variations*.

sur place, literally in place, term used of any step performed on the spot, without travelling.

SVETLANA, a ballet. Choreography, Popko, Posspekhine, Radunsky; music, Klebanov. First performed, 1939, at the Bolshoi Theatre, Moscow. Principal dancers, **Olga Lepeshinskaya,** Yuri Kondratov, Sulamith Messerer. The work is a spy story, the action taking place in a forest.

SWAN LAKE or **Le Lac des Cygnes,** a ballet in four acts. Libretto, V. P. Begitcha and Vasily Geltzer; choreography, Julius Reisinger; music, Peter Tchaikovsky; decor, Shangin, Valtz, Groppius. First performed, 4 March 1877, at the Bolshoi Theatre, Moscow. Principal dancers, Pauline Karpakova (Odette-Odile), Gillbert (Siegfried). This production was a failure. Much of the music was considered unsuitable for dancing, and the choreography and decor were poor. Subsequently the score was cut in places and dances from other ballets introduced. This version was revived in 1880 and 1882, again unsuccessfully. For a new version, **Marius Petipa** choreographed Acts 1 and 3, and **Lev Ivanov** choreographed Acts 2 and 4. Decor, Botcharov, Levogt. First performed, 27 January 1895, at the Maryinsky Theatre, St. Petersburg. Principal dancers, **Pierina Legnani** (Odette-Odile), **Paul Gerdt** (Siegfried). This version had instant success. The two separate choreographic exercises complemented one another perfectly. Revived at the Bolshoi Theatre, Moscow, 1911, by **Alexander Gorsky. Asaf Messerer** choreographed Act 4 and an important variation was the introduction of a jester. Mime was introduced into Act 1. The famous 32 fouettés were introduced in an Odile variation in Act 3. **Vladimir Bourmeister** choreographed Acts 1, 3 and 4 of yet another Russian version. Act 2 followed Ivanov's 1895 score. Decor, Anatole Lushin. First performed, 24 April 1953, at the Stanislavsky Nemirovich-Danchenko Lyric Theatre, Moscow. Principal dancers, Violetta Bovt (Odette-Odile), Oleg Chichinadze (Siegfried). Repeated, 1956, at the Châtelet Theatre, Paris and, 21 December 1960, for the **Paris Opéra Ballet.** Principal dancers,

Josette Amiel (Odette-Odile), **Peter van Dijk** (Siegfried). First performed in Britain, 16 May 1910, at the Hippodrome, London. A complete version by **Nicholas Sergeyev** was staged at Sadler's Wells Theatre, London, 24 November 1934, for Vic-Wells Ballet. Decor, Hugh Stevenson. Principal dancers, **Alicia Markova** (Odette-Odile), **Robert Helpmann** (Siegfried). A new version was staged, 7 September 1943, at the New Theatre, London. Decor, Leslie Hurry. Principal dancers, **Margot Fonteyn** (Odette-Odile), Robert Helpmann (Siegfried). Leslie Hurry redesigned this same version, 18 December 1952, at the Royal Opera House, Covent Garden, London. Principal dancers, **Beryl Grey, John Field.** Nicholas Sergeyev staged the full-length work at the Adelphi Theatre, London, 18 March 1947, for **International Ballet.** A new production was staged in 1963 by Robert Helpmann for **The Royal Ballet,** with parts re-choreographed by **Frederick Ashton.** Another production was staged by Frederick Ashton and **John Field** in 1965. London's **Festival Ballet** presented a version in 1964, by Vaslav Orlikovsky. Also staged for the same company by **Jack Carter,** 12 February 1966, at Teatro la Fenice, Venice. Principal dancers, Maryon Lane, **Lucette Aldous, John Gilpin.** A new production following Ivanov and Petipa was choreographed by **Beryl Grey** for London Festival Ballet, 1972. Principal dancers, **Galina Samtsova, André Prokovsky.** First performed in the United States, 19 December 1911, at the Metropolitan Opera House, New York. Principal dancer, **Yekaterina Geltzer. George Balanchine** choreographed and staged his own version of Act 2, 20 November 1951, for **The New York City Ballet.** He retained the **pas de quatre** of the Little Swans. Principal dancers, **Maria Tallchief, André Eglevsky.** In 1941 **Alexandra Fedorova** revived Act 3 (the ballroom scene) under the title *The Magic Swan* for **Ballet Russe de Monte Carlo.** First performed in France, 10 April 1912, by the **Diaghilev** Ballets Russes. Principal dancer, **Mathilda Kchessinska.** In Den-

Swan Lake: performed by The Royal Ballet. Ph. Roger Houston.

mark, 8 February 1938, at the Royal Theatre, Copenhagen. Principal dancer, **Toni Lander.** In Germany, 3 December 1959, in Munich. Principal dancers, Dulce Anaya, **Heino Hallhuber.** In Sweden, by Mary Skeaping, 1953. Principal dancers, **Mariane Orlando,** Teddy Rhodin. In the full version, Odette the Swan Queen is really a princess under the spell of a wicked magician, Rothbart. Only at night can she revert to being human, and the spell can only be broken permanently when a young man falls in love with her and with her only. Prince Siegfried falls in love with Odette and to prevent the spell being broken, Rothbart has his daughter, Odile, impersonate Odette. At first Siegfried is misled but realizes his mistake in time to prevent a broken-hearted Odette killing herself. In the Russian version, the spell is broken when Siegfried defeats Rothbart in combat. The roles of Odette and Odile are frequently danced by the same ballerina.

SWEDEN, history of ballet in.
1638 The first ballet performance in Sweden takes place at the court.
1773 King Gustav III founds an opera in Stockholm. Louis Gallodier, a Frenchman, becomes ballet master.
1781 Antoine Bournonville, a pupil of **Noverre,** becomes choreographer.
1818 Filippo Taglioni becomes a ballet master. He redesigns the costumes, making greater movement possible.
1833 Anders Selinder becomes first Swedish ballet master of the Royal Swedish Ballet.
1837–41 Christian Johansson is premier danseur in Stockholm.
1841 Maria Taglioni dances in *La Sylphide* and *Le Lac des Fées* in Stockholm. She goes to Russia with Christian Johansson.
1845 Royal Swedish Ballet stages *Giselle.* After 1860 it undergoes a decline.
1906 Isadora Duncan dances in Stockholm.
1908 Anna Pavlova dances in Stockholm.
1913 Michel Fokine is guest artist with the Royal Swedish Ballet.
1920–5 Les Ballets Suédois performs, with **Jean Börlin** as choreographer.
1950 Antony Tudor becomes director of the Royal Swedish Ballet. He stages *Giselle*

and *The Lilac Garden*. **Birgit Cullberg** stages *Miss Julie* and, as choreographer during the 1950s, creates *Romeo and Juliet, Moon Reindeer, Odysseus* and *The Lady from the Sea*. Elsa-Marianne von Rosen is première danseuse.

1953 **Mary Skeaping** stages *Swan Lake*, and becomes director of the Royal Swedish Ballet. **Mariane Orlando** becomes ballerina.

1954 **Mary Skeaping** becomes ballet director.

1957 Ivo Cramér's *The Prodigal Son* is staged.

1958 **Gerd Andersson** becomes ballerina.

1960 **Birgit Cullberg** becomes director and choreographer of Stockholm City Theatre and organizes a group of dancers. Contact with **Yuri Grigorovich** and the USSR influences Swedish ballet in the 1960s.

1967 **Erik Bruhn** is appointed director of ballet at the Royal Swedish Opera House. He stages *La Sylphide* and *Giselle*, invites **Nureyev, Fonteyn** and **Carla Fracci** to appear as guest artists, and choreographers **Kenneth MacMillan** and **Jerome Robbins** to stage works.

1969 First European performance of **Jerome Robbins**'s *Les Noces*.

1970 MacMillan's *Romeo and Juliet* is staged. The Cullberg Ballet takes first prize at the Paris International Dance Festival.

Swedish Ballet *see* **Sweden, history of ballet in.**

SYLPHIDE, LA, a romantic ballet in two acts. Libretto, Adolphe Nourrit; choreography, **Filippo Taglioni**; music, Jean Schneitzhoffer; decor, Pierre Ciceri; costumes, Eugène Lami. First performed, 12 March 1832, at **L'Académie Royale de Musique**, Paris. Principal dancers, **Maria Taglioni** (La Sylphide), Mme. Elie (Sorceress), Joseph Mazilier, Lise Noblet. Repeated 28 July 1832, at Covent Garden, London; 6 September 1837 in St. Petersburg; 29 May 1841 at **Teatro alla Scala**, Milan. After a period of neglect, *La Sylphide* was revived by **Marius Petipa**

at the Imperial Theatre, St. Petersburg. Again revived, 1945, by **Les Ballets des Champs-Elysées**. Decor, A. Serebriakov; costumes, Christian Bérard. Another version was choreographed by **August Bournonville**. First performed, 28 November 1836, by the Royal Danish Ballet. Music, Herman von Løvenskjold. Principal dancers, **Lucile Grahn** (La Sylphide), August Bournonville (James). Restaged by **Harald Lander** at the Théâtre de l'Empire, Paris, 9 December 1953, for **Grand Ballet du Marquis de Cuevas**. Principal dancers, **Rosella Hightower, Serge Golovine**. Repeated, 1962, at Teatro alla Scala, Milan. Principal dancers, **Carla Fracci,** Mario Pistoni. Repeated, 1963, for Nederlands Nationaal Ballet. Principal dancers, Sonja van Beers, Ben de Rochement. Lander's version, with additional music by Edgar Cosma and new decor by Robert O'Hearn, was first performed at San Antonio, Texas, 11 November 1964, by American Ballet Theatre. Principal dancers, **Toni Lander, Royes Fernandez**. Restaged, 18 March 1965, in New York, with the same principals. August Bournonville's version was staged by Elsa-Marianne von Rosen, under the title, *The Sylphide*, at Sadler's Wells Theatre, London, 20 July 1960, by **Ballet Rambert**. Choreography adapted by Ellen Price de Plane; decor, Robin and Christopher Ironside. Principal dancers, Elsa-Marianne von Rosen, **Flemming Flindt**, Gillian Martlew, Shirley Dixon. The ballet has remained in the repertoire of the Royal Danish Ballet. Notable Sylphides have included Juliette Price, **Margrethe Schanne, Anna Laerkesen** and **Kirsten Simone.** The story is set in Scotland. The mortals, James and Effie, are to marry, but on their wedding day James falls in love with the Sylphide, a fairy. The Sorceress causes James to be the means of the Sylphide's death. In this ballet Maria Taglioni introduced the romantic **tutu** of the female dancer and danced on points. Until then the practice had been to dance only very short passages on points.

SYLPHIDES, LES or **Chopiniana,** a

Les Sylphides: performed by the Paris Opéra Ballet. Ph. Lipnitzki.

plotless romantic ballet in one act. Choreography, **Michel Fokine**; music, Chopin; decor, **Alexandre Benois**. First performed, as *Chopiniana*, 8 March 1908, at the Maryinsky Theatre, St. Petersburg. Principal dancers, **Olga Preobrajenska, Anna Pavlova, Tamara Karsavina,** Vera Fokina, **Vaslav Nijinsky**. This production was a series of scenes danced in national costumes. Anna Pavlova wore a long white tutu (after **Maria Taglioni** in *La Sylphide*) and this inspired **Diaghilev** to stage the work as a **ballet blanc**. First performed at the Théâtre du Châtelet, Paris, 2 June 1909, by his Ballets Russes. Principal dancers, Anna Pavlova and Vaslav Nijinsky (mazurkas and waltz pas de deux), Tamara Karsavina (waltz), Alexandra Baldina (prelude). Michel Fokine staged the ballet under its original title of *Chopiniana* for the Royal Danish Ballet in 1925, for **René Blum**'s Ballet de Monte Carlo in 1936 and for **Ballet Theatre** in 1940. This is a ballet of mood, an interpretation of music in terms of movement, demanding faultless technique from soloist and corps de ballet.

SYLVIA or **La Nymphe de Diane**, a ballet in three acts. Libretto, Jules Barbier, Baron de Reinach; choreography, **Louis Mérante**; music, Léo Delibes; decor, Chéret, Rubé, Chaperon; costumes, Eugène Lacoste. First performed at the Paris Opéra, 14 June 1876, by the **Paris Opéra Ballet**. Principal dancers, **Rita Sangalli** (Sylvia), Louis Mérante (Shepherd). Staged, 1891, at the Maly Theatre, St. Petersburg. Choreography, M. Saracco. Principal dancer, Adelina Rossi. Staged, 15 December 1901, at the **Maryinsky Theatre**. Choreography, **Lev Ivanov, Paul Gerdt**. Revived, 17 May 1916, for **Tamara Karsavina**. A one-act version by C. Wilhelm and Fred Farren was presented, 18 May 1911, at the Empire Theatre, London. Principal dancer, **Lydia Kyasht** (Sylvia). For Act 3 of the full length version, **George Balanchine** arranged a brilliant pas de deux which includes the well known Pizzicato Polka. First performed, 1 December 1951, in New York City Center. Principal dancers, **Maria Tallchief, Patricia Wilde, Melissa Hayden** (Sylvia), **Nicholas Magallanes, André Eglevsky** (Shepherd). Another three act version was choreographed by **Frederick Ashton**. Music, Léo Delibes; decor, Robin and Christopher Ironside. First performed at the Royal Opera House, Covent Garden, London, 3 September 1952, by Sadler's

Sylvia: Lycette Darsonval. Ph. Victor Dibilio.

Wells Ballet. Principal dancers, **Margot Fonteyn** (Sylvia), **Michael Somes** (Aminta), John Hart (Orion) **Julia Farron** (Diana), **Alexander Grant** (Eros). Revived 1963. Principal dancers, **Doreen Wells** (Sylvia), **Christopher Gable** (Aminta). This was a simplified version of the original. The Shepherd, Aminta, surprises the Huntress, Sylvia, while she dances in celebration of the hunt. As she confronts him angrily, an arrow from the bow of Eros strikes her. She is captured by the huntsman, Orion, but rescued by Eros and restored to Aminta. This angers Diana who relents, however, when she remembers that she once loved a shepherd.

SYMPHONIC VARIATIONS, a plotless ballet in one act, for six dancers. Choreography, **Frederick Ashton**; music, César Franck (*Symphonic Variations for Piano and Orchestra*); decor, Sophie Fedorovich. First performed at the Royal Opera House, Covent Garden, London, 24 April 1946, by Sadler's Wells Ballet. Principal dancers, **Margot Fonteyn, Pamela May, Moira Shearer, Michael Somes.**

SYMPHONIE CONCERTANTE, a ballet in four movements. Choreography, **George Balanchine**; music, Mozart (*Symphonie Concertante in E flat*); decor, James Morcam. First performed in New York City Center, 12 November 1947, by Ballet Society. Principal dancers, **Maria Tallchief, Tanaquil LeClercq, Todd Bolender.** This work is a ballet of pure dancing.

SYMPHONIE FANTASTIQUE, a ballet in five scenes. Libretto, Hector Berlioz; choreography, **Léonide Massine**; music, Berlioz; decor, Christian Bérard. First performed at the Royal Opera House, Covent Garden, London, 24 July 1936, by **Colonel de Basil's Ballet Russe de Monte Carlo.** Principal dancers, **Léonide Massine** (Young Musician), **Tamara Toumanova** (His Beloved). The subtitle of the music, *Episodes de la Vie d'un Artiste*, describes the plot of the ballet. The musician, tormented under the influence of opium, dreams of his beloved and follows her to a lonely countryside. After a Black Sabbath passage, the ballet ends on a note of hope.

SYMPHONIE POUR UN HOMME SEUL, a plotless ballet in one act. Choreography, **Maurice Béjart**; music, Pierre Schaeffer, Pierre Henry. First performed at the Théâtre de l'Étoile, Paris, 3 August 1955, by Ballets de l'Étoile. Principal dancers, Michele Seigneuret, Maurice Béjart. The ballet, danced to musique concrète, depicts man as a prisoner of the life around him. **Merce Cunningham,** in his work *Collage* (1952), used part of the music in New York, when it was the first musique concrète to be heard in the United States.

SYMPHONY FOR FUN, a ballet in one act. Choreography, **Michael Charnley**; music, Don Gillis; decor, Tom Lingwood. First performed at the Festival Hall, London, 1 September 1952, by London's **Festival Ballet.** Principal dancers, Noel Rossana, Anita Landa, **John Gilpin.** This is an inconsequential ballet of young people happily jiving.

SYMPHONY IN C *see* **Palais de Cristal, Le.**

T

Maria Taglioni. Ph. Lipnitzki.

TAGLIONI, Filippo (1778–1871), Italian dancer and choreographer. He studied with his father and made his debut in Pisa (1794). After dancing with his family in Italy, he went to study with Coulon (1799) and appeared at the Paris Opéra in *La Caravane du Caire*. He was premier danseur in Florence, Venice and Paris and chief dancer and ballet master in Stockholm. He presented members of his family in ballets throughout Europe; these included *The Reception of a Young Nymph at the Court of Terpsichore* (1822), *Le Dieu et la Bayadère* (1830), *La Sylphide* (1832), *La Gitana* (1838) and *L'Ombre* (1839). He retired in 1852. He was the father of **Paul** and **Maria Taglioni**.

TAGLIONI, Maria (1804–84), Italian ballerina. She studied with her father, **Filippo Taglioni**, and later in Paris, making her debut at Hoftheater, Vienna (1822) in *The Reception of a Young Nymph at the Court of Terpsichore*, choreographed by her father. In 1823 she danced in Germany and Italy, and with the **Paris Opéra Ballet** (1827–32). She created the title role in *La Sylphide* (1832), which she danced on points. She introduced the conventional Romantic ballet dress or tutu. Her repertoire included *La Fille du Danube*, *Flore et Zéphyr*, *La Gitana*, *Le Dieu et la Bayadère* and **Perrot**'s *Pas de Quatre* (1845). After **Elssler** became her rival at the Paris Opéra (1834), she went to the Imperial Theatre, St. Petersburg (1837–40). Afterwards she returned to Europe, dancing regularly in London (1830–47), and retired in 1848. She later taught in London and Paris, and choreographed *Le Papillon* (1861). Taglioni's influence on ballet stemmed from the spiritual quality she brought to her interpretations, which was heightened by her technique and **élévation**.

TAGLIONI, Marie Paul (1830–91), Italian dancer, niece of **Maria Taglioni**, daughter of **Paul Taglioni**. She made her debut as soloist at Her Majesty's Theatre, London (1847–9) and danced in *Thea*, *Fiorita* and *Electra* (1847–9). Her roles as prima ballerina with the Berlin State Opera (1848–65) include *Flick and Flock* and *The Metamorphosis*, choreographed by her father. She made guest appearances in all the capitals of Europe, and retired in 1866.

TAGLIONI, Paul (1808–84), Italian dancer and choreographer, son of **Filippo Taglioni** and brother of **Maria Taglioni**. He studied with his father and with Coulon, making his debut in Stuttgart (1825) in

Zémir et Azore. He appeared in Paris, Vienna and Munich. His choreographic works include *Thea,* or *The Flower Fairy* (1847), *Fiorita* (1848), *Electra* (1849), *La Prima Ballerina* and *Les Patineurs* (1849), *The Metamorphosis* (1850) and *Flick and Flock* (1862). All but the last were premièred in London and restaged in Berlin.

TAGLIONI, Salvatore (1790–1868), Italian dancer and choreographer, brother of **Filippo Taglioni.** He studied at the Paris Opéra school and made his debut in 1806 with his sister, Luisa. For nearly fifty years he was principal dancer and ballet master at Naples where he created over fifty works, among which were his own versions of *La Sylphide, L'Eridita* and *Tolomeo Evergete* (1834). His daughter Louise (1823–93) was a principal dancer at the **Paris Opéra Ballet** (1848–57).

TALLCHIEF, Maria (1925–), American ballerina, of American Indian origin. She studied with **Nijinska,** Ernest Belcher, **Lichine** and **Balanchine,** at the School of American Ballet, and appeared in Nijinska's *Chopin Concerto* when she was only 15. As soloist with **Ballet Russe de Monte Carlo** (1942–7) she created Coquette in *Night Shadow,* and danced in *Ballet Impérial, Serenade, Le Baiser de la Fée, Gaieté Parisienne* and *Schéhérazade.* She was guest artist with the **Paris Opéra Ballet** in 1947 and danced *Apollo, Serenade* and *Le Baiser de la Fée.* Later that year she joined Ballet Society and stayed with the company when it became **The New York City Ballet.** Her Odette in *Swan Lake* was a great success. She danced with Ballet Russe de Monte Carlo (1954–5); with **American Ballet Theatre** on its Russian tour (1960), dancing the title role in *Miss Julie* and ballerina in *Grand Pas-Glazounov.* She has appeared with **Ruth Page**'s Chicago Opera Ballet and the Royal Danish Ballet (1961); and Chicago Lyric Opera (1962). For The New York City Ballet she created many roles including title roles in Balanchine's *Firebird* and *Sylvia Pas de Deux,*

Eurydice in *Orpheus,* Swan Queen in Act 2 of *Swan Lake,* Sugar Plum Fairy in *The Nutcracker* and leading girl in *Divertimento.* In 1965 she resigned from The New York City Ballet saying 'I don't mind being listed alphabetically, but I'm not going to be treated alphabetically.' She was married to **George Balanchine.**

TALLCHIEF, Marjorie (1927–), American ballerina, sister of **Maria Tallchief.** She studied with **Bronislava Nijinska** and **David Lichine.** Her early roles include Queen of the Wilis in *Giselle,* and leading roles in *On Stage!* and *Graduation Ball* with **Ballet Theatre** (1944–6). She danced with Original Ballet Russe (1946–7) and was ballerina (1947–1956) with Grand Ballet de Monte Carlo, which became **Grand Ballet du Marquis de Cuevas.** Her repertoire included the classical and dramatic roles in *Les Biches, Brahms Variations, Aubade, Concerto Barocco, Night Shadow, Idylle,* **Skibine**'s *Romeo and Juliet,* and she created the leading roles in *Annabel Lee* and *Prisoner of the Caucasus.* She was the first American invited to dance at the **Paris Opéra Ballet** in 1957 as première

Marjorie Tallchief. Ph. Michel Petit.

danseuse étoile. While with the company (1957–62) she danced *Firebird*, *Les Noces Fantastiques* and *Giselle*, and created roles in *Concerto* (1958), *Pastorale* and others. During the same period she toured America with **Ruth Page**'s Chicago Opera Ballet (1956–8), creating the title role in *Camille* and dancing *The Merry Widow* and *Revenge*; and in 1961 danced *Metamorphoses* and *Concerto* at Teatro Colón, Buenos Aires. After she and her husband **George Skibine** resigned from the Paris Opéra, they toured Europe with a troupe of dancers. She became guest prima ballerina with **Harkness Ballet** in 1964 and resigned in 1966.

TAMIRIS, Helen (Helen Becker, 1905–1966), American dancer, choreographer, teacher and director. After study with Metropolitan Opera Ballet and **Michel Fokine**, she danced three seasons at the **Metropolitan Ballet**, and toured South America as ballerina with the Bracale Opera Company. She made her concert debut at the Little Theatre, New York (1927); and brought Negro spirituals and American folk songs to the Salzburg Festival. Every year from 1930 she presented her own company in New York. She was director and teacher at the School of American Dance (1930–45) and choreographed for Dance Project (1937–9). During the next fifteen years she lectured to actors and directors throughout the country, and choreographed many works. She returned from choreographing for films to modern dance in 1957, staging *Pioneer Memories* (1957) and *Memoir* (1959). With her husband she founded Tamiris-Nagrin Dance Company (1960) and choreographed *Women's Song* (1960) and *Once Upon a Time* (1961).

TARAS, John (1919–   ), American dancer, choreographer and ballet master. He began by studying drama, then studied ballet with **Fokine, Vilzak** and Shollar. He danced with American Ballet Caravan at the New York World's Fair (1940), Littlefield Ballet (1940–1), American Ballet on its South American tour (1941), and **Ballet**

John Taras. Ph. S. Lido.

Theatre (1942–6) where he rose from the corps de ballet to soloist and ballet master, choreographing his first work *Graziana* in 1945. He presented *Tchaikovsky Waltz* for the Markova-Dolin ballet and *Camille* for Original Ballet Russe (1946), which he joined in 1947 as dancer and ballet master for its European Tour. He choreographed *The Minotaur* for Ballet Society, and *Designs with Strings* for Metropolitan Ballet (1948), Ballet Theatre and **Grand Ballet du Marquis de Cuevas** (1949), and the Royal Danish Ballet (1953); and *Persephone* for San Francisco Ballet (1948). As ballet master for **Grand Ballet du Marquis de Cuevas** (1948–52, 1955–1956, 1958–9) he choreographed *Élégie*, *Fête Polonaise*, *Nuit d'Été*, and his most important work, the exotic *Piège de Lumière* (1952) which has since entered the repertoire of many companies. In 1959 he revived Night Shadow for **The New York City Ballet**, and danced the role of Baron. As assistant to **Balanchine** with The New York City Ballet he choreographed *Variaciones Concertantes* and *Ebony Concerto* (1960), *Arcade* and *Fantasy* (1963) and staged *Piège de Lumière* (1964), *Shadow'd Ground* (1965), *La Guirlande de Campra* (1966) and his own version of *Jeux*. He has staged works for a number of ballet companies including *Variaciones Concertantes* for Teatro Colón, Buenos Aires, and National Ballet of Chile; choreographed *Scènes de Ballet* and *Night Shadow* for Het Nederlands Ballet, *Fanfare for a Prince* for the Monte Carlo Opéra specially for Prince Rainier's wedding, *Les Griffes* for Les Ballets 1956, and choreographed the first and third acts of Sagan's *Le Rendez-vous Manqué*. Most recently for The New York City Ballet he has choreographed *Haydn Concerto*. He became ballet master for a short time at the **Paris Opéra Ballet** in 1969, and was later appointed director of the Deutsche Oper, Berlin.

TAYLOR, Paul (Paul Bellville Taylor Jr.' 1930–), American modern dancer and choreographer. He studied at Juilliard School of Music Dance Department, Martha Graham School and Metropolitan Opera Ballet School. For his own company he choreographed *Three Epitaphs* and *Tropes* (1956), *The Tower* (1957), *Images and Reflections* (1958). For Het Nederlands Ballet he choreographed *The White Salamander* (1960). As a dancer he was leading soloist with **Martha Graham**'s company (1955–61) and created Aegisthus in *Clytemnestra*, Hercules in *Alcestis*, Samson the Destroyer in *Samson Agonistes*, and danced Tiresias in *Night Journey* and Stranger in *Embattled Garden*. As guest artist with **The New York City Ballet**, he danced special variations in *Episodes* (1959) created for him by **Balanchine**. He toured South America, Europe, North Africa and the Near East (1965–6). His *Orbs* was premièred at the Holland Festival (1966). He founded the Paul Taylor Dance Company, staging new works such as *Churchyard*, *Piece Period*, *Aureole* and *Junction*. His works betray his strong sense of humour, and his aim is to entertain rather than philosophize.

TCHERINA, Ludmilla (Monique Avenirovna Tchemerzina, 1925–), French dancer. She studied with **Ivan Clustine** and **Preobrajenska**. She was ballerina with Monte Carlo Opéra (1940–4), and guest ballerina with **Les Ballets des Champs-Elysées** (1945). As ballerina with **Nouveau Ballet de Monte Carlo** (1946) she created the leading roles in *A La Memoire d'un Héros* and *Mephisto Valse*. She appeared at **Teatro alla Scala**, Milan (1954), and in 1957 danced at the Paris Opéra in *The Martyrdom of St. Sebastian*, a role which established her as a great dancer. She formed her own company in Paris (1959); the repertoire included *Les Amants de Teruel* and *Feu aux Poudres*. She toured Russia in 1960 and danced *Giselle* at the Bolshoi. In Venice (1961) she appeared in Salvador Dali's *Gala*. She was created Chevalier of the Légion d'Honneur in 1970.

TCHERNICHEVA, Lubov (1890–), Russian dancer and teacher. A graduate of the Imperial School, St. Petersburg (1908), she danced at the Maryinsky Theatre and with **Diaghilev**'s Ballets Russes in 1911. In 1912 she resigned from the Imperial Theatre and joined Diaghilev's company (1912–29) dancing leading roles. She became ballet mistress in 1926. In 1932 she joined **Colonel de Basil**'s **Ballet Russe de Monte Carlo**. She continued with the company when it became Original Ballet Russe (1937) and was ballet mistress in its last years. Her notable roles include Zobéide in *Schéhérazade*, Miller's Wife in *The Three-Cornered Hat*, Constanza in *The Good-Humoured Ladies*, the title roles in *Francesca da Rimini*, which she created, and *Thamar*. With her husband, **Serge Grigoriev**, she restaged *Firebird*, *Les Sylphides* and *Petrouchka* for Sadler's Wells Ballet, and for **Teatro alla Scala**, Milan (1955).

Teatro alla Scala *see* **Scala, Teatro alla**.

temps de cuisse *see* **cuisse, temps de**.

temps de flèche *see* **flèche, temps de**.

temps de poisson *see* **poisson, temps de.**

temps levé, literally a raised movement, a step like a hop.

temps lié, a step involving change of weight from front to back foot, crossing and uncrossing the legs. Also term used for connected series of classroom exercises forming part of the **adagio.**

terre à terre, literally earth to earth, term used for steps in which feet are only raised from the ground sufficiently to allow them to be pointed, as opposed to steps performed en l'air.

TERRY, Walter (1913–　), American critic and lecturer. He studied various forms of dance. He was dance critic of the Boston *Herald* (1936–9), the New York *Herald-Tribune* (1939–42; 1945–66) and the *Saturday Review* (1967–　). His published works include *Ballet in Action, The Dance in America* and *Isadora Duncan, Her Life, Her Art, Her Legacy* as well as numerous contributions to magazines and journals.

TER WEEME, Mascha, Dutch dancer and artistic director. He studied with **Mary Wigman, Yvonne Georgi, Igor Schwezov, Victor Gsovsky, Léo Staats** and **Preobrajenska,** and was assistant to Yvonne Georgi from 1936–44. He was artistic director of Het Ballet der Lage Landen (1947–59), and of Het Amsterdams Ballet (1959–61). In 1961 he became head of the Opera Ballet Department of Het Nederlands Nationaal Ballet.

TETLEY, Glen (1926–　), American modern dancer and choreographer. He studied with Hanya Holm, Margaret Craske and **Antony Tudor.** He danced in *Amahl and the Night Visitors* (1951), and was premier danseur with New York City Opera (1952–4; 1959). He toured Europe in 1955. He was guest artist with Robert Joffrey Ballet (1956–7), joining **Martha Graham**'s company in 1958 and American Ballet Theatre in 1960, touring Europe and the Soviet Union. He again toured Europe in 1961 with Ballets: USA. He joined Nederlands Dans Theater in 1962 as dancer and choreographer. His roles include Jean in *Miss Julie,* and Alias in *Billy the Kid.* Among his choreographic works are *Pierrot Lunaire* (1962), *The Anatomy Lesson* (1964), *Game of Noah* (1965), *Sargasso* (1965), *Freefall* (1967), *Field Figures* (1969) and *Mutations* (1970). In 1969 Tetley became joint artistic director of Het Nederlands Dans Theater. He created *Small Parades* for Het Nederlands Dans Theater, and *Threshold* for Hamburg Opera (1972).

THAMAR, a ballet in one act. Libretto, **Léon Bakst**; choreography, **Michel Fokine**; music, Mily Balakirev (*Thamar*); decor, Bakst. First performed in the Théâtre du Châtelet, Paris, 20 May 1912, by **Diaghilev**'s Ballets Russes. Principal dancers, **Tamara Karsavina** (Thamar), **Adolph Bolm** (Prince). Later revived by Colonel de Basil's **Ballet Russe de Monte Carlo.** Thamar, Queen of Georgia, seduces then murders a visiting Prince. Included in the ballet are a notable pas de deux for the Queen and the Prince, and several Caucasian dances. Karsavina's portrayal of the vicious Queen was unforgettable.

Théâtre National de l'Opéra *see* **Académie Royale de Musique, L',** and **Paris Opéra Ballet.**

THEILADE, Nini (1916–　), Danish dancer and choreographer, born in Java. She studied with **Egorova, Von Laban** and **Wigman,** and started her career as a leading dancer in Max Reinhardt's theatrical productions. As soloist with **Ballet Russe de Monte Carlo** (1938–40), she created Venus in *Bacchanale* and Stream in *Seventh Symphony,* also dancing in *Les Sylphides* and *Coppélia.* She has been guest artist with Rio de Janeiro Opera where she choreographed *Psyche, Les Nuages* and *Metaphore.* In 1970 she opened the Danish Ballet Group Academy in Svendborg, Denmark.

THEME AND VARIATIONS, a ballet in one act. Choreography, **George Balanchine**; music, Tchaikovsky (*Suite No. 3 in G*); decor, Woodman Thompson. First performed at Richmond, Virginia, 27 September 1947, by **Ballet Theatre**. Staged at New York City Center, 26 November 1947, by the same company. Principal dancers, **Alicia Alonso, Igor Youskevitch**. Revived in 1958 by American Ballet Theatre. Principal dancers, **Violette Verdy, Royes Fernandez**. Lupe Serrano was notable in the ballerina role. Presented by **The New York City Ballet**, 1960. Principal dancers, **Violette Verdy, Edward Villella**. This is an abstract classical ballet, the variations consisting of a series of pas, and a final polonaise.

THIBON, Nanon (1944–), French dancer. Studied at the Paris Opéra Ballet school. She subsequently joined the company and was promoted to première danseuse when 19, and étoile in 1965. Notable in her repertoire is her dancing of pas de trois in *Swan Lake* and first movement in *Scotch Symphony*.

Nanon Thibon. Ph. Liseg.

THREE-CORNERED HAT, THE or **Le Tricorne**, a ballet in one act, based on the play *El Sombrero de Tres Picos* by Antonio de Alarcón. Libretto, Martinez Sierra; choreography, **Léonide Massine**; music, Manuel de Falla; decor, Pablo Picasso. First performed at the Alhambra Theatre, London, 22 July 1919, by **Diaghilev**'s Ballets Russes. Principal dancers, Léonide Massine (The Miller), **Tamara Karsavina, Lubov Tchernicheva** (His Wife), **Léon Woizikowsky** (Corregidor), **Stanislas Idzikowsky** (Dandy). Colonel de Basil took the ballet into the repertoire of his **Ballet Russe de Monte Carlo**. Principal dancers, Léonide Massine, **Tamara Toumanova**. Revived by Léonide Massine, 1943 for **Ballet Theatre**, 1947 for Sadler's Wells Ballet, and for the Royal Swedish Ballet. Staged at the New York City Center, 25 September 1969, by the City Center Joffrey Ballet. The most famous dances in the ballet are the farucca danced by the Miller, the fandango danced by His Wife, and the jota for the corps de ballet; these were choreographed by Massine in classical terms. The Corregidor (governor of the province) orders his bodyguard to kidnap the Miller so that he can be alone with the Miller's Wife. She pushes him into the river. Climbing out he dons the Miller's dressing gown, is mistaken by his own bodyguard for the Miller and is beaten. The Miller and his Wife are reunited, and join in the beating.

THREE GIFTS, THE or **The Kermesse at Bruges**, a Romantic ballet in three acts. Choreography, **August Bournonville**; music, H. S. Paulli. First performed at the Royal Theatre, Copenhagen, 6 May 1849, by the Royal Danish Ballet. It has had many revivals by the same company. Staged by **Flemming Flindt** in 1966, with decor and costumes by Jacques Nokl. In 17th century Bruges, the brothers Geert, Adrian and Carelis rescue Eleonore, daughter of Mirewelt the Alchemist. Mirewelt gives Geert a ring which wins all hearts, Adrian a sword which cannot be vanquished, and Carelis a fiddle which makes everyone dance. Geert, Adrian and Mirewelt are to be burned for alleged witchcraft, but are rescued by Carelis, who finally wins Eleonore's hand. The inspiration for the scenes in the ballet was drawn from Dutch Old Masters.

THREE VIRGINS AND A DEVIL, a ballet in one act. Libretto, Ramon Reed ; choreography, **Agnes de Mille** ; music, Ottorino Respighi (*Antiche Danze ed Arie*) ; decor, Arne Lundborg. First performed at the Majestic Theatre, New York, 11 February 1941, by **Ballet Theatre**. Principal dancers, Agnes de Mille, Annabelle Lyon, **Lucia Chase**, Eugene Loring, **Jerome Robbins**. This ballet, with music by Walford Hayden, was originally an item in a revue, presented in 1934 at the Palace Theatre, London.

TIKHOMIRNOVA, Irina Victorovna (1917–), Russian ballerina, Honoured Artist of the RSFSR, wife of **Asaf Messerer**. She studied in Moscow and was a soloist with the Bolshoi company (1936–59). Her roles included Aurora in *The Sleeping Beauty* and Odette-Odile in *Swan Lake*.

TIKHOMIROV, Vassily (1876–1956), Russian dancer and teacher, Peoples' Artist of the RSFSR. He was placed in the Bolshoi School at the age of nine, graduating in 1891. He then studied at the St. Petersburg School under **Christian Johansson** and **Paul Gerdt**, who greatly influenced his style and teaching methods. He made his debut at the Bolshoi Theatre, in *Robert and Bertram* with Lubov Roslavleva, and so began a long career as teacher, choreographer and dancer. He trained many male dancers, among them **Mikhail Mordkin, Alexandre Volinine** and **Asaf Messerer**, using his own energetic teaching system. He also trained many leading ballerinas. His partner and wife, **Yekaterina Geltzer**, studied with him for most of her career. Tikhomirov became first teacher at the Bolshoi school in 1896. He was considered one of the greatest teachers of the era. He danced in London at the Alhambra Theatre in *Dance*

Dream (1911), and with **Pavlova** in 1914. His major roles included Jean de Brienne in *Raymonda* and Conrad in *Le Corsaire*. After the 1917 Revolution Tikhomirov helped to maintain the Moscow ballet school. His productions include revivals of *La Bayadère* and *The Sleeping Beauty* (1924), a different version of *La Esmeralda* (1926), and in 1927 collaborated with Laschilin on a new version of *The Red Poppy* with **Yekaterina Geltzer**. He retired from the Bolshoi school in 1937 for reasons of ill health, having previously been made a director.

TIKHONOV, Vladimir Petrovich (1935–), Russian dancer, Honoured Artist of the Moldavian SSR. He studied in Leningrad, joining the Kirov Ballet in 1960. His roles include Siegfried in *Swan Lake* and Poet in *Straussiana*. He was a Gold Medallist at Varna in 1965.

TIL EULENSPIEGEL, a ballet in one act. Choreography, **Jean Babilée** ; music, Richard Strauss ; decor, Tom Keogh. First performed at the Théâtre des Champs-Elysées, Paris, 9 November 1949, by **Les Ballets des Champs-Elysées**. Principal dancers, Jean Babilée, Elise Vallée, Danielle Darmance. **Vaslav Nijinsky** had choreographed a ballet using the same title and music. Decor, Robert Jones. First performed, 23 October 1916, at the Metropolitan Opera House, New York. Principal dancer, Nijinsky. The story is based on the Flemish folk tales of Til whose mischief, at the expense of those in authority, leads him to the gallows. The action takes place during the Spanish occupation of the Netherlands. *See* **Tyl Ulenspiegel**.

TIMOFEYEVA or **TIMOFIEVA, Nina Vladimirovna** (1935–), Russian ballerina, Honoured Artist of the RSFSR. She studied in Leningrad, joining the Kirov Ballet in 1953, and the Bolshoi Ballet in 1956. Her extensive repertoire includes Odette-Odile in *Swan Lake*, Kitri and Street Dancer in *Don Quixote* and Myrtha in *Giselle*. She has danced in Europe, North

America and Japan. She excels not only in classical ballets, but also shows ability as a character dancer as in **Leonid Lavrovsky**'s *The Night City* in which she created the role of the Girl. In 1969 she danced *Swan Lake* with the Bolshoi on its London visit.

tire-bouchon, en, literally like a corkscrew, position in which the working leg is bent so that the toe touches the knee of the supporting leg.

TIRESIAS, a ballet in three scenes. Choreography, **Frederick Ashton**; music, Constant Lambert; decor, Isabel Lambert. First performed at the Royal Opera House, Covent Garden, London, 9 July 1951, by Sadler's Wells Ballet. Principal dancers **Margot Fonteyn, Michael Somes,** **Margaret Dale, John Field,** Alfred Rodrigues. The ballet recounts the Greek legend of Tiresias who becomes a woman, then reverts to being a man. Hera and Zeus then ask him whether man or woman enjoys love more. His answer of woman infuriates Hera who blinds him. To compensate for his loss of sight, Zeus makes him the gift of prophecy.

TOBY, Harriet (Harriet Katzman, 1929–1952), American dancer, born in Paris. At eight years of age she studied with **Volinine,** then with **Shollar** and **Vilzak,** and at the School of American Ballet during the Second World War. She made her debut with Markova-Dolin Ballet in *The Seven Lively Arts* (1944). She danced with **Ballet Russe de Monte Carlo** (1946), **Les Ballets de Paris de Roland Petit** (1948) and finally with **Grand Ballet du Marquis de Cuevas** where she achieved outstanding success. Her repertoire included *Les Biches, Constantia, Concerto Barocco* and Blue Bird pas de deux in *The Sleeping Beauty*. Her brilliant career came to an abrupt end when she was killed in an air crash at Nice.

tombé, literally fallen, term used for a step in which the dancer appears to fall, by bending the knee of the working leg when landing on it.

TOUMANOVA, Tamara (1919–), Russian ballerina. Taught by **Preobrajenska,** she made her debut at the **Paris Opéra Ballet** in *L'Éventail de Jeanne* when only eleven and became ballerina two years later. She was engaged for Ballet Russe de Monte Carlo by **Balanchine,** who choreographed *Cotillon, Concurrence* and *Jeux d'Enfants* for her (1932). He also created *Les Songes* for her, which she danced with Les Ballets 1933. She rejoined Ballet Russe in 1934 as one of the **baby ballerinas,** and danced the title role in *Firebird*, Ballerina in *Petrouchka*, Aurora in *Aurora's Wedding*, and created The Beloved in *Symphonie Fantastique*. When the company split in 1937 she joined **Massine's Ballet Russe de Monte**

Harriet Toby. Ph. Liseg.

Carlo, adding *Giselle* to her repertoire. She was guest ballerina with **Paris Opéra Ballet**, where she created the title role in the Cocteau-Auric-Lifar production of *Phèdre* (1950). She also danced with **Grand Ballet du Marquis de Cuevas** (1949), **Teatro alla Scala**, Milan (1951 and 1952) and London's **Festival Ballet** (1952 and 1954). She has given many concert performances in South America and Europe. She embodied the popular conception of a Russian ballerina.

tour en l'air, an acrobatic step usually performed by male dancers, involving one or more complete turns made without touching the ground.

TRAGEDY OF FASHION, A or **The Scarlet Scissors**, a ballet in one act. Choreography, **Frederick Ashton**; music, Eugene Goossens (*Kaleidoscope*); decor, Sophie Fedorovich. First performed at the Lyric Theatre, Hammersmith, London, 15 June 1926, as part of the revue *Riverside Nights*. Principal dancers, Frederick Ashton (Monsieur Duchic), **Marie Rambert** (Orchidée). This was Ashton's first choreographic work, and was presented by Marie Rambert. A couturier kills himself with his scissors when his creation fails to satisfy his wealthiest customer.

TRAIN BLEU, LE, a ballet in one act. Libretto, Jean Cocteau; choreography, **Bronislava Nijinska**; music, Darius Milhaud; decor, Henri Laurens; curtain, Pablo Picasso. First performed at the Théâtre des Champs-Elysées, Paris, 20 June 1924, by **Diaghilev**'s Ballets Russes. Principal dancers, Nijinska, **Lydia Sokolova, Anton Dolin, Léon Woizikowsky**. The action is based on the movements of dancing, swimming, tennis and golf, and was designed to display Anton Dolin's acrobatic dancing. This ballet was a tremendous success.

TREFILOVA, Vera (1875–1943), Russian ballerina. A graduate of the Imperial School, St. Petersburg (1894), she entered the Maryinsky Theatre where she became ballerina in 1904, and prima ballerina in 1906. She danced the classic repertoire and was noted for her Aurora in *The Sleeping Beauty*. She retired in 1910, but returned to the stage (1915) as an actress. She left Russia in 1917 and went to Paris. Persuaded by **Diaghilev** to dance Aurora, she alternated in the role (1921) with **Egorova, Lopokova** and **Spessivtzeva**. She trained **Andrée Howard**.

TRICORNE, LE *see* **Three-Cornered Hat, The.**

TRIOMPHE DE L'AMOUR, LE, a ballet in twenty-five entrées. Libretto, Isaac de Benserade and Philippe Quinault; choreography, Charles Beauchamp and Louis Pécour; music, **Jean-Baptiste Lully**; decor, Jean Bérain. First performed at the Court of Louis XIV of France, 21 January 1681. Repeated at **L'Académie Royale de Musique**, 16 May 1681, when a professional woman dancer appeared for the first time in French ballet. This was Mademoiselle Lafontaine, the first of a long line of dancers to be called 'La Reine de la Danse'. Until this time, the Queen and the ladies of the court had danced the female roles. A new version, but with the original libretto and music, was staged by **Harald Lander** for the Royal Danish Ballet in 1962.

TRISTAN FOU or **Mad Tristan**, a ballet in two scenes, based on the legend of Tristan and Isolde. Libretto, Salvador Dali; choreography, **Léonide Massine**; music, Wagner; decor, Dali. First performed at the International Theatre, New York, 1944, by **Ballet International**. Principal dancers, **Francisco Moncion**, Toni Worth, Lisa Maslova. Revived at Monte Carlo, 1949, by **Grand Ballet du Marquis de Cuevas**. Principal dancers, **André Eglevsky, Ethéry Pagava, Marjorie Tallchief**. The story of the ballet departs from the legend. Tristan, in despair over the absence of his beloved and terrified of loneliness, goes mad. Isolde becomes a vision to him and at the end he is left with only his illusion.

TRIUMPH OF BACCHUS AND ARIADNE, THE, a ballet-cantata, based on a Florentine carnival song by Lorenzo de Medici. Choreography, **George Balanchine**; music, Vittorio Rieti; decor, Corrado Cagli. First performed in New York City Center, 9 February 1948, by Ballet Society. Principal dancers, **Nicholas Magallanes** (Bacchus), **Tanaquil Le-Clercq** (Ariadne), Herbert Bliss, **Francisco Moncion**. There was also a choir of forty singers. Repeated, 1 November 1948, by **The New York City Ballet**, with the same principals. The work consists of tableaux of mythological characters, and ends with a Bacchanale.

TRIUMPH OF NEPTUNE, THE, a ballet in two acts. Libretto, Sacheverell Sitwell; choreography, **George Balanchine**; music, Lord Berners; decor and costumes based on 19th century toy theatres. First performed at the Lyceum Theatre, London, 3 December 1926, by **Diaghilev**'s Ballets Russes. Principal dancers, **Alexandra Danilova, Serge Lifar, Lydia Sokolova, Lubov Tchernicheva**, George Balanchine, **Stanislas Idzikowsky**. This ballet was specially created for the English pantomime audience and evoked the Victorian pantomime spirit. It was notable for a solo danced by Balanchine.

TUDOR, Antony (1909–), British dancer, choreographer and teacher. He studied with **Rambert**, Craske, **Legat, Pearl Argyle** and **Harold Turner** and was dancer and choreographer with Ballet Club (1930–8), as well as dancer with the Vic-Wells Ballet and Sadler's Wells Ballet (1933–5). His first choreographic work was *Crossgarter'd* in 1931 for Ballet Club. He founded The London Ballet in 1938, choreographing *Judgement of Paris* and *Gala Performance*. He went to America in 1939, and as choreographer and artistic director of **Ballet Theatre** (1940–50), he staged *Pillar of Fire, Romeo and Juliet, Shadow of the Wind* and *Nimbus*, as well as restaging earlier works. Among the roles he created as a dancer were The Man She Must Marry in *Lilac Garden*, Drunken

Guest in *Judgement of Paris*, Tybalt in *Romeo and Juliet*, and leading roles in *Dark Elegies* and *Dim Lustre*. As guest choreographer, he staged *Time Table* for Ballet Caravan (1941), *Lady of the Camellias* (1951) and *La Gloire* (1952) for **The New York City Ballet**, *Offenbach in the Underworld* for National Ballet of Canada (1955), and *Pillar of Fire* and *Romeo and Juliet* for Royal Swedish Ballet. Concurrently he held the posts of artistic director of The Royal Swedish Ballet, principal of the Metropolitan Ballet School, New York and teacher at Juilliard School of Music, New York. For **The Royal Ballet**, London, he choreographed *Shadowplay* (1967) and *Knight Errant* (1968).

TURNER, Harold (1909–62), British dancer and teacher. He studied with **Marie Rambert** and Alfred Haines, making his debut with Haines's company in 1927. He became a principal dancer with Ballet Rambert, partnering **Tamara Karsavina** in *Le Spectre de la Rose* (1930). He was guest artist with Vic-Wells Ballet (1929–30) and a member of the company (1935–55), except for a brief time with **Mona Inglesby**'s **International Ballet**. The first virtuoso male dancer produced by British ballet, he was noted for his *Swan Lake* pas de trois, Peasant pas de deux in *Giselle*, Miller in *The Three-Cornered Hat*; and he created Blue Skater in *Les Patineurs*, Red Knight in *Checkmate*, and Dancing Master and Man with a Rope in *The Rake's Progress*. He taught at the Royal Academy of Dancing until his death.

turn-out, term for the position of the hip-joints achieved by fully trained dancers in which one leg can be extended to form an angle of 90° with the other. As result of suitable exercises the thigh bones are able to rotate fully in their sockets, giving the dancer control of movement in every direction. It was first taught by **Carlo Blasis**.

tutu, popular name for the classical short frilly ballet skirt, also sometimes applied to the longer version worn in Romantic ballets. Skirts were gradually shortened to give the freedom of movement required for the steps of **élévation**, and the brief type appears to have been introduced for the Italian dancers of the later 19th century; the longer one was apparently first used in *La Sylphide*.

TWO PIGEONS, THE or **Les Deux Pigeons**, a ballet in three acts, based on a tale of La Fontaine. Choreography, **Louis Mérante**; music, André Messager; decor, Rubé, Chaperon, Lavastre. First performed, 18 October 1886, at the Paris Opéra. Principal dancers, Marie Sanlaville, **Rosita Mauri**. Revived, 1952, by **Albert Aveline**. Frederick Ashton choreographed a two-act version, using the same music. Decor, Jacques Dupont. First performed at the Royal Opera House, Covent Garden, London, 14 February 1961, by **The Royal Ballet**. Principal dancers, **Lynn Seymour**,

Merle Park (Young Girl), **Christopher Gable, Alexander Grant,** Kenneth Mason (Young Man), Elizabeth Anderson, Georgina Parkinson, Monica Mason (Gypsy), Robert Mead (Gypsy Chief).

TYL ULENSPIEGEL, a ballet in two scenes. Choreography, **George Balanchine**; music, Richard Strauss; decor, Esteban Francés. First performed in New York City Center, 14 November 1951, by **The New York City Ballet**. Principal dancer, **Jerome Robbins**. The story is basically the same as that of *Til Eulenspiegel*. Balanchine, however, added a new twist. Tyl and the child King Philip of Spain play a game, Tyl with a loaf and Philip with a ship. The ship pushes the bread off the table, and thereafter Tyl directs his mischief against the occupying Spanish. The ballet ends with King Philip and his armies leaving the Netherlands. *See* **Til Eulenspiegel**.

Galina Ulanova in Giselle. Ph. Reyna.

ULANOVA, Galina (1910–   ), Russian prima ballerina assoluta, Peoples' Artist of the USSR. After studying with her mother and **Agrippina Vaganova,** she danced her first major role as Odette in *Swan Lake.* For her graduation in 1928 she danced Waltz and Mazurka in *Chopiniana* and the Sugar Plum Fairy Variation from *The Nutcracker.* During her first season with the Kirov Ballet she danced Princess Florine in Blue Bird pas de deux and Aurora in *The Sleeping Beauty,* and in her second season added Odette-Odile in *Swan Lake* to her repertoire. She added *Giselle* in 1932 (later filmed), and in 1934 created Maria in *The Fountain of Bakhchisarai,* an interpretation which has not been equalled by any other dancer. In 1940 she created the leading role in Prokofiev's *Romeo and Juliet* which made her famous ; and *The Stone Flower* was created especially for her. After the War, in 1944 she moved to the Bolshoi Ballet where she re-created her previous roles. In 1949 she created Tao-Hoa in **Lavrovsky**'s first version of *The Red Poppy.* From about 1959 she danced more infrequently, though still continuing with *Chopiniana* and *The Fountain of Bakhchisarai.* Her appearances outside Russia came late in her dancing career. In 1951 she danced at the Fourteenth Maggio Musicale, Florence. Until their European tour, Russian Ballet was virtually unknown, except for the legendary fame of the great Ulanova. She danced with the Bolshoi when they appeared in Berlin (1954), London (1956), Japan (1957), Paris (1958), the United States and Canada (1959, 1962) and Egypt (1961), and she was artistic director of the company for its 1961 Hungarian tour. Her unforgettable interpretations included the roles of Masha and 'The Golden Waltz' in *The Nutcracker* (1929, 1934), Young Communist Girl of the West in *The Golden Age* (1930), Mireille de Poitiers in *Flames of Paris* (1932), Diana in *Esmeralda* (1935), Coralli in *Lost Illusions* (1936), *Raymonda* (1938), Nikia in *La Bayadère* (1941) and *The Dying Swan* which she danced in recitals. She danced well into her fifties. In 1959 she became ballet mistress of the Bolshoi Theatre, coaching young dancers in important roles. She has also judged ballet festivals and competitions in Eastern Europe, and has written articles on ballet.

UNDERTOW, a ballet in prologue, one act and epilogue. Libretto and choreography, **Antony Tudor**; music, William Schuman; decor, Raymond Breinin. First performed at the Metropolitan Opera House, New York, 10 April 1945, by **Ballet Theatre**. Principal dancers, **Hugh Laing** (Transgressor), **Nana Gollner** (Medusa), **Alicia Alonso** (Ate), **Diana Adams** (Cybele), **Lucia Chase** (Polyhymnia), Patricia Barker (Aganippe), Shirley Eckl (Volupia), **John Kriza** (Pollox). This is a dramatic psychological ballet in a modern setting. Unwanted at home, a young man falls into a terrible depression and eventually kills Medusa in the depths of his disillusionment.

UNION PACIFIC, a ballet in one act. Libretto, Archibald MacLeish; choreography, **Léonide Massine**; music, Nicholas Nabokov; decor, Albert Johnson; costumes, Irene Sharaff. First performed at the Forrest Theatre, Philadelphia, 6 April 1934, by **Colonel de Basil's Ballet Russe de Monte Carlo**. Principal dancers, **Tamara Toumanova, André Eglevsky**, Léonide Massine, **David Lichine, Sono Osata**, Eugenia Delarova. This was an early attempt to portray the American way of life in terms of ballet. The story is of the Wild West and the building of the Union Pacific Railroad in 1869.

V

VAGANOVA, Agrippina Yakolevna (1879–1951), Russian ballerina and teacher, Peoples' Artist of the RSFSR. She had a classical training with **Ivanov, Gerdt** and **Legat** at the Imperial School, St. Petersburg, and was able to watch Cecchetti's work with **Preobrajenska.** Première soloist at 27, she did not receive the title ballerina until 1915, just a year before she retired. Her repertoire included Odette-Odile in *Swan Lake* (first danced when only 18), Mazurka in *Chopiniana*, Czar-Maiden in *The Humpbacked Horse* and *Giselle*. She taught at the School of Russian Ballet (1919–21), where **Vera Volkova** was greatly influenced by her. In 1921 she started teaching at the Leningrad Choreographic School, formerly the Maryinsky, and became its leading teacher. Among her pupils were **Nicholas Sergeyev, Natalia Dudinskaya, Galina Ulanova** and **Irina Kolpakova.** She established the Russian system of ballet education and is regarded as one of the greatest ballet teachers of all time, though a strict and exacting one. She was also a great influence on the style of male dancing and on the works of the Soviet choreographers. Her influence stemmed not only from her book *Fundamentals of the Classic Dance* (1934), but from the fact that her methods were adopted by other teachers. She stressed harmonious co-ordination of the body linked with total stability and great strength in her pupils' backs, to enable them to soar through the air and manoeuvre their bodies in flight. The 'Vaganova back' is recognizable to balletomanes throughout the world. From 1934–41 she taught in the various departments at the Leningrad Ballet School, and held the Chair of Choreography at the Leningrad Conservatory (1946–51). At the Kirov in 1931 she revived *Chopiniana*, but *Swan Lake* is considered her most impor-

tant work (1933); she staged a new version of *Esmeralda* for Tatiana Vecheslova (1935), and *Diana and Acteon* pas de deux for Ulanova and **Chabukiany.**

VAINONEN, Vassily (1898–1964), Soviet dancer and choreographer, Honoured Artist of the RSFSR. He studied at the Maryinsky Theatre school, graduated in 1919, and joined the Kirov Ballet. He became associated with the Young Ballet in the 1920s, together with Georgi Balanchivadze (**George Balanchine**), **Leonid Lavrovsky** and **Alexei Yermolayev,** and choreographed dances including the acrobatic *Moszkowski Waltz*, which is still popular today. After 1925 Vainonen gave up dancing to concentrate on choreography. In 1932 he created *Flames of Paris*, an innovation in Soviet ballet, using national and character dances. Subsequent ballets include *The Golden Age* (1930) and *Gayane* (1957); and new versions of *The Nutcracker* (1934), notable for its dance of the Snowflakes, and *Raymonda* (1938). He staged *Flames of Paris* and *The Nutcracker* in Budapest, became director of the Budapest company in 1948, and did much to revive Hungarian ballet during the next few years. He was chief choreographer of the Novosibirsk Theatre of Opera and Ballet (1952–3), choreographing *The Sleeping Beauty*. His production of *The Nutcracker* was revived at the newly opened Palace of Congresses, Moscow, in 1961. Although his earlier experimental ballets have not survived, Vainonen became an important transmitter of the classical repertoire.

VALSE, LA, a choreographic poem to music by Maurice Ravel (*La Valse*). The first version was choreographed by **Bronislava Nijinska**; decor, **Alexandre Benois.** First performed at the Paris Opéra,

23 May 1929, by the **Ida Rubinstein** company. Principal dancers, Ida Rubinstein, **Anatole Vilzak**. Revived, 25 June 1931, at the Paris Opéra. Choreography, **Michel Fokine**. The music was known in concert before it was finally produced as ballet. Swirling clouds vanish to reveal a magnificent ballroom with colourful dancers. A new ballet to Ravel's *La Valse* and *Valses Nobles et Sentimentales* with choreography by **George Balanchine** was first performed in New York City Center, 20 February 1951, by **The New York City Ballet**. Principal dancers, **Tanaquil LeClercq, Nicholas Magallanes, Francisco Moncion**. Revived, 1 May 1962. Principal dancers, **Patricia McBride**, Nicholas Magallanes, Francisco Moncion. In this version, a forbidding note is struck amid the gaiety of a dance. This is heightened by the arrival of a·young girl attending her first ball and culminates in the entry of Death. A new version, choreographed by **Frederick Ashton**, was first performed at **Teatro alla Scala**, Milan, 1 February 1958. Decor, André Levasseur. Staged at the Royal Opera House, Covent Garden, London, 10 March 1959, by **The Royal Ballet**.

Claire Motte in La Valse. Ph. Bernand.

VALSES ET VARIATIONS *see* **Raymonda Variations**.

VANCE, Norma (Norma Kaplan, 1927–1956), American dancer. She studied with Swoboda-Yurieva, and was a member of **Mia Slavenska**'s group (1944–5). As soloist with **Ballet Theatre,** her repertoire included Youngest Sister in *Pillar of Fire,* French Ballerina in *Gala Performance* and Prelude in *Les Sylphides*. Until 1946 she danced under the name of Vaslavina.

VAN DANTZIG, Rudi (1933–), Dutch dancer and choreographer. He studied with **Sonia Gaskell** and danced with Het Nederlands Ballet. As a choreographer, he staged *Night Island* (1954) and *Spring Concerto* (1958) for Het Nederlands Ballet; *Giovinezza* and *Looking Back* (1959) for Het Nederlands Dans Theater; *Jungle* (1961), *Moments* (1968) and *Painted Birds* (1971) for Het Nederlands Nationaal Ballet; *The Ropes of Time* (1970) for **The Royal Ballet**. *Monument for a Dead Boy* is probably his best known work. He became chief choreographer and later joint artistic director of Het Nederlands Nationaal Ballet.

VAN DIJK or **VAN DYK, Peter** (1929–), German dancer and choreographer. He studied with Tatiana Gsovska, **Boris Kniasev** and **Serge Lifar**. He made his debut at the Berlin Opera in Blue Bird pas de deux, *Firebird* and *La Boutique Fantasque*, and was soloist (1946–50). After a period as choreographer and soloist with Wiesbaden Opera (1952), he joined Ballets de France de Janine Charrat the same year as principal dancer. There he created the leading male role in *Les Algues* (1953), and toured Europe and Africa with the company. As premier danseur étoile of the **Paris Opéra Ballet** (1955), he created the leading roles in *Les Noces Fantastiques* (1955) and *Chemin de Lumière* (1957); he also danced Prince Siegfried in *Swan Lake*. As a choreographer his works include *Pelléas et Mélisande* for Wiesbaden Opera (1952), *Symphonie Inachevée* and *Peau de Chagrin* for Opéra Comique, and *Romeo and Juliet* for Hamburg Opera, where he was guest artist and choreographer. He became ballet director, resident ballet master and choreographer with the Hamburg State Opera Ballet. In 1963 he created Phlegmatic Variation in Balanchine's *The Four Temperaments*, and in 1965 partnered **Maria Tallchief** at Jacob's Pillow Dance Festival. Later that year he and Tallchief danced his *Poème* for the Third International Dance Festival in Paris.

VAN MANEN, Hans (1932–), Dutch dancer and choreographer. He trained with **Sonia Gaskell** (1952–3), and became soloist (1953–8), choreographer and guest artist with the Netherlands Opera Ballet Company. From 1959–60 he danced with **Les Ballets de Paris de Roland Petit**. In 1960 he joined Het Nederlands Dans Theater, of which he became joint artistic director and choreographer (1961).

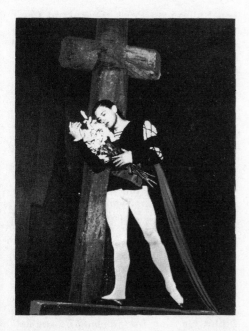

Peter van Dijk in Giselle. Ph. Michel Petit.

Among his works for this company were *Intermezzo*, *Mouvements Symphoniques*, *Concertino*, *Metaphors* and *Solo for Voice I*. He has staged a series of plotless pieces which present a view of dance as emotion, for example, *Three Pieces* (1968). Recent experimental works have included *Twice*, *Situation* and *Grosse Flügge*. In 1970 he resigned from his post at Het Nederlands Dans Theater, but continued to choreograph works for this and other companies, and for television.

VAN PRAAGH, Peggy (1910–), British dancer, ballet mistress, teacher and director, Dame of the Order of the British Empire. She studied ballet with Aimée Phipps, Craske, **Sokolova** and **Volkova**, mime with **Tamara Karsavina** and modern dance with Gertrud Bodenweiser and **Agnes de Mille,** making her debut with **Dolin** (1929). She was soloist with Ballet Rambert (1933–8) and principal dancer with **Antony Tudor**'s London Ballet (1938). She created Episode in His Past in *The Lilac Garden*, Bolero in *Soirée Musicale*, Russian Ballerina in *Gala Performance*, Mortal Under Mercury in *The Planets*, and the leading role in *Dark Elegies*. She also danced Châtelaine in *La Fête Étrange*, Venus in *Judgement of Paris* and Caroline in *The Lilac Garden*. In 1940 she inaugurated Lunch-Hour Ballet at the Arts Theatre in London. Included in her repertoire as principal dancer with Sadler's Wells (1941) were Swanilda in *Coppélia* and Blue Girl in *Les Patineurs*. De Valois invited her to be ballet mistress of the new Sadler's Wells Theatre Ballet (1946), and she was assistant director (1951–5). She directed tours in Munich, Scandinavia, Canada and New York. She became artistic director of Borovansky's Australian company on his death (1960) and was also guest teacher with Ballet International du Marquis de Cuevas (1961). In 1962 she became the first artistic director of Australian Ballet. She wrote *The Art of Choreography* (1963) with Peter Brinson.

variation, term used for a solo dance, for

example the Sugar Plum Fairy variation in
The Sleeping Beauty.

Varna *see* **Competitions.**

VASSILIEV, Vladimir (1940–   ), Russian dancer. A graduate of the Bolshoi
Theatre School, he danced Danila in *The
Stone Flower* during his first season with
the Bolshoi Ballet (1958–9), and again on
tour in America and Canada. He created
Ivan in *The Humpbacked Horse* and
danced Lukash in *Song of the Woods*,
Faun in 'Walpurgis Night' from *Faust*,
Andrei in *Pages of Life*, and the title role in
Grigorovich's *Spartacus*.

VAUSSARD, Christiane (1923–   ),
French ballerina. She studied with **Carlotta Zambelli** at the Paris Opéra school
(1933), became première danseuse with
the **Paris Opéra Ballet** in 1945, and
étoile in 1947. Her repertoire included
Swan Lake, *Giselle*, *Coppélia*, *Les Deux
Pigeons*, *Serenade*, *Le Baiser de la Fée* and
Suite de Danses, and she created the
leading roles in *Le Chevalier Errant* (1950),
Variations (1953), *Firebird* (1954), *La
Symphonie Fantastique* (1957) and *Pas de
Quatre* (1960).

VECHESLOVA, Tatiana (1910–   ),
Russian ballerina and teacher, Honoured
Art Worker of the RSFSR, Honoured Artist
of the RSFSR. She studied at the Petrograd
school (1919–28), joining the Kirov Ballet,
and becoming ballerina. In 1931 she
toured the United States with **Vakhtang
Chabukiany**. Her repertoire included the
title role in *Esmeralda*, Zarema in *The
Fountain of Bakhchisarai* and Noune in
Gayané. On her retiral from dancing in
1953 she became ballet mistress of the
Kirov company. She directed the Leningrad
school (1952–4).

VERDY, Violette (Nelly Guillerm,
1933–   ), American ballerina, born in
France. She studied under **Victor Gsovsky**, making her debut when only twelve,
as girl acrobat in *Les Forains* with **Les
Ballets des Champs-Elysées**. With

Violette Verdy. Ph. M. Seymour.

Les Ballets de Paris de Roland Petit
(1950–4), she became principal dancer in
1953, creating Bride in Petit's dramatic
Le Loup, and dancing Danäe in *Les Amours
de Jupiter*. In 1954 she toured the United
States as principal dancer with London's
Festival Ballet, in 1955 danced with
Ballet Rambert, and was ballerina with
Teatro alla Scala, Milan. As leading
dancer with American Ballet Theatre
(1957–8), she created the title role in *Miss
Julie*. In 1958 she joined **The New York
City Ballet** as principal dancer, making
her debut in *Divertimento No. 15* and the
1st movement in *Symphony in C*. Her
repertoire included *Stars and Stripes* and
Apollo, and she created the leading roles
in *Medea*, *Liebeslieder Walzer* and *Episodes*. In 1962 she danced in *Tchaikovsky
Pas de Deux* with **Edward Villella** at
Fonteyn's Annual Gala Performance at the
Royal Academy of Dancing, London. In
1964 she was guest artist with **The Royal
Ballet,** dancing *The Sleeping Beauty* and
Tchaikovsky Pas de Deux, which she

staged for the company. She returned to **The New York City Ballet** in 1966. Star of film *Ballerina* (1949).

VERT-VERT, a ballet in three acts. Choreography, **Joseph Mazilier**; music, Deldevez and Tolbecque; decor, Cambon and Thierry; costumes, Lormier. First performed, 25 November 1851, by the **Paris Opéra Ballet.** Principal dancers, Adeline Plunkett, Priora. The work depicts the French Court.

VESTRIS, Auguste (Marie Augustin Vestris, also known as Vestr'Allard, 1760–1842), French dancer. Son of **Gaetan Vestris** and his mistress **Marie Allard,** he was taught by his father, and made his debut at the **Paris Opéra Ballet** (1772) in *Cinquantaine*, a divertissement in which he performed a chaconne. In 1773 he danced Eros in *Endymion*. He was premier danseur at the Opéra for nearly 36 years, and for a time, ballet master at the King's Theatre, London. He made his last appearance at the age of 75, partnering **Marie Taglioni.** Among his pupils were **Fanny Elssler, Charles Didelot** and **Jules Perrot.**

VESTRIS, Gaetan Balthazar (1729–1808), Italian dancer. He entered the French Royal Academy in 1748, studying under **Dupré,** whom he succeeded as soloist (1751–4). In 1755 he produced his first ballet in Turin but returned to the **Paris Opéra Ballet** (1756) and in 1761 became ballet master and assistant to Lany. He was also dancing master to Louis XVI. During his leave from the Opéra he worked and danced with **Jean-Georges Noverre** in Stuttgart, and was instrumental in taking Noverre to Paris (1765) to produce *Médée*, with Vestris and **Marie Allard** dancing the leading roles. In *Castor et Pollux* (1772) he discarded the mask, showing himself to be an accomplished mime. He was known as the greatest male dancer of his time, and influenced male dancing of the next century. His wife was the German dancer Anne Heinel who is credited with the invention of the pirouette.

Vic-Wells Ballet *see* **Royal Ballet, The.**

VIGANO, Salvatore (1769–1821), Italian dancer, choreographer and teacher. One of a family of dancers, he made his debut in a female role in Rome, and then went to Madrid and London. In 1790 he danced in Venice and produced his first ballet in 1791. He met and was influenced by **Dauberval** in Madrid. He went to Italy then settled in Vienna (1798–1803). He produced ballets in Milan, Padua and Venice, and in 1812 became ballet master at **Teatro alla Scala,** Milan. Using the music of several composers as well as his own, he created dramatic ballets. Beethoven composed *Prometheus* for him in 1801. Vigano created many ballets including *Gli Strelizzi* (1809), *Dedalo* (1813), *Otello* (1818), *La Vestale* (1818) and *I Titani* (1819). He was married to dancer Maria Medina.

VILLELLA, Edward (1936–), American dancer. A student at the School of American Ballet (1946–51, 1955), he joined **The New York City Ballet** in 1957 and danced his first solo, Faun in Robbins's *Après-midi d'un Faune*. His extensive repertoire also includes *Symphony in C*, *Stars and Stripes* and *Agon*, as well as the title role he created in *The Prodigal Son*, a notable achievement; and he created Harlequin in *La Sonnambula*, Sweep in *Creation of the World*, Oberon in *A Midsummer Night's Dream*, First Couple (with **Patricia McBride**) in *Fantasy*, and *Tarantella* pas de deux. In 1962 he had a major success in *Tchaikovsky Pas de Deux* with **Violette Verdy** at **Fonteyn**'s annual Gala Performance at the Royal Academy of Dancing, London, and in 1962 and 1963 danced as guest artist with the Royal Danish Ballet. Balanchine created a special pas de deux for him and Patricia McBride in *Tarantella* (1964).

VILZAK, Anatole (1896–), Russian dancer and teacher. He studied with **Fokine** and graduated from the Imperial School, St. Petersburg, in 1915. He became premier danseur at the Maryinsky Theatre three years later, and partnered **Mathilda Kchessinska, Vera Trefilova, Tamara Karsavina** and **Olga Spessivtzeva,** in the whole classical repertoire. He left Russia in 1921 to join **Diaghilev**'s Ballets Russes as premier danseur in the London revival of *The Sleeping Beauty.* He was noted for his roles of Favourite Slave in *Schéhérazade,* male role in *Les Sylphides* and in *Les Biches.* For **Ida Rubinstein**'s company he created the leading male roles in *La Bien-Aimée* and *Bolero* (1928), and *La Valse* (1929). With Karsavina and **Shollar** he formed a company which appeared in London ; was premier danseur, ballet master and choreographer for the State Opera House, Riga, Latvia ; and with **René Blum**'s **Ballet Russe de Monte Carlo** he created the title role in *Don Juan* (1936), and danced Harlequin in *Carnaval.* He was premier danseur at the Metropolitan Opera House, New York (1936–7), and taught at the School of American Ballet. He established the Vilzak-Shollar School in New York (1940). He also taught at the Ballet Russe de Monte Carlo School, New York, the Washington School of Ballet, and joined the San Francisco Ballet School staff in 1965. He excelled as both danseur noble and character dancer.

VIRSKY, Pavel Pavlovich (1905–   ), Russian dancer and choreographer, Peoples' Artist of the USSR. He studied music and drama in Odessa (1927) and Moscow (1928), and was a dancer and choreographer with the Odessa troupe (1923–30). He was artistic director of the Khalkov troupe (1930–7). His choreographic works included *Swan Lake, Raymonda, Esmeralda, The Red Poppy* and *Don Quixote.* In 1937 he organized the Ukraine Dance Ensemble and from 1940–1953 choreographed works for the Soviet Army dance troupes. In 1955 he became artistic director of the State Ensemble of National Dancing of the Ukraine.

VLASSI, Christiane, French dancer. She studied at the Paris Opéra school and rose from the corps de ballet to première danseuse étoile at the **Paris Opéra Ballet**

Christiane Vlassi and Attilio Labis in Swan Lake. Ph. Lipnitzki.

in 1963. She dances the leading roles in *Swan Lake, Suite en Blanc, Les Sylphides, Palais de Cristal, Giselle, Études* and *Arcades.*

VOLININE, Alexandre (1882–1955), Russian dancer and teacher. He studied at the Imperial School, Moscow, graduating in 1901. In 1910 he danced with the **Diaghilev** Ballets Russes at the Théâtre Châtelet, Paris, as partner to **Yekaterina Geltzer,** dancing *Les Orientales* and other roles. He later toured Australia and the US (1912, 1913) with **Adeline Genée** ; and made a world tour (1914–25) as partner to **Anna Pavlova.** On his retirement he opened a school in Paris ; among his pupils were **André Eglevsky, David Lichine, Tatiana Riabouchinska** and **Jean Babilée.** His repertoire included *Coppélia* and *Swan Lake.*

VOLKONSKY, Sergei Mikhailovich (1860–1937), Russian critic and theorist. As director of the Russian Imperial Theatres (1899–1902), he encouraged **Michel Fokine,** and advocated the use of the methods of **Emile Jaques Dalcroze.** Volkonsky left Russia after the Revolution and went to live in the United States. His published works include *Man on Stage* and *Art and Gesture.*

VOLKOV, Boris (Boris Baskakov, 1902–), Russian dancer, teacher and choreographer. He studied at the Moscow State Ballet School and was first character dancer at the Opera House, Baku (1916–1918), and with Mordkin Ballet, Moscow (1922). In 1924 he toured Siberia with the Moscow State Ballet, becoming dancer and choreographer with Carlton Café, Shanghai, the same year. He became leading dancer with Adolph Bolm Ballet (1928). In 1929 he directed ballet at the Uptown Theatre, Toronto, and opened his own studio in Toronto (1930). His own group, the Volkov Dancers, represented Canada at the XIIth Olympiad, Berlin, in 1936. In 1937 he staged a number of works for the Opera Guild of Toronto, and in 1939 his Volkov Canadian Ballet gave its first performance. His choreographic works for this company included *The Nutcracker*, and *Classical Symphony* to music by Prokofiev.

VOLKOVA, Vera (1904–), British teacher, born in Russia. She studied with Maria Romanova (**Ulanova**'s mother) and **Agrippina Vaganova**, making her debut in Russia. She danced in China with George Goncharov and briefly with **International Ballet** (1941). Importing Vaganova's methods she started teaching in London in 1943; dancers, including **Fonteyn** and **Elvin**, came from both English and all major visiting companies to her classes. Considered a leading teacher of the contemporary classical style, she taught the company dancers at **Teatro alla Scala**, Milan (1950); she was teacher and artistic adviser to the Royal Danish Ballet (1952) and guest instructor for the **Harkness Ballet** in the summers of 1964 and 1965. With the Royal Danish Ballet she toured the United States as artistic adviser and instructor (1966). She later took a teaching post at the Royal Theatre, Copenhagen.

VON LABAN, Rudolf (1897–1958), Czech teacher and theorist. He studied in Paris and in 1911 founded the Central European School, Munich, which introduced a new system of dance that greatly influenced modern dance and ballet. Among his pupils were **Mary Wigman** and **Kurt Jooss**. He taught in Zürich and Hamburg, and became choreographer at the Berlin Opera. In collaboration with Jooss he explored the co-ordination between mind, nerves and muscles, and classified his results as laws of physical expression. These enable dancers to categorize both dynamics and expression of their bodies. Until his death Laban conducted his Art of Movement Studio in England. His system of Dance Notation, *Kinetographie Laban*, was published in 1928.

VYROUBOVA, Nina (1921–), French ballerina. She studied with **Vera Trefilova, Preobrajenska, Victor Gsovsky, Boris Kniasev, Lubov Egorova** and **Serge Lifar**. She appeared in Soirées de la Danse (1944), dancing with **Roland Petit** in *Giselle* and *Nightingale and the Rose*, and created the principal role in his *Les Forains* (1945). A member of **Les Ballets des Champs-Elysées**, she created the title role in *La Sylphide* (1946), and was première danseuse étoile of the **Paris Opéra Ballet** (1949–56). She danced the classical ballerina roles, as well as leading roles in *Blanche Neige*, *Les Mirages* and *Les Noces Fantastiques*; her *Giselle* won the Prix Pavlova at the Institut Chorégraphique de Paris (1957). As ballerina with **Grand Ballet du Marquis de Cuevas** (1957–61), she danced in *Giselle*, *The Song of Unending Sorrow* and *The Sleeping Beauty*. She was guest ballerina with **Ballet Russe de Monte Carlo** (1961–2) on their United States tour, and with Teatro Colón, Buenos Aires (1964).

W

WALL, David (1946–   ), British dancer. He joined the Royal Ballet School in 1956, danced in **Kenneth MacMillan**'s *Motus* at the Royal Ballet School Matinée in 1963, and graduated into the Touring Section of **The Royal Ballet** the following year. He danced the leading roles in *La Fille Mal Gardée* and *Swan Lake* while still a member of the corps de ballet, and in 1966 he became a principal. His roles include Prince Florimund in *The Sleeping Beauty*, Albrecht in *Giselle*, Oberon in *The Dream* and Solor in *La Bayadère*. He created roles in *Knight Errant* (1969), *Creatures of Prometheus* (1970), *Anastasia* (1971) and *Triad* (1972).

WANDERER, THE, a plotless ballet in four movements. Libretto and choreography, **Frederick Ashton**; music, Franz Schubert (*Wanderer Fantasia*); decor, Graham Sutherland. First performed at the New Theatre, London, 27 January 1941, by Sadler's Wells Ballet. Principal dancers, Robert Helpmann (The Wanderer), **Margot Fonteyn** (Success), **Pamela May, Michael Somes**. In his imagination the Wanderer re-creates his loves, successes and failures. Ashton created the role of Success for Margot Fonteyn.

WEAVER, John (1673–1760), British dancer, choreographer and teacher. He danced the demi-caractère or comic roles, particularly Clown in English pantomime, a new theatrical genre at that time. He was the first producer of the **ballet d'action** (pantomime ballet) long before **Hilverding, Noverre** or **Angiolini**. His first, *The Tavern Bilkers*, was danced at Drury Lane in 1702. His first large-scale work, *The Loves of Mars and Venus*, was produced in 1716 with **Dupré**. Hester Santlow, the ballerina who created the principal roles in his ballets, and the first

British ballerina, danced the leading roles, while Weaver danced Vulcan. From 1717–1733 he created a number of similar works. As well as his own libretti, he wrote *A Small Treatise of Time and Cadence in Dancing* (1706), *History of Mimes and Pantomimes* (1728), and the first English translation of Feuillet's *Chorégraphie*, titled *Orchesography* (1706). Although remembered in histories of drama and music, he is seldom mentioned in ballet histories.

WEDDING BOUQUET, A, a ballet in one act based on Gertrude Stein's *They Must be Wedded to Their Wife*. Libretto, Lord Berners; choreography, **Frederick Ashton**; music and decor, Berners; verses, Gertrude Stein. First performed at Sadler's Wells Theatre, London, 27 April 1937, by Vic-Wells Ballet. Principal dancers, **Robert Helpmann** (Bridegroom), **Margot Fonteyn** (Julia), Mary Honer (Bride), **June Brae** (Josephine), **Julia Farron** (Pepe, the dog), **Ninette de Valois** (Webster, a maid). Revived at the Royal Opera House, Covent Garden, London, 17 February 1949, by the same company. Principal dancers, Robert Helpmann, **Margaret Dale, Moira Shearer**. Staged by Pieter van der Sloot, 1947, in Holland. Revived, 1965, for a tour of the United States. Principal dancers, **Alexander Grant,** Stanley Holden, **Merle Park**. Gertrude Stein's verses were originally sung, but later recited by Constant Lambert. The story is of a wedding in France, to which the Groom's former sweetheart comes to embarrass him, at which a bridesmaid is tipsy, and a little dog wants to be a ballerina.

WEIDMAN, Charles (1901–   ), American dancer, choreographer and teacher. He studied with Eleanor Frampton, **Ruth St. Denis, Ted Shawn** and Theodore

Koslov, making his first professional appearance with **Martha Graham** in *Xochitl*. As a member of Denishawn for eight years, he toured the United States, England and the Orient. With **Doris Humphrey** (1927–45) he co-directed the Humphrey-Weidman company for which he created *And Daddy was a Fireman* and *Lynchtown* (1936). In 1945 he established his own school and in 1948 his own dance group, for which he choreographed his best known work *Fables of Our Time* (1948), to fables by James Thurber, and *The War Between Men and Women* (1954). With Mikhail Santaro he established the Expression of Two Arts Theatre, where dance performances involve music, painting and sculpture. Weidman continued to teach at the Arts Theatre and to conduct master classes in many colleges in the United States. Among his pupils have been many modern dancers.

WELLS, Doreen (1937–), British dancer. She studied at the Bush-Davies School and won the Genée Gold Medal of the Royal Academy of Dancing. In 1955 she joined Sadler's Wells Theatre Ballet which became part of **The Royal Ballet** in 1956. She became a ballerina with the touring section of the company. Frequently partnering **David Wall,** her repertoire includes title role in *Giselle*, Odette-Odile in *Swan Lake*, Swanilda in *Coppélia*, The Girl in *The Two Pigeons*, The Girl in *The Invitation*, *Don Quixote* pas de deux and Lise in *La Fille Mal Gardée*. In 1964 she danced *Raymonda* with Nureyev at Spoleto Festival of Two Worlds. She made her American debut as Aurora in *The Sleeping Beauty* in 1967. She created Juliet in *Creatures of Prometheus* (1969) with The Royal Ballet, and became a principal after its re-organization in 1970.

WESLOW, William (1925–), American dancer. He studied with Mary Ann Wells, Edward Caton, **Vilzak, Balanchine, Nemtchinova** and **Igor Schwezov.** Initially a soloist with American Ballet Theatre, he joined **The New York City Ballet** where he became soloist

in 1959. His roles included Sailor in *Con Amore*, Tea-Chinese Dance in *The Nutcracker*, Blackamoor in *La Sonnambula*, and he danced many of Balanchine's abstract works.

WESTERN SYMPHONY, a plotless ballet in four movements. Choreography, **George Balanchine**; music (based on American folk tunes), Hershy Kay; decor, John Boyt; costumes, Barbara Karinska. First performed at the City Center, New York, 7 September 1954, by **The New York City Ballet.** Principal dancers, **Diana Adams,** Herbert Bliss, Janet Reed, **Nicholas Magallanes, Patricia Wilde, André Eglevsky, Tanaquil LeClercq, Jacques d'Amboise.** At first the ballet was danced in practice costumes, but in 1955 decor and costumes were introduced. The action is set in a 19th century Western village. Classical ballet steps were set to American folk tunes like *Red River Valley* complete with saloon piano.

Western Theatre Ballet *see* **DARRELL, Peter.**

WIGMAN, Mary (1886–), German dancer and teacher. She studied with **Emile Jacques Dalcroze** and with **Rudolf von Laban,** whose assistant she became in 1914. In 1918 she created *The Seven Dances of Life,* which marked the beginning of her career on the concert stage. The Mary Wigman Central Institute was opened in 1920 at Dresden to train dancers and experiment in choreography, and she toured frequently with her group, making her London debut in 1928, and her American debut in 1930. During World War II she taught in Leipzig, while a prisoner of the Nazis. After the war, she opened a school in West Berlin and choreographed *Le Sacré du Printemps* for the 1957 Berlin Festival. Her early works, tense and sombre, danced without music or with percussive accompaniment, made her one of the pioneers of modern dance in Europe. Her pupils included Hanya Holm, **Harald Kreutzberg** and **Yvonne Georgi.**

Patricia Wilde: with Anthony Blum in Divertissements. Ph. New York City Ballet.

WILDE, Patricia (Patricia White, 1930–), American dancer, born in Canada. She studied at the School of American Ballet, making her debut with Concert Ballet in 1943. She danced with **Ballet International** (1944–5) and was soloist with **Ballet Russe de Monte Carlo** (1945–9), creating Hoop Dance in *Night Shadow* and dancing leading roles in *Concerto Barocco*, *Rodeo* and *Pas de Quatre* with **Alexandra Danilova, Mia Slavenska** and **Alicia Markova**. She was guest artist with **Les Ballets de Paris de Roland Petit** (1950) and guest ballerina with Metropolitan Ballet on its Netherlands tour and for the London season. In 1950 she joined **The New York City Ballet** where she danced a large repertoire of Balanchine ballets, creating the principal roles in *Swan Lake*, *La Valse*, *Scotch Symphony*, *Western Symphony*, *Glinka Pas de Trois*, *Square Dance*, *Divertimento No. 15* and *Raymonda Variations*. She is noted especially for her speed and her magnificent jump. She made guest appearances for special performances in the United States, Canada, Mexico and the Caribbean Islands, and choreographed for herself and a small group programmes presented by the New York Philharmonic Promenade Concerts (1964, 1965). In 1965 the Harkness House for Ballet Arts invited her to be head of their Dance Department.

WILLIAMS, Peter (1914–), British ballet critic and designer. He was assistant editor of *Ballet* (1949–50), ballet critic of the *Daily Mail* (1950–3) and founder editor of *Dance and Dancers* from 1950. He created the designs for **Taras's** *Designs with Strings* and for the first British production of **Fokine's** *Prince Igor* (1947) ; and *Selina* for the Sadler's Wells Theatre Ballet (1949). He is a member of a number of advisory panels connected with the dance, and was chiefly responsible for the Ballet Section in the *Arts Council Report on Opera and Ballet in the United Kingdom 1966–9*. He was awarded the OBE in 1971 for 21 years as editor of *Dance and Dancers*.

WILSON, Sallie (1932–), American dancer. She studied with Dorothy Colter Edwards, Margaret Craske and **Antony Tudor**. She joined **Ballet Theatre** (1949) ; danced with Metropolitan Opera Ballet (1950–5) ; and rejoined American Ballet Theatre, becoming soloist (1957). From 1958–60 she was with **The New York City Ballet**, dancing in *The Cage*, *Symphony in C*, *Stars and Stripes*, and creating Queen Elizabeth in *Episodes*. When American Ballet Theatre was again functioning, she re-joined as first soloist (1960), and danced Boulotte in *Bluebeard* and Young Mother in *Fall River Legend*. In 1962 she became ballerina. Her roles have included Mazurka and pas de deux in *Les Sylphides* and Russian Ballerina in *Gala Performance*. For American Ballet Theatre's 25th anniversary season she danced the title role in *Sargasso*. Hagar in *Pillar of Fire* (1966) is considered her finest achievement. She has danced at Jacob's Pillow Dance Festival, and has made guest appearances with other companies.

Winnipeg Ballet *see* **Canada, history of ballet in.**

WITCH BOY, a ballet in one act, based on the ballad *Barbara Allen*. Choreography, **Jack Carter**; music, Leonard Salzedo; decor, Norman McDowell. First performed, 24 May 1956, by the Ballet der Lage Landen, Amsterdam. Principal dancers, Norman McDowell, Angela Bayley. Staged at the Opera House, Manchester, 27 November 1957, by London's **Festival Ballet.** Principal dancers, **John Gilpin**, Anita Landa. The Witch Boy falls in love with the girl, is lynched by the villagers who suspect him of witchcraft. However, the Conjurman appears, and Witch Boy is reborn.

WOIZIKOWSKY, Léon (1897–), Polish dancer, ballet master and teacher. He was discovered by **Diaghilev** in 1915, and danced with the Ballets Russes (1915–29) and with **Ballet Russe de Monte Carlo.** In Paris (1935–6) he organized his own company which toured Europe. He was ballet master and teacher at the New Theatre, Warsaw (1958), but left to revise *Petrouchka* (1958) and *Schéhérazade* (1959) for London's **Festival Ballet.** Later the same year he joined **Massine**'s Ballets Européens of Nervi as ballet master, but returned to Festival Ballet in 1961. He was also ballet master with Opera Ballet, Cologne, Germany. The finest character dancer of his day, he had the marvellous qualities of suppleness, precision and vitality. He was considered outstanding as Polovetsian Chief in *Prince Igor*, for the leading role in *Petrouchka*, Niccolo in *The Good-Humoured Ladies*, Corregidor in *The Three-Cornered Hat*, Conductor of the Dance in *Cotillon* and Tatterdemalion in *Concurrence*. Other roles include *Contes Russes*, *La Boutique Fantasque*, *Les Biches*, *Pas d'Acier*, *Les Noces* and *The Gods Go a'Begging*.

WRIGHT, Belinda (1929–), British dancer. She studied with Dorothea Halliwell, **Preobrajenska** and Kathleen Crofton. She joined Ballet Rambert in 1945

Belinda Wright. Ph. Mike Davis.

and toured Australia. In 1949 she joined **Les Ballets de Paris de Roland Petit** and in 1951 London's **Festival Ballet**, where she became ballerina. She moved to **Grand Ballet du Marquis de Cuevas** in 1954 and re-joined Festival Ballet as prima ballerina (1955–7). In 1959 she danced at the Festival of Basel, Switzerland, again re-joining Festival Ballet until 1962. In her large repertoire she excels in both modern and Romantic ballets. She created Marguerite in *Vision of Marguerite*, Alice in *Alice in Wonderland*, Swanilda in *Coppélia*, Sugar Plum Fairy in *The Nutcracker* and the title role in *Giselle*. In 1960 she made a concert tour of South Africa with **Anton Dolin** and **John Gilpin**, and has been a guest artist in many countries with her husband, the Yugoslav dancer Jelko Yuresha.

WRIGHT, Peter (1926–), English dancer and choreographer. He studied with **Kurt Jooss, Vera Volkova** and **Peggy van Praagh**, and danced with Metropolitan Ballet (1947) and St. James's Ballet

(1948). He was soloist with Sadler's Wells Theatre Ballet (1949–51, 1952–5) and assistant ballet master (1955). He danced roles in *Pineapple Poll* and *Blood Wedding*, among others. As assistant dance director of Edinburgh International Ballet (1958), he choreographed *The Great Peacock* ; and he has choreographed for many companies, including *Giselle* and *The Sleeping Beauty* for **The Royal Ballet.** He taught at the Royal Ballet School (1957–9) and became ballet master of the Stuttgart Ballet. He was appointed associate director of The Royal Ballet in 1971.

Y

YERMOLAYEV, Alexei (1910–), Russian premier danseur and choreographer, Peoples' Artist of the RSFSR. He studied at the Leningrad School under **Vaganova**, and graduated when only sixteen. For his memorable graduation performance (1926) he danced Vayu, God of the Wind, in *The Talisman*. For the Kirov Ballet he danced the leading roles in the classical repertoire; transferred to the Bolshoi Ballet (1930), he danced over twenty important roles and was considered an outstanding principal dancer-actor. His Tybalt in *Romeo and Juliet*, Yevgeny in *The Bronze Horseman* and Albrecht in *Giselle* were remarkable feats of virtuosity. He was the first male dancer to develop the heroic manner of dancing, and had enormous influence on the Soviet School of the 1920s. His ballon has been compared with that of **Nijinsky**. In 1959 he retired from the stage to devote himself to teaching at the Bolshoi school. He began teaching the graduating male class in 1961. His teaching methods soon won him a well-deserved reputation as an effective and original teacher. Author of several libretti, he also choreographed *The Nightingale* (1939) for the Minsk Opera Ballet.

YOUSKEVITCH, Igor (1912–), American premier danseur and teacher, born in Russia. A member of the famous athletic organization, Sokol, he was invited to partner Xenia Grunt, the Yugoslav ballerina, in 1932, having had no previous ballet training. After one year of intensive ballet lessons he danced with her in Paris (1933). He studied for two years with **Preobrajenska** and danced with **Bronislava Nijinska**'s Les Ballets de Paris (1934), and **Léon Woizikowsky**'s company (1935), continuing with the group under **Colonel de Basil** for its 1937 Australian tour. In 1938 he joined the Massine-Blum **Ballet Russe de Monte Carlo** as premier danseur, creating Officer in *La Gaieté Parisienne*, the god in 3rd movement of *Seventh Symphony*, Man in *Rouge et Noir* and dancing the classical repertoire. After serving in the Navy during the Second World War, he was guest artist with **Massine**'s Ballet Russe Highlights, then joined **Ballet Theatre** (1946–55). He created the leading male role in *Theme and Variations*, and danced *La Gaieté Parisienne*, **Tudor**'s *Romeo and Juliet*, *Helen of Troy* and *Black Swan*. He partnered **Alicia Alonso** in a number of classical ballets, including *Giselle*, and established himself as a great classical dancer. In 1955 he re-joined Ballet Russe de Monte Carlo and created Harlequin in *Harlequinade*, and after 1957 appeared as guest artist with the company until 1962. He appeared with Ballet Alicia Alonso in South America and Cuba and, in 1963, at the Metropolitan Opera House. On his retirement he taught in his own school.

YUGOSLAVIA, history of ballet in.
1892 Performance in Zagreb of *Die Puppenfee*, first ballet performance in Yugoslavia.
1894 Under the direction of Stjepan Miletic, Otokar Bartic becomes ballet master at Zagreb Theatre. Emma Grondone, Luisa Viscusi and Achille Viscusi are the leading dancers.
1895 The Zagreb company performs *Coppélia*.
1897 now a full-size company, the Zagreb Ballet performs *Giselle*.
1898 The company presents *Jela* and *At the Plitvica Lakes*, new works on Croation themes.
1918–39 Ballet companies are formed in Belgrade, Zagreb, Ljubljana, Orijek, Rijeka and Split. Margarita Froman organizes the Belgrade and Zagreb companies. She

stages the first national ballet, *The Ginger-bread Heart* (1927). Natalia Boskovic is the first prima ballerina at Belgrade. Ana Roje and Oskar Harmos are prominent figures.

1945 Ballet companies are established in Sarajevo, Skoplje, Maribor and Novi Sad.

Dimitri Parlic choreographs works from the classical repertoire for the Belgrade National Ballet. Among outstanding Yugoslav dancers have been Mia Slavenska, **Milorad Miskovitch, Pino** and **Veronika Mlakar,** and Vassili Sulich.

Z

ZABOTKINA, Olga Leonidovna (1936–), Russian dancer, Honoured Artist of the RSFSR. She studied in Leningrad, becoming a soloist with the Kirov Ballet in 1953. Her roles include Cleopatra, Mercedes in *Don Quixote* and Aisha in *Gayané*.

ZAKHAROV, Rotislav (1907–), Russian choreographer and teacher, Peoples' Artist of the RSFSR. He studied in Leningrad (1920–5) and worked as a choreographer in different parts of the Soviet Union until 1932 when he went to the Kirov Theatre, producing *The Fountain of Bakhchisarai*, his best known work, in 1934. He went on to stage the dramatic ballets, *Lost Illusions* (1936) and *The Prisoner of the Caucasus* (1938), *Cinderella* (1945), *Mistress into Maid* (1946) and *The Bronze Horseman* (1949). Many of his ballets are creations from works by Pushkin. Zakharov was artistic director of the Bolshoi Ballet (1936–9) and headed the Bolshoi school (1946–9). He helped found the Choreographers' Faculty of the Theatre Institute, Moscow, and was later appointed professor of choreography. He set out his theories in *The Choreographer's Art* (1954). His remarkable talents as a theatrical director are also demonstrated in his opera productions.

ZAMBELLI, Carlotta (1877–), Italian ballerina and teacher. She studied at the Milan Conservatory and danced at **Teatro alla Scala.** In 1894 she made her debut at the **Paris Opéra Ballet** as one of the Courtesans in *Faust* and was soon promoted to étoile. Her first important role was Snow Fairy in *La Maladetta*. Her repertoire included *La Korrigane, Namouna, Les Deux Pigeons, Sylvia* and *Coppélia*, and she created the leading role in *Cydalise et le Chèvre-pied*. She was the last foreign ballerina to be invited to Czarist Russia, at the Maryinsky Theatre (1901). She retired in 1927 and until 1955 taught at the Paris Opéra school. In 1956 she was created an Officer of the Légion d'Honneur.

ZÉPHYR ET FLORE *see* **Flore et Zéphyr.**

ZIMMERL, Christl (1939–), Austrian dancer. She studied at the Vienna State Opera and with teachers of the Royal Ballet School, London. She joined the Vienna State Opera company in 1953, becoming soloist in 1956. Her roles include the title role in *Medusa*, Myrtha in *Giselle*, Elvira in *Don Juan*, Prelude in *Les Sylphides*, Lilac Fairy in *The Sleeping Beauty*; and in 1964 she danced Odette-Odile in Rudolph Nureyev's version of *Swan Lake*, **Fonteyn**'s former role.

ZIMMERMANN, Klaus (1927–), German dancer. He studied with Tatiana Gsovska and Edith Feifferle, and danced initially in opera and operetta. He danced the leading roles of the classical repertoire in Berlin, Cologne and Malmö, Sweden.

ZUCCHI, Virginia (1847–1930), Italian ballerina. A pupil of **Carlo Blasis,** she started dancing in the corps de ballet, later becoming ballerina at Padua. Her first ballet was *Brahma*. She was guest artist in many European capitals. She went to St. Petersburg in 1885 to dance *A Trip to the Moon* in summer theatre. She danced at the Maryinsky Theatre (1885–92) in *The Daughter of Pharaoh, Coppélia, Paquita, La Fille Mal Gardée, Esmeralda* and many other works.

ZVEREV, Nicholas (1897–1965), Russian dancer and ballet master. He joined **Diaghilev's Ballets Russes** in 1912, became soloist, and remained with the company until 1926. His roles included Moor in *Petrouchka*, Male Acrobat in *Parade* and Cossack Chief in *La Boutique Fantasque* (1919). With his wife, **Nemtchinova,** he toured from 1926–36. He became ballet master with Les Ballets de Monte Carlo, and remained until 1945. He revived *Petrouchka* (1948), *Prince Igor* (1949) and *Le Spectre de la Rose* for **Paris Opera Ballet.** Taught at **Teatro alla Scala**, Milan.